SOLAR ARCHITECTURE
in COOL CLIMATES

COLIN PORTEOUS WITH KERR MACGREGOR

EARTHSCAN
London • Sterling, VA

Hartness Library
Vermont Technical College
One Main St.
Randolph Center, VT 05061

First published by Earthscan in the UK and USA in 2005
Copyright © Colin Porteous and Kerr MacGregor
All rights reserved
ISBN-10: 1-84407-281-9
ISBN-13: 978-1-84407-281-1
Page design by The Graphics Company
Printed and bound in the UK by Cromwell Press
Cover design by Yvonne Booth

For a full list of publications please contact:
Earthscan
8–12 Camden High Street
London, NW1 0JH, UK
Tel: +44 (0)20 7387 8558
Fax: +44 (0)20 7387 8998
Email: earthinfo@earthscan.co.uk
Web: www.earthscan.co.uk
22883 Quicksilver Drive, Sterling, VA 20166-2012, USA

Earthscan is an imprint of James and James (Science Publishers) Ltd
and publishes in association with the International Institute for Environment
and Development

A catalogue record for this book is available from the British Library

Library of Congress Cataloging-in-Publication Data:

Porteous, Colin.
Solar architecture in cool climates / Colin Porteous with Kerr MacGregor.
p. cm.
Includes bibliographical references and index.
ISBN 1-902916-62-X (pbk.)
1. Solar houses--Climatic factors. 2. Sustainable architecture. 3. Solar heating.
I. MacGregor, Kerr. II. Title.
TH7414.P67 2005
728'.370472--dc22
2005008379

Printed on elemental chlorine-free paper

Photograph on previous page by Colin Porteous of Kunstbygning, Århus, Denmark (architect M. Møller)

Contents

LIST OF BOXES   vii

LIST OF FIGURES   ix

PREFACE   xiii

ACKNOWLEDGEMENTS   xix

Chapter 1 North Sun Context   1

Latitude myths challenged   2
    Brighton breakthrough / 3

Dynamic complexity – direct versus indirect passive solar models   5
    direct gain model – detached house / 5
    indirect gain model – dense terrace / 7
    sunspaces work due to diverse climatic influences / 10
    further modelling confirms North–South trend in UK / 11

Widening the solar agenda   13
    institutional divergence – Northern Europe and Canada / 14

Chapter 2 Multiple and Added Solar Value   23

The case for integration   25
    flat-plate solar thermal collectors / 25
    active experiment – matching supply to demand / 26
    passive exploitation of triangular section / 28
    formal issues and shed vernacular / 29
    multiple active–passive solar roofs / 34
    solar retrofit – collection isolated from storage / 36
    scope for geometric diversity / 37
    aesthetic ambiguity and nuance of solar collection – arcades and atria / 42
    solar retrofit as a means of rebranding / 47

The case for isolation   48
    multilateral advantage / 49

Chapter 3 Environmental Comfort and Well-being   57

Microclimatic opportunities   59

ancient precedent to modern urban paradigm / 60

architect as occupant – rural exposure / 64

extroversion and ability of occupants to interact / 67

Quality versus quantity tensions   71

ventilating – evidence from recent Scottish housing / 73

mass as a mediator for open windows / 74

Chapter 4 Adaptive Control   81

Owning the means of proaction   82

participatory bilateralism / 83

early passive solar precedents – bifurcation / 86

solar thermal storage walls inhibit adaptive control / 88

Trombe-Michel principle moves north to Ireland / 89

thermal storage wall in England with movable insulation / 90

thermal storage wall in Scotland with transparent insulation / 91

thermal storage wall in Sweden with isolated solar supply / 93

the case for a 'human interaction factor' in predictions / 94

Conservatories conserving?   96

new-build Scottish demonstration / 97

further insights from Scottish urban retrofit / 102

other sunspace paradigms / 108

further thoughts on options for mechanically assisted ventilation / 114

raising architectural stakes – widening performance gap / 116

Sociodemography in focus   118

Scottish experience / 119

Danish and German experiences / 120

Chapter 5 Passive Control   127

Plan and section   128

light orchestration – Nordjyllands Kunstmuseum / 128

light and air – Kuntsbygning in Århus / 135

relevance of latitude to designing for daylight / 138

daylight and air for utilitarian use – sport, production and transport / 139 daylight and air for educational buildings / *141*

sectional consequences of stack-dominated ventilation / *146*

Thermal mass dilemmas   **147**

embedded fluids for heating and cooling / *150*

solid solar masonry walls / *153*

thermal mass and timber construction / *156*

composite construction / *157*

cladding, colour and other storage media / *158*

Optimizing heat and light balance through glazing   **159**

mirror-optics and other progress in variable transmission / *159*

alternative integrated innovations / *163*

external screens – competition for advanced glazing? / *165*

transparent insulation / *167*

Chapter 6 Machine Control   **173**

Diffusing, shading and opening – glazing controls   **173**

wear and tear / *173*

optimizing control / *176*

shading with heat as a useful by-product / *180*

shading with heat as a useless by-product / *180*

selective versus exclusive modes / *182*

Harvesting hot air – integrated collectors   **183**

early development and general principles of solar air collectors / *184*

development of glazed solar air collectors in Scotland / *185*

development of unglazed solar air collectors in Scotland / *188*

small window-integrated options / *190*

further work on absorbers and dynamic insulation / *190*

large-scale, multi-faceted proposal / *191*

Fuelling competition – interactive control and management   **191**

lessons from a solar primary school / *192*

tutorials at a university campus / *194*

risks of partially heating buffer spaces / *197*

free heat to buffers and related energy-efficiency measures / *198*

heat pumps versus boilers / *200*

small-scale CHP and heat exchangers / *205*

wider questions / *206*

Chapter 7 Green Solar Future **211**

Conflicting views on global warming and environmental sustainability   212
    dimensions of sustainable architecture / 213
    solar–green, green–solar interface / 214
    eco-footprint, ambitions and constraints / 215
    merit and diversity in environmental architecture / 218

The work of two North American practices   219
    contextual commonalities and differences / 220
    coastal Pacific projects / 223
    ubiquitous environmental concerns / 231
    coastal Atlantic projects / 233

The need for a 'value system of complexity'   237

PICTURE CREDITS   247

INDEX OF SOLAR BUILDINGS AND PROJECTS   249

INDEX OF PEOPLE, PRACTICES, INSTITUTIONS, ETC.   254

INDEX OF DEFINED TERMS AND PRODUCTS   261

INDEX OF ACRONYMS AND ABBREVIATIONS   265

LIST OF BOXES

■ **1.1** Terms, units and numbers with comparative examples   2
    1.2 Basic 'steady-state' methodology for estimating space heating loads   3
    1.3 Hypothetical dimensions for 1981 theoretical model   4
    1.4 Theoretical predictions of useful solar gain in various UK locations, 1981   4
    1.5 Context of dynamic modelling and key results for direct gain model, 1984   5
    1.6 Theoretical performance data for back-to-back indirect gain model, 1984   10
    1.7 Contrasting Lerwick and London (Kew): some climatic detail   11
    1.8 Sunspace modelling: Glasgow compared to Kew in dimensional and climatic detail   12
    1.9 Germany, Denmark, Sweden and the Netherlands: solar activity   14
    1.10 Norway, Finland, UK, Scotland and Canada: solar activity   16
    1.11 Global to national statistics on fossil fuel consumption and CO_2 emissions   18

■ **2.1** Passive solar gain: basic definition and critical angle for sunbeam   23
    2.2 Flat-plate collectors: specification options   26
    2.3 Solar geometry: supplementary notes (refer also to Tables 2.1–2.6)   38
    2.4 Transparent insulation   41
    2.5 Thermos principle applied to dwellings in the 1930s and 1990s   41

■ **3.1** Monitored housing in Glasgow: notes on terms and data   73
    3.2 Specification at Hockerton   76

■ **4.1** Details of the 1967 and 1974 Trombe-Michel wall experiments   88
    4.2 Christopher Taylor Court: variable estimates of U-values   90
    4.3 Strathclyde student residence: air change rate from monitored data   93
    4.4 Details of the Stornoway climate, sunspaces and predicted savings   98
    4.5 Realization of the Stornoway project: energy consumption factors   100
    4.6 More details of the Stornoway project and monitoring   101
    4.7 'Heatfest' and its organizers: Easthall, Glasgow   102
    4.8 Initial predictions for the Easthall project compared to Stornoway   103
    4.9 Political birth pangs of the Easthall European solar demonstration project   103
    4.10 Easthall: ventilation and temperature as key influences   105
    4.11 Easthall: consumption influenced by distribution of demand for heat   106
    4.12 Easthall: auxiliary heating and window opening   107
    4.13 Easthall: real versus effective rates of ventilation   108
    4.14 Easthall compared to Stornoway: consumption range – influence of advice   108
    4.15 Ballantrae rural housing: supplementary information   114
    4.16 Graham Square urban housing: supplementary information   117
    4.17 Easthall: ventilation related to smoking, children and pets   120
    4.18 Ottrupgård Fjernewarme rural co-housing: energy efficiency values   120
    4.19 Vauban, Freiburg: details of monitored energy   123

■ 5.1 Predictive methods used for Queens Building in Leicester   147
5.2 Open and closed systems for ducting air   148
5.3 Units of thermal capacitance   149
5.4 Thermal admittance, response and damping   152
5.5 TI saving: Freiburg compared to Glasgow   153
5.6 Impact of TI on length of heating season: Freiburg compared to Glasgow   154
5.7 Influence of selective coating on mass wall   156
5.8 Timber versus concrete and an innovative Austrian solar wall   157
5.9 Colour, mass and phase-change materials   159
5.10 Light-grid: vital statistics for solar versus light transmission   163
5.11 Transparent insulation variants   167

■ 6.1 Leslie Jesch: a solar champion   175
6.2 The chemistry of ETFE   179
6.3 Examples of earth cooling   182
6.4 George Löf's breathing solar air collector in Colorado   184
6.5 Simple solar air collectors in Stornoway   185
6.6 Breathing solar air collectors in Easthall   187
6.7 Unglazed air collectors: details of tests   188
6.8 Airing windows: details of PASSYS tests   190
6.9 Airing walls: details of PASSYS tests   192
6.10 LPG family   192
6.11 Netley Abbey design team   192
6.12 Details of monitoring at Netley   194
6.13 Details of monitoring at Jubilee Campus   196
6.14 Monitoring and predictions at Trondheim   198
6.15 PV performance at Petten   199
6.16 PV predictions in Glasgow   200
6.17 Shettleston housing, Glasgow: thermal storage   201
6.18 Lumphinnans housing, Fife: thermal storage and performance   203
6.19 Background to Helliwell + Smith's home and studio   204
6.20 Proposed floating dwellings in the Netherlands: quantitative detail   205
6.21 Task XIII apartments, Amstelveen: performance detail and comparison   206

■ 7.1 Global warming: Mauna Loa, Keeling curve, Vostok ice core, Kyoto etc   212
7.2 Active thermal and electrical systems: barriers challenged   215
7.3 Eco-footprint numbers   216
7.4 Frank Lloyd Wright and Usonia   233
7.5 Vitruvian triad: sense and sensibility?   241

LIST OF FIGURES

Chapter 1 North Sun Context

1.1	Plan of 'direct gain' passive solar house by Stillman and Eastwick-Field	6
1.2	3-dimensional 'cutaway' of 'indirect gain' solar house by Malcolm Newton	8
1.3	First Scottish passive solar housing in Stornoway by Western Isles Islands Council	13
1.4	villaVISION in Tasstrup, Denmark, by the Danish Technological Institute	15

Chapter 2 Multiple and Added Solar Value

2.1	a	Rooftop of the Joan Miro gallery in Barcelona	24
	b	Rooftop sculpture court of gallery in Århus	24
	c	Nordjyllands Kuntsmuseum in Ålborg	25
2.2		'Fantasy' solar house in Almere: a) active flat plate collector doubles as a south-facing roof; b) seasonal thermal store makes a statement on the public side of the house	27–28
2.3		Solar terrace in Zollikofen, Berne: a) PV array visually echoes opening windows at top of façade; b) blanked by blinds in warm weather	29
2.4		Passive solar house at Garriston, near Dublin	30
2.5		Passive solar house at West Pennant, near Halifax, Nova Scotia	31
2.6		Gymnasium at Oberhambach, by Peter Hübner: a) schematics for different weather and seasons displayed next to plant room; b) ventilating slot looking west to triangular sunspace; c) flat plate solar thermal collectors on south-east façade	32
2.7		Multiple solar roof of Energiebalanswoning by Van Straalen, Zeist & BOOM	34
2.8		EVA Lanxmeer eco-village at Culemborg: a) integrated solar roof; b) private side of another solar terrace – solar array not visible	35
2.9		Detail of roof of swimming pool in Gouda – solar collector replacing former glazing	36
2.10		Two projects in Göteborg: a) solar retrofit of 1950s housing block – roof collector; b) new-build solar housing with wall collector	37
2.11		Southern façade of Scottish dementia unit	40
2.12		Solar house in Freiburg: a) detail of façade; b) plan; c) section	42
2.13		Wasa City shopping market in atrium at Gävle	43
2.14		New atrium between old terraces at Söderhamn	44
2.15		John Darling Mall at Eastleigh in Hampshire: a) plan; b) view of south end	45
2.16		Inside Akademie Mont-Cenis during construction in the summer of 1999	46
2.17		Images from the proposed BIPV retrofit project for Strathclyde University	47
2.18		The solar cladding features of the STinG project in Glasgow	49
2.19	a	Terraced housing in Niewland, Amersfoort – PV arrays on flat roofs are not visible	51
	b	Flats in Freiburg – solar thermal and PV arrays crown the free aesthetics	51

Chapter 3 Environmental Comfort and Well-being

3.1 a Looking east in Gravinnehof (mid afternoon in August) 60
b Cross section through access promenades, detailing glass and timber screen 61
c Upper deck with diagonal roof-lights looking west 62

3.2 The Edwards sunspace from a first floor window, with the owner and visitors 65

3.3 'Hill House', South Coast Nova Scotia, looking south 68

3.4 Entrance court of 'Messenger II' in Kingsburg – looking south 68

3.5 a The glaciated rock shelf as a terrace for the Kutcher house near Halifax 69
b The paved terrace of the Greenwood or 'Fishbones' house on Galiano Island 70

3.6 The outdoor room of the Murphy house on Gambier Island: a) looking inwards to north; b) outwards to south 71

3.7 The south façade of one of the Hockerton houses 75

Chapter 4 Adaptive Control

4.1 General view of the JUgend FOrum 83

4.2 Schematics for the rotating roof 83

4.3 Internal view of 'city of mud' 85

4.4 Trombe-Michel principle applied to Irish agricultural cottage in Carlow – south façade 89

4.5 South façade of Christopher Taylor Court: a) general view; b) close-up 91

4.6 Solar TI façade of a student residence in Glasgow, facing slightly west of south 92

4.7 Schematic of Stile Park solar housing in Stornoway – stacked sun-porches 99

4.8 Plan view of model of passive solar flats at Easthall, with original chimney breast in key location – stacked glazed-in balconies face southeast or west in demonstration 102

4.9 Solar house at Ayton with double-height, recessed glazed sun-porch 109

4.10 Maisonettes over flats in Ballerup with double-height, corner glazed sun-porch 110

4.11 Self-build, cooperative passive solar houses at Paxton Court, Sheffield: a) two-storey houses; b) single-storey houses 111

4.12 Lean-to sunspaces at Coldstream 112

4.13 Semi-recessed, double-height sunspaces at Ballantrae 113

4.14 Semi-recessed, double-height and single-height stacked sunspaces at Deventer 115

4.15 Stacked sunspaces at Graham Square in Glasgow – facing 15° north of west 116

4.16 South façade of the 'Wohnen & Arbeiten' (Living & Working) block in Freiburg 121

Chapter 5 Passive Control

5.1 Cross section of roof monitor at Nordjyllands Kunstmuseum 130

5.2 Nordjyllands Kunstmuseum: a) gallery from entrance looking southeast; b) still looking southeast, monitors at right angles to southwest edge; c) turning round to northwest: small galleries to left of corridor 131

5.3 Nordjyllands Kunstmuseum: a) shadows of light fittings enliven light-scoops; b) sunlight edits floor and display surfaces on summer solstice 132

5.4	Kuntsbygning in Århus. Curving southwesterly wall of 1993 extension	136
5.5	Kuntsbygning in Århus: a) looking southwest into 2003 extension; b) looking up into glazed lantern of 2003 extension	137
5.6	Kunsthaus in Bregenz: a) detail of glass rain-screen at external corner on sunny day; b) looking down staircase, with indirect daylight through ceiling on sunny day	138
5.7	Inside the lighting void over gallery at Davos	139
5.8	Fondation Beyeler, Basel: a) detail at edge of glass roof; b) general view from west	139
5.9	Sports 'factory' – schematic section showing system for natural light and ventilation	140
5.10	'Showroom' for PV factory in Freiburg – louvres functionally advertise the product	140
5.11	Bus station at Göteborg: a) inside concourse; b) west-south-west façade	141
5.12	The cone sheds daylight deep into the library at Delft Technical University	142
5.13	Learning Centre, Kirkintilloch – cross section maximises opportunity for natural light	143
5.14	De Kleine Aarde, Boxtel – inside the atrium with all south and north windows open	144
5.15 a	Looking up 'shark's fin' tower of atrium at Wasa City at Gävle	147
b	Looking up triangular tower of atrium at the Eco-Centre in Jarrow	147
5.16	Bridges in the multi-level circulation spine of Queens Building enliven spatial drama	148
5.17	View into gymnasium at Gleneagles Community Centre, looking towards thermal wall	150
5.18 a	Main living space of Howard House, West Pennant, with polished concrete floor	158
b	Living space of guest wing, Coastal House 22, with polished concrete floor	158
5.19 a	Koster's mirror-optics – typical sections	161
b	'Ökasolar' used at Ökohuis, Frankfurt	161
5.20	Detail of south façade of Brundtland Centre in Toftlund with glazing hierarchy	162
5.21	'Visi Heat' and 'Thermascrene' glazing by Solaglas at Whalley house	164
5.22	Berlingske Tidene extension in Copenhagen at night	166

Chapter 6 Machine Control

6.1	External shading mechanisms, Burrell Museum, Glasgow	174
6.2	View looking north past west façade of R & D building in the Rheinelbe Science Park	175
6.3	South façade of school in Glasgow, showing louvres and glazing with blinds	176
6.4	Atrium of Rijkswaterstaat – windows closed with weather sunny but windy	178
6.5	ETFE canopy at Kingsdale School – artificial lights inside while outside is sunlit	179
6.6 a	The structural glass roof over the atrium of the Wolfson Building	181
b	The inside of the 'study landscape' with cedar-slatted blinds occluding daylight	181
6.7	Close-up of the solar absorber in the 'Trisol' system used at Dingwall	186
6.8	A roof-integrated solar air collector at Easthall, aligned with the glazed-in balcony	186
6.9 a	Mock-up of window integrated solar air collectors on PASSYS test cell	191
b	Detail of fabric absorber and air inlet slot	191
6.10	View within linear sunspace at Netley Abbey Infants' School	193

6.11   Inside atrium at Jubilee Campus looking east towards service stack   195

6.12   Conical cowls and cleaning gantry at east end of atrium at Jubilee Campus   197

6.13   Atrium at the Technical University Campus, Trondheim   197

6.14   Winter garden located on top of boiler house at Kilwinning   200

6.15   Solar house at Stokkan: a) cross section showing mechanical servicing;
        b) double-height winter garden above plant room   201

6.16   The combined geothermal heat pump and solar system for Shettleston   202

6.17   Solar-geothermal retrofit at Lumphinnans: a) schematic; b) sunspaces   203

6.18   General view of south façade of Task XIII solar apartment block in Amstelveen   206

Chapter 7 Green Solar Future

7.1   The concept of three overlapping dimensions of sustainability – people, place and
        prosperity – per William Heath Robinson   213

7.2   Part of south façade of BedZED terrace   217

7.3   Inside and outside the 1985 conversion of the MacKay-Lyons house at Kingsburg   222

7.4   Inside the main living space of the Graham house – note the sectional device for
        providing daylight and ventilation deep within the floor plate   223

7.5   Helliwell + Smith's cliff-side home and studio on Hornby Island   223

7.6   The West Vancouver studio of Blue Sky Architecture: a) curved west facade;
        b) straight façade opposite, facing to the north of due east   224

7.7   The Murphy house: a) curvaceous front; b) angular back   225

7.8   The Greenwood or 'Fishbones' house on Galiano Island: a) plan; b) elevation;
        c) cross section; d) interior view   227

7.9   Japanese Centre for Art and Technology, Kracow: a) external view; b) internal view   228

7.10   The spinal beam of the Murphy house, looking west into the main room   229

7.11   The Gadsby house looking into living area west towards entrance porch   230

7.12   Coastal House 22: a) view south to guesthouse; b) view north to estuary   234

7.13   Coastal House 22: architect's drawings – plans and elevations   234–235

7.14   Coastal House 22: structure integrated in the main bedroom, looking north   236

7.15   The atrium of the computing technology centre at Dalhousie University, looking west   237

7.16   The 'look at me' and 'look at this' of the new Scottish Parliament's exterior   238

It is perhaps odd that many architects are so nervous of science – at least the kind of physics and engineering that is mostly found in the proceedings of solar conferences or illustrious journals. After all, they have to deal in quantities in order to create buildings and are happy to take on the general concept of firmness – structural stability and the provision of adequate shelter relative to a particular function. However, they commonly perceive a large gulf between physical spatial constructs and the physics of energy flux. For a start, the dimensions of the latter are not static. But then, as soon as people occupy buildings and move around in them, we have a fourth dimension which is also not static. It seems that most architects grapple with visible, spatial awareness, coupled with movement, much more easily than with mainly invisible transfers of energy. Of course sunlight and daylight are visual phenomena, which are inspirational. But the implications of energy in terms of its modes of transfer and the elusive characteristics of thermal admittance, damping and time lag are tougher to take on and exploit aesthetically. Then we have specialist consultants who tend to be happier with the engineering certainties of discrete active or mechanical systems than with the more subtle synergies of building-integrated passive or inert ones. In any event, evidence of relatively limited uptake suggests that trying to nourish architects with technical textbooks on solar architecture is problematic. On the other hand, coffee-table books with seductive photographs, but minimal accompanying information regarding performance, are unlikely to be useful. Certain principles do need to be understood.

Thus one aim of this book is to prime architects and other members of their teams who are working in cool climates, generally associated with higher latitudes, to design solar buildings, which it is increasingly recognized should or could also be green or environmental buildings. The implication of high latitudes is that buildings have to mediate with ambient temperatures, which are well below acceptable internal comfort levels for a significant part of the year. However, even in such cool climates, they may also have to tackle overheating in warm, sunny weather. The stance taken in this book is, firstly, that basic natural techniques, possibly solar assisted, can get rid of unwanted heat. Secondly, and more importantly, it is that free solar energy can make a significant impact in bridging the 'cold gap', even where winters tend towards cloud and rain. In simple terms of supply and demand, the contention is that the solar supply diminishes less rapidly than the demand for heat increases as one moves away from the tropics of Cancer and Capricorn. This provides opportunities, particularly for passive solar design. This is where a building contributes to the capture, storage and delivery of the sun's energy. Quantitatively, the sun will displace traditional fuels for space heating, which are predominantly non-renewable and have damaging combustion products. Qualitatively, it should also be possible to add to the sensory drama of the architecture, thus adding pleasure to the lives of occupants.

The competing climatic characteristics that held sway over many of the pioneering passive solar experiments from the late 1930s up to the 1970s related to distance from the sea and altitude as well as to solar geometry. There are many areas, with relatively low latitude, that have considerable heating loads in winter but also significant amounts of winter sunshine. Supply is well aligned with demand. Thus it was in the latitudinal zone of 42–43°N in the vicinity of Chicago in the USA, where many of George Keck's pioneering solar houses were built in the 1940s, and also in southern France, where the renowned Trombe-Michel experiment took place in 1967. Many of the following passive solar experiments in the 1970s were even further south in locations such as New Mexico and Colorado, where demand for heat is more influenced by geographical characteristics other than the distance from the Equator. This book assumes that lack of drive to address both solar heating and cooling at higher latitudes, with less obvious attributes in terms of weather, is not primarily due to paucity of information. That is there if one searches for it. The basic problem is lack of confidence and conviction. To give this a boost, architects need palatable information on the one hand and convincing arguments on the other.

The geographical scope of this book in terms of case studies could have included regions such as southern Chile, northern Japan or the South Island of New Zealand. However, the principle of the authorship being enhanced by direct personal knowledge of solar buildings used as case studies would have been compromised in these countries. Such experience underpins the case to be discussed and developed in successive chapters. The focus has therefore been pragmatically limited to more populous northern European countries, with a coastline to the Atlantic Ocean, North Sea, Norwegian Sea and Baltic Sea, and to part of the Pacific edge and Atlantic edge of North America. These regions are also ones where there is an established, but far from fully developed, market for solar architecture.

Underdevelopment is due to a number of reasons. One is that there is political scepticism about renewable technologies in general and solar energy in particular. Also political is a prevailing attitude by elected representatives that tends to equate energy with the generation of electricity rather than the demand for heat. This of course handicaps development of solar thermal systems, especially if they are integrated building design techniques, rather than discrete products. Then there is a commonly held, and not unnatural, lay view that solar energy cannot really work in countries or regions where it rains a lot.

Hence the book consciously targets areas with frequent rainfall, winters that demand that buildings are heated, and summers where high temperatures, such as those experienced in Northern Europe in 2003, have been historically quite rare. This does not mean that passive heating techniques suitable for the climatic zones thus identified are not transferable to more extreme southern or continental climates, providing some adjustment is made to take account of varying solar geometry and intensity. Rather, propositions that have been tried and tested in regions with significant amounts of winter sunshine do not tend to transfer so readily to those without. This point will emerge more clearly through the case studies, but is an important one to make at the outset, when defining geographical and climatic scope.

The 'cool' in the title is not quite the same as the meteorological temperate since some locations are included that are quite some distance from the sea and could thus be regarded as continental. Rather than define territory too tightly by northerly latitude, although this aspect is undoubtedly relevant, approximate climatic boundaries are taken as moderate July mean daily temperatures (say, no higher than 20–22°C) and annual rainfall of not less than 0.5 metres. The first limit excludes most of southern Europe, roughly beyond a line from below Brittany to the southern boundary of Poland, even though there are regions here that do have a significant demand for space heating in winter. It also targets regions such as the coastal part of British Columbia and all of Nova Scotia, and could include other continental locations with specific climatic moderators, and some high altitude locations at lower latitudes. The second limit implies relatively low levels of sunshine, commonly during winter in particular, when the demand for heat is highest. One might imagine that this intrinsic out-of-phase characteristic is too great a handicap, but this will be shown to be not necessarily the case.

Accordingly, the strategy adopted is to show that solar savings can be brought to the architectural marketplace in apparently challenging territory. The text will progressively introduce and explore scientific principles and concepts embedded in the design of buildings, and it will do so predominantly in an experiential and thematic way. This is done mainly through the medium of first hand knowledge of their performance, or at least a critical aspect of it. Inevitably, by choosing particular buildings to discuss key parameters, many other similarly deserving exemplars are missed. Hence the transference of principles is left to the reader. Predictive modelling also has a role, initially setting out some of the key issues for a solar space-heating capability relative to climate and built form. Unbuilt Scottish projects are included as well as built ones. Since Scotland has strong historical links to both Canada and Northern Europe, it might be regarded as a centre of gravity or pivot from which to look east and west. In any case, its position between the Atlantic and the North Sea might indicate that it would be one of the least favoured of all the climatic locations examined.

Insights with regard to innovative solar architecture have thus been garnered through a combination of theory, measurement, observation and dialogue. A predominant thrust is on how buildings and their systems have performed compared with the pre-contract expectation. Empirical data are gained partly through detailed monitoring programmes, which can be compared with predictive modelling. It is also acquired simply by visiting and speaking to the occupants, as well as getting into physical contact with the environmental aura in order to become sensitized to particular thermal attributes or shortcomings. This can be particularly valuable when visiting at a time of some climatic spike, in areas where these are relatively rare, and where control systems are not functioning as intended at design stage. In other words, there is an appropriate mix of first-hand hard and soft research. Source material includes published papers by many authors with expertise in the field, mainly from the mid 1980s onwards, as well as Scottish Solar Energy Group archives.

The language is consciously architect-friendly, without avoiding necessary numerical comparators that are also useful to the scientific and engineering community. Having decided not to dodge physical quantities, their relationships and the units that define them, the problem is then how to avoid excessive interruption to thematic flow. The device chosen is to provide in-depth supporting information as required in blocks of notes parallel to the main text. Readers then have more choice as to how they engage with the issues. Also, although there is a coherent structure to successive chapters, each has a stand-alone quality. The other characteristic of the structure of chapters is to adopt a position that is sometimes biased more towards the intentions of the originators than the experience of the users of the built environment, and sometimes vice versa. In order to give vent to such differences of emphasis there is also deliberate overlap of the themes that are tackled.

The first two chapters are in the former category, Chapter 1 setting out the context for solar architecture at high latitudes, Chapter 2 then addressing how additional costs can be diluted through diverse aesthetic and tectonic means. The next two chapters swing attention more to the user. Chapter 3 covers aspects of comfort and microclimate, and then tensions between energy efficiency and environmental quality. Then Chapter 4 moves into the realm of proactive control, the manner in which users affect the performance of small domestic sunspaces and socio-demographic influences. The following two chapters continue with issues of control, but shift the discourse back more to the aims of the design team. Chapter 5, in addressing passive configurations, starts with plan and section, then gets to grips with thermal mass and ends with the transparent surfaces, summarizing innovation with respect to the balance of light and heat at various levels of sophistication. Chapter 6, in dealing with active configurations, continues this line of enquiry, adding in mechanical and electronic means of control. It then moves on to cover progress with solar air heating systems and ends by probing a number of performance shortfalls and surprises arising from multiple parametric interactions between static built components and dynamic systems of control. The seventh and final chapter widens the agenda to solar architecture, which may also be described as green or environmental architecture, and how this is viewed relative to sustainability and sustainable development. The perspective may be perceived as mainly an architectural or technical one, but the meshing with the aspirations of the users through the mutual development of the architectural programme means that this chapter embraces the role of lay players, mainly clients, who effectively sponsor responsible environmental innovation.

Thus the book is structured to progressively excavate myths, tensions, dilemmas and cruxes in a way that should promote flexibility and opportunity to a relatively diverse audience, including those who use, procure and finance buildings. The fundamental aim is to facilitate solar architecture in cool climates out of its current experimental and special interest status and into the mainstream. This includes refurbishment as well as new-build, recognizing the potential for solar energy to play a much more significant role in the former than is presently the case. An explicit objective is that the built environment should actually shoulder some responsibility in terms of CO_2 reduction. This is simple common sense, but expressly does not imply moving towards an eco-morality that might be perceived as obsessive. Neither is it intended to further hem architectural professionals in with unnecessary rules or obligations. Rather, there is an acceptance that people inhabiting parts of the world with relatively long dark winters are naturally sympathetic to architecture that makes the most of daylight and sunlight. Solar knowledge is just the means to an end that has emotionally uplifting, as well as physically grounded, altruistic dimensions. Thus it is a straightforward win–win solar sales pitch. It very much embraces good design, but endeavours to steer clear of the dispiriting political language of best value, which seems to be synonymous with worst architecture.

Colin Porteous
Glasgow, spring 2005

ACKNOWLEDGEMENTS

Since this book draws on many case studies, nearly all of which have been visited with extremely hospitable and informative guides or hosts, there are many people to thank. Where there have been several years of involvement from inception to completion, including monitoring and dissemination, the list of those to whom gratitude is due is lengthy just for a single project. Therefore, I find it difficult not to be selective and trust that those who have not been named, but have played a part in imparting their knowledge and experience to a wider audience through this medium, will be aware that their contribution is not forgotten or ignored. I am extremely grateful to all of them.

My own solar research journey began with unheated sunspaces and I have devoted considerable space to the findings of two particular Scottish projects. The one in Stornoway would not have happened without my old climbing friend and architect Alan Holling having the insight to see the potential for a south sloping site at the same time that I had started in-depth research into passive solar applications in Scotland. A few years later, when I was leading an urban community technical aid project, I met up with a remarkable group of tenant activists in the east end of Glasgow – Easthall Residents' Association. Three of their leading lights were David Humble, Helen Martin and Cathy McCormack. The European Solar Demonstration Project at Easthall would never have happened without their persistent resolve to tackle fuel poverty in their community and the cold, damp and mouldy homes that went with it. A spin-off of the widely publicized solar solution was community and personal empowerment. Their play, *The Damp Busters*, was Easthall's humorous contribution to Glasgow, City of Culture 1990. Cathy, its main script writer, went on to become involved on the global health scene, travelling widely to countries such as Nicaragua, and taking part in follow-up events to the 1992 Rio Earth Summit such as the one in New York. I also have fond memories of travelling around Eastern Europe in 1996 with David – our mission to spread Easthall's bottom-up story, strewn with political obstacles, to other communities with similar problems.

Within the international solar village, I am very grateful to the encouragement and steer of leading Anglo-Hungarian solar luminary Leslie Jesch. While Leslie is no longer an active solar researcher and campaigner, I am glad that he is still in good health and still travelling to interesting places with his wife – even volcanoes! It was Leslie who valued and publicized solar work in Scotland through Sun at Work in Great Britain, Sun at Work in Europe and Sun World, with the able help of Alison Patterson. It was also Leslie who helped to give the Scottish Solar Energy Group a political voice within Europe. As I indicated, there are very many people in Europe to whom I owe thanks. Torben Esbensen is another individual who, like Leslie, has been very supportive of Scottish solar activity, who hosted our visit to a very special solar building in Denmark and who has contributed valuable Scandinavian experience to the Scottish North Sun meetings of 1984 and 1994, not to mention a smaller international meeting in 1998. Similarly, I would like to thank the architects Christer and Kirsten Nordström, not only for their warm hospitality to our group when in Göteborg, but also to Christer for helping to inform and enliven a conference in Glasgow, and more recently updating me on the tactics with regard to occupants and performance in his solar housing. Bart Jan van den Brink is another person who has allowed his small Dutch solar home to be invaded on two occasions by a party from Scotland, and more recently travelled to visit us in Scotland in order to help dispel solar myths at a symposium. Such exchanges are invaluable.

In Canada, my partner Mary and I were overwhelmed by the friendliness and generosity of people in general, but in particular from our architectural hosts. Readers will note North American solar threads complementing the weave of European ones, especially the work of Bo Helliwell and Kim Smith (Blue Sky Architecture) in the west and Brian MacKay-Lyons in the east. Not only did Bo and Kim put us up and show us around in Vancouver, but also they lent us their home on Hornby Island. I had been nurturing a desire to visit Hornby ever since the special issue of Architectural Design was published in the

1970s. The fulfilment of this ambition, with Bo and Kim's stunning cliffside home as our base, was exhilarating, and to meet up with Bo's former partner Michael McNamara, still leading Blue Sky Design, an added bonus – not to mention the ambience of jazz in the local pub. We had not met Brian before, but both found an immediate rapport with his intense take on architecture that is just as rooted in the culture and geography of Nova Scotia as that of Bo and Kim's is in British Columbia. Within two hours of meeting him, Brian also offered a second home as our base, only warning us to be careful not to set the house on fire as Aldo van Eyck had apparently nearly done! Moreover, we owe a vote of thanks to his administrator, Constance Gould, for rapidly organizing an itinerary of visits to a number of dwellings along the southern coastal trail of Nova Scotia. Regardless of how good the relationship between architect and client may be, gaining access to private homes can be difficult. But in terms of soft environmental research, it is necessary to both experience the buildings inside, and to learn of the experiences and attitudes of the users.

Closer to home, I am indebted to the Glasgow School of Art for allowing a term's sabbatical, without which timely completion of the script would not have been possible. Particular colleagues have also made important contributions – David Buri, our architectural librarian, Vivian Carvalho and Craig Laurie for scanning many images, and Paul Simpson for reading the script and making helpful suggestions as to navigating within and between chapters. Outside the 'Mac', I thank Sally Patrick for her useful library of newspaper cuttings. Then I owe a special debt to Mary Patrick, who has patiently supported me in this venture throughout and provided invaluable advice on the initial draft. Mary also later did a fine job with the typesetting and layout for the Graphics Company, a workers' cooperative in Edinburgh with which I have had a long and fruitful relationship. I am also grateful to Alison Neathey, a founder member of the cooperative and its link with the publishers. Finally, having got to James & James and Earthscan, I warmly thank Guy Robinson and Hamish Ironside for their support and editorial input.

CP, Mackintosh School of Architecture (the 'Mac'), May 2005

Chapter 1   North Sun Context

The case for solar architecture in cool climates rests to a large extent on a truth that was revealed to the international solar community well over two decades ago and then followed up by many other solar scientists and architects keen to promote the 'north sun context'. It is therefore fundamental to the thrust of this book and involves the presentation of certain thermal principles at the outset. Fortunately, these are not excessively daunting.

In 1981 at the International Solar Energy Society (ISES) World Solar Congress in Brighton, UK, a paper was presented with analytical information that indicated that northern European latitudes could be better for solar space heating than southern ones (MacGregor, 1981). This is not actually as surprising as it might seem, but requires explanation. For many solar energy applications in the northern hemisphere, both electrical and thermal, the potential increases with the supply of solar radiation as one moves south – at least to the vicinity of the Tropic of Cancer. For example, this is the case for solar photovoltaic (PV) arrays, provided almost all the collected electrical energy can be utilized. The same applies to solar heated water for hygienic and utilitarian uses, where there is a year-round thermal demand. In warmer and sunnier climates, however, there is more demand for cooling spaces than for heating them. Solar energy can still be used to offset cooling by other means, but its usefulness for heating becomes marginal. This generalization is of course subject to topography and regional climatic factors. A town located at a high altitude, but relatively low latitude and in a continental setting that is subject to high daily and seasonal swings in temperature, may have both heating and cooling demands. In essence, the north is better trend for solar displacement of space heating acknowledges that as latitude rises, the solar supply diminishes. But it does so more slowly than the increasing intensity of climatic factors that drive the demand – lower ambient temperature and higher wind speeds, especially accompanied by rain. It has to be accepted that the relative merits of latitude are not immediately obvious. Indeed, in the 1970s a view or prejudice against solar space heating in the north of the British Isles was certainly apparent.

■1.1 Terms, units and numbers with comparative examples

1.1(1) Flat-plate collectors are more fully described in Chapter 2. At this stage it is sufficient to say that they belong within the specialist sphere of plumbing and engineering. Such solar components are also termed 'active', signifying movement and mechanical intervention, as opposed to 'passive', indicating more static modes of energy exchange.

1.1(2) 'Global solar radiation' means all the sun's energy, both direct (clear sky) and diffuse (through cloud and haze), falling on a surface, which is taken to be horizontal unless otherwise stated. 'Irradiation' and 'insolation' are used to express this energy quantified over a period of time (units: joule, J; watt x seconds, Ws; watt x hours, Wh; kilowatts x hours, kWh etc.). 'Irradiance' is the flow of energy at a given moment (units: joules per second, J/s; $1J/s = 1W$). 'Degree days' (DDs) are the difference over time between an average internal temperature, usually a 'base' value having deducted for the impact of free gains (solar and incidental from people, lighting and appliances), and that outside. It is added up over a relevant period – as long as base temperature remains above that outside (ambient).

1.1(3) From 1983–1987 Stornoway in the Western Isles at 58.2°N averaged 469kWh/m² from September to May on a south-facing vertical surface (Porteous, 1990, p26). This compares with 281kWh/m² for Kew in London at 51.5°N from November to April (Page and Lebens, 1986, p162). This six month period shares a similar average temperature as Stornoway over nine months: 6.1°C. If we then deduct 6.1°C from the base temperature of 15.6°C used by UK-ISES, we get 9.5 to be multiplied by 273 days (= 2593.5DDs). The same difference for London from November to April is multiplied by 181 days (= 1719.5DDs). Respective supply–demand ratios are then 0.18 for Stornoway and 0.16 for London, assuming all of the supply is useful in each case. This is a very different answer to that given by the raw UK-ISES method. It indicates that Stornoway has 12.5 per cent better solar heating potential. As the methodology becomes less crude, the ratio now favours the more northerly location.

Latitude myths challenged

Going back several decades, the UK section of the International Solar Energy Society (UK-ISES) published a review of solar energy (UK-ISES, 1976). It stated: 'South-west England and south-west Wales are the best areas for solar space heating from the meteorological point of view.' A government report in the same year (Long, 1976, pp25–44) was worthy in some respects, but naïve and misleading in others. It recognized the supply–demand dilemma, but omitted to mention the significance of demand extending the duration of the heating season, and did not engage with the potential for using unheated glazed spaces as a means of preheating air for ventilation. The term 'solar ventilation preheat' is now commonly used. It is possible for solar energy to tackle a thermal niche market, which complements other less sensitive enablers of energy efficiency such as insulation.

The report also rightly emphasized the issue of long-term and medium-term thermal storage, but was incredibly tentative and misleading with respect to solar energy and architecture. For example, having given complete misinformation with respect to the 'Trombe' wall (see Chapter 4), the second part of the following statement probably belongs in the territory of wishing in hindsight that it could have been erased from the record (Long, 1976, p37): 'In practice, a very important distinction is that flat-plate collectors [■1.1(1)] can be installed on suitably oriented existing buildings, while, by definition, techniques involving novel architectural design are applicable only to new properties.' That is hard to beat for myopic ignorance. Even though solar heating at that time was mainly contemplated from an additive engineering perspective, the logic of denying existing buildings scope for an integrative architectural one is obscure. At any rate, the received wisdom that opportunities for solar heating in the UK were confined to the south still prevailed at the time of MacGregor's counter proposition at Brighton. A book published that year (Oppenheim, 1981), which set out to explore the potential for solar buildings in cold northern climates, stated: '… the most favourable areas lie to the south of Britain, and the least favourable areas to the north.' Oppenheim supported his assertion with numbers, similar to the ones used in the scientific reports five years previously. Therefore, in mounting a challenge, a limited amount of mathematical investigation is necessary.

Numbers, which are used evidentially, must have a sound basis. However, the methodology used by UK-ISES and Oppenheim relied on a proportional relationship, both parts of which were fundamentally flawed. A crude index of climatic suitability was derived from a supply–demand ratio of 'global solar radiation' to 'degree days' ■1.1(2). In the first place, the warmer the climate, the more this index will indicate strong solar potential for heating. Yet, in reality, the reverse is true. At the point when there is minimal demand for heat, there is minimal scope for the solar supply to play a useful part. Most, if not all, of the numerator then has to be discounted. Conversely, the supply should all be counted in as long as there is a heating demand. But a second flaw is that the demand side of the ratio assumes a standard length of heating season for all locations. The same number of days is used everywhere, although the UK-ISES report did acknowledge that northern UK could have a percentage of 'degree days' in summer twice that of a sunnier south. So both the supply and demand is less than it should be as one moves north, while not all the supply computed is likely to be useful in the south. For example, the relevant period of time for solar radiation and 'degree days' might be six months for London, but at least nine months for the Western Isles in Scotland ■1.1(3). Indicative ratios would improve for both locations as a building becomes more energy-efficient, the proportional gap diminishing somewhat and both heating seasons shrinking. It is always subject to all the solar supply being able to usefully contribute to heating, which becomes less likely the warmer the climate and the more efficient the construction.

If the impacts of wind and rain are also evaluated, the contrast will increase. A further problem is that the totals for degree days are based on an initial assumption with regard to the energy efficiency of the buildings. The more thermally efficient a building becomes, the shorter will be the period in each case, as well as the lower the gap in temperature driving the need for heat. But a significant geographical time difference would remain and, in reality, the relativity of supply and demand is very dependent on the design of buildings, even for one location. Moreover, solar radiation on a horizontal surface is not particularly relevant to solar geometry in winter. That falling on a south-facing vertical surface, or a steeply sloping surface, is more likely to displace fossil fuels for heating. So, for example, one might expect the incident irradiation from September to May in the Western Isles to be greater than that from November to April in London. Overall, although the idea of such a ratio as a ready reckoner of potential may appeal, it would need to be carefully devised to eliminate an erroneous southern bias.

Brighton breakthrough

The analysis presented at Brighton was subject to assumptions for a simple theoretical model for a small dwelling, which was well insulated. It was such a powerful dispeller of previous myths that some numerical detail is required. The house was not designed, but rather assumed to have a low specific heat loss or heat loss coefficient, as well as a particular size and efficiency of solar collection. ■1.2(1) For a representative UK location, this suggested a contribution of about 2500kWh over a heating season from October to April. Residual or net space heating loads would then be in the order of 3000kWh. ■1.2(2) These numbers are important in that they signify a considerable level of energy efficiency. Most householders would be pleasantly surprised if they found that they had only

■1.2 Basic 'steady-state' methodology for estimating space heating loads

1.2(1) The 'heat loss coefficient' was given as 100 W/K (watts, a flow of energy, per degree kelvin: 1K equals 1°C, but a convention is to use the Kelvin scale for differences in temperature and Celsius for absolute values.) 'Specific heat loss' or 'heat loss coefficient' is energy lost by ventilation added to that lost by conduction through the fabric of a building. The model assumed a 30 per cent efficient 26m^2 vertical, south-facing solar collector, but this could also be conceived as a smaller collector plus passive solar heat gained through windows.

1.2(2) The following scenario fleshes out the computation: if free gains from lighting and appliances amount to 400W, and are divided by the specific heat loss of 100W/K, the resultant differential of 4K represents the free heating effect. Deducted from an average demand setting of 20°C, normal for a well-insulated dwelling, it gives a first 'base' level of 16°C. Solar gains can be similarly computed (ie deducting the ratio of solar gains in watts to the specific heat loss) to arrive at a final internal 'base' temperature. It is the difference between this and the temperature outside that drives the space-heating load. If the outside temperature averages 5°C over 212 days from October to April, and the solar gain effectively contributes 5K (500W divided by 100W/K), the internal 'base' temperature falls to 11°C. If the product of the heat loss coefficient of 100W/K and 6K (ie 11 – 5) is then multiplied by 212 days and a coefficient of 0.024 (to convert from watts x days to kWh), we arrive at an approximate net demand for space heating of 3000kWh. At the same time, useful solar contribution is over 2500kWh (500W x 212 days x 0.024). This is a basic 'steady state' analysis, which does not allow for the fluctuating climatic characteristics such as driving rain or dynamic effects of thermal storage, noting that fluxes of energy in and out of storage tend to cancel out in dwellings with a 24-hour occupancy cycle.

■1.3 Hypothetical dimensions for 1981 theoretical model

If, for example, the model takes plan dimensions of 12m x 4.5m (giving a footprint of 54m²), the height rises from 2.35m to 4.35m, the south-facing windows and glazed doors are 9m², the solar collector is 17m² and other windows are kept to a minimum, then the heat loss through the fabric with U-values (thermal transmittance coefficients) circa 0.2W/m²K would be about two-thirds of an assumed total of 100W/K. The balance due to ventilation implies an average hourly rate of air change of 0.6, a value that is more likely to be achieved with the aid of mechanical heat recovery than by reliance on natural ventilation. The residual space-heating load expressed per unit area would then typically be in the range 50–60kWh/m².

■1.4 Theoretical predictions of useful solar gain in various UK locations, 1981

1.4(1) The useful solar gain was predicted to be 4240kWh in Lerwick compared to 2670 in London.

1.4(2) The useful solar gain was predicted to be 4250kWh in Eskdalemuir, only 10kWh higher than Lerwick; and respective net loads for space heating were 3500kWh and 3160kWh.

used 3000 units for heating in a year. They might also be surprised that their bill could have been more than eighty per cent higher but for the contribution from the sun.

By assuming an energy-efficient model, the analysis was both forward-looking and avoided southern locations being deceptively favoured. Although a poorly insulated model would have lengthened the heating season for all locations, an efficient model moves towards eliminating space heating entirely. It is also important to emphasize that all the values used are reasonable and could translate into built form. The house might, for example, have a relatively long and high south façade, with a mono-pitched roof sloping down to the north across a relatively narrow depth. ■1.3 This is an archetypal passive solar form. Roughly half of this might be either collector or window, with minimal glazing elsewhere and impressively low U-values or thermal transmittance coefficients for all opaque surfaces. Alternatively, if conceived as part of a terrace, the U-values could afford to rise a bit. This kind of solar dwelling could match the assumed heat loss coefficient.

The results showed higher solar savings with increasing latitude. For example, at the most northerly latitude of Lerwick in the Shetland Isles at 60°N the solar contribution was nearly four times greater than in the most southerly location of Messina in Sicily at 38°N. Even within the UK, Lerwick's solar input was nearly 60 per cent greater than that for London ■1.4(1). The explanation for this surprising conclusion was the better usefulness of solar energy at high latitudes due to the greater, longer and flatter profile for heating demand. This more than compensated for the slightly lower solar radiation levels, the reduction, as already stated, being a lot less marked on vertical surfaces than on tilted or horizontal ones. Altitude was also relevant. For example, at Eskdalemuir in the Scottish Borders at 250m, the solar contribution was predicted to be marginally greater than for Lerwick at sea level, while the residual demand for space heating was also somewhat higher ■1.4(2). Later work, which examined the relative climatic suitability for solar space heating in different parts of Scotland (MacGregor and Balmbro, 1984), found that the best location was in the north at Wick (58.4°N), while the worst was in the south at Greenock (55.9°N), the difference being 45 per cent.

In Norway, Olseth and Skartveit (1986), using another analytical method known as 'F-chart', investigated the relative performance of an active solar heated building in different locations. Again it was found that solar savings are generally greater at higher latitudes, for example 10 per cent higher at Tromso (69.7°N) compared with Oslo (60°N). An earlier study in North America (Duffie, Beckman and Dekker, 1977) also concluded that solar savings for space heating generally increase with latitude and altitude.

A review of all the above studies (MacGregor, 1987) came to the clear conclusion that high latitudes offer more scope for solar space heating. This is a fundamentally important finding because it completely contravenes the previous beliefs and opens up new possibilities for solar energy. Indeed, the initial study in 1981 provided the impetus to inaugurate the North Sun series of conferences with their consistent theme of 'solar energy at high latitudes'. The findings are now generally accepted within the solar community, but the common perception outside it is still that solar energy only works at low latitudes. Clearly, there is a major task of education to be done! Although it is conceded that the performance of solar water heating systems generally gets poorer at higher latitudes, there is a countervailing northern compensation even for this technology. Lower ambient water temperatures yield higher heating loads and so give solar energy more potential work to do. Similarly, for PV the lower ambient temperatures at higher latitudes and altitudes allow modules to work more efficiently.

Quite apart from the supply–demand play-off between solar intensity and geometry relative to the surfaces of buildings and the ambient temperature, there is also a tendency for the weather to become windier and wetter with rising latitude and altitude, especially in maritime locations. Again, this increases the demand for heat. Consequently, anything that shields a building against these elements, such as a sunspace or glazed solar skin, will have a greater energy conservation benefit at high latitudes. In addition, the amenity benefits of usable buffer spaces of this kind are likely to be greater in areas with much wind and rain.

Dynamic complexity – direct versus indirect passive solar models

Having thrown a fairly challenging, if perfectly logical, broad-brush 'north is better' hypothesis at the solar community, inevitably, when more specific models are subjected to more rigorous dynamic thermal analysis, matters become more complex. For example, a paper presented at the inaugural North Sun 84 in Edinburgh (Bartholomew, 1985), three years after the congress in Brighton, compared simulated results for two very different passive solar houses, with reference houses in contrasting UK locations. These were London, the Southern Uplands of Scotland and Shetland, all with detailed meteorological records, including solar radiation. ■1.5(1)

direct gain model – detached house

One solar house was categorized as 'direct gain' (solar transmission through windows directly into rooms) with most rooms on a relatively long south façade (Figure 1.1). This 150m² detached model was designed by Stillman and Eastwick-Field, Architects (Stephens, 1983). It included night shutters to main windows on the south façade and both walls and roof were well insulated in the context of the UK in the early 1980s. ■1.5(2) Walls were more than three times as efficient as most dwellings built at this time, and the roof four times as much.

■1.5 Context of dynamic modelling and key results for direct gain model, 1984

1.5(1) Respective meteorological stations were Kew (London), Eskdalemuir (Scottish Borders) and Lerwick (Shetland Islands). The proposed dwelling models were part of a series organized by A5 Architects for the Energy Technology Support Unit (ETSU), then directed by Dr David Bartholomew, as part of its programme of passive solar performance studies.

1.5(2) Respective U-values (thermal transmittance coefficients) for walls and roof of 0.3W/m²K and 0.15W/m²K were less than one third and exactly one quarter of the minimum statutory standards (1981). U-values for the ground floor was allowed to rise to 0.6W/m²K, as computer modelling had shown that extra insulation was not particularly advantageous here.

1.5(3) At an average internal temperature of 18°C, the passive solar advantage over the upgraded reference model was twice as great in Kew as in Lerwick (3000kWh compared to 1500kWh). Moreover, the residual annual space heating load for this achieved temperature was substantially less at Kew than Lerwick – about 5000kWh compared with 12,500kWh, or 60 per cent less.

1.1 Plan of 'direct gain' passive solar house by Stillman and Eastwick-Field

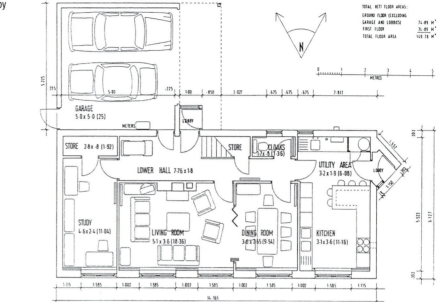

Indeed, a concern was that the standards of conserving heat were such that potentially useful solar gain in the autumn and spring would be displaced. As stated earlier, it is axiomatic that the more energy-efficient a building becomes, the shorter will be its heating season.

This appears to indicate that passive solar performance, implying significant investment in glass, is in competition with good standards of insulation, since the latter is much more cheaply purchased. In reality, the value of energy efficiency relative to passive solar measures is subtler. For example, the solar contribution may primarily tackle the ventilating or convective component of heating demand, while insulation is dealing mainly with heat lost by conduction. Thus it is possible for them to complement each other rather than compete. These are important issues, which will be elucidated in succeeding chapters.

The comparative modelling for this particular 'direct gain' dwelling, reported at North Sun 84, showed that the southern English location was more effective than the northern Scottish one, once the insulation levels in the reference model were matched to the solar one. ■1.5(3) However, much of this difference is taken up with respective thermal losses through windows, two thirds greater in the case of Lerwick.

Since the heating season for an energy-efficient house would still be significantly longer in Shetland compared with the London area, one has to be careful in assuming that respective solar contributions are decisive. Even if the amount of useful solar gain in Lerwick is greater than that of Kew, climatic factors such as the ambient temperature and wind strength, especially together with rain, are influential. The southern location constitutes the softer option in this regard. Although the former aspect, that of solar supply, is shown to favour Lerwick over Kew by 1800kWh for a typical heating regime, and hence supports the 'north is better' contention, the losses through the windows far outweigh this apparent strength. It is the relativity of gain to loss that is critical. It is also known that the final sizing of windows, as well as the specification of single glazing to all four bedrooms, the study and the kitchen, were both influenced by the initial thermal modelling in the southern climate (Stephens, 1983). Those decisions certainly disadvantaged the two Scottish locations, one high in altitude and the other in latitude.

indirect gain model – dense terrace

The second house was a modern solar interpretation of a 19th century English 'back-to-back' terraced house, accessed either from the east or west (Figure 1.2). Although it was single-aspect, it included a generous unheated atrium or conservatory with the main windows facing south on to it. This then offered the opportunity for 'indirect' solar gain, where the 'greenhouse effect' within the atrium should have an indirect impact on the adjacent heated spaces. In the words of its author, architect Malcolm Newton (Newton, 1983), this 'has the advantage that fresh air from the sunspace can be brought into the house through the heating system and this ensures that a known quantity of fresh air enters and a corresponding quantity of moisture laden air leaves.' The important aspect from an energy-saving viewpoint is that the air in the atrium averages a significantly higher temperature than outside. It is as if the air bounding the heated core had changed season – say, April when it is really January, and the core wishes to provide the environment of July.

The heating system to which Malcolm Newton refers was a '4.5kW gas fired central warm air unit with short ducts to all rooms.' This addresses the small space-heating load, a result of a combination of the solar buffer, the small exposed perimeter afforded by the back-to-back terrace and, again, relatively low U-values (ranging from 0.3–0.35W/m²K for roof, walls and floor). It also addresses the difficulty of slow response heating systems displacing potentially useful solar heat gains. The atrium itself tackles this problem by virtue of being unheated. But there are still significant direct solar gains to all the heated rooms to consider, even though solar radiation often has to pass through the atrium on the way to the heated rooms.

Some of the earliest consciously designed passive solar houses failed to adequately acknowledge the issue of the central heating usurping solar heat. A famous example is Frank Lloyd Wright's 'solar hemicycle' designed in 1943 for Herbert Jacobs, and located in Middleton, Wisconsin. This is an area where mean January temperatures are well below freezing point, but in the same month the percentage of sunshine is a promising 44 per cent of the maximum

1.2   3-dimensional 'cutaway' of 'indirect gain'
      solar house by Malcolm Newton

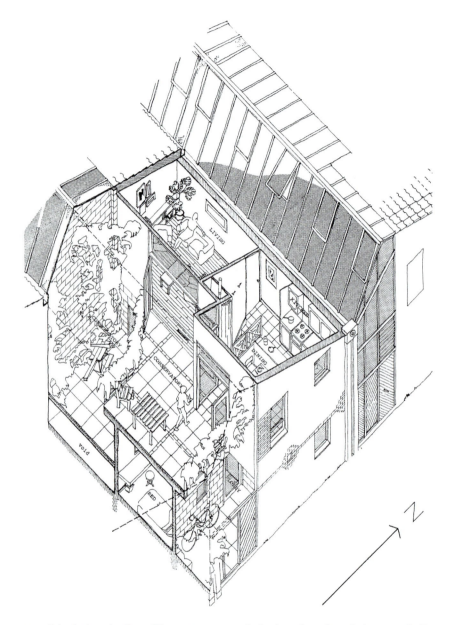

possible during daytime. The concave, south-facing glass façade hence admits significant amounts of solar radiation, to be stored directly in the concrete floor slab. However, the same floor slab accommodates large diameter hot water coils, termed 'gravity heating' by Wright (1977). Jacobs (1978), in writing his memoir, acknowledged that the thermostat regularly switched off shortly after the sun began to shine on fine days in winter: 'We had almost daily evidence of winter solar heating. Usually by nine o'clock on a sunny morning, even in below-zero weather, the heating system stopped, and did not resume again until late afternoon.' Regardless of the client's glowing perception of performance, the fact remains that the already consumed supply of energy to the furnace would have its heat stored in the concrete slab for some considerable period after the heating switched off. Thus some of the apparently useful solar gain would have been displaced. On the other hand, we also have the 'late afternoon' assertion of Jacobs in terms of the heating coming back on again. One might optimistically assume that 'late' signified after sunset. It is then the sun's heat that is displacing fuel that would otherwise be required, and we might reasonably conclude that this cancels out the morning deficit. However, looked at from the point of view of maximizing solar gain, one would wish for the best of both worlds – minimizing fossil fuel displacement of potentially useful solar heat after dawn and maximizing solar thermal storage after sunset.

Jacob's observations had actually been confirmed by measurement some years earlier in relation to the 1941 Duncan house by architects Keck and Keck. Of the two brothers it was George Fred Keck who continually explored new boundaries in technical experimentation, with the first serious passive solar prototype built in 1935. This was also the year that Libby-Owens-Ford Glass Company introduced double-pane glazing. In October 1941, the year-long monitoring of the Duncan house commenced under the direction of Professor James C. Peebles of the Illinois Institute of Technology, funded by Libby-Owens-Ford. Similar to the observations of Herbert Jacobs in Wright's Solar Hemicycle, Peebles noted that on a sunny day in January, the furnace shut off from 8.30am until 8.30pm (Boyce, 1993). Indeed, since the temperature inside the living space rose above 29°C, it was necessary to open windows. However, the monitoring also acknowledged that part of the heat gained during that period was '…due to the hot water in the dark brown concrete floor slab, which continued to radiate heat even when the furnace was shut off.'

This particular aspect, among others such as the temptation to heat conservatories in winter, will be explored in greater depth in subsequent chapters. It is important that such issues are well aired, since it is quite dispiriting for the solar community that they are still not always taken seriously by either architects or occupants. It is right to challenge why this should be the case, given the increasing emphasis on continuing professional development for the architectural team, and when a well publicized proposal from the mid-1980s, such as that by Malcolm Newton, appears to have such a logical foundation. The heating system he recommended could respond rapidly to solar gain, thus maximizing its potential, and the modest amount of glass enclosing the winter garden relative to its volume would increase the amount of time it could be comfortably occupied, even in cold cloudy weather.

One must not forget that such semi-outdoor spaces are the recipient of heat lost from the host rooms, as well as from the sun. The consequence is that

■1.6 Theoretical performance data for back-to-back indirect gain model, 1984

1.6(1) The 'solar' advantage for the Newton design relative to the reference model was an impressive 6000kWh for the Shetlands compared to 4000kWh for the London location.

1.6(2) Heating demand was predicted to be approximately 1000kWh in Kew compared with 2750kWh in Lerwick, a difference now reduced from 7500kWh in the direct gain model to only 1750kWh for the Newton design.

1.6(3) Heat predicted to be lost through windows in Lerwick reduced from 10,480kWh for the first direct gain design to 540kWh for the Newton design.

in cold, overcast weather, or during the night, taking the supply of air for ventilation from the conservatory into the house constitutes a basic form of passive heat recovery. Another advantage of such unheated spaces, provided they remain only heated for free by the sun or from donations from heated rooms, is that high thermal capacitance is advantageous. It does not compete with the fast response needed for auxiliary heating. Moreover, it is worth emphasizing the character of this particular conservatory as a rain-free and wind-sheltered garden, which is divided into three functional zones – entry, alfresco eating and multipurpose – as opposed to an extra room or rooms. This tends to encourage rational use relative to weather and possibly less rational serendipitous use, rather than treating it as an all-year-round space.

Theoretical predictions are able to simulate form and constructional specification accurately. They can also make reasonable assumptions with regard to the regimes adopted by occupants for heating and ventilation, as well as use of lighting and appliances. However, it has to be accepted that the introduction of unheated glazed spaces introduces a further set of possible variables in this regard. These are explored in more depth in Chapter 4. At any rate, the comparative northern Scotland versus southern England computer modelling showed that in this instance 'north was best'. Taking the same average internal temperature as the 'direct gain' house, the apparent passive solar advantage over the upgraded reference model was now reversed to 50 per cent greater in Lerwick than Kew. ■1.6(1) Furthermore, although the residual annual space-heating load for this achieved temperature was still less at Kew than Lerwick, the difference was now much more modest. ■1.6(2) Expressed per square metre of heated floor, the figures translate to 14kWh/m^2 and 38kWh/m^2 for Kew and Lerwick respectively. The value of risking numerical overdose at this early stage is that it establishes benchmarks for comparison with other case studies, both real and theoretical, as the chapters proceed. Critical to this improvement, in the case of Lerwick, is that the energy lost through windows bounding the heated part of the house has been reduced by a factor of almost 20 for a typical heating regime. ■1.6(3) Although Kew also benefits from a significant reduction, it is not of quite such an impressive order – close to a factor of 17.

sunspaces work due to diverse climatic influences

Given that rainfall in Lerwick during winter is high, and that corresponding sunshine is low, the results are impressive, even puzzlingly so. Kew, of course, fares somewhat better in these terms. The annual rainfall is approximately half that of Lerwick, while the proportion of possible sunshine is considerably greater during winter. ■1.7(1) Therefore a question arises: how does Newton's house manage to attribute so much increased efficiency to the solar design features? Bear in mind also that respective savings are related to reference models insulated to the same relatively high standard as the Newton design and it therefore follows that insulation does not seem to be in direct competition with the passive solar features.

To move closer to the explanation for the success of the Newton design in both locations, but particularly in Lerwick, it is necessary to view climatic differences in slightly more detail. ■1.7(2) The differentials in favour of Kew suggest that variables over and above solar radiation and temperature strongly influence Lerwick's larger saving relative to the reference house. Clearly the atrium protects the inner façades between atrium and heated rooms from wind and rain. ■1.7(3) Moreover, the climate severity index or CSI (Markus, 1984), which combines the effect of air temperature, solar radiation and wind, demonstrates an even greater disparity. ■1.7(4) But by sheltering much of the bounding surface of heated spaces with the atrium, especially the windows, and other external surfaces by means of the back-to-back terraced form, this negative impact is greatly reduced. The heating season in Lerwick remains longer than that of Kew, and the residual demand for heat remains higher, but overall the specific design attributes are able to work harder in terms of energy saving.

Therefore, a tentative conclusion to be drawn for indirect gain solutions is that the apparent solar contribution will rise with latitude, and that this is likely to be partly due to other benefits afforded by the passive design features. However, the Newton back-to-back solution is so particular that such a conclusion should be treated with some caution.

further modelling confirms North–South trend in UK

More detailed modelling work carried out after North Sun 84 (Porteous, 1990, pp55–57, 80–93), and using a more conventional terraced house, also found that the indirect versus direct passive solar solutions favoured northerly latitudes. Viewed quantitatively, the useful 'solar' saving in heating, which was attributable to the indirect system compared with the direct one, was significantly higher in central Scotland than southern England. But as in the two theoretical case studies discussed above, which used more extreme models in more contrasting geographical locations, that is not the complete picture.

A five-person living–dining room with generous direct gain double-glazing ■1.8(1) was compared with the same space completely buffered with a single-glazed conservatory, its combined vertical and tilted area of glass being twice that of the direct gain double-glazing. Two UK locations, Glasgow and Kew, were modelled in March, each assuming a young family as occupants. This implied relatively intensive occupation of the living room over a daily cycle with a relatively high thermostat setting, so the simulation included a relatively large amount of incidental or casual heat gain from occupants themselves, lighting and appliances. Responsive convectors, similar to those specified by Malcolm Newton, were built into the model for heating. Levels of insulation were also similar. ■1.8(2)

■1.7 Contrasting Lerwick and London (Kew): some climatic detail

1.7(1) Lerwick's rainfall from 1951–1980 averaged nearly 1.2m annually, over 80 per cent of which occurred from September to May. Average sunshine in January is only 12 per cent and, from September to May, 21 per cent of what is theoretically possible in cloudless conditions (compared with 44 per cent in the location of Frank Lloyd Wright's 'solar hemi-cycle'). London's rainfall from 1951–1980 averaged 0.6m annually, 80 per cent occurring from September to May, while its proportion of possible sunshine in this period rises to 30 per cent. The relative differences in possible sunshine translate to Lerwick being disadvantaged relative to Kew by some 20 per cent, taking respective incident solar irradiation on a south-facing vertical surface.

1.7(2) The main glazed surfaces in Newton's design are to the south at a 45° tilt, and vertical surfaces facing east or west. There is a significant incident solar fall-off in the central winter period (November to March) from Kew to Lerwick of approximately 35 per cent for both orientations. Extending the period from September to May, the outer margins of autumn and spring probably still being relevant for Lerwick, slightly reduces the deficit to 21 per cent for the tilted surface and 17 per cent for the vertical surface. However, it makes no sense to compare the respective solar supplies over the same period. Each should correspond to the period when the internal base temperature is higher than that outside.

1.7(3) The driving rain index or DRI (Lacy, 1977) for Lerwick is estimated to be nearly four times that in Kew. The index in Lerwick is $10.6m^2/s$, while that in Kew is only $2.75m^2/s$.

1.7(4) The climate severity index is 169 for Lerwick as opposed to 100 for Kew – ie one would expect Lerwick to have a heating demand some 69 per cent greater than that of Kew.

■1.8 Sunspace modelling: Glasgow compared to Kew in dimensional and climatic detail

1.8(1) The area of the room was 21m² and the double-glazing was some 44 per cent of this.

1.8(2) U-values were calculated to be 0.27W/m²K for walls and 0.37W/m²K for the floor.

1.8(3) Glasgow has 15 per cent of sunshine theoretically available in January compared with Lerwick's 12 per cent, and 24 per cent from September to May, compared with Lerwick's 21 per cent. This is still well below Kew's respective 19 per cent for January and 30 per cent for September to May, but when the amount of solar radiation falling on a south-facing vertical surface is compared, the difference between Glasgow and Kew is not so marked. Indeed, average values from September to May are only 6 per cent less in Glasgow than in Kew. Glasgow's mean ambient air temperature from September to May is 6.9°C, compared with Kew's 8.5°C.

1.8(4) Glasgow's DRI of 5.5m²/s is roughly twice the Kew value and half that for Lerwick.

1.8(5) From November to March, the temperature in Glasgow is 1.4K less than in London, while Glasgow's incident radiation on a south wall is 14 per cent less than in London: 181kWh/m² compared to 210kWh/m² (Page and Lebens, 1986, pp162, 171, 208, 217).

Glasgow has about two thirds of the annual rainfall of Lerwick, while there is also a somewhat greater amount of sunshine, and of course it is wetter and less sunny than Kew. The difference in temperature from September to May between the two locations is more marked than the difference in solar availability. ■1.8(3) Also, the driving rain index now lies between that for Lerwick and that for Kew. ■1.8(4) This means that, given a particular energy-efficient design, the heating season will shrink more for Kew than for Glasgow. If we then compare the narrower time-frame of November to March, the difference in temperature actually drops marginally, but the difference in solar availability is more marked. ■1.8(5) Effectively, this means that the sheltering effect and the heat-recovery aspect of the buffer space will start to dominate its energy-saving ability in the relatively sunless parts of winter.

The computer modelling for the month of March confirmed that, although the indirect solution works significantly better than direct in the northerly location, the residual space-heating load still remains higher in Scotland than in Kew for the same design with the same occupancy and heating schedule. The following summarizes the main aspects of the output:

Direct gain system:
- residual space heating demand for Kew is less than half that of Glasgow;
- Kew's useful solar supply as percentage of demand is more than twice that of Glasgow;
- Kew's absolute useful solar supply (kWh) is about 20 per cent more than that of Glasgow.

Indirect gain system (30m³ sunspace, outer glass twice area of inner):
- residual space heating demand for Kew is less than half that of Glasgow;
- Kew's useful solar supply as percentage of demand is more than twice that of Glasgow;
- Kew's absolute useful solar supply (kWh) is slightly less than that of Glasgow;
- percentage saving compared to direct system lower in Glasgow than Kew (31% compared to 35%);
- kWh saving compared to direct system higher in Glasgow than Kew.

Modelled over a complete heating season from September to May, the space-heating load for Kew maintained its 'less than half' position relative to Glasgow. Nevertheless, expressed per square metre of floor area of the living room, Glasgow at 78kWh/m² compares favourably with the direct gain model of 113kWh/m². This is a saving of 31 per cent, exactly as for the March-only simulation.

Having established certain comparative aspects of performance for an economic, rectilinear terraced house type, and noting the more beneficial latitudinal impact of Malcolm Newton's rather complex solution, further modelling was carried out on an L-shaped house form (Porteous, 1990, pp58, 80–89). This embraced a square double-height atrium and was again capable of being built in terraced or, alternatively, semi-detached form. In other words, it was slightly more ambitious in terms of design, and probably cost, compared with a simple rectangle, but still not as radical as Newton's back-to-back proposal.

Taking the living room on its own, the residual September to May space-heating load for this model in Glasgow reduced by some 23 per cent from 78kWh/m^2 to 60kWh/m^2. Taking the entire house over the same period, and using the same volume of unheated solar space in each case, the relative saving reduced to 14 per cent, but quantitatively it came down to a very respectable 24.5kWh/m^2. One can compare this with the Newton value of 38kWh/m^2 for a different design in a much more severe climatic location. If one took a hard line, it could be said that such comparisons are spurious. There are just too many variables from location to location, project to project. However, the more energy-efficient buildings become, the less influential are the variables. This means that in monitored projects, as opposed to predictive models, human factors tend to become much greater drivers of differences than climate or detailed design.

1.3   First Scottish passive solar housing in Stornoway by Western Isles Islands Council

Without real people, the differential in the above theoretical studies naturally leads on to the question 'which variable caused the saving?' Any significant alteration to the plan and section of a building is bound to affect the outcome in a number of ways: by varying solar geometry, varying thermal mass, etc. Nevertheless, the numerical indicators given above provide some idea of what one might expect both quantitatively and proportionately at different locations. Results from two different researchers, using different computer programmes, appear to correlate logically and also provide some comfort for the context of the passive solar period of the early 1980s to the early 1990s in the UK and its neighbours. Unarguably, climatic buffer spaces were used extensively in northern Europe and parts of North America during this period and beyond. Interestingly, they remain to this day contentious in terms of their ability to save energy. However, at least we know from the above that, albeit by diverse means, they are theoretically capable of saving energy, even in relatively extreme locations such as Shetland, where the climate appears to be rather hostile to solar applications. Indeed, following hard on the heels of North Sun 84, Scotland's first new-build passive solar housing (Figure 1.3) was completed in 1985 by the Western Isles Islands Council in Stornoway. The main town of the Outer Hebrides, it has a climate with marked similarities to that of Shetland, perhaps especially that of driving rain.

Widening the solar agenda

Some of these live projects have included other solar components, such as air collectors (see Chapters 2 and 6) and flat-plate water-heating collectors (see Chapter 2), the latter not of course limited to the space-heating season. Others have successfully linked passive solar buffer spaces to mechanical heat

■ 1.9 Germany, Denmark, Sweden and the Netherlands: solar activity

1.9(1) Germany's Energy Research and Technology Programme, launched in 1990, gave significantly more government funds to PV (50 million Deutschmarks for a 1990s monitoring programme) than any of the other nine energy categories in the programme. This was more than five times as much as for wind in the first three years, the latter also being about 18 per cent less than the budget for 'rational user of energy and solar energy in buildings' (Lottner, 1992). With solar electricity in the limelight, 1997 – five years after the Earth Summit at Rio – marked a critical 100MWp (megawatt peak) per annum on an exponential curve of increasing PV output (Luther, 2002). Active solar thermal systems also maintained a strong presence. By 2001, Germany had circa 2,290,000m^2 flat-plate collectors (Bosselaar, 2001). The cost of PV still inhibits uptake, but it is falling: 0.6€/kWh in Northern Europe in 2000, and hoped to fall to 0.22€/kWh by 2020 (Luther, 2002).

1.9(2) Five aims of a new Danish Energy Plan were outlined at a seminar in Scotland, February 1999:

1) 20 per cent reduction CO_2 from 1998 to 2005;
2) share of renewable sources 12–14 per cent total energy supply by 2005;
3) share of renewable sources 33 per cent total energy supply by 2030;
4) CO_2 reduction of 50 per cent overall and 25 per cent from transport by 2030; and
5) overall reduction of energy consumption by 2030. The plan had six initiatives:

1) special effort with respect to building-integrated systems;
2) better motivation for commercial and industrial buildings;
3) promotion of solar applications in rural areas (outside gas and district heated zones);
4) promotion of large thermal plants – 8,000m^2 plus seasonal stores;
5) fine-tune storage and control – day/night and summer/winter; and
6) promotion of international dissemination – eg via new IEA groups.

recovery systems. In fact one such scheme, completed in 1987, was as far north as 69.6 degrees latitude – a day-care centre in Alta, Norway. This particular project was monitored by SINTEF, the Norwegian Solar Energy Research Centre at the Norwegian Institute of Technology, Trondheim. This was one case study out of 48 undertaken under the auspices of the International Energy Agency (IEA), Task XI: Passive and Hybrid Solar Commercial Buildings (Hildon and Seager, 1989).

Out of twelve countries represented in this study, six were in northern Europe and one in Canada. A large majority of these case studies were occupied between 1984 and 1987, and reported performance gave some encouragement at that time to pursue such technology further. This was particularly so within regions, such as Scandinavia, that might be considered as solar-challenged during winter. Apart from extensive use of glazed atria and arcades, it was Scandinavia that took a lead in large-scale arrays of flat-plate collectors combined with seasonal storage. In other words, they were addressing the long-term mismatch between supply of solar energy and the demand for heat. Of course, these arrays were detached from the buildings they served, but that is one of the themes to be explored further in the next chapter. An attempt to integrate a sufficient area of collector on to the roof of a small house to charge a seasonal thermal store, also integrated with the house, was made in the late 1980s in Holland. Such projects partly reflected the experimental spirit of some architects, engineers and physicists, and partly the willingness of governments to pump-prime renewable technology.

In this regard, there was and is by no means an even-handed approach across national boundaries. While there is a considerable amount of continuing dissemination within the scientific solar community, getting the message across to a large cross section of architects and their clients is more problematic. Even more critically, while technical opportunities and obstacles tend to vary within quite a narrow spectrum (taking examples from the climatic zones as defined in the Preface), the political and economic ones have a large range.

institutional divergence – Northern Europe and Canada

The leading countries in Northern Europe are Germany, Denmark, Sweden and the Netherlands. They all have, and have had for some time, ambitious programmes for both solar thermal and photovoltaic (PV) systems. Germany now has a 100,000 programme for PV installations, starting from an initial 2000 in the early 1990s, and it is also the leading EU market for solar thermal applications. ■1.9(1) Denmark is a strong player in solar thermal research and the development and manufacture of large-scale solar thermal arrays. A 30 per cent government subsidy helped to secure this position as well as a generously funded regional campaign to build up the market (Windeleff, 1994). Part of the marketing strategy was a highly symbolic 'villaVISION', an evocative 'dream house of the future' (Figure 1.4) (Danish Technological Institute, 1994). This is located at the Danish Technological Institute and was realized through the sponsorship of several government agencies as well as trade unions and trade associations. It embodies both passive and active solar features, thermal and electrical, as well as taking on a holistic green agenda. By 1999, the Danish Energy Directorate had an ambitious new energy plan, ■1.9(2) an extension of their 'Solar Energy Plan of Action 1998–2000' (Danish Technological Institute, 1998). Sweden has a similar system of subsidy, this time 25 per cent, and has established a lead in the design of very large-scale solar thermal projects with inter-seasonal storage. ■1.9(3) In the Netherlands, there is excellent cooperation between national and local government agencies, and also energy utilities, to install both electrical and thermal solar panels. ■1.9(4) It is now recognized that the critical mass for the market has been achieved in this small, densely populated country, which was also, until recently, home to the largest building-integrated PV system in the world – a 2 megawatt (MW) roof over a large exhibition area near Schiphol Airport (now overtaken by a 40,000m^2 roof over a logistics building in Bürstadt, Germany).

1.9(3) A Swedish programme to demonstrate larger systems began in the 1990s. The aim was to replace oil in heating plants at an annual rate of 7–32GWh (gigawatts x hours), the maximum level of government support being 50 per cent (Rantil, 1994). In 2002, it was reported that the costs for large systems had fallen below 250€/m^2 (Dalenback, 2002).

1.9(4) In the Netherlands, while recycling and generation of electricity by wind are now seen as important, there is a commitment to grid-connected PV, with about 20MWp installed (compared with 3MWp off grid in 2003). There is a 3.5€/Wp (euros per watt peak) subsidy for private people and other fiscal incentives for companies, the price per watt peak having fallen from €20 in 1990 to €5 in 2002. PV unit cost in 2003 on a net metering system was 0.08€/kWh. The Dutch government's energy research centre, ECN, is currently investigating the potential for combined PV thermal (PVT) collectors. This reduces the thermal efficiency by 30–40 per cent. Roughly 5000 normal flat-plate collectors systems are sold annually. This is an 80 per cent increase since the start of a Beldezon (Call the Sun) campaign by the Ecostream marketing arm of the international consultancy Ecofys, with a target of 1.2 million m^2 by 2010. Typically, the collection area for drain-back systems (see also Chapter 2) is 3m^2, with 100 litres storage. There are time-limited subsidies of up to 40 per cent and a standard cost in 2003 of €2200 (£1700), including installation (information from a visit to ECN, August 2003, and from Giel Linthorst of Ecofys in Glasgow, December 2002.) Dutch subsidies have extended to more than specific solar components – eg IEA solar apartments in Amstelveen of mid-1990s, (Chapter 6) received 2.5 million guilders for research, 1 million for risk and 1 million for a land discount. This translates to over £40,000 per unit (information given by developer, April 1995).

1.4   villaVISION in Tasstrup, Denmark, by the Danish Technological Institute

■1.10 Norway, Finland, UK, Scotland and Canada: solar activity

1.10(1) The area of solar thermal collectors in 1992 in Norway was estimated to be less than 7000m² from about 1750 installations. At that time, two years after a government fund was started to establish a solar energy market in Norway, it was estimated that there were only some 500 active solar domestic installations in Finland, compared with 70,000–100,000m² of agricultural drying systems. Concurrently, Scotland had approximately 2000 systems, which were mainly domestic. The UK market for active solar thermal systems has remained sluggish. In 2001, it was estimated that the total area of collectors was 141,000m². This is one sixteenth of the comparable market in Germany (Bosselaar, 2001).

1.10(2) Professor Anne Grete Hestnes has been a leading light relative to SINTEF for many years. Two SINTEF projects are discussed in Chapter 6. She has also been very involved in the regional and global solar community, becoming President first of ISES Europe and then ISES worldwide.

1.10(3) An example of Røstvik's architectural work is the near-autonomous 1988 Parmann house constructed in Stavanger, in southwest Norway, for a Swedish couple. The climate here is relatively mild, no month averaging below 0°C, but the area still has a long heating season. The house utilizes a combination of active and passive solar features, as well as integrating a small wind turbine. Solar thermal provided about 4700kWh annually, solar electrical about 800kWh and wind is estimated to provide 700kWh. The balance of the thermal load is met by a 97 per cent efficient 'kakkeloven' tiled log-stove, built from 'olivienstone', while the annual electrical balance from the grid was estimated to be only about 900 kWh.

1.10(4) An example of statistical information given by Røstvik is: 'Every Norwegian is responsible for twice the world average of CO_2 emissions.' He also claims: 'Pollution for the drilling rigs in the North Sea equals the pollution from all the private cars in Norway.' He adds that it is the car users who are left with a bad

Other Northern European countries such as Norway and Finland developed niche markets for PV to power isolated weekend and holiday huts and cottages. Active domestic solar thermal systems in Norway and Finland were a minority interest when reported in 1992, the year of the Earth Summit at Rio de Janeiro. The number of installations in the latter was, for example, significantly less than in Scotland. There was more interest in agricultural solar drying applications in both Scandinavian countries, as well as a stronger interest in PV (Lund, 1992; Porteous, 1992; Salvesen, 1992). ■1.10(1) As indicated above, Norway has also given quite a strong architectural lead through leading characters in SINTEF ■1.10(2) and other individuals such as Harald Røstvik, who made a reputation both in terms of radical built projects ■1.10(3) (Røstvik, 1990) and in terms of political perspective (Røstvik, 1992a, 1992b). In essence, Røstvik has been attacking the unfair distribution of resources, the playing field powerfully tilted by the traditional energy oligarchies away from renewable technologies in general and solar development in particular. His complaint was targeted nationally and globally. In Norway, he made the point that the combination of oil wealth, gas wealth and hydro-wealth was starving solar research and was not appeased in terms of hydro-electricity being a renewable source. ■1.10(4) Globally, it was the same kind of picture, with multinational companies desperate to dominate the developing countries. The problem with solar energy for such interests is that it lends itself to small, community-controlled structures. In any event, along with other prominent political environmentalists such as Hermann Scheer (Scheer, 1994), Røstvik was heavily involved in getting solar energy on the agenda at Rio. Political and institutional barriers were among the main themes to be addressed for both developed and developing countries.

Across the Atlantic in Canada, there is some commonality with countries such as Norway and Finland. Today, individual architects such as Peter Busby champion fine architecture that is both solar and environmental in spirit – for example the Institute of Technology in Merritt, British Columbia (Gregory, 2004). Others, such as Martin Liefhebber in Toronto, have promoted an aesthetically more confrontational and holistic formula, as in the community-led design for a 'healthy house' in 1999 (Liefhebber, undated). The active solar arrays of this condominium are visually dominant and raise issues to be tackled in more depth relative to other case studies in the next chapter. Back in 1992, at the time of the Earth Summit in Rio, Canada had a national research and development programme, which included solar energy (Carpenter 1992). But this was funded through the Canadian Centre for Mineral and Energy Technologies (CANMET). Such funds that CANMET disbursed generally went to 'centres of expertise' such as at the University of Waterloo and Queen's University. In other words, their progress relied on small budgets and the impetus given by individual academics. This is very similar to the situation reported for Scotland at the same time (Porteous, 1992). However, like Scotland, Norway and Finland, the commercial status of Canada was not strong. ■1.10(5) It has to be accepted that the energy context of a huge and sparsely populated country like Canada is different from a small, mainly densely populated country like the UK. In Canada, the World Energy Atlas indicated that in 1985 the energy consumption per capita was two thirds greater than that of Northern Europe (Scheer, 1994, p14), while statistics from 1995 showed that three quarters of greenhouse gas emissions were attributable to transport, electricity generation, industry and fossil fuel production (Sharpe, 1999). ■1.10(6)

This is very different from the global picture ■1.11(1) (Smith, 1996; Vale and Vale, 1991) or that in the UK ■1.11(2) (Bell, Lowe and Roberts, 1996), where architecture is more in the frame. Although differing regional statistics are hard to compare directly, it is evident that both consumption of fossil fuels and emissions from buildings, and particularly housing, will vary downwards with the falling density of the population. On the other hand, in large countries, the distended infrastructure for transport and industry will skew these values upwards. Such variations are bound to occur even if approximate parity of wealth exists for varying densities. But there are also large cultural differences in terms of vehicular size and fuel efficiency, not to mention from one oil company to another (Macalister, 2004). ■1.11(3) In terms of changing the status quo, Peter Smith in the UK has many recommendations, for example extolling the virtues of geothermal energy compared with gas or oil, or indeed coal (Smith, 2003). There is still an output of CO_2, but it is a small fraction compared with fossil fuels. ■1.11(4) It is also self-evident that the existing stock of buildings must be made energy efficient, in parallel with the slow annual replenishment of new-build, in order to make much of an impact on the emissions of greenhouses gases… easier said than done.

When discussing active and passive solar expansion, it should be borne in mind that electricity accounts for less than 20 per cent of the delivered energy in most European countries. Also, as stated at the outset of this chapter, while the demand for heat rises with increasing latitude, the opportunities for utilizing solar energy passively can also rise, depending on the skill of the architect. Thus any programme that sidelines the much bigger market for heat is deficient. In the UK there is now a modest subsidy system for installing solar thermal systems, mainly for domestic hot water, as well as PV systems. Unfortunately there is no target for renewable sources to provide heat. The emphasis is restricted to the generation of electricity, for which there are reasonably ambitious targets dominated by wind. Broadly speaking, the countries that have advanced solar programmes for heat and electricity have politically intervened to make this possible. This tends to go hand in hand with the level of democracy, embracing some form of proportional representation, which can allow specific altruistic interests to flourish. One can take the potency of the Green Party in Germany as an example, with added muscle provided by solar champions such

conscience, and that the surplus of hydro-electric power could be used to reduce emissions from the North Sea.

1.10(5) Within the whole of Canada in 1992, the annual installations of residential active solar systems was only around 200, plus about 500 pool preheat systems. Similarly to Norway and Finland, there was another niche market – this time for large-scale, unglazed commercial solar air-heating systems (see Chapter 6). These were commercialized as Solarwall in conjunction with the aluminium company Alcan, amounting at that time to about 1200m² annually in Canada with limited exports. PV also had a minor presence: annual sales in the order of 650kWp, approximately one hundredth of the German output at the same time.

1.10(6) 75 per cent of greenhouse emissions in Canada in 1995 were given as follows: 26 per cent transportation by road, rail and air, 17 per cent electricity generation, 16 per cent industry and 16 per cent fossil fuel production. The balance was attributed to: 12 per cent non-energy, 8 per cent residential and 5 per cent commercial.

■1.11 Global to national statistics on fossil fuel consumption and CO_2 emissions

1.11(1) Brenda and Robert Vale give approximate values of 50 per cent for global consumption of fossil fuel related to 'the servicing of buildings'. They also point out that, since CO_2 constitutes roughly half of the total greenhouse gases, one quarter of the total is 'under the control of the designers or inhabitants of buildings'. Five years later, Peter Smith again quotes the 50 per cent value for all carbon emissions 'attributable to buildings in one form or another', and adds a further probable 20 per cent to take account of transport 'directly generated by buildings'.

1.11(2) Bell, Lowe and Roberts quote an official 1992 Department of Trade and Industry figure of just less than 30 per cent of CO_2 emissions from housing in the UK.

1.11(3) Macalister reports that the CO_2 emissions of the Texan oil firm, Exxon Mobil, are more than 60 per cent higher than those of British BP, when its production is less than 16 per cent higher. Exxon produced 4.4 million barrels in 2003 and BP 3.8 million. BP's estimated annual output of greenhouse gases is 83.3 million tonnes compared with Exxon's figure of 135.6, which is more than twice Norway's output of CO_2. A consultancy in Colorado believes that Exxon's output is far greater than 60 per cent above this figure once power to run its petrol stations and tankers is taken into account. Its estimate is 379 million tonnes.

1.11(4) From a survey of 5000MW of installed geothermal capacity, the average emission of CO_2 per kWh was found to be 65 grams. This is one seventh of that for gas, one fourteenth of that for oil and one sixteenth of that for coal.

as Hermann Scheer. He is the social scientist and economist who became a member of the German Bundestag in 1980. Even though his manifesto explaining 'the need for a total solar energy supply … and how to achieve it' may have had little chance of implementation, he showed that it is theoretically possible (Scheer, 1994, pp75–104).

The other political condition, which favours progressive regulation as a means to allow solar markets to flourish, is that of relatively high progressive taxation. The low taxation, 'let market forces rule' culture of countries such as the UK has inhibited progress over several decades. Other fiscal incentives, as opposed to barriers, are also required. Despite a strong, architect-led campaign against Value Added Tax (VAT) on building materials for refurbished properties, this tax remains a major disincentive for brown-field regeneration. Susannah Hagan refers to 'the ideological battle between environmentalism and consumerism' (Hagan, 2001). Put another way, this could be seen as the opposition between regulation and deregulation, ironically both perceived as progressive by respective advocates. Hagan points out that perception is all. Pursuing this theme in the context of priming solar architecture in cool climates, the interventionist policies with regard to solar energy by the Danes and the Dutch are undoubtedly perceived positively as progressively innovative by at least the politicians who introduced them. On the other hand, the politically opposed parties or party within the same government, as well as different governments, which are more driven by consumerist neo-liberalism, would view the same policies as regressive. Not only that; each side is likely to claim its position as 'sustainable', confirming that the term is politically ambiguous – one may assume deliberately so since a key product of governing is law, and lawyers thrive on ambiguity. In terms of the potency of architecture within the 'sustainability' debate, Hagan suggests that the influence of exemplars far exceeds their literal contribution.

However, exemplars must grapple with the hard economics of payback as well as with the aesthetics that the architectural community find acceptably free of constraint. Here the principles of added value and multi-functionality become relevant and merit discussion.

REFERENCES

Andresen, I. and Hestnes, A. G. (eds) (1992) *North Sun 92, Solar Energy at High Latitudes,* proceedings of conference (Trondheim, Norway, 24–26 June), SINTEF Architecture and Building Technology, Trondheim.

Bartholomew, D. M. L. (1985) 'Possibilities for passive solar house design in Scotland', *International Journal of Ambient Energy,* vol 6, no 3, July, pp147–158.

Bell, M. M., Lowe, R. and Roberts, P. (1996) 'Energy, climate change and housing', in *Energy Efficiency in Housing,* Avebury Ashgate Publishing Ltd., Aldershot, UK, p17.

Bosselaar, L. (2001) 'Solar heating is a major source of renewable energy', in van der Leun, K. and van der Ree, B (eds), *North Sun 2001: A Solar Odyssey, Technology Meets Market in the Solar Age,* proceedings of conference (6–8 May), Ecofys, Leiden, the Netherlands.

Boyce, R. (1993) 'Development of a Passive Solar House', in *Keck and Keck,* Princeton Architectural Press, New York, pp78–79.

Carpenter, A. M. (1992) 'Canadian solar energy research and development activities', in Andresen and Hestnes (1992), pp31–33.

Dalenback, J.-O. (2002) 'Solar thermal market in Europe – integration', from notes of verbal presentation at *Eurosun 2002: The 4th ISES Europe Solar Congress,* 23–26 June, Bologna, Italy.

Danish Technological Institute (1994) *villaVISION.* World Pictures, Danish Technological Institute, Taastrup, Denmark.

Danish Technological Institute (1998) *Solar Energy Plan of Action 1998–2000,* The Solar Energy Committee, Renewable Energy Information Centre, Danish Technological Institute, Taastrup, Denmark.

Duffie, J. A., Beckman, W. A. and Dekker, J. E. (1977) 'Solar heating in North America', *Mechanical Engineering,* November, pp36–45.

Gregory, R. (2004) 'Merritt distinction', *The Architectural Review,* Oct. 2004, vol CCXVI, no 1292, pp76–79.

Hagan, S. (2001) 'Introduction', in *Taking Shape: A New Contract between Architecture and Nature,* Architectural Press, Oxford, UK, ppx–xix.

Hildon, A. and Seager, A. (1989) 'Introduction', in *International Energy Agency Task XI, Passive and Hybrid Solar Commercial Buildings,* The New and Renewable Energy Promotion Group (REPG), Energy Technology Support Unit, Harwell, UK, ppx–xvii.

Jacobs, H. with Jacobs K. (1978) 'From cellar to solar', in *Building with Frank Lloyd Wright: An Illustrated Memoir,* Chronicle Books, San Francisco, p121.

Lacy, R. E. (1977) 'The effects of climate on the design of buildings', in *Climate and Building in Britain,* Department of the Environment, Building Research Establishment, HMSO, London, pp104–110.

Liefhebber, M. (undated) *Healthy Housing: A Winning Design,* Canadian Housing Information Centre, Toronto, Canada.

Long, G. (ed) (1976) 'Collection of solar energy as heat', in *Solar Energy: Its Potential Contribution Within the United Kingdom* (report prepared for the Department of Energy by the Energy Technology Support Unit, Harwell), HMSO, London.

Lottner, V. (1992) 'Solar Energy Programme of Germany', in Andresen and Hestnes (1992), pp24–25.

Lund, P. (1992) 'Solar Energy Activities in Finland', in Andresen and Hestnes (1992), p23.

Luther, J. (2002) 'Solar research and development – roads to a stronger market', from notes of verbal presentation at *Eurosun 2002: The 4th ISES Europe Solar Congress,* 23–26 June, Bologna, Italy.

Macalister, T. (2004) 'Exxon admits greenhouse gas increase', *The Guardian,* London, 7 October, p21.

MacGregor, A. W. K. (1981) 'A comparison of the climatic suitability of various locations in the European Community for solar space heating', in *World Solar Forum,* proceedings of conference, UK Section of the International Solar Energy Society, Brighton, UK, August, pp1852–1857.

MacGregor, A. W. K. (1987) 'Is north really best for solar heating of buildings?' in Bloss, W. H. and Pfisterer, F. (eds) *Advances in Solar Energy Technology,* proceedings of conference (Biennial Congress of the International Solar Energy Society, Hamburg, Germany, 13–18 September), Pergamon Press, vol 4, pp3395–3398.

MacGregor, A. W. K. and Balmbro, D. (1984) 'Where are the best places in Scotland for solar space heating?' in MacGregor, K. (ed), *North Sun 84, Solar Energy at High Latitudes,* proceedings of conference (4–6 September), Scottish Solar Energy Group, Edinburgh, UK, p76.

MacGregor, A. W. K. and Porteous, C. (eds) (1994) North Sun 94, *Solar Energy at High Latitudes, 6th Biennial International Conference,* proceedings of conference (7–9 September, Glasgow, Scotland), James & James (Science Publishers) Ltd., London, UK.

Markus, T. A. (1984) 'Development of a Cold Climate Severity Index', *Energy and Buildings,* no 4, August, pp277–283.

Newton, M. (1983) 'Design study for 3B4P public sector house with attached sunspace' in *Design Methods for Passive Solar Buildings,* proceedings of conference (7 October), UK-ISES, pp6:48–6:58.

Olseth, J. A. and Skartveit, A. (1986) 'The solar radiation climate of Norway', *Solar Energy,* vol 37, pp423–428.

Oppenheim, D. (1981) 'Climate', in Small Solar Buildings in *Cold Northern Climates,* Architectural Press, London, pp6–7.

Page, J. and Lebens R. (1986) *Climate in the United Kingdom: A Handbook of Solar Radiation, Temperature and Other Data for Thirteen Principal Cities and Towns* (for the Energy Technology Support Unit, Harwell), HMSO, London, pp162, 171, 208, 217.

Porteous, C. D. A. (1990) 'Performance Characteristics of Solar Buffer Zones for Scottish Housing', PhD thesis, Department of Architecture and Building Science, University of Strathclyde, Glasgow, October.

Porteous, C. D. A. (1992) 'Scottish Solar Position 1992', in Andresen and Hestnes (1992), pp26–28.

Rantil, M. (1994) 'Solar energy activities in Sweden', in MacGregor and Porteous (1994), pp447–452.

Røstvik, H. (1990) 'Building for the Future: An autonomous house in Norway', *Sun at Work in Europe,* vol 3, no 5, pp14–15.

Røstvik, H. N. (1992a) 'The Environmental Challenges', in *The Sunshine Revolution,* trans. Stoner, D., SUN-LAB publishers, Stavanger, Norway, pp6–21.

Røstvik, H. N. (1992b) 'Solar Energy on the International agenda at the Rio Earth Summit?', *Sun at Work in Europe,* vol 7, no 2, pp18–19.

Salvesen, F. (1992) 'Norwegian Solar Energy Program', in Andresen and Hestnes (1992), pp15–18.

Scheer, H. (1994) *A Solar Manifesto: The Need for a Total Solar Energy Supply... and How to Achieve It,* James & James (Science Publishers) Ltd., London.

Sharpe, S. (1999) 'Industries warm to the challenge', *Sustainable Energy & the Environment,* supplement with The Calgary Sun, July, pp2–3.

Smith, P. F. (1996) *Options for a Flexible Planet: The Evidence, the Policies and Possible Remedies,* Sustainability Network, School of Architectural Studies, University of Sheffield, Sheffield, UK, p58.

Smith, P. F. (2003) 'Geothermal Energy', in *Sustainability at the Cutting Edge: Emerging Technologies for Low Energy Buildings,* Architectural Press, Oxford, UK, p45.

Stephens, M. (1983) 'Passive solar house design study for an "upmarket" private large detached house with direct gain', in *Design Methods for Passive Solar Buildings,* proceedings of conference (October 7), UK-ISES, pp9:80–9:95.

UK-ISES (1976) 'Solar Energy and Architecture' in *Solar Energy: A UK Assessment,* UK-ISES, London, May, pp180–181.

Vale, B. and Vale, R. (1991) 'Purpose, architecture and the survival of the planet', in *Green Architecture: Design for a Sustainable Future,* Thames & Hudson Ltd., London, p23.

Windeleff, J. (1994) 'Solar energy campaigning in Denmark', in MacGregor and Porteous (1994), pp429–433.

Wright, F. L. (1977) 'Gravity Heat', in Book 5 ('Form') of *An Autobiography,* Quartet Books, London, pp520–522.

Chapter 2   Multiple and Added Solar Value

This chapter deals with alternative approaches to maximizing opportunities for stimulating solar architecture. Windows intrinsically imply multiple and added solar value, but they can simultaneously present problems. They provide daylight, which can and should displace electrical lighting. However, realizing this benefit is not nearly as easy as it sounds. They can provide the means to capture useful solar heat, although orientation is naturally significant and they can lose more heat than they gain. They can also provide the means to limit solar overheating and glare. This aspect may be dealt with passively ■2.1(1) by the tilt and orientation of the glass relative to solar geometry, bearing in mind that transmission of solar radiation falls off rapidly once the angle of incidence ■2.1(2) exceeds fifty degrees. It can also be tackled by the physics of the glass itself, or by a discrete screening or shading device – blinds, awnings, louvres etc. Glazing technology to tackle these conflicting characteristics became increasingly sophisticated during the 20th century, and the quest to improve on current technology and to bring it further into the marketplace continues apace.

It is perhaps interesting to remember that there was a patent application in 1891 by a physician, William van der Heyden, for a thermo-chromatic glazing sandwich. In the context of trying to secure healthier and more comfortable Japanese dwellings, van der Heyden proposed that a chemical solution be encapsulated between two layers of glass. The solution remained transparent in cool weather, thus allowing transmission of useful solar heat and light, but it became translucent in hot weather, hence avoiding overheating, while still allowing adequate transmission of daylight. More than a hundred years later, advanced glazing technology is still very much concerned with producing products that will improve energy efficiency and environmental comfort, but their share of the market remains disappointing. It is a commercial reality that the running costs for energy are a relatively small percentage of overheads in all non-domestic buildings and the capital cost of energy-efficient glazing has always been an issue, especially for the housing market.

Also, one has to bear in mind that other benefits of windows are not dependent on energy-efficiency. A single glazed window offers the same advantage of viewing the outside world, psychologically connecting and

■2.1 Passive solar gain: basic definition and critical angle for sunbeam

2.1(1) The term passive signifies a system where the constructional design and form of the building itself, as opposed to its servicing, is mainly responsible for the capture, storage and distribution of solar energy, normally with the aim of displacing other fuels for space heating.

2.1(2) The angle of incidence is the angle between a line normal to the surface of the glass and the direction of the beam of sunlight.

2.1a Rooftop of the Joan Miro gallery in Barcelona

2.1b Rooftop sculpture court of gallery in Århus

reducing isolation in a living or working situation. Indeed, increasing transparency, a health hallmark of the modern movement in the early part of the 20th century, has had a significant resurgence in the last decade or so. This may be partly attributable to technical advances, such as those flagged above, and also to frameless and structural fenestration. But it is above all rooted in aesthetics, whether or not further justified as denoting or promoting well-being, political openness and so forth.

Similarly, the opportunity for free natural ventilation is not dependent on glazing cost or sophistication, although single glazing is likely to introduce condensation, as well as discomfort from downdraughts and radiation loss to the cold surface in winter. Natural ventilation reinforces sensory contact with the environment, but in certain situations this may be problematic. For example, noise from traffic may cause undue disturbance within a building, and opening windows in windy conditions may be impracticable unless the capability of fine-tuning control is built into the design. Passive solutions to such dilemmas include an outer layer of fixed glass, constituting a shield against ambient noise and wind, in conjunction with an inner thermal layer with opening capability. The gap between the two layers, whether continuous or interrupted at each floor level, also requires the means for controlling the passage of air in and out, and may well include a layer for adjustably controlling solar heat and light. However, there are potential pitfalls to such systems, including loss of daylight, and a recent Scottish case study, where the basic principles have not been observed, is included in Chapter 6. A theoretical study for a double façade with a multiple environmental agenda will also be introduced later in this chapter.

Another take on windows is that, although we are used to their diverse attributes, including that of dissolving barriers between the inside and outside of buildings, we are also used to a specific emphasis for specific building types. We do not necessarily expect a view out from an art gallery. However, in such cases, although the main emphasis may be on maximizing the opportunities for daylight, with 'windows' not even visible from within the gallery, there may still be dual or triple purposefulness. For example, the diffuse glazing elements of the Joan Miro gallery in Barcelona by architect Josep Lluis Sert form part of the enclosing landscape of the rooftop sculpture terrace (Figure 2.1a). Similarly, the various glazing lanterns of the 2003 underground extension to the modern art gallery (Kuntsbygning) in Århus by architect Mads Møller contribute essentially to the sculpture court above it. This, in turn, is an outdoor visual complement to Møller's addition of one decade earlier (Figure 2.1b). Not only that; opening lights on the glazed projections provide natural ventilation to the new basement. Another notable art museum where contact with the external landscape occurs periodically as one circulates inside, perhaps, surprisingly, along with delightful splashes of sunlight, is again Danish, that in Ålborg by Elissa and Alvar Aalto with Jean Jacques Baruël, (Figure 2.1c).

The passive effectiveness of the two Danish galleries, together with curatorial influences, will be discussed more fully in Chapter 5 together with other galleries and building types where there is an interplay between daylight, sunlight and ventilation. It suffices to say at this stage that windows can provide multiple values to which solar energy contributes. However, we still have to resolve certain conflicts of environmental interest. These are likely to be different for every building's function and every facet of its external surface, as well as different for each specific climatic and morphological context from dense urban situations to open rural ones. What will not change, however, is the axiom that all windows, including those associated with glazed spaces which buffer the main heated or cooled accommodation, are of necessity building-integrated, while for other solar components this is not necessarily the case.

Although the integrative scenario has accumulated currency across the solar sector in the last two decades, most recently relative to the push for building integrated photovoltaic arrays (BIPV), there is still a case to be made for isolating solar components from the building or buildings they serve. This does not necessarily mean total visual and architectural isolation, but rather liberation from full tectonic integration, for example as a roof covering. The merits and handicaps of these two approaches are best discussed through built case studies.

2.1c Nordjyllands Kuntsmuseum in Ålborg

The case for integration

Following from the introductory setting out of ground rules, it is apparent that such a case may be broken down into systems or components for which it is not possible to dissociate from the immediate building design, and others where a choice exists. One might imagine that the former category is not worth discussing. Such an argument might even assert that form will follow function. In other words, if passive solar gain to displace winter heating is the primary aim, then solar geometry will dictate the area, tilt and orientation of glazing in order to maximize collection. However, the potential variables in engaging building geometry with solar geometry to produce viable solar buildings are subtly manifest, as will be seen below. In any case, the extent to which this is formally expressed inevitably becomes an issue for the architect. In some buildings the capture and storage of solar energy is deliberately given aesthetic prominence, while in others it is equally consciously suppressed.

flat-plate solar thermal collectors

A common solar component, where a frequently tricky visual choice exists with regard to integration, is the active ■2.2(1) flat-plate collector. As the workhorse of active solar technology, its basic characteristics are worth summarizing in order to preface a case study that uses it.

It normally consists of a high conductivity metal plate, finished with a highly absorptive black surface, which is exposed to solar radiation, enclosed in a box

■2.2 Flat-plate collectors: specification options

2.2(1) The term active signifies a system that is largely reliant on mechanical help and/or plumbing or other servicing systems in order to store and deliver captured solar energy to displace other fuels for space or water heating.

2.2(2) In cold climates most flat-plate collectors use a water–antifreeze mix for heat transfer to avoid freezing damage. This means that a heat exchanger (with consequent performance penalties) must be used to transfer heat to the fresh water tank. Other methods of freeze protection include 'drain-back' or 'drain-down', where the water in the collector drains away when the pump stops (popular in the Netherlands), and auxiliary heating, where heat is injected when freezing is likely (wasteful in climates where freezing is common). An ingenious UK invention uses a solar collector that is inherently 'freeze-tolerant' (not damaged by freezing) so that fresh water can be heated directly in the collector, and is allowed to freeze. (see www.solartwin.com)

2.2(3) The rate of pumping the heat transfer fluid through a collector has traditionally been quite high, giving a temperature lift of 5–10K for each pass, and having multiple passes. However, recent research (Furbo and Knudsen, 2000) has shown a performance advantage in having much lower flow rates ('microflow') and aiming to achieve temperature stratification in the storage tank. A central heating 50W centrifugal type of pump is usual, its operation controlled by a 'differential temperature' thermostat, which switches it on only when the absorber is hotter than the heat storage tank. An interesting alternative method is to use a small PV cell to directly drive a small direct current (DC) pump (Grassie and MacGregor, 1999). This has advantages in that no mains power is used or needed and the pump has a variable speed, depending on solar irradiance. With careful matching of components, it is possible to get a near constant delivery temperature to the storage tank.

2.2(4) A non-selective black surface absorbs shortwave solar radiation well, but it also radiates long wave or infrared heat outwards. A selective

or casing with a transparent front and an insulating back. The plate has water passages built into it through which a heat transfer fluid, either water or a water–antifreeze mixture ■2.2(2), is circulated by means of a pump or by natural thermo-syphonic action. ■2.2(3) The collector is normally mounted in a fixed position on a roof surface or on the ground. Tracking collectors (ie moving to stay at right angles to the sunbeam over a daily cycle) have been used, but the extra complexity and cost is usually not considered worthwhile. The surface of the absorber plate can be either selective or non-selective, the former providing optimum performance. ■2.2(4) The transparent front to the collector can be made of either glass or plastic. ■2.2(5) An important feature of all flat-plate collectors is that they are most efficient at low operating temperatures. This is because their loss of heat becomes less as the temperature of the absorber plate falls. Thus a collector is more effective relative to a system with a low temperature demand, such as a swimming pool, than one with a high demand, such as an industrial process.

To give an idea of the performance of flat-plate collectors, most collection efficiencies are in the range 40–60 per cent. Thus in the UK, with annual incident solar irradiation of about 1000kWh/m^2, the delivered heat over a year should be approximately 400–600kWh/m^2. It may be noted that such values are presently some three times better than for PV cells. It follows that solar heating is more cost-effective than solar electricity.

Many flat-plate collectors are retrofitted on top of an existing roof surface, with fixings through slates or tiles to the structure below, and sealed with silicone. For new-build the opportunity exists to fully integrate the collectors with the roof. This can be done using commercial collectors. Alternatively it is relatively easy, and much cheaper, to build the collectors on site. Sweden and Denmark in particular have pioneered techniques for building very large-scale collectors on rooftops or on the ground. Clearly the latter locus tends to lie in the category of isolation as opposed to integration, while the former implies a visual challenge for architects.

active experiment – matching supply to demand

One example of explicit and integrated flat-plate solar advertisement is the small house of 100m^2 designed by architect Bart Jan van den Brink and built in 1988 as one of seventeen experimental (and intended to be temporary) dwellings. This was organized as the first phase of the 'Fantasy' competition on the outskirts of Almere, one of the new polder towns in the Netherlands within easy commuting distance of Amsterdam. The van den Brink dwelling is conceived boldly, stretching the technology of building-integrated active solar collection. In particular it attempts to tackle the seasonal mismatch between supply and demand – the greatest amount of solar irradiation naturally occurring in summer. The concept is therefore to provide a suitable area of flat-plate collector to charge an adequate seasonal store of water to meet most of the thermal load – both space-heating and hot water – of a single small home from autumn through to spring. In his scenario, it is accepted that the topping up of solar heat in autumn, winter and spring, albeit the lowest amount of top-up coinciding with the highest demand, remains essential to the overall viability.

The 70m² collector is tilted at 45° to form the waterproof and insulated cover of a combined wall-roof on the south facing edge (Figure 2.2a). The cost of what would otherwise have been required for this part of the external envelope thus offsets the cost of the collector and its associated plumbing. In order to achieve an orientation directly to the south, the axis of the house lies diagonally across the rectilinear plot. The tilt is actually close to the optimum for maximum average annual daily incident irradiation from the sun. While a lower pitch of say 30° would have increased the summer contribution by around 6 per cent, there were practical spatial constraints. The chosen pitch of 45° allows useable internal space quite close up to the junction between floor and the sloping surface. The thermal store is a vertical cylinder with a 40,000 litre capacity, and this is located provocatively half inside and half outside the north-facing façade (Figure 2.2b). It is provocative in part because it is a highly visible servicing element of the kind where the norm is to conceal, whether above or below ground. It is also exposed to ambient weather for about two thirds of its bounding surface and is therefore very reliant on its 'jacket' of insulation in terms of conserving its heat over long periods.

The Fantasy competition viewed all the dwellings as temporary, having minimal impact on the site in terms of excavations for foundations and restoration after demolition. This presented a particular challenge for a solar house where a significant mass was an essential part of the strategy. Here the problem of the blunt point load of the thermal store located at the northern extremity of the plan was solved by means of a concrete raft, which projects beyond the south, east and west edges as a water filled tray. This not only functions as a counterweight to the thermal store, but also provides a reflective surface to increase solar capture by the flat-plate collector. The slab also increases thermal storage for any direct solar gain through east and west fenestration, while the active or mechanical delivery of the heat stored in the cylinder to the occupied spaces is by air.

The remainder of the north, east and west façades are fully glazed. This in turn raises the issue of heat balance, particularly for the north-facing sections, but the problem has been countered by the use of external folding shutters. These are 6.8m high and well insulated. Even so, structural rigidity is needed, and it is perhaps surprising that the users seemed to be able to manhandle them without too much difficulty. They could be drawn across the northeast and northwest corners during very cold spells or at night, leaving the triangular east and west facing glazed sections to rely solely on the specification of the triple-glazed units.

surface absorbs a much higher proportion of solar radiation, but emits and absorbs in long wave poorly, further enhancing the performance. A selective surface should yield 10–15 per cent more than a non-selective one.

2.2(5) Plastics used include polycarbonate, acrylic and polyester. In the last case, if twin skinned (as in a collector made in the Highlands of Scotland by AES Ltd.) the outer skin may be a material called Tedlar and the inner one Teflon. Tedlar is more robust and ultra-violet resistant than Teflon. Justification for more than one glazing sheet depends partly on the temperature required – more so for domestic hot water than an under-floor space heating system. The primary purpose of the transparent cover is to trap shortwave solar radiation. All transparent materials are relatively transparent to incoming shortwave radiation, and opaque to outgoing long wave emissions. Thin membranes such as Tedlar and Teflon have better shortwave transmission characteristics than thicker plastics, such as polycarbonate, or glass.

2.2a 'Fantasy' solar house in Almere: active flat-plate collector doubles as a south-facing roof

2.2b 'Fantasy' solar house in Almere: seasonal thermal store makes a statement on the public side of the house

Although, with all shutters closed, the balance of glazing is more than adequate for daylight at 36 per cent of the total ground and first floor area, the solar collector does block out the opportunity for views to the south as well as direct solar gain to the interior. In this particular case the south side also happens to be the most private side. The access road lies to the northwest while there are other dwellings quite close to the southwest and northeast. The same sacrifice of aspect for opaque south-facing surface would occur for other indirect passive solar methods such as thermal mass storage walls or solar air collectors.

In terms of performance, the architect subjected the design to thermal modelling prior to construction. True to form, the predictions proved to be over-optimistic and more will be said about performance and control issues in succeeding chapters. It is enough to say at this stage that the store lost heat too rapidly and was not ideally matched to the collector. Significantly more auxiliary heat than envisaged was required during winter, and the active system was modified some ten years after it was first built. Nevertheless, it remains a valuable pioneer. The thermal store could have been provided below the floor. This might have involved a deeper raft and hidden one half of the iconic solar imagery, but it would have been a significantly more thermally efficient solution, with much of the thermal loss contributing usefully to the interior in winter and spring. Even though it might be argued that it would also increase unwanted incidental gain to the interior on a warm day in summer, overheating could have been readily avoided by opening windows in all but the most exceptional weather. Then, the loss of heat through the high north wall could have been addressed by eliminating the glazing altogether, rather than by movable insulation.

passive exploitation of triangular section

Moving from a single experimental house to experimental housing, and still with the triangle as a dominant sectional device, it is interesting to compare the solar tactics of AARPLAN's terrace in Zollikofen, a suburb to the northeast of Berne in Switzerland. In this case a glazed south-facing façade is tilted at 60° from the horizontal and forms the outer cover of a three-storey high, unheated sunspace, which buffers all the heated accommodation. To ventilate the heated rooms it is therefore necessary to open both inner and outer glazing, the latter operated electrically. The fenestration is capped by a linear array of PV panels at a somewhat shallower tilt. This complements the faceted, overlapping effect of the upper opening hoppers, especially when open, as well as concealing the depth of the roof (Figure 2.3a). Although structurally slim, there is some 20cm of turf over 25cm of insulation. The rectangular hollow steel sections, which support the outer glazing, also constitute essential ties to a steel catenary roof structure, with vertical columns in compression just behind the inner glazed screen. Moreover, the geometry of the section provides most space within the sunspace at the lowest level where it is needed (for example, for relaxation, drying clothes and growing food). Therefore, in this case, the overt solar geometry is completely in tune with structural and other functional requirements and the passive solar system does not inherently clash with views out and connection with gardens.

The sunspace additionally serves as the entrance porch or storm lobby to each house, so that in winter the sliding outer door can be closed before the inner door to the heated interior is opened. Energy-efficiency in winter is therefore addressed on at least five fronts: direct solar gain through both outer and inner windows; indirect gain by means of a preheated supply of air from the sunspace; the solar-enhanced thermal resistance of the sunspace; the sheltering effect of the buffer space from wind and rain, (particularly since it doubles as the entrance and dries clothes passively); and its structural and amenity value. The scheme very much conforms to the title of this chapter.

There is also an ingenious method to avoid overheating in summer. Air is supplied via an underground cellar, forming a cool buffer on the north side of the accommodation and leaving via the high level glazed hoppers on the south side. The outer glazing is also shaded by means of internal blinds. However, on visiting this building during a hot and sunny afternoon in May, the visual effect of so many blinds being down gave a closed appearance to the façade (Figure 2.3b). Therefore, although on the face of it there is no prohibition of prospect as by the active collector in the case of the Dutch Fantasy house, one of the means to avoid overheating does form a visual barrier. From the outside, the appearance is predominantly opaque. Depending on viewpoint, lighting conditions and precise specification of blind, they may be less so from inside. Overall, however, transparency is undoubtedly interrupted during the very times when many people would most want to dissipate the inside–outside distinction, and so may be regarded as a negative consequence of the solar section.

A point about the evident solar character of this small suburban scheme is that an enquiry at the local library, which consisted only of a 'hand language' version of the cross section, elicited an immediate response with full directions. Also, although the project stood out visually as being very different from its more traditional neighbours, the lay opinion of the librarian and one occupant who happened to be at the desk seemed very positive.

formal issues and shed vernacular

In terms of its architectural form, the housing at Zollikofen represents a special condition of a prototypical cross section. Essentially, it is a mono-pitch rising to the south to maximize free solar gain and falling to the north to minimize expensive thermal loss. In this case, the low curve and turf covering of the roof allows it to merge with natural ground level on the north side. This does slightly soften the impact of the east and west ends, but formally a question remains. Could the bookends have not been stronger visual variants of the standard single-aspect intermediate houses, receiving some additional benefit from east-

2.3   Solar terrace in Zollikofen, Berne:
a   PV array visually echoes opening windows at
      top of façade
b   blanked by blinds in warm weather

and west-facing windows respectively? Also, although the concave green surface of the roof eliminates overshadowing to other dwellings located to the north, as well as enhancing their privacy, it creates an awkward dilemma in terms of the suburban landscape. The grass is not public space and consequently is rather clumsily fenced off. It is also home not only to a series of projecting roof-lights, which might be considered to carry some visual authority, but also to ventilating terminals, which are awkwardly intrusive.

Reduced to a single dwelling on a flat site, and with a flat mono-pitch, the AARPLAN version of the prototype is reminiscent of the 1980s house designed for John Cash and his family at Garriston, about 20 miles north of Dublin in Ireland (Figure 2.4). Interestingly, a non-architect member of the Scottish Solar Energy Group who visited the Cash house in 1988 was fulsome in his praise: 'The two-storey high, single-room deep, massively constructed house with its towering cliff of south-facing glazing offers eloquent testimony to the belief that uncompromising passive solar design are wholly compatible – providing that like John and his collaborators, such as architect Duncan Stewart, you have faith in your idea and a sound grasp of the principles and of the technology involved.' (Talbot, 1988). The interesting question is whether many architects would endorse such uncompromising passive solar design. A related question is whether the multi-functionality of designs such as that at Zollikofen, including the structural justification for the basic geometry, helps to dilute the radicalism of the passive solar design, and consequently to make it more acceptable.

2.4   Passive solar house at Garriston, near Dublin

The simple mono-pitched form is also used by Canadian architect Brian MacKay-Lyons in several of his houses in Nova Scotia. For example, the gently sloping roof of the 1999 Howard house in West Pennant, close to Halifax, takes the main living space up to a lofty 8.4m at its southern end (Figure 2.5). The lower two thirds of this is glazed, and the fenestration wraps round east and west facades by over 2m, providing a net total of about 40m^2 of solar aperture, which directly serves a floor area of 30m^2. Muted yet explicit multi-functionality relates here to the views towards the bay, as well as the architectural concept of a slim wall at right angles to contours and coastline, which deliberately divides the external maritime realm into three picturesque zones. The basic shape also provides a low surface to volume ratio, which is appropriate to the climate in Nova Scotia. Even in June the maximum ambient temperature can drop into single figures, making this a valuable strategy for energy-efficiency. Where the prismatic form is modified, there is also a complementary multifarious logic. The concrete projection on the west façade that accommodates stairs and a double-sided spine of bookshelves, the latter in turn absorbing the hearth, is subtly straightforward in terms of its variable functionality. The reinforced structural U-shape on plan constitutes an essential buttress to the prevailing winds, which effortlessly absorbed the force of a major equinoctial hurricane in the autumn of 2003. But it also economically houses the vertical circulation and leaves the narrow 3.6m width of the floor uninterrupted.

2.5   Passive solar house at West Pennant, near Halifax, Nova Scotia

MacKay-Lyons draws analogies for this type of project to the vernacular sheds of the province (MacKay-Lyons, 1995). In this regard he acknowledges its multinational heritage, the early name of Acadia given by the 17th and 18th century French settlers (expelled by New England planters in 1755), and he talks of the vernacular as a 'process or cultural view'. His expansion of this assertion is imbued with his poetic and strongly rooted clarity, as well as underlying passion:

Also contributing to the pragmatic and spartan aesthetic of Nova Scotia sheds is a strong cultural ethic.
This is a deeply democratic ethic which elevates simplicity to a moral idea where modesty is considered a virtue,
while ostentation or the display of wealth are discouraged.
This is not hard to understand given the tragic, peasant background of the Scots, Irish, Germans and Acadians that settled here.

Another shed, which plays a degree of ascetism against sophistication, is that of the gymnasium for the Odenwaldeschule at Oberhambach in Germany by architect Peter Hübner (Figures 2.6a–c). Located among the Odenwald hills, roughly halfway between Stuttgart and Frankfurt, the site slopes down a full two storeys across the width of the building to the west, with a sunspace taking advantage of the height along this edge. Its triangular section, similar to that at Zollikofen, accommodates both entrance and fitness equipment lobby. The tilt of its glazing, at about 68°, is even steeper than at Zollikofen and the cross-

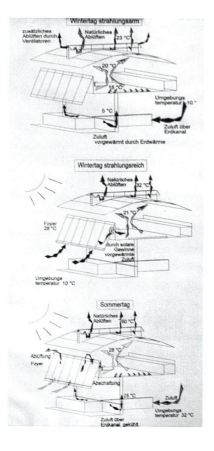

2.6 Gymnasium at Oberhambach, by Peter Hübner

a schematics for different weather and seasons displayed next to plant room

b ventilating slot looking west to triangular sunspace

c flat-plate solar thermal collectors on southeast façade

section suits its utilitarian purpose as well as forming an integral part of the structure, this time as a buttress to resist the outward thrust of the low barrel-vaulted roof. Another difference is that the roof beams cantilever downward well beyond the sloping glass surface of the sunspace, with tilted louvres set between them providing significant shading during the summer. In turn, deciduous planting inside the sunspace augments cooling.

The net result is that the space is adequately self-shading in summer, and so does not suffer from the defensiveness of Zollikofen with its blinds down. This is important, since the space functions as a welcoming threshold to the gymnasium. Moreover, unlike Zollikofen, with its concave roof, the convex surface of the roof vault is visually dominant relative to the sunspace, and the structural raison d'être of the buttressing seems more obvious than the tensioning function of the equivalent structural member at Zollikofen. The downward slope of the ground also adds to the anticipation of the steeply upward tilted surface of glass. It is a transparent counterpoint to the ground, clothing the supporting structure for the gentle vault which in turn is launched from a low base forming the upper eastern edge to the building.

Still dealing with the passive syntax of Hübner's building, there is a second glazed component slicing across the curve of the roof. This also has more than one function. Firstly, it is the means of exhausting stale air at a level higher than the highest part of the roof, thus assisting natural thermal buoyancy. Secondly, it houses a dividing screen, a giant folding blind which, when lowered, allows two different sports activities to take place simultaneously. Whether up or down, this screening device also performs the function of a solar absorber, so acting as an accelerator for the passive exhaust system and making the feature triply functional. Perhaps more importantly, it is another formal architectural statement, which cleverly punctuates the flow from east to west across the site. The only contentious aspect of this device is the decision to only open up the narrow ends rather than having a continuous strip of opening windows at the highest level along its flanks. The risk is that the relatively small area of opening windows, as built, will not provide an adequate rate of exhaust for warm vitiated air.

Then this building has a third solar element: a series of flat-plate solar collectors for preheating hot water, which step down the southern gable. These are explicitly solar with no secondary function. The generous overhang of the roof provides shading of the south facing glazing from steep summer sunlight. The solar collectors are therefore only incidentally integrated, the lower part of the south gable being a convenient place to mount them. Having said that, they do contribute positively to the whole ensemble. The array enlivens the gable, referring to the slope of the ground rather than slavishly following it.

2.7   Multiple solar roof of Energiebalanswoning
by Van Straalen, Zeist & BOOM

multiple active–passive solar roofs

Returning to the domestic scale, traditional pitched roofs inevitably present themselves as targets for highly visible arrays of solar collectors. The Van den Brink house configured the roof as a wall and, by doing so, broke with traditional norms. An experimental pair of dwellings where a shallower and extensive mono-pitched roof is raised one floor above the ground, but encloses a further two floors along the north edge, is the Energiebalanswoning or 'energy balance house' in Amersfoort, the Netherlands. Designed by Architectenbureau Van Straalen, Zeist & BOOM of Delft, it is one of the main living experiments in the Waterkwartier Nieuwland solar suburb, forming the northern extremity of a rapidly expanding Amersfoort at the time of a visit in 2003. The relatively low mono-pitch of about 21.5° accommodates a mix of translucent and opaque PV panels, generating electricity, flat-plate collectors preheating hot water, and transparent windows, allowing direct solar gain and natural ventilation ('translucent' here referring to a glazing sandwich containing PV cells, spaced out to leave a proportion of the roof completely transparent). Sections of the roof landscape are also treated as voids. Each dwelling has a small patio recessed below roof level on the first floor, while fixed louvres on the plane of the roof protect the south-facing windows to ground and first floors.

In this case, the rational solar-collecting language appears direct and authoritative, all the more so because all collectors are fully integrated as a principal part of the waterproof skin of the building (Figure 2.7). However, there is a functional flaw. Not only is the pitch rather low for effective self-cleansing, dirt accumulates behind the raised horizontal framing separating PV panels and this will have a negative effect on performance. Indeed, if any of the cells in a particular PV 'string' or circuit are obscured, the entire string can be knocked out.

The other aspect to PV as waterproof skin is that, similarly to any sheet material with a high resistance to water vapour, a ventilated air space is required below it in order to limit risk of interstitial condensation. The more the air moves, the closer its temperature and vapour pressure will come to the ambient conditions and hence the less the chance of condensation occurring within the cavity. In the case of PV, this has an added advantage. The flow of air will help to remove heat from the underside of the cells, thus helping to keep the efficiency of their generation of electricity as high as possible. This raises the possibility of using the air below the cells as a preheated supply in winter, bearing in mind that this technique would also recycle heat already lost by conduction from the interior. However, in this case, the decision was made not to do this.

Not too far to the south, in the small EVA Lanxmeer eco-village located next to the railway station of Culemborg, there is another attempt to integrate PV, flat-plate collectors and roof windows (Figure 2.8a). The roof pitch is steeper in this

2.8 EVA Lanxmeer eco-village at Culemborg
a integrated solar roof of terrace on the north side of access road
b private side of solar terrace to the south of access road – solar array not visible

case, but the thrust of integration seems very similar to that of Energiebalanswoning. However, the detail of a strip of profiled pantiles above the party walls, together with similarly profiled ridge tiles, somehow grates relative to the solar arrays. Either the latter's smooth surfaces seem to intrude on textured traditionalism, or vice versa. This may seem like aesthetic nit-picking, especially since the dwellings are designed by carefully selected architects – in this case Peter van der Cammen of Orta Nova, Amersfoort. But most architects are like that. They are hyper-critical of the work of their own peer group, and if we are to significantly increase the uptake of solar technology, architects must be reassured that they can remain fully in charge of every detail.

It is evident from these two examples that such aesthetic nuances are prepared to forego optimum performance based on orientation and tilt. The terrace in Culemborg shown here contains the same active solar ingredients as that of the Energiebalanswoning in Amersfoort, but the respective pitches are very different. Diagonally across from the Orta Nova terrace in EVA Lanxmeer there is another terrace by Joachim Eble, well known for his ecologically-sensitive oeuvre. In this case, the cross section rises up somewhat east of north to the road to gain a third floor. An active solar array is located along that highest edge with what appears to be an appropriate tilt and facing slightly west of south. This means that it cannot be seen from the street or from close in to the dwelling on the private side (Figure 2.8b).

2.9   Detail of roof of swimming pool in Gouda –
      solar collector replacing former glazing

solar retrofit – collection isolated from storage

Sometimes, especially with retrofit projects, the architect has very little choice. For example, staying in the Netherlands, a listed swimming pool in Gouda, which was the Dutch 'solar city' in 1995, had its original roof glazing replaced with solar air collectors (Figure 2.9). These faced east and west, with a medium pitch, somewhere between the Amersfoort and Culemborg examples. One array preheated the pool itself, while the other did the same for the air handling system. In terms of having a function other than collecting solar energy, rather unusually in this case, their very presence was used to facilitate the absence of any significant aesthetic alteration to the building. The solar collectors are effective – the new array provides over 400kWh/m^2 annually, totalling approximately 40,000kWh to heat the pool itself and 30,000kWh to heat the air around it – but do not appear very different from the former skylights, while the original pantiles are still the appropriately dominant texture. Moreover, even though the original overhead skylights had gone, windows in each gable were still able to provide adequate amounts of daylight.

Another project with a roof-integrated solar air collector is the 1986 retrofit of a 1950s housing block in Göteborg in Sweden by architects Christer and Kirsten Nordström. Here the complete south-facing roof surface has been replaced with an air collector, which then delivers the heat to externally insulated walls via a serpentine system of cavities. These are achieved by spacing out a new brick skin, lined internally with 80mm mineral wool from the original 'no-fines' (a form of concrete with no fine aggregate and consequently with air voids) solid concrete wall. Thus both roof and wall have a new solar function. That in the wall is invisible and, because the collector covers the entire roof and the interval of glazing supports from ridge to eaves sets up a rhythm not dissimilar to a Scandinavian copper or zinc roof, the system barely declares itself as solar. Indeed, the new greenhouse at ground level, installed more as a social engineering exercise than to improve energy efficiency, gives a stronger solar signal (Figure 2.10a). However, vertical solar air collectors, also by the Nordströms, on new-build housing in another suburban district of Göteborg are more contentious (Figure 2.10b). They occupy a large proportion of the main façade, facing on to the street, and although this may work well in terms of privacy they do appear to compete with normal windows. The two projects also raise a functional question as to whether a low south-facing pitch of around 30° is better or worse for space-heating than a vertical wall. The answer is quite complex. It is dependent partly on the local climate and partly on the general level of energy efficiency. The latter aspect, mainly driven by quantity of insulation, dictates the months when heating is required and so defines the solar geometry for these months.

2.10 Two projects in Göteborg
a   solar retrofit of 1950s housing block – roof
     collector does not compete with windows
b   new-build solar housing – wall collector
     competes with windows for share of façade

scope for geometric diversity

Staying with the issue of orientation and tilt of solar collectors, the situation is naturally different when the emphasis is on domestic hot water or electricity. The steeply pitched example in Culemborg is not ideal for the two domestic hot water (DHW) collectors located above the two roof windows. In order to maximize solar preheat over a year, it makes sense to prioritize collection in summer. If the collector had been targeting space heating, then a steeper pitch would be appropriate. Also for PV, it makes sense to collect as much as possible during summer, especially when the system is grid-connected. A general rule in Northern Europe is for a pitch of some 20° below that of the latitude angle (Thomas and Fordham, 2001). On this basis, the lower pitch of the two experimental dwellings in Amersfoort can again be expected to outperform the Orta Nova terrace at Culemborg.

Having made this point, the annual differences for a south-facing roof are relatively minor. ■2.3(1) However, as the orientation moves away from south, the use of steeper tilts becomes progressively more critical for annual performance, as shown in Table 2.1 below.

Table 2.1 Mean Annual Incident Solar Irradiation Predicted for Glasgow (kWh/m²)

	30°	45°	60°	90° tilt
South	987	975	919	701
SE/SW	944	923	863	664
E/W	836	786	720	548

Source: Page and Lebens, 1986, p171

■2.3 Solar geometry – supplementary notes (refer also to Tables 2.1–2.6)

2.3(1) Incident solar radiation on a 60° pitch in Glasgow is 7 per cent less than on a 30° pitch over a complete year. Then a 30° pitch, facing due east or west, compared with one facing due south, collects about 15 per cent less, with a further 14 per cent loss if the east–west pitch increases to 60°.

2.3(2) A 30-year mean at Glasgow Airport (Plant, 1967) gives 3.44°C for November compared with 3.78°C for April; while the same means for Edinburgh Airport (Plant, 1968) are even closer at 2.94°C and 3.06°C respectively.

2.3(3) At Glasgow's latitude of 56°N, the mid-April maximum solar altitude (at solar noon) is 44°, while in mid-November it is just less than 15°. The length of the day also increases by 50 per cent from eight hours in mid-November to twelve hours in mid-April.

2.3(4) Table 2.4 shows that there is a 4 per cent increase in incident solar irradiation from a 30° to a 45° south-facing tilt, dropping slightly to 3 per cent as the pitch increases to 60°. When we move from 30° to a vertical south-facing surface, there is now more a significant fall in availability of 13.5 per cent. For surfaces facing due east or west, vertical surfaces now receive 30 per cent less than for 30°, which is best for this orientation, but 27 per cent less than for the due south 45° equivalent.

2.3(5) It is estimated that the range of transmitted solar heat gain would be approximately 100kWh/m² at east- and west-facing extremities, 150kWh/m² for southeast- and southwest-facing, and up to 175kWh/m² on the south-facing centre line.

Table 2.2 indicates that a similar pattern emerges if the collecting season disregards October to February. It should be noted that the omission of these five months has a greater impact the closer to south the orientation is, as shown below in Table 2.3; and also, once the orientation has drifted by as much as 90°, the effect of tilt is less important. These data also confirm that the relatively low pitch of around 30° is quite favourable for active systems.

Table 2.2   Mean Incident Solar Irradiation Predicted for Glasgow from March–September (kWh/m²)

	30°	45°	60°	90° tilt
South	821	794	732	529
SE/SW	795	765	704	524
E/W	724	678	618	467

Source: Page and Lebens, 1986, p171

Table 2.3   Percentage Reduction in Mean Incident Solar Irradiation for Glasgow: Annual (Table 2.1) compared to March–September (Table 2.2)

	30°	45°	60°	90° tilt
South	16.8	18.6	20.3	24.5
SE/SW	15.8	17.1	18.4	21.1
E/W	13.4	13.7	14.2	14.8

Source: Page and Lebens, 1986, p171

Returning to the low-pitched roof versus vertical wall for solar space heating in Göteborg, we have a latitude and climate that is quite similar to that of Glasgow. When the emphasis shifts to heating in winter, say from November to April, the expectation arising from a seasonal perception of sunlight is for steeper pitches to become much more relevant. Hence one might anticipate that the collector on the wall is best, since it would be at a more favourable angle in relation to a sunbeam than a low-pitched roof. However, the picture is not as clear-cut as one might imagine. A November–April heating season provides rough symmetry in terms of external air temperature for most 'cool climate' locations. ■2.3(2) On the other hand there is a large amount of asymmetry when it comes to solar geometry. ■2.3(3)

Thus, although in Glasgow there is a slight increase in incident solar irradiation from low to medium south-facing tilts, when we move up to the vertical south-facing surface, there is a significant fall in availability. Then, as we move away from south to southeast or southwest, the vertical surface becomes nearly one fifth less than a low pitch, while a medium pitch remains optimal, even though it is less than for due south. Finally, addressing surfaces facing due east or west, vertical surfaces now receive substantially less than for a low pitch, which is best for this orientation. ■2.3(4) Table 2.4 summarizes this situation.

Table 2.4 Mean Incident Solar Irradiation Predicted for Glasgow from November–April (kWh/m²)

	30°	45°	60°	90° tilt
South	304	317	313	263
SE/SW	283	288	279	230
E/W	231	221	205	160

Source: Page and Lebens, 1986, p171

Such vital statistics are difficult to assimilate at a glance, but they do start to make sense of some of the varying geometries described for the buildings above. For example, the combination of direct gain through low-pitched roof-lights and vertical windows in the Energiebalanswoning appears quite logical. So also does the 60° tilt at Zollikofen and a relatively similar steep tilt for direct gain in the Orta Nova example at Culemborg.

There is one further note of caution, however. In cloudless conditions, when the angle between a sunbeam and a line normal to a glazed surface (the angle of incidence) exceeds 50°, there is a rapid decrease in transmitted solar heat. This would certainly apply to the 21.5° roof windows of the Energiebalanswoning throughout the day in November, and for parts of the day in other months. Having said that, much of the radiation during winter in temperate or 'cool winter' climates is diffuse or directionless. Overall, solar irradiation, which has been predicted to be transmitted through south facing double-glazing in Glasgow (Page and Lebens, 1986), keeps the same ranking for the various tilts as for incident irradiation, with vertical windows again receiving about 13.5 per cent less than that transmitted through roof windows with a 30° tilt (Table 2.5). On the other hand, as one moves away from due south orientation, the loss of transmitted irradiation due to high angles of incidence has a greater impact. The percentage reduction, comparing incident energy and that transmitted, is at or just below one third for the due south orientation, increasing a little for southeast and southwest, but quite significantly for due east and west (Table 2.6).

Table 2.5 Mean Solar Irradiation Predicted to be Transmitted Through Double-glazing for Glasgow from November–April (kWh/m²)

	30°	45°	60°	90° tilt
South	202	214	213	175
SE/SW	185	191	186	150
E/W	146	141	132	100

Source: Page and Lebens, 1986, p171

2.11 Southern façade of Scottish dementia unit

Table 2.6 Percentage Reduction in Mean Solar Irradiation for Glasgow: Incident Compared to Through Double-glazing

	30°	45°	60°	90° tilt
South	33.6	32.5	31.9	33.5 %
SE/SW	34.6	33.7	33.3	34.8
E/W	36.8	36.2	35.6	37.5

Source: Page and Lebens, 1986, p171

This information simply reflects the asymmetrical solar geometry relative to the demand for heat. In particular, the solar angles in March and April make a more favourable impact on tilted surfaces as the orientation veers away from due south. This does not mean to say that architects should avoid vertical east- and west-facing windows. It suggests rather that, where opportunities occur, tilted glazing should also have a passive solar role in winter, even at relatively low angles. Alternatively, if tilted glazing is not an option, then east or west vertical glazed area could increase by 75 per cent to bring it up to the same level as vertical south glazing, or roughly double to compete with optimum south-facing tilts. Such increases would require to be complemented by an appropriately high specification for the glazing and its frame in order to minimize conducted thermal loss. The aim must be to achieve a net gain over the heating season. The strategy of the case studies used so far in this section has tended to be driven by the north–south cross section. But it is evident that the plan and east–west sections can also play a crucial part in terms of multiple and added solar value.

Mention was made earlier of the 'solar hemi-cycle' by Frank Lloyd Wright. This presented a concave surface to the main daytime rooms and a convex surface to the sleeping accommodation. The same planning device is employed in a dementia unit located near Larbert in central Scotland by Foster and Partners. There is more length for bedrooms on the outer edge relative to inward-facing sitting rooms (Figure 2.11). The curve also counteracts the negative aspect of an economic linear plan with accommodation on either side of a central corridor – that of long narrow vistas, with a perspective of receding doors. In terms of free energy, it means that the transmitted solar heat to the day-rooms, as well as through clerestory glazing to the main internal circulatory street, from November to April will vary by about 75 per cent. ■2.3(5) The concave shape also provides a sense of enclosure to a garden court. Indeed, it will have a beneficial effect on the microclimate of the court, including enhanced radiant comfort due to solar capture, as well as shelter from the wind. On the outer northerly edge to the bedrooms, solar gain is not so much the issue. Rather, the geometry allows some sunlight to enter bedrooms, particularly during spring and summer, and this may well help to enliven the rooms, and possibly the emotional responses for some of the residents.

Another building with a strongly evocative form is the 'solar house' in Freiburg by architects Hölken & Berghoff in association with the Fraunhofer Institut fur Solare Energiesysteme (ISE), Figure 2.12. The plan is symmetrical with a convex curved façade, partly energy-efficient windows for direct gain and partly thermal storage walls augmented by transparent insulation (TI). ■2.4 The primary curved spaces are attached to a service spine along the north edge, punctuated by a small semi-circular porch. The plan of the spine and porch is then extruded on section as a south-facing mono-pitch, which is covered in active solar arrays. Thus when the building is viewed from the south, the radial curve of the north-facing porch is axially expressed as the zenith of the active collection, reflecting the larger radial thrust of the main accommodation. However, although solar collection is manifestly expressed, a secondary function is limited to simply being part of the external skin. There are no fringe benefits such as the curving corridor or the outdoor courtyard of the Scottish dementia unit. On the other hand – and this limitation applies equally to some of the examples above explored primarily through their cross section – the act of collection for both active devices will result in heating of the fabric behind the collector. This will increase the effectiveness of the insulating ability of the surfaces (ie lower U-values) during cold and sunny weather. In the case of the passive TI, heating up a storage wall is its rationale, aiming at negative effective U-values in sunny weather (ie gain to the interior) and close to zero on average.

During a visit in 1999, Dr Klaus Heideler of ISE likened the house to the principle of a thermos flask. It has to be admitted that this is not a new idea in architecture. The Italian 'thermos' casa of 1933 by architect Luigi Figini comes to mind. ■2.5(1) However, while Figini's house may well have been very energy-efficient for its time, the solar house in Freiburg is very close to claiming a 'zero energy' label. ■2.5(2) Detailed aspects of this impressive performance will be discussed in a later chapter. At this stage it is sufficient to say that the strongly integrated solar aesthetic is an issue. Axial symmetry is definitely part of this, with its historical association with power – the politically authoritarian sort. It is not that symmetry has disappeared altogether from normal domestic architecture – the work of Mario Botta is a case in point. But, in conjunction with the patently engineered technology, where symmetry is also a common idiom, the building emanates a message. It combatively declares itself as an 'experiment'. This is what it is, rather than a 'home'. Nevertheless it is a domestic concept that ISE is trying to promote, together with the solar technology. This poses a question as to the viability of a 'solar house' (as conceived and named by ISE) which is also so overtly a 'solar experiment' (and one that could only be replicated in detached form).

■2.4 Transparent insulation

Like any other form of insulation, TI relies on trapping pockets of air, which are small enough to inhibit transfer of heat by convection. This results in a low rate of thermal conductivity, while at the same time the transmittance of light and radiant heat is quite high. Therefore, solar heat can be absorbed by surfaces on the inside of the TI, where most of it can be stored and usefully delivered to the space after a certain time lag, while relatively little is conducted back out in overcast and nocturnal periods. Types of TI vary in terms of precise geometrical structure (eg foams and capillaries) and material (eg aerogel, acrylic or polycarbonate). Further technical information on products such as foamed acrylic and the highly porous aerogel is given in the third part of Chapter 5. One of the more common plastics used is polycarbonate, with a capillary structure at right angles to the plane of the surface where it is applied. It may be bonded on to a single sheet of glass, used as its weatherproof cover and secured in front of a storage wall, as at Freiburg, or held in place in a freestanding manner between outer glazing and storage wall (as in the student residences in Scotland, cited in Chapters 4 and 5). Alternatively it may be bonded between two sheets of glass or plastic and used as an alternative to normal fenestration.

■2.5 Thermos principle applied to dwellings in the 1930s and 1990s

2.5(1) Figini's 'thermos' casa was exhibited in the Lighthouse, Glasgow, in 2003 as the UK premiere of 'One Hundred Houses for One Hundred Architects of the XX Century'.

2.5(2) Dr Heideler presented the following figures for annual energy loads in kWh/m² for heating and hot water in German dwellings: 160 as average; 50 for low energy standards; 20 for a low energy, passive solar exemplar; and 2.7 for the Freiburg solar house. One must assume that the values of 2.7kWh/m² and 20kWh/m² exclude the space heating contribution made by ventilation heat recovery.

2.12 Solar house in Freiburg
a   detail of façade
b   plan
c   section

aesthetic ambiguity and nuance of solar collection – arcades and atria

Taking other stances – those of visual diffidence, neutrality or subtlety in terms of solar collection – a number of diverse approaches are feasible. For example, glazed streets or arcades have a history of association with urban grain which, although acknowledged in terms of protection from wind and rain, are not necessarily perceived in terms of solar gain. Similarly, early atria, say in Parisian department stores, were not so much about daylight, often heavily muted through stained glass, as about legibility for the shopper – scents below, clothes in the middle and furnishings on top, all at a glance. Therefore, it can be argued that the solar purpose of a considerable number of such modern spaces, both in the UK and within continental Europe, may be at least partly neutralized by precedent.

This is important for at least some architects who fear that too much direct expression of solar collection risks shallow, formulaic cliché. On the other hand, some applications of ostensibly passive solar devices, such as atria in commercial developments, have become almost ubiquitous in marketing terms. One can imagine an advertising hoarding: '10,000 m² fully air-conditioned luxury office space on eight floors, with full-height atrium'. Of course in terms of energy-efficiency, atria should go hand in hand with natural or 'mixed mode' ventilation. They are capable of saving energy and improving the organic quality of air, as well as boosting the whole psychological and metaphysical experience of the working day. But the reality for many atria is a poor reflection of the marketing hype. They can be dull and austere spaces, where the potential environmental assets are completely unexploited.

Past reactions are interesting here, quoting from the report of a UK-ISES tour as the postscript of its September 1987 Atria Conference:

> The afternoon started with an unrelentingly grey atrium in a typical new 'dealer floor' building (Merrill Lynch) and gave the impression that there would be little joy for employees, let alone the general public, when all was

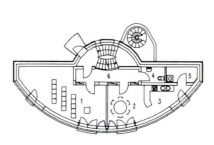

Ground floor
1. Lecture room   2. Dining area
3. Kitchen   4. WC
5. Store-room   6. Corridor

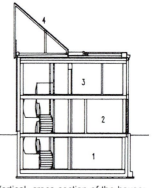

Vertical cross-section of the house:
1. Basement   2. Ground floor
3. First floor   4 Photovoltaic & collector
                     systems

complete. The next stop, Triton Court, was cheerier and open to the public, but I am none the wiser with respect to its energy saving role, if indeed that has any relevance for the developer. The next (3 Finsbury Avenue) was not open to the public, and its energy saving function appeared to be venting unwanted gains generated by the over-glazed, double-skin main façade. The same 'stable door' logic applies to another detail of the moment, much in evidence on the new generation of atria buildings – maintenance platforms at each floor level as passive solar shading devices. First over-glaze the envelope, and then shade it. To add insult to injury, the detail is applied equally to all orientations. So we have a design gimmick to replace the travelling cradle, but we do not have an energy-conscious façade. Similarly atria, merely by virtue of their presence, do not even necessarily constitute energy or visual assets. They are simply products of market forces, and I will not be surprised when they begin to be filled in by – yes – more dealer floors! (Porteous, 1988)

2.13 Wasa City shopping market in atrium at Gävle

Nevertheless, having provided a further platform for such critique, the fact that atria continue to carry commercial clout means that solar designers have a suitable environmental Trojan horse, which does not in itself carry overt green symbolism. The same applies to buildings with a social or cultural function. Atria have a credibility for both lay users and architects over and above that ultimately concerned with global warming.

Two Swedish examples illustrate retrofit potential for atria. Wasa City, at latitude 60.7°N in Gävle to the north of Stockholm, was one of the International Energy Agency (IEA) Task XI Solar Heating and Cooling projects. It is very much in the genre of glazed markets, but is in this case a market held within a courtyard bounded by housing constructed in 1964. Commerce flourishes at ground level (Figure 2.13), while there is a residential promenade overlooking the marketplace at first floor level. In 1987 architect Thurfjell introduced a simple propped 30° dual-pitch roof structure, which is terminated at the southern end with a 'shark's fin' tower, the south slope at 45°, where air is exhausted by natural thermo-circulation. There are detailed aspects of the performance that will be discussed in a later chapter. The important point to make at this stage is that the ambience is pleasant, with planting playing a significant role. Commercially, of course, the courtyard is now able to generate significant income. As a local shopping experience, it seems a much better option for areas with severe winters than the internalized 'pedway' (pedestrian walkway) systems to be found in cities such as Edmonton in Canada. Overall, it is a humane intervention, rooted in historical precedent and, visually, it is uncontroversial.

In Söderhamn, not far to the north of Gävle, there is another slightly earlier retrofit, which follows a similar rational and functional logic. In 1983, architect Jack Hanson opportunistically linked a three-storey, flat-roofed terrace of 1960s housing to a two-storey one by means of a gently sloping mono-pitch roof

2.14 New atrium between old terraces at Söderhamn – note second layer of glazing to servicing accommodation at ground level

(Figure 2.14). The aim here was to provide some services within the new enclosed space for occupants with special needs. Effectively the roof encloses a village street with cafeteria, library and other communal facilities. Fortuitously, the higher block lay to the north so that the roof tilted to the south, but only by some 9°. Thus solar gain in winter will inevitably be modest, with the emphasis more on buffering and recovering heat from the microclimatic space. Interestingly, in terms of daylight, apart from a continuous strip of fenestration along the north junction with the original terrace, opaque and transparent bays alternate. This is where the low pitch assists. By pointing at the brightest part of the sky, the relatively low proportion of glass, some 60 per cent of the available roofscape, provides plenty of natural light. Hanson's pragmatic intervention at Söderhamn also introduces a sort of Russian doll concept of buildings within buildings. Here the communal elements of a new village street have their own skin, again part solid and part glazed. Thus the climate steps from true outdoor to semi-outdoor to fully indoor conditions.

An English project, which adopts much the same strategy, is the John Darling Mall at Eastleigh in Hampshire. The County Architect's Department here, under the leadership of Colin Stansfield Smith, rightly gained a considerable reputation for solar and bioclimatic projects in the 1980s. The John Darling Mall is one of Hampshire's projects designed by the late David White together with Malcolm Gates as structural engineer. White laid out two irregular terraces of flats, bedsits and communal rooms for disabled residents running roughly north–south, so that flats had both east- and west-facing windows (bedsits faced mainly east and shared lounges to the west, Figure 2.15a). Over these two terraces Gates designed a lightly structured, umbrella covered with clear polyvinyl chloride (PVC) (Figure 2.15b). This had a lively section from east to west, with opening smoke vents at the highest point above the central avenue, widening at intervals to form sociable patios. The umbrella is open along all its edges. Thus the effect on microclimate is significant, but not the same as for an enclosed atrium. Formally, the dwellings are suppressed, simply rectilinear pedestals, with load-bearing party walls supporting the imaginatively engineered space-frame. Also the integral relationship between roof and dwellings is relatively loose. The roof must cover the units of accommodation, but the latter are free to meander relative to the discipline of the extruded structure above. Moreover, had the residents been able-bodied, it would have been logical to occupy the roofs as further landscaped semi-outdoor spaces.

An architectural practice that has long been interested in the separation of a roof from the accommodation below it is that of Jourda and Perraudin. A 1990s commission of theirs, in association with the German practice of Hegger, Hegger and Schleiff, is the Akademie Mont-Cenis in Herne-Sodingen, Germany. The umbrella to individual buildings in this instance has developed sides. However, both roof and walls are liberally permeable, allowing the microclimate

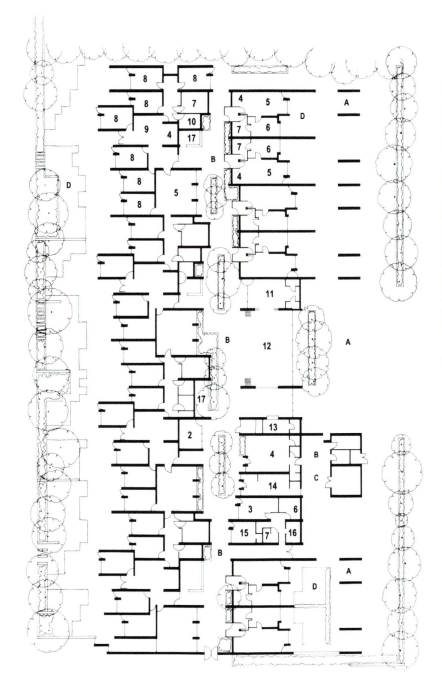

2.15 John Darling Mall at Eastleigh in Hampshire
a   plan
b   view of south end

0   8m

1 RECEPTION **2** OFFICE **3** STAFF **4** KITCHEN **5** LOUNGE **6** BEDROOM **7** BATH
8 BED/SITTING ROOM **9** DINING ROOM **10** SHOWER **11** BAR **12** FORUM **13** SHOP
14 LAUNDRY **15** HAIRDRESSING **16** LOCKER ROOM **17** BATTERY RECHARGEANT
18 PLANT **A** PARKING **B** MALL **C** SERVICE YARD **D** GARDEN

2.16 Inside Akademie Mont-Cenis during
construction in the summer of 1999

of the interstitial space between buildings and their outer cover to adjust in harmony with the weather. In terms of solar visibility, this building definitely takes a soft line. For a start, the orientation of the glazed enclosure is such that vertical surfaces face roughly northeast, southeast, southwest and northwest. This means that all will be penetrated by sunlight at some time, but although the best for solar collection are unarguably the southerly ones, the southeast façade is apparently perversely shaded by a large roof projection. Only two elevations are used actively for PV solar collection, the one facing southwest and the roof. The latter has a shallow saw-tooth profile with the long surfaces tilted slightly up to the southeast. Their PV cells are incorporated within the glass at different densities, reportedly in order to convey cloud-like effects (Kugel, 1999). In other words an artificial construct alludes to nature. Whether such a strategy has been successful is a matter of subjectivity. But what is interesting is that although at the time of building this was the biggest example of building integrated BIPV, it was done relatively effortlessly without maximizing or optimizing use of potential collecting planes.

Another characteristic of this building, which at first sight seems to contradict the concept, is that the support structure for the outer transparent and translucent skin has not been delicately minimized as at the John Darling Mall. It is robust in the extreme and, from certain angles inside, the skin is barely visible through it. The impression is rather of being in a forest glade, with tall pine trunks capped by a thick canopy of branches. Indeed, the columns are literally trunks – large pines transported from the Black Forest, their lower branches shaved off, and provided with appropriate structural fixings at top and bottom to emphasize their new role. Their primary branches are standard rugged trusses, using rectangular timber sections, and supporting primary and secondary purlins or crossbeams. Then, as one looks closer at the canopy, slender diagonal steel tie-rods become apparent, as do actuators to open the roof windows (Figure 2.16). Continuing the sylvan imagery, this might be new growth and twigs. Finally there are the PV cells. These are perhaps more like leaves than clouds, with their shadows on the branches in sunny conditions adding to this effect.

An adjusted or manicured 'dendriform' hierarchy is complete (dendriform being the term Frank Lloyd Wright used for his columns in the Johnson Administration Wax Building, although whether they were tree-like is open to interpretation). From the outside, of course, the order of the hierarchy is reversed. One is only vaguely aware of the timber forest within the taut glass skin. Here again it is the wider picture, the container as a whole, that dominates, rather than the detail. Even quite close-up, the manner in which opening windows pop out from the façade attracts more attention than the presence of PV cells. Indeed, although the PV is an essential part of the energy strategy for this complex, its presence is virtually incidental to the concept of contained buildings. The outer cover, as climatic filter, may just be regarded as a convenient support system for the cells.

Therefore, in terms of the multi-functionality of the solar collecting device, there are two points to make. Firstly, whether they are metaphoric clouds or leaves, the role of the PV cells in providing partial shade is vigorously assisted by the timber structure. Secondly, the passive presence of the glazed box constitutes a powerful moderator of microclimate within it, and that includes reduction of daylight to the individual buildings. This might in turn lead to increased use of electricity for lighting, which represents something of a paradox, since the purpose of the second skin is to both generate renewable energy and displace fossil fuel. In any event, the box is an inescapable statement, which passively edits or interprets climate for the users of the building, as well as generating electricity. One might optimistically assume a net benefit in energy efficiency. But equally, there should be awareness that the materiality and geometry of the enclosure relative to the buildings within it simply defines a formal agenda, which provides no guarantee of this. Indeed, without its flexible permeability, the buildings inside might well require full air conditioning.

solar retrofit as a means of rebranding

A theoretical postgraduate student project for the solar refurbishment of a large 1950s–1960s building, belonging to the University of Strathclyde in Glasgow, has tackled similar issues (Kondratenko, 2003). This proposal also used BIPV as one component of a multi-faceted environmental project. Quite apart from testing the technology, the student wished to create a new image. This was effectively to rebrand the building, in today's marketing jargon. In broad terms, the expression of the solar nature of the retrofit was not seen as problematic. Glazed atria and double skin façades were openly expressed. On the other hand, many urban buildings are now being reborn in a more transparent mode, but without becoming solar buildings. In other words, they are not solar in the sense of the sun saving energy. As stated already, features such as atria do not in themselves guarantee energy savings, or any other form of environmental consciousness on the part of the architect.

The aesthetic dilemma here is that the student was concerned with image as well as solar functionality. Without any sacrifice to a new, 21st century look, she wanted the new second skin to make some reference to the original chequerboard elevation of windows and solid panels (Figure 2.17). Fortuitously, this coincided with the best place to position the PV cells. This was not opposite the windows, where they might have reduced daylight too much, but opposite the alternating solid panels. She also wished to visually enrich the vertical glass wall to a new entry atrium. PV shading lamellas, set out from the glazing, were intended to be both functional and enlivening.

In terms of its multiple and added solar value, both the double skin system and the atria were required primarily to enable natural ventilation without disturbance from traffic. The PV was not an afterthought; it was integral to the idea. Metaphorically, it was a passenger on a free transport system. One does

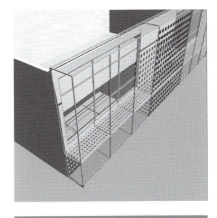

2.17 Images from the proposed BIPV retrofit project for Strathclyde University

not need to delve into life-cycle costing to see that this is a major advantage for an intrinsically expensive system. It is the very essence of integration. Indeed, it is such an advantage that it might be argued that the alternative case for isolation is untenable. Moreover, the formation of the new atria, economically obtained since most of the walls already existed, provided extra usable, and very desirable, break-out space. In turn, this adds capital value, which may more than offset the initial building cost. Nonetheless, there are issues around the predicted hybrid electrical, thermal and daylight impact of the PV skin, to be discussed later, that cast doubt on their specific efficacy in the total package.

Another unrealized retrofit proposal in Scotland was given the acronym STinG, denoting Solar Towers in Glasgow, (Sharpe, Porteous and MacGregor, 1998). This was an idea promoted by Glasgow City Council in the late 1990s. Having already recognized the need to refurbish a large number of identical eight-storey towers, including new roofs and cladding to walls, it seemed logical to try to go one step further and use them as beacons for practical solar technology. It was hoped that the solar addition to costs would be relatively modest. Effectively, this meant that every available surface had to play a part. All windows to living rooms and bedrooms faced east or west, with the opportunity to glaze over existing recessed balconies and provide window-integrated solar air collectors. Even the north-facing, largely windowless façade was to be the recipient of a solar donation from the southern counterpart. This, innovatively, was to have had a seven-storey high transpired or breathing air collector, part opaque, part glazed and with a small array of PVs to power fans.

However, the issue of aesthetics was not simple. For a start, there is now a history of roughly two decades of badly designed recladding of tower blocks, much of it in arbitrarily patterned, panelled rain-screens. This leads to a tin can expectation, to which a solar overclad solution would not ideally wish to conform. Also, if the roof was to be an effective collector, it naturally had to tilt to the south. Thus, by following function together with the dictates of an existing building, much of the visual impact in terms of integration was preordained. Finally, there is the discrediting of the very idea of tower blocks for social housing. While some notable housing towers in the UK, mainly in London, have acquired desirable status, this has not happened so far in Scotland to an identifiable extent. Therefore, although the image of 21st century renewal, with renewable solar technology as a principal enabler, seems very attractive, it is by no means easy to achieve (Figure 2.18).

The case for isolation

Having inclusively shown that the case for integration can be made in terms of economical, organizational and environmental advantage, and apparently without undue aesthetic prescription, can a counter-case be made for isolation?

Perhaps paradoxically, an argument for isolation can again be made from

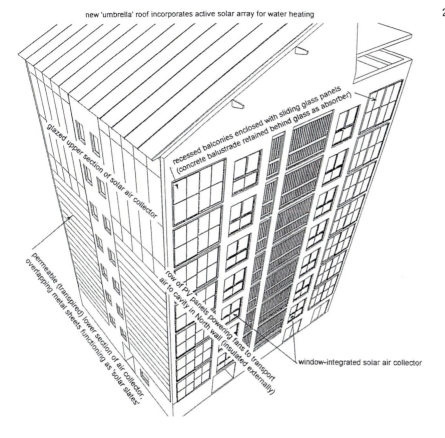

new 'umbrella' roof incorporates active solar array for water heating

recessed balconies enclosed with sliding glass panels (concrete balustrade retained behind glass as absorber)

glazed upper section of solar air collector

permeable (transpired) lower section of air collector, overlapping metal sheets functioning as solar slates'

row of PV panels powering fans to transport air to cavity in North wall (insulated externally)

window-integrated solar air collector

2.18 The solar cladding features of the STinG project in Glasgow

the point of view of both architectural design and economics. Costs for large-scale solar thermal arrays drop dramatically. By locating them remotely from buildings, the arrays can maximize solar collection and enable seasonal storage for groups of buildings, while architects are totally unconstrained in terms of form and materiality. Such schemes can go hand in hand with renewable district heating or combined heat and power (CHP) systems, and there may be even more added economic value by selling to the grid.

multilateral advantage

One such thermal project is that of Ottrupgård Fjernewarme, a Danish rural co-housing project near Skörping in Northern Jutland at 56.8°N.

The solar technology was reasonably remote from the dwellings, just beyond a vegetable garden. There seemed to be an appropriateness about locating the solar collectors and the seasonal clay-lined store just beyond the cabbages and carrots. (Porteous, 1996)

In this case the area of collectors is 562.5m², while the volume of the store is

1528m^3. The first thing to note is that the ratio of collector area to volume is very much reduced compared with the single-house system in Almere. One may assume that this partly reflects the economy of scale of the store and its location below ground. It is certainly now much larger relative to the collection area. But it is also not attempting to produce all of the energy required.

> *It met up to 50 per cent of the community's space heating load, the balance supplied by a wood-pellet fuelled boiler sited in converted farm buildings. These also housed communal dining room, kitchen, laundry, drying rooms and so forth, leaving the twenty houses to cope with much less in the way of processes which demand a high rate of air change.* (Porteous, 1996)

Thus, in this case, the isolation of the solar collection and storage goes hand in hand with grouping particular wet functions remotely from dwellings. The dwellings themselves, as part of their overall co-housing strategy, were freed from the tectonic, aesthetic and performance constraints of solar housing schemes such as those at Culemborg in Holland, as discussed above. That of course did not prevent them from exploiting passive solar design in a fairly routine manner – window size and orientation, sun-porches, etc. In addition, the isolationist technical aspects encouraged social cohesion, conceivably including activities such as communally cleaning collectors in the course of harvesting vegetables. So, although it might be considered ironic, the isolated mono-functionality of the active solar system should be viewed as part of an integrated multilateral approach to environmental sustainability.

It was stated earlier that there could be middle ground in terms of isolation. In certain sunny countries, such as Greece, we have become used to the sight of flat-plate collectors as one component of a set of rooftop paraphernalia such as television aerials and reinforcement rods for potential vertical extensions. They simply constitute plumbing clutter, which often inhibits other useful functions, for flat roofs at least. The case can be made that such systems are not building-integrated. However, the advantage of such lack of integration is that collectors may be optimally positioned relative to shading obstructions, as well as optimally tilted and oriented. Thus there is a functional argument for what most people would agree is an eyesore.

That being the case, it follows that all solar collectors, which are located on buildings, but otherwise make no positive architectural contribution, should be categorized as isolated systems. Such a definition would then include many projects that have hitherto been classed as building-integrated. It would include, for instance, the terraced housing in Niewland, Amersfoort, by Dutch architects Galis Architectenbureau BNA and Van Straalen. Here six rows of narrow, 4-cell high PV arrays are sited on flat roofs in such a way as not to be visible to passers by (Figure 2.19a). Essentially, the architects wanted the renewable electricity but did not want any visual intrusion or expression. Also, in a more densely populated urban situation compared with that of the quiet rural setting of the

Danish Ottrupgård co-housing, the hidden rooftop location provides security. For any minority of people in higher buildings, who can look down on such roofs, the orderly PV arrays at least break up the monotony of typical flat membrane roofs, even when covered in stone pebbles as in this case.

Still removed from the skin of the building, but clearly visible and with a tentative function, the solar thermal and PV arrays of Thomas Spiegelhalter's flats in Freiburg might be said to veer more towards being integrated than isolated (Figure 2.19b). They do shade the south-facing windows of the top storey, but are only one component of a compound filigree of balconies, louvres

2.19a Terraced housing in Niewland, Amersfoort – PV arrays on flat roofs are not visible

2.19b Flats in Freiburg – solar thermal and PV arrays crown the free aesthetics and planting trellises which adorn an otherwise unremarkable apartment block, terminating the east end of a considerably less extrovert terrace. This is now a well recognized dialectical game, where the permanent structural and insulating core lies within much more ephemeral environmental clothing, specifically addressing solar heat gain, air quality, biodiversity and opportunities for extending living out of doors.

The case studies discussed in this chapter appear to have presented a stronger case for integration than for isolation. It might be argued that there is an inevitability that integration is likely to be the technique that will most challenge and intrigue architects. But the more important conclusion to draw is that the scope for architectural diversity is considerable. With respect to passive and active solar collection for space heating, Tables 2.4 to 2.6 provide useful guidance, while Tables 2.1 to 2.3 provide useful indicators for annual collection for hot water and electricity. What stands out above all from this data is that seasonal storage can provide the opportunity for a three times greater solar contribution to space heating. If this were to prevail, it could well tip the balance in favour of isolated active systems in tandem with integrated passive ones, as used at the Ottrupgård Fjernewarme project in Denmark.

Naturally solar availability will vary with geographical location, but, relatively, the principle of seasonal storage enabling a three times greater exploitation of solar energy will hold good. If one compares annual and winter incident solar radiation for Lerwick (in Shetland) and London, two reference locations discussed in the first chapter, the ratios of respective values do not vary significantly. Indeed, Tables 2.7 to 2.10 show that the annual to winter ratios remain virtually identical in London to those for Glasgow, while they increase somewhat in Lerwick. Thus, although London would gain more in absolute terms from an annual system with seasonal storage, once again the northern island location would be relatively better off.

Table 2.7 Mean Annual Incident Solar Irradiation Predicted for Lerwick (kWh/m²)

	30°	45°	60°	90° tilt
South	893	883	835	642
SE/SW	856	838	788	611
E/W	759	721	664	513

Source: Page and Lebens, 1986, p173

Table 2.8 Mean Incident Solar Irradiation Predicted for Lerwick from November–April (kWh/m²)

	30°	45°	60°	90° tilt
South	255	266	263	223
SE/SW	237	242	236	196
E/W	194	187	175	138

Source: Page and Lebens, 1986, pp173

Table 2.9 Mean Annual Incident Solar Irradiation Predicted for London (kWh/m²)

	30°	45°	60°	90° tilt
South	1067	1053	990	745
SE/SW	1018	992	925	704
E/W	897	840	765	577

Source: Page and Lebens, 1986, pp162

Table 2.10 Mean Incident Solar Irradiation Predicted for London from November–April (kWh/m²)

	30°	45°	60°	90° tilt
South	331	343	338	281
SE/SW	307	310	300	244
E/W	251	238	220	170

Source: Page and Lebens, 1986, pp162

Without labouring the 'north is best' angle, but rather making the case for seasonal storage in cool, cloudy regions, it may be noted that Skörping is at virtually the same latitude as Falkenborg in Sweden. Here there is over 5000m² of flat-plate collection serving a huge water-filled subterranean cavern, in turn linked to a local district heating system. These are not the only Scandinavian examples of such systems. Their presence makes a strong case for similar installations in other areas with relatively overcast winters. The populous Central Lowlands of Scotland, for example, share the same latitudinal zone as Skörping and Falkenborg. Not only will the solar geometry be the same, but also, since all are subject to maritime influence, one can expect their other climatic characteristics to be fairly similar.

Having acknowledged that a strategy of isolation can paradoxically have a positive impact on lifestyle, while integration may have both positive and negative effects depending on the skill of architects, it is a suitable stage to move more into the realm of the user.

REFERENCES

Furbo, S. and Knudsen, S. (2000) 'Small domestic hot water systems based on smart solar tanks', in proceedings of conference (*Eurosun 2000*,19–22 June), ISES Europe, Copenhagen.

Grassie, T. and MacGregor, K. (1999) 'Optimizing flow control in a novel solar domestic water heating system', in proceedings of conference (*North Sun 99, 11–14 August*), Canadian Solar Energy Society, Edmonton, Canada.

Kondratenko, I. (2003) 'Double Skin Façade with BIPV Case Study Building', Chapter 4 of 'Urban retrofit building integrated photovoltaics (BIPV) in Scotland, with particular reference to double skin façades', PhD thesis, Mackintosh School of Architecture, Glasgow School of Art, University of Glasgow, pp103–121.

Kugel, C. (1999) 'Green Academy', *The Architectural Review,* Oct. 1999, vol CCVI, no 1232, pp51–55.

MacKay-Lyons, B. (1995) 'Seven stories from a village architect', *Design Quarterly* no 165, Summer, p12.

Page, J. and Lebens R. (1986) 'Hourly incident solar radiation averaged over all weather conditions', in *Climate in the United Kingdom: A Handbook of Solar Radiation, Temperature and Other Data for Thirteen Principal Cities and Towns* (for the Energy Technology Support Unit, Harwell), HMSO, London.

Plant, J. A. (1967) *Climatological Memorandum No. 60: The Climate of Glasgow,* Climatological Services (Met. 0.3), July (revised September 1973), Table 2a.

Plant, J. A. (1968) *Climatological Memorandum No. 54A: The Climate of Edinburgh,* Climatological Services (Met. 0.3), November (revised September 1973), Table 2, p39.

Porteous, C. (1988) 'UK-ISES Atria Conference, September 1987', *Scottish Solar Energy Group Newsletter,* no 1, June, Mackintosh School of Architecture, Glasgow, p8.

Porteous, C. (1996) 'Roam with a view', *Scottish Solar Energy Group Newsletter,* no 17, December, Mackintosh School of Architecture, Glasgow, p6.

Sharpe, T. R., Porteous, C. D. A. and MacGregor, A. W. K. (1998) 'Integrated solar thermal upgrading of multi-storey housing blocks in Glasgow', in Maldonado E. and Yannas S. (eds), *PLEA 98 Environmentally Friendly Cities* (proceedings of conference, Lisbon, Portugal, June), James & James (Science Publishers) Ltd., London, pp287–290.

Talbot, R. (1988) 'SSEG four day visit to Ireland: April 1988', *Scottish Solar Energy Group Newsletter,* no 1, June, Mackintosh School of Architecture, Glasgow, p5.

Thomas, R. and Fordham, M. (2001) 'What are photovoltaics?', in *Photovoltaics and Architecture,* Spon Press, London, p11.

Chapter 3   Environmental Comfort and Well-being

The two principal sections of this chapter deal primarily with physiology, while each also acknowledges psychological influences, which are not always adequately valued. It is self-evident that any discussion of environmental comfort and well-being within buildings is bound to bring into play a certain complexity with both subjective and objective facets. Despite many attempts at quantification, with tools and guidelines of widely varying sophistication, people inevitably adopt individualistic attitudes and responses to their surroundings. One person's comfort can be another's discomfort in identical spaces even though the level of clothing and activity is the same.

Outside, we are very accustomed to the weather assailing our senses. Most of us can recognize the sumptuously sensuous smells of rainfall interacting with pavements and vegetation, and rain certainly touches us. Tasting it might depend on whether we walk with our mouths open into the wind or, less directly, if we drink from a mountain stream or live in an autonomous house. If we concentrate, we can listen to the impacts of sunshine on nature and buildings, and taste the consequence of sun on our bodies as our own saltiness. We also say that we feel cold or warm, but does that feeling indicate that our sense of touch is involved? In reality, the five traditional senses, as one well-known architect in a less celebrated book, *Survival Through Design* (Neutra, 1954, pp199–201), points out quite forcefully, constitute a misleading simplification. He tells us that we have 'surface senses' ranked numerically for pain, pressure and heat. In addition to three to four million pain receptors, we have some 500,000 'pressure points', which will record masses as low as 0.0004g, and 150,000 'warm points', again minute points or receptors on the skin, which are sensitive to 'contact-cold', or 'contact-heat'. Put another way, this is awareness of temperature by conduction and convection. Then we have 'teleceptives', the most obvious of which are the eyes, the ears and the nose, but also include 'receptors for radiant heat and cold'. The surface receptors and teleceptives are two of a group of four, the other two being 'proprioceptives' and 'interoceptives'. The former group 'record for us the movements and positions of our body', while the latter record 'impulses from various visceral organs within the body.'

Thus we can see that experiencing our immediate environment is rather subtle. Over and above the variability of physical interactions, we are used to emotional responses – perhaps negative in wind and rain, usually positive in the sun, provided there is adequate shade or a cooling breeze. But whether we are up or down in the way we feel when outdoors, there tends to be a greater level of acceptance or tolerance compared with indoors. Once we are inside buildings, different mindsets are adopted, especially when we become sedentary with a lower metabolic output – say down by a third from 300W while walking to 100W while sitting. Then the movement of air around us may become an irritating draught, when previously it was refreshing. We are also likely to be more sensitive to being in radiant contact with the sun when behind glass than we are outside. We might also feel neutral, in which case the very lack of awareness may lead to dissatisfaction by default – boredom and lethargy. Then there are the issues of habit and acclimatization, both of these related in turn to individual organic differences such as weight, blood pressure and circulation.

Researchers and environmental engineers have long been concerned with tying down thermal comfort within quite tight parametric ranges according to clothing, activity level and so forth. The same applies to aural and lighting comfort. On the other hand, there is now an increasingly prevalent counterview that suggests a loosening up. For example, audiences may forgive bad acoustics in deference to the atmospheric character of a converted market, ferry or any other building with a high heritage rating. The psycho-social aura prevails over the specific quality of sound. It is also increasingly recognized that people generally welcome the opportunity to take more personal control of their immediate indoor environment. Depending on what they are doing, they are likely to be quite content with a lower than recommended level of luminance or more than recommended contrast between brightness and shade. Indeed, shadows are now being recognized as having positive environmental worth, as opposed to the dominant commercial insistence on high, uniform luminance.

Workers may well also appreciate individual adjustment of ventilation, especially when it is natural, provided the capability for fine tuning has been provided. We have long been able to address quite large swings in temperature by adding and removing clothing, although the modern shirt-sleeve culture is now an issue. Attitudes to background noise are very variable, but there is undoubtedly a point where traffic noise heard through open windows can make a working meeting untenable. However, there are again relatively simple architectural solutions to this problem. Modern workplaces also often include 'breakout' spaces so that staff may choose from a range of visual, aural, olfactory and thermal environments during the day.

The critical factor in buildings where we tend to spend long periods of time, usually at work or at home, is the scope for enjoying one's immediate microclimate, taking into account the emotional impacts of the physiological ambience. Somehow we have been programmed to expect psycho-sensory surges in particular types of buildings, which we visit for short periods such as cathedrals or art galleries, but not in others, such as offices or factories, where we tend to spend long periods of time. Individuality inside the home can have some expression, but basic issues such as access to sunlight are usually constrained by the architect rather than imposed standards. Just as importantly, the adjacent territory outside the home, where it is reasonable to expect a stimulating environment, too frequently lacks fundamental attributes such as privacy, shelter from wind and exposure to sunshine.

Microclimatic opportunities

As indicated above, Richard Neutra's half-century old book *Survival Through Design* provides significant insights into interactive sensory responses relative to environmental comfort and well-being. He discusses at some length our scope to change or improve our circumstances in this regard, using both the terms 'kinesthesis' (movement of body parts) and 'somesthesis' (inner perception of body position) (Neutra, 1954, p160). Clearly both relate to the 'proprioceptives' already mentioned. Moving into the psychological, and probably 'interoceptive', relevance of 'somesthesis', we can see a connection with what Neutra calls 'stereognostic cross-filing' (Neutra, 1954, pp153–155) and his description of the 'Mystery House on Confusion Hill'. This could be said to presage the experience of late 20th century buildings by renowned architects such as Zaha Hadid and others: 'The floor, walls, ceiling, although tilted, keep their usual relationship, so that the eyes are deceived and report the situation as normal. But the other up and down senses differ in their report and are brought disturbingly out of joint with the eye. Gravity, always taken for granted, becomes a surprising phenomenon of almost painful intensity and of a direction which makes it over into something we believe we have never experienced before.' Then, when discussing 'defense reflex' (Neutra, 1954, pp219–220, 247) in conditions without distorted geometry, Neutra asserts 'we welcome a solid or opaque enclosure, especially a sheltering feature behind us.' It seems likely that our DNA programmes us not to risk getting attacked from behind. On the other hand he states that while generally we also like to 'maintain clear visibility' in front, a view through a wide unobstructed window might induce anxiety. Forty years later another commentator (Etlin, 1994) discusses this same issue in terms of the 'prospect-refuge' theory of Appleton and relates it to 'the dialectic of small and large… the paired experiences of concentration and expansion'.

One might ask what has all this to do with solar buildings and microclimatic opportunities? The first point is that these concepts are important relative to a holistic interpretation of the impacts made on us by our natural, quasi-natural and artificial surroundings. More specifically, we can also see that our 'somesthesis' relative to opaque and transparent enclosure could relate directly

3.1a Looking east in Gravinnehof (mid afternoon in August) – glass roof of communal lounge in foreground and glass and timber screen to access promenades to left

to solar access and the ability of bounding materials to absorb, store and emit energy. Probably, at this stage, it is most useful to describe and discuss direct experience of microclimatic opportunities through case studies.

ancient precedent to modern urban paradigm

Gravinnehof – roughly, Dutch for Earl's Court – is a recent passive solar housing project at 52.4°N in Haarlem, the Netherlands, for residents who are aged over 55 and with limited income. On the occasion of two visits, guided by the secretary of the Residents' Committee and respectively in May and August, the weather was sunny and warm. He was pleased to give access to his own home, one of 26, and all communal spaces, including a small laundry, a bicycle store, a hobby room and an attractive glass-roofed lounge and kitchen. This last space faces east into the wedge-shaped courtyard towards the narrow double-height entrance below a two-storey 'gatehouse' (Figure 3.1a). It is a relaxing social space, a counterpoint to the transitory nature of threshold. Courts, similar to the open Roman atria, are what hofs or hofjes ('little hofs') are all about. It is what the word means, and it is an old traditional form of Dutch housing, designed to offer the residents security and sanctuary together with sociability. The occupants of Gravinnehof, completed in 2001, are immensely pleased to be in the first hof to be built in the Netherlands for a considerable time.

It is not only an excellent example of urban regeneration, which is generally sensitive to the needs of occupants, it has also managed to maximize particular opportunities for a beneficial microclimate on its constrained site. In passive solar terms, it is the stepped-back, south-facing section, devised by architect Dolf Floors, which is of most interest. This linear arrangement on plan, which is aligned so that the main façade faces just west of due south, accommodates most of the flats, while there are special flats at east and west ends of the complex, both rising a further floor. This means that the flats are accessed either directly from the court at ground level, or by generously wide decks or galleries at first and second floor level (Figure 3.1b). Their width is much the same as the floor-to-floor height and they are separated from the court by a glass and timber screen. This tilts outwards by 6° and allows some capture of solar radiation and significant wind shelter. In other words, the screen impinges on both the radiant teleceptives as well as the warm points of the surface senses, with residents able to freely interact through movement and position (the kinesthesis and somesthesis of proprioceptives in Neutra's terminology). Horizontal timber louvres are about 20cm deep, and are spaced out to provide about 40–50 per cent shading on the first floor concrete deck during afternoons in summer (as in the case of the visits in May and August), and complete shading on the walls of the first floor apartments. The first two louvres are set about 90cm apart, with the next five gaps up to the roof reduced by one third. In terms of wind shelter, the first two spaces between the louvres are glazed, and then there are alternate air gaps, three in all. The wind is therefore broken, but the experience of moving

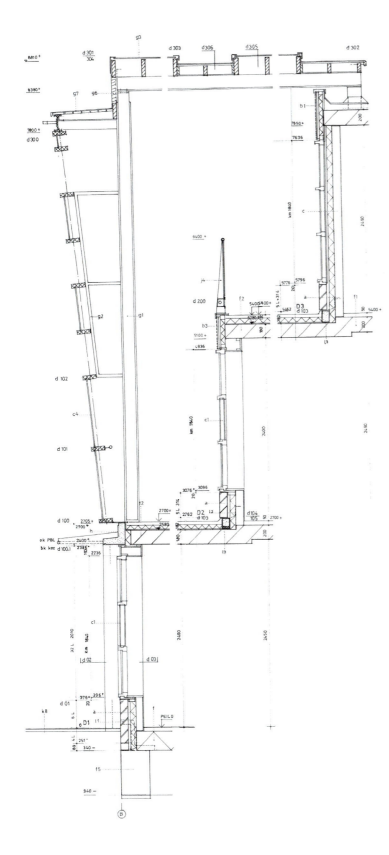

3.1b Cross section through access promenades,
detailing glass and timber screen

3.1c Upper deck with diagonal roof-lights looking west

along or pausing on the decks still feels like being outside. Indeed, they are outdoor spaces in terms of such mundane, but important, matters as smoke dispersal and fire escape.

In winter, the screen will allow more sunlight to fall on to the façade of the flats as well as the floor. Nearly two-thirds of the screen will trap solar radiation due to the greenhouse effect. The stained timber panels below and between windows to the dwellings will constitute lightweight absorbers, providing a rapid response to solar gain. This means that the surface factor is close to unity (1.0), so that unshaded parts of the wall initially absorb a substantial proportion of incoming sunshine before rapidly re-emitting it in a cooler long-wave form. One would expect the impact on comfort to occur in less than half an hour. Similarly, the proportion of solar radiation that is reflected from windows will have an immediate effect, in contrast to the solid floor, with its lower surface factor (say 0.6), and significantly slower response to solar gain. It would probably take more than two hours for long-wave re-emission to occur after absorption. Thus, sitting with one's back to the timber and glass screen in winter sunshine could provide relatively immediate radiant comfort from the front and behind, depending on time of day, while the floor provides longer term thermal stability, as well as some additional reflected long-wave radiation. From the point of view of the residents, it is a social space in the immediate vicinity of their homes that can be comfortably enjoyed for much of the year, although still dependant to some extent on the weather.

The roof over the double-height deck space has relatively narrow strips of roof-lights running diagonally across the space, aligned roughly northeast to southwest (Figure 3.1c). Spaces between the roof-lights are approximately the same width. In other words, glazing is about half of the area of roof above the promenades. Its design dictates summer shading on to the threshold and façade of the second floor dwellings, and what is especially significant is that a vertical fin of the same depth as the roof subdivides each strip of glass. At least two thirds of both the upper floor deck and façade were shaded at the time of each visit. It should be noted that these occurred during the hottest time of day, circa three o'clock, and taking into account the shade and air movement, both lower and upper decks seemed very comfortable. However, during the worst of the August 2003 heat wave only days before the second visit, the decks had apparently got up to 41°C in spite of the shading. This does raise the issue as to whether the diagonal alignment should not have been rotated by 90° in order to completely exclude direct solar gain on a sunny afternoon in summer, whilst admitting it during the cooler mornings. That would have satisfied strict thermal logic. It would also not have compromised the wonderfully dynamic impact of sunlight and shade over time. On the other hand, ambient temperatures in the mid-30s Celsius are hardly a common phenomenon in Haarlem.

In winter, there will be little direct solar gain through these roof-lights. Nevertheless, they will still admit a generous amount of daylight from the brightest sector of the sky, as well as help to trap long-wave radiation in the same way as the tilted screen. Apparently it was often all right to sit out in cold weather when it was not too windy. The west end of the decks had originally been unglazed and had allowed driving rain from this direction to form puddles on the deck. Now, at the behest of the residents, this defect has been remedied with an adjustable louvred glass screen. Interestingly, in terms of the screening to the decks, this is the only element where the residents can operate movable controls, other than moving chairs in or out of patches of sunshine, or not choosing to sit in the space in the first place.

The court itself offers some more movable shading choice in the form of traditional garden parasols. However, intrinsically, it is the fixed passive features that drive its microclimate. The geometry of the site itself is quite limiting. The eastern boundary is only about half the width of the western one, and once the three-storey stepped flats are accommodated, the court is narrowed to some 5m at the open part of the east end, and narrows even further below the entry block. A storey-height wall provides privacy along its southern boundary to a lane and, in turn, the buildings along its southern side form an upper visual backdrop to the Gravinnehof. It will also, of course, provide significant shading to the court in winter, as will the four-storey high east and west end-pieces to the development. It is really only the northwest part of the court that will enjoy some morning sunlight in the depths of winter. However, by March and April, solar penetration will be quite good. Remembering that the Dutch spring is predominantly pretty cold, any direct solar gain to the court at this time will be very welcome for residents. Even though the weather on the occasion of the first visit at the beginning of the second week in May had been hot and sunny, only three days previously it had been sunny, but bitingly raw. Under such circumstances, the same combination of lightweight timber panelling and heavy paving should ensure a satisfyingly complementary microclimate. When it does get hot, then the linear pool, on an east–west axis and parallel to the south boundary wall, provides some valuable passive evaporative cooling and extra thermal mass. Bear in mind that the capacity of water to store heat is approximately five times greater than dense concrete per unit mass, and two and a half times greater per unit volume. Thus not only will the passive thermal character of the court change dramatically according to season and weather, there is also a great deal of opportunity to appreciate it from different thermal vantage points, as well as to exploit simple modifiers such as the parasols.

Finally, it is worth mentioning the environmental subtleties of the short transition from communal outdoor hofje into the inner communal sanctuary of the lounge and kitchen. Although now fully indoors, this space remains in visual contact with the court as well as the upper galleries and, importantly, very much to the sky, since this internal space has a glass roof. On the other hand, the geometry and location of the roof within the complex means that it will not receive direct solar radiation during afternoons, when ambient temperatures normally peak. During sunny mornings in summer one would expect that opening windows would avoid overheating.

In summary, the architect has achieved a consistently successful passive solar strategy, tied in with favourable stages of external, semi-external and internal microclimate, on a tight site within the medieval grain of Haarlem. Moreover, from the wider viewpoint of sustainability, it is a project where the stakeholding dimension is very high. This characteristic of ownership, as opposed to alienation, is of course multi-faceted. It concerns practical convenience, feeling safe and so on. But it is in turn partly due to both secluded and social microclimatic opportunities on the doorstep, which the architect manifested as an inclusive part of the process of the design. Because of this inclusiveness, the residents feel free to adapt and enhance… to inhabit and personalize specific territory.

architect as occupant – rural exposure

Although set in a very different context, upland rural as opposed to low-country urban, a similar project in many ways is the home of Professor Brian Edwards, architect, planner, critic, author and academic. Here again one is aware of layers of microclimate from a fully outdoor terrace, with some sheltering and shading features, to a recessed solar buffer space, still very much outdoor in character, and thence to an internal double-height stair hall, which accesses all other individual rooms. Given its elevated and open position of some 300 metres altitude near Kirknewton in the Pentland foothills southwest of Edinburgh in Scotland, and also its relatively high latitude of circa 56°N, this microclimatic hierarchy is intrinsic to the upgrading and habitability of the dwelling.

Originally designed by Edinburgh's New Town architect James Gillespie Graham as a coaching inn in 1822, and then becoming a schoolhouse, it was acquired in a somewhat ruinous state back in the owner's student days. The south leg of the original T-plan was most dilapidated, and so the decision was taken to demolish it, leaving only the lower portion of the outer wall to define a projecting stone-paved terrace. The gap left by the T-leg in the centre of the south façade was initially a paved part of this, embedded within the main body of the house, and with a small lean-to back-porch constructed in the internal eastern corner. Some years later, it was decided to glaze over the entire void in line with the roof and outer south walls, leaving the porch as a small thermal lock within a larger one, and having the added function of nurturing vulnerable plants and shrubs in frosty weather. Although the building was listed, this tactic of respecting the profile of the existing roof and walls with the new glazed insert was deemed acceptable by the planning authority.

This stage, complete by the time of a visit early in October 1987, also included glazing the remainder of the recessed south façade at ground level into the stairwell of the entrance hall (Figure 3.2). The first floor section of wall above this screen is clad in Scottish Ballachulish slates, and pierced by two windows, one of these lighting the upper part of the stairwell and landing, the other a first floor bedroom. The two sidewalls are rendered – 'wet dash harling' is the Scottish terminology – and the floor remains paved in rough stone flags. The roof glazing is the simplest of single, fixed, overlapping sheets of toughened glass, spanning sturdy rough-sawn rafters, while the outer glazed wall is marginally more sophisticated, with one off-centre hinged glass door and an opening light located directly above it. Both structure and choice of glass respects the loading from wind and snow. Relative to the external glazing, which both gains and loses heat, the area of surfaces that may either donate heat from the house, or transmit heat to it, are about 10 per cent greater, while the 'heat sink' of the paving is about 50 per cent less. Aside from the sheltered and solar-enhanced amenity provided within this spacious new enclosed patio, there is reportedly also a discernibly beneficial thermal impact on the rooms within the house itself, compared with the former situation.

In terms of microclimate, there are several significant points to make. The terrace is partly defined, sheltered and shaded by the remnant of the original wall and two clusters of deciduous trees. The larger of these, with fairly dense and generous spans of leaf cover, is located somewhat to the southwest. It is both in a good location to break the prevailing winds and to provide valuable shading to the sunspace in hot anticyclonic weather. What at first seems surprising is the limited amount of opening windows to the glazed skin, but the entire assemblage is intrinsically air-leaky, and the topographical position is exposed.

During the visit in 1987, the weather was typically autumnal. Sitting out on the terrace would have been chilly and draughty. However, behind the glazed screen it was a different matter, and the beauty of it was that it still felt more like outside than inside. The rough paving, slate and roughcast walls and stacks of cut logs, all helped this outdoor feel, while a painting on one of the side-walls provided some ambiguity. Indeed, condensation on the single glazing, and the occasional drip falling on to the paving or occupants added to an outdoor ambience.

Passing into the hallway through a glass door connecting directly to the foot of the stairs, the atmosphere changes. Thermally, there is still plenty of capacitance and although there are still some sections of wall in exposed masonry, the more dominant finishes are now polished quarry tiles and smooth plastered walls. In other words, they are the kind of finishes that tend to be associated with internal spaces. Also, although the hallway is spacious and airy, the level of daylight is more distinctly graded. In the stairwell itself it is sufficient to display some 20 pictures under conditions of natural lighting, but daylight is much more muted further back into the centre of the plan. In terms of thermal

3.2 The Edwards sunspace from a first floor window, with the owner and visitors

comfort, it is a zone of transience, which puts it on a somewhat similar footing to the sunspace. The latter is used both for passing through to the garden and for relaxation, while psychologically it represents captured or modified outdoor territory – a true winter garden. The hallway is definitely an indoor space, but one in which movement to and fro is the norm. Thus both are liable to be relatively robust in terms of the range of thermal parameters that will satisfy. Importantly also, there appears to be no temptation to heat the sunspace. Its status as semi-outdoor territory, to be used fortuitously according to weather and occasion, seems to preclude this temptation in exactly the same way as the terrace beyond.

The other interesting aspect in terms of movement between hallway and sunspace is that of air circulation. In sunny conditions, warm air entering from the sunspace into the stairwell at high level is likely to become cooler in the internal space, descending back to ground floor, where it might re-enter the sunspace and continue a natural convective loop. During cold and overcast winter weather, this thermo-circulation might reverse. Warm internal air could enter the sunspace from the upper stairwell window, cool against the glass and fall to the floor. However, since both this and the window to the bedroom are centrally pivoted, it is more likely that there could be simultaneous ingress and egress of air. In particular, in the case of the larger window to the upper floor bedroom, one would always expect a two-way exchange of air, especially when the door to the room is closed. The presence of the buffer space as a source of fresh air, with its temperature well above that outside, would also mean that liberal nocturnal ventilation to the bedroom will not constitute energy profligacy. Then, looking at another possibility, if both connecting windows are closed in cold weather, the movement of air in the sunspace should tend to be upwards from the warmer surfaces at the rear and sides, and downwards towards the front.

Regardless of whether such scenarios would or would not be perceived as thermally beneficial in terms of comfort, convective transfer of air driven by differentials in temperature within and between respective inner and outer spaces will inevitably be a microclimatic characteristic. Furthermore, given the recessed geometry of the sunspace, the self-shading during sunny weather will provide further contrasts of surface temperature, which will in turn help to drive varying convective patterns. Since such spaces are very close to the natural world, it is likely that attitude towards all the environmental nuances will be more in tune with the outdoors. Sitting in the Edwards's conservatory could be more akin to resting on a hillside than facing a keyboard and monitor in an office. Awareness of convective movement of air and radiant warmth may be heightened in an optimistically receptive way – perhaps analogous to floating in the sea on a sunny day.

It is also of historical note that the presence of the slate-clad wall, as well as the slated roof over the lean-to porch, gave rise to a considerable amount of subsequent research work at Napier University in Edinburgh. 'Solar slates' have since become a commonly used technique to introduce preheated fresh air into buildings. Cladding of this sort functions as the absorber of an unglazed, 'transpired' or breathing, low-temperature solar air collector (see Chapter 6). However, even without exploiting this potential, such a surface still has a relatively rapid impact on the radiant microclimate within the space, much in the same way as the timber panelling at Gravinnehof.

extroversion and ability of occupants to interact

One of the main points to be derived from these two examples is that opportunities for satisfying microclimatic experiences, linked in turn to strategies for energy efficiency, need not rely on sophisticated controls. Other than opening windows, the adaptability of the environmental experience depended firstly on the static architectural decisions and secondly on dynamic decisions of occupants, both interacting with the variabilities and vagaries of daily and seasonal climatic cycles. In terms of the architectural input, one can say that given a suitable analytical computer model, all this can be accurately predicted. This is so, but relatively basic empirical and intuitive architectural knowledge should not be underestimated.

Both case studies were designed on this basis. In one case the interactivity of the users was also reasonably foreseeable, since the architect was also the client. In the other, the architect seems to have developed a post-occupancy relationship with the users, which has them 'onside', and the users also clearly do have scope for making the most of their microclimate. A concept of wide to narrow environmental zoning is posited not only as valuable relative to these case studies but also as a general principle, recognizing that people are more forgiving of temperature, air movement, glare and so on when outside, and still quite forgiving when on the move inside. Corresponding to this, there is the aspect of extroversion relative to captured or modified outdoor space compared with relative introversion in the fully indoor condition, especially when working or socializing. In other words the theory of 'prospect and refuge' has relevance to microclimatic opportunity through the kinesthesis and somesthesis as explained by Neutra.

Brian MacKay-Lyons uses the term 'prospect and refuge' when describing the walled garden or patio that separates a guest wing from the main part of the 2004 'Hill House' roughly 100km southwest of Halifax in Nova Scotia at 44.2°N. This latitude is the same as 65km south of Bordeaux in France, but one has to appreciate that the climate is more like that near Helsinki in Finland. The cold Labrador Current and the cold mass of continental land to the north constitute strong influences. On the other hand, to the south lies the much warmer Gulf Stream, and winds can also approach Nova Scotia from the direction of Florida. This means that within two days in early summer, the maximum ambient

3.3 'Hill House', South Coast Nova Scotia (late afternoon in June), looking south towards garage and guest wing before courtyard has been landscaped

3.4 Entrance court of 'Messenger II' in Kingsburg – misty June morning looking south

temperature can swing by some 20 degrees from single figures to the high twenties Celsius. By offsetting the two components of accommodation, MacKay-Lyons has not significantly compromised the patio as a wind-sheltered refuge, but there are also oblique views outward (Figure 3.3). In terms of sensory impact, the proposed use as a herb garden will also mingle scents with those of the sea and shore, as the hilltop is on a peninsula with the Atlantic Ocean on three sides.

In several of his other projects, such outdoor rooms are further protected with transparent roofs, while large sliding screens provide the opportunity for variable climatic shielding. The entrance court of the Messenger II house on another vantage point just to the west is an example of this (Figure 3.4), as is the Howard house, already mentioned in the second chapter. Both of these also have open timber decks, while his Kutcher house at Herring Cove, at 44.5°N and much closer to Halifax, exploits a natural rock shelf as an outdoor terrace along the south edge of the main living space (Figure 3.5a). The light surface of the granite, long since swept by retreating glaciers, will have its own impact on the microclimate. Not only will it help to reflect solar heat into the house, it will hang on longer to warmth collected during a sunny day, whilst remaining relatively cooler earlier on compared with a wooden deck.

It is interesting to compare these projects with examples in the vicinity of Vancouver from another notable Canadian practice, that of Helliwell + Smith: Blue Sky Architecture. Roughly five degrees of latitude to the north, the climate close to sea level is much more temperate. Winds tend to be from the southwest during winter and are often from the northwest during summer, whilst the North Pacific Drift has a similar influence to that of the Gulf Stream on the maritime areas of northern Europe. This means that cities such as Vancouver have much

3.5a The glaciated rock shelf as a terrace for the
Kutcher house at Herring Cove near Halifax –
looking east at midday in June

more rain in winter and less sunshine than Halifax. For example, in December and January Nova Scotia's capital receives respectively 33 per cent and 34 per cent of possible sunshine, compared to 13 per cent and 16 per cent in Vancouver. On the other hand there is rough parity from April to September. There are of course comparable differences to be found within the areas of Europe being considered here.

What can be said is that the south-facing terrace of rock of the Kutcher house seems just as appropriate in terms of its microclimate as that of the west-facing one (stone paving set over rock) of the Greenwood or 'Fishbones' house by Helliwell + Smith (Figure 3.5b). This is sited on a narrow and steeply sloping strip of land between road and sea at the northwest tip of Galiano Island, almost exactly on the 49th parallel. The spatial ambience of the minimally manicured natural terrace is enhanced by the curve given to the glazed west façade of the house. It may well be that the more temperate climate of Galiano, not to mention its lower rainfall compared with Vancouver and somewhat longer summer days compared with Herring Cove, will provide more frequent opportunities to comfortably occupy the terrace. But natural variations in respective climates will result in very similar experiences during an annual cycle.

The common factor is that, given adequate privacy and shelter, most people like to frequent and enjoy outdoor spaces associated with their homes. Given the movement of the sun over a day, it is also likely that more than one space may be required to satisfy this need. The Kutcher house has an east-facing deck and a lower west-facing patio as well as the rock shelf along the longer south façade. Another project by Helliwell + Smith, the Murphy house on Gambier Island, slightly further north at 49.5°N and closer to Vancouver's bounding mountains, has a recessed and covered outdoor room (Figure 3.6).

3.5b The paved terrace of the Greenwood or 'Fishbones' house on Galiano Island – looking southeast, late afternoon in May

This space has a granite fireplace as well as a barbecue, thus enabling multi-seasonal, nocturnal and diurnal use. It also separates the owner's sleeping accommodation from the main living space, and a sliding glass panel on the south edge of a glazed linking passage further accentuates the indoor–outdoor synergy. When this is completely opened, disappearing inside a wall in the bedroom wing, the whole of the outdoor room operates as the day–night or public–private mediator. Also, since the fixed glass screen forms its northern boundary, its southern edge is free to extend outwards beyond the line of the southern façade. In terms of solar access, the house has been deliberately set back and almost completely hidden from the sea behind a screen of pine trees. Although more low-angle sunlight will reach this space in winter, the trees provide substantial shading by early summer. In doing so they lend the particular qualities of a forest glade, heavily scented with resinous pine and still close enough to salt water for that to exert its influence. Hummingbirds are a bonus. In any case, if relaxing in full sunlight is desired, the site also offers sufficient scope for an unshaded deck on the point of rock that projects to the south of the house, not to mention other natural sunlit promontories.

One could go on ad infinitum with examples of outdoor rooms, which make valuable microclimatic contributions to life-style. This section has only discussed two specific case studies in depth and given a brief contextual sense of a few others. In doing so, it has fleshed out aspects of comfort and well-being that were also implicit in the second chapter relative to the serial added solar value of a wide range of other semi-outdoor spaces. Some of these were quite radical and large in scale, such as the glazed box of Akademie Mont-Cenis at Herne in Germany. However, domestic projects on a much smaller scale are useful in getting a focus on specific contentious issues. It has also been mentioned in passing that the relatively liberal ventilation of a bedroom, which is likely to promote health and well-being, does not necessarily clash with energy efficiency. Nevertheless, such an attitude signals a potential conflict, which deserves further attention.

Quality versus quantity tensions

Many would argue that generous ventilation in winter, even when associated with a solar buffer space, does run counter to serious attempts to conserve energy. Therefore, it is necessary to dig further into the potential clash between energy efficiency and health or well-being with regard to the adequacy of fresh air introduced into buildings. From the viewpoint of energy conservers, ventilation constitutes a demand for heat over a significant proportion of the year in cool climates, and so should be carefully regulated to provide enough, but not more than enough. The latter will not only increase consumption of fuel in the depths of winter, but it may also extend the length of the heating season in autumn and spring. On the other hand, users are likely to view ventilation as a valuable resource in all seasons, unless of course it presents itself as a

3.6 The outdoor room of the Murphy house on Gambier Island – looking inwards to north and outwards to south, late afternoon in May

nuisance in the form of draught. There is also much research to support the hypothesis that lack of control is a major stressor relative to 'sick building syndrome' (Tong and Wilson, 1990). This is particularly evident relative to ventilation, with evidence of a negative perception of lack of control in air-conditioned buildings compared with those with natural or mixed-mode systems (Wilson and Hedge, 1987). Air remains a crucial environmental issue and, irrespective of the system provided, it would appear that users are generally able to compromise energy efficiency.

Sometimes they may do this inadvertently, and sometimes in a deliberate quest for health or well-being. Conversely, if constrained by 'fuel poverty' or a phobia of draughts, they may degrade their environment in terms of stuffiness or humidity. This then is a matter of qualitative aspirations, usually those of users, pitted against mainly quantitative, conservationist goals of designers. In the relatively rare circumstance when the designer is also the user, disciplined commitment may resolve the potential conflict. However, in most cases the designer's hope is to provide workable systems, which will be reasonably robust relative to anticipated usage. Returning to Gravinnehof, the flats are fitted with whole-house heat recovery systems. The aim here is two-fold: firstly, to provide an efficiently controlled supply and exhaust to and from all spaces; and, secondly, to save energy, as well as the cost to the consumer for it.

The first motive is a powerful one, in that it should also ensure health and well-being. The controlled extract and supply will tend to lower relative humidity and, consequently, populations of dust mites as well as the risk of fungal growth. Both mites and mould are thought to be triggers for respiratory ailments such as asthma (Howieson et al, 2003). In addition, it would theoretically provide an adequate level of freshness of air, thus reducing the temptation to open windows so frequently during cold weather. It may be noted in passing that mechanically assisted ventilation of dwellings is routine in many parts of continental Europe and Canada. It was present in the eastern and western coastal examples brought up in the previous section. Warm water coils embedded in floors provide a relatively steady supply of heat, which may then be rapidly fine-tuned by means of the small air-handling system, accommodated within the timber superstructure.

However, the latter aim is actually quite difficult to achieve, either in terms of the consumption of primary energy or the economy of attempting this. The norm is that fans are powered by inefficiently generated electricity. On the other hand, heating, certainly in the Netherlands, is supplied much more efficiently by gas from the North Sea. The gas is also normally significantly cheaper than electricity, although tariffs vary according to location.

Accepting that the first aim of a heat recovery system is worthwhile and that any saving of energy may be problematic, the device should at least be as economic as possible. This is where the user may further compromise matters. To work properly, an air-to-air heat recovery unit should be correctly balanced. The mechanically introduced air, together with any slight natural air leakage, should match the rate of extraction. Alternative systems, which supply preheated air from attics, below roof tiles or from solar air collectors, are normally intended to slightly pressurize the dwelling, with air escaping through carefully designed routes. In either case, it means that the envelope of the dwelling must be as airtight as is reasonably feasible. If external doors or windows are left open, the systems will not work as intended. Ventilation will tend to be dominated by wind and will therefore be largely uncontrolled. If it is uncontrolled at a time when the heating system is still switched on, and especially if thermostats are set high, the net result will be greater energy use, with a heat recovery or preheat system an irrelevance. Whether or not this is a problem at Gravinnehof is not known, but the potential exists wherever there are opening windows and doors. All dwellings have entry doors, but only some, such as the Edwards house in Scotland, have double-doors with thermal locks – porches of one kind or another. At Gravinnehof the flats have a single entrance door into a hallway, but at least the doors are protected from direct blasts of wind.

ventilating – evidence from recent Scottish housing

The asymmetry between temperature and solar geometry has already been highlighted. Cold and sunny weather in spring may well tempt users to open windows whilst thermostats are still in operation. In a recent survey of four houses from early May to early June this was found to be so (Kondratenko, Porteous and Sharpe, 2004). These were located in Castlemilk, an estate to the south of Glasgow. During this period, the ratio of free solar and incidental gains to the heat loss was much lower than would have been the case had the rates of ventilation been as predicted by the Standard Assessment Procedure (SAP) ■3.1(1). The culprit for this rise was the high rate of air change. Together with high settings for the heating this significantly raised the threshold for heating demand. The relatively exposed site of Castlemilk, some 150m above sea level, is a further contributory factor together with lack of adequate thermal capacitance. If a building has a high level of thermal storage, and a regular regime of heating so that it is kept warm, it will be much less sensitive to intermittent opening of windows and doors than one that is lightweight. Since there is now a tendency in many countries, including Scotland, to favour light timber construction, the issue of controlling ventilation is all the more crucial. Overall, it is quite a serious finding, because these are new houses designed to high theoretical efficiencies.

The specification for this particular project did not include heat recovery and, ironically, the nocturnal rates of ventilation in bedrooms were borderline in terms of high humidity. The question to be posed is whether heat recovery systems would have inhibited daytime window opening and provided more appropriate levels of ventilation overnight. The monitoring of another project in Priesthill, Glasgow, where energy efficiency combined with health and well-

■3.1 Monitored housing in Glasgow: notes on terms and data

3.1(1) SAP is accepted as a means of energy rating in the UK building regulations. If the flow of free gains in Watts is divided by the specific heat loss or heat loss coefficient in W/K, the resultant value in K or °C may be subtracted from the internal temperature to give the internal base temperature. It is the difference between the base temperature and that outside that drives the heating demand. (See also Chapter 1).

3.1(2) Temperatures in living rooms averaged 19.5°C over 100 days in the winter, and daily gas consumption in kWh/m^2 (space and water heating plus cooking) varied from 0.4 in two dwellings up to 0.7 in the third. Since the floor area is $72.7m^2$, the third household is consuming 50kWh daily, while the other two are just below 30kWh. These might be viewed as rather high values, given the low fabric losses (theoretical U-values of $0.15W/m^2K$ for roofs and floors, and less than 0.2 for walls). However, the first two correspond reasonably well to predictions. If the heating season were restricted to the period from October to April, the total demand for gas would be approximately $75kWh/m^2$. Bearing in mind that the energy for heating water and cooking accounts for roughly half of the total annual load, the balance for space heating in these six months may be of the order of $56kWh/m^2$.

In at least one house, heat recovery seems to have completely lost the battle against the user-induced regime of ventilation. Using available data, there was an attempt to match theory to practice. Temperatures were adjusted to conform to measurements. U-values were raised to allow for possible shortcomings in workmanship or over-optimistic theory. Water heating was increased to allow for young children, and ventilation rates were doubled. The last was again partly justified to take account of the habits of young children, such as running in and out of doors without closing them. These modifications gave a very close match to measured consumption, providing some indication of sensitivity to variables. Ventilation is undoubtedly potent, particularly in the absence of significant thermal storage.

being was the goal, suggests that this is doubtful (Sharpe and Porteous, 2001). The hilltop site is similarly exposed and there is a lack of front and back entrance lobbies. There are also other apparent symptoms of air leakiness, low thermal mass and a mixed approach to thermal comfort and ventilation. Only three dwellings were monitored, but one of these consumed more than 80 per cent more than the other two. ■3.1(2) Moreover, given the experience of the survey at Castlemilk, an assumption of heating not drifting into other months is probably unduly optimistic. Since the temperature in the dwelling with the highest consumption was not the highest of the three monitored, it is clear that ventilation is the critical variable. The heat recovery units may have helped in some measure to improve air distribution. Mean relative humidity levels were 31 per cent and never exceeded 50 per cent, but this information also reflects the relatively high temperatures achieved.

mass as a mediator for open windows

A notable project which consciously specified a very large amount of thermal capacitance in conjunction with passive solar gain, heat recovery and thermal locks, is that constructed in the tiny hamlet of Hockerton in Nottinghamshire, UK. Hockerton is close to the small minster town of Southwell, host to the second autonomous house designed by Robert and Brenda Vale for themselves in the 1990s (Vale and Vale, 2000). The Vales were also the architects of the Hockerton Housing Project, and it very much embodies their zero-energy, CO_2-neutral, autonomous and holistic approach. First and foremost the plan, section and constructional strategy are all extremely simple. Moreover, the systems for heating and ventilation are very much embedded in these aspects of the design. This is true synergetic integration.

There are five dwellings in a simple linear terrace (Figure 3.7). The entire 6m deep section of living space, with approximately 18m wide frontage for each dwelling, planned in six structural bays, is earth sheltered. The mono-pitch over the rooms slopes up to the south to capture as much solar light and heat as possible, while the insulated roof is covered in a generous layer of turf and the similarly insulated rear wall retains an artificial bank of earth. In front of this, five bays in each dwelling have a south-sloping glazed lean-to, enclosing an unheated glazed conservatory, which is over 3m deep. The sixth bay functions as a storm porch, and has a slated roof. All bays have roof windows, roughly 1.2m square, and located at the highest point of the mono-pitch. The vertical wall of the conservatory is glazed down close to the floor and there are two opening lights corresponding to the roof windows on three of the bays and double French windows on the remaining two. There is therefore the traditional ability to naturally ventilate the conservatory, in the same way as any greenhouse, with fresh air supplied through the lower windows and leaving via the roof windows.

The walls between the inner and outer parts of each house alternate between approximately 1.2m wide solid insulated sections, and 1.8m wide by

3.7 The south façade of one of the Hockerton houses – late morning in April before PV array added on top of the wall between sunspaces and heated rooms

some 3m high glazed sections with fanlights above doors. Thus again there is the capability for natural exchange of air between the heated interior rooms and the conservatory, but none of the rooms have any direct glazed contact with the outside. Accordingly, the size and south-facing orientation of the protected inner windows compensates. They are about 60 per cent of the façade area and 30 per cent of the area of the inner floor. ■3.2(1) With regard to the topic in hand, comfort and well-being, there is an interesting dichotomy. Most people would probably instinctively perceive the conservatory as the most attractive space due to its greater spatiality, light, openness and proximity to the outdoor realm. Despite the relatively generous area of south-facing windows, the inner rooms seem cave-like in comparison to the conservatory. On the other hand, the inner rooms provide an unusual degree of stability with respect to the main parameters of comfort, while the conservatory will be subject to much greater fluctuations and asymmetry. It can be argued that the two environments in tandem offer the best of both worlds. The steady predictability of the inner sanctum is complemented by the lively vagaries of the outer space, much more directly tuned in to the environment and weather outside.

As indicated, the protected thermal capacitance is crucial to the lack of climatic editing within the buffered accommodation. The opaque parts of the house, the roof, rear wall and floor, have 30cm of 'Dritherm' insulation. This is halved to 15cm in the dividing sections of wall and the low base course to the conservatory. The insulation encapsulates a large quantity of dense concrete. ■3.2(2) All internal block-work is finished in cement-lime plaster. Finally, floors are clay quarry tiles on a concrete slab. In terms of potential replication of the

■3.2 Specification at Hockerton

3.2(1) The specification for the inner windows is argon-filled, triple-glazed, Swedish timber frames, with a U-value of 1.4 W/m²K; while outer glazing to the conservatory is standard double-glazed 'Pilkington-k', with a U-value about 1.0 W/m²K higher. Taken separately, each specification should gain more energy than is lost over the duration of the heating period. Taken together, the balance of thermal gain and loss to and from the inner spaces should be very favourable.

3.2(2) Excluding the 30cm insulation, the rear retaining wall is 45cm thick overall, two skins of concrete block having been used as permanent shuttering to 25cm of concrete fill. The roof consists of inverted pre-cast concrete T-beams at about 75cm centres, with 10cm concrete blocks as infill. Load-bearing block cross walls are 20cm thick, while there is 10cm block and brick respectively on inner and outer surfaces of the dividing wall.

3.2(3) To put some figures on ventilation, if the average velocity through the ducts was about 4m/s, the system could replenish the air in all the inner spaces 0.9 times every hour (0.9 ac/h). Provided there was reasonable mixing of air between spaces and assuming the members of the family move from one space to the other in a normal manner over the daily cycle, the quality of the air would be satisfactory. However, even with most of the doors ajar, it can be confirmed by calculation that eight people would overstress any one space.

basic strategy on a larger scale, the large amount of plastered masonry and poured concrete raises issues of speed, particularly competing with dry timber construction. Is there a case to be made, for example, for mixed heavy and light prefabricated construction?

The large mass of 'wet' construction at Hockerton also involved a considerable period of drying out, and it was noted that there had been an interim period when condensation had been troublesome. However, this was before the ventilation system had been installed. Fresh air is delivered to all inner rooms except the kitchen and bathroom. It is supplied at low velocity though a 15cm diameter fireclay pipe via an air-to-air heat exchanger, which is located over the lowered ceiling above the storm porch. Air is then extracted to the heat exchanger from the kitchen, utility area and bathroom. The use of fireclay ducts seemed not only notionally earthier or greener than either plastic or metal ducting, but also to have the physical advantage of being able to absorb and desorb moisture from supply and extract.

However, during a visit to the house on a lightly overcast morning in late April, it soon began to feel stuffy in the living room. A party of eight people was clearly too much for the rate of supply from the heat exchanger. Given that there was no direct sunshine at that time, and that it was distinctly chilly outside, the rapid contrast came as something of a shock to our sensory receptors. Apparently the temperature within the internal rooms normally drops to no lower than 18°C in winter and rises to no higher than 22°C in summer. However, this is not the main determinant of air quality. Too much CO_2 exhaled along with all the bad gaseous company it keeps, not to mention rather still air, will result in stuffiness. ■3.2(3)

Environmental science usually backs up experienced perception. In any case, the visiting group welcomed a move from the living room into the conservatory. This internal climatic shift might well have corresponded to any equivalent situation, where the intensity of occupation significantly exceeds the norm. Since part of Hockerton's income comes from paying visitors, display material was much in evidence. It covered at least a quarter of the vertical windows, thus interfering to some extent with the incoming solar radiation. Nevertheless, the space seemed very comfortably warm, but also noticeably fresher than the previous internal pausing space. Even though all windows remained closed, the extra volume of air, and probably also the gentle radiant loss to the cloudy sky, was beneficial to its microclimate.

This experience raises the issue of how else to cope with social gatherings, when the demand for fresh air inside will tend to outstrip the ducted supply. For example, a group of people may wish to remain in the living or dining area, rather than occupy the conservatory, depending on weather, time of year and time of day. However, under such circumstances, the air supply may be readily supplemented naturally, firstly by opening up to the conservatory, and secondly, if this still does not satisfy, by opening the windows of the conservatory directly to the outside. The mechanically extracted air from the service areas at the north side of the plan will also encourage some cross-ventilation in this single-aspect situation. Given the amount of thermal storage, it may reasonably be inferred that intermittent natural flushing with fresh air should not significantly compromise either energy efficiency or thermal comfort. The storage effect should also be able to accommodate normal rural family life during winter, when children in particular may not tend to respect the draught lobby procedure of closing inner and outer doors.

However, a potential concern is that in the event of the conservatory being used to refresh an overcrowded interior during a summer heat wave, its supply might be too warm. Dwellings in hot climates normally attempt to exclude ambient air during daytime for this reason. In connection with such a scenario, it is worth noting that the conservatory is already the ambient source for a heat pump, which sits alongside the heat exchanger and addresses the demand for domestic hot water. Since the pump extracts thermal energy from the air in the conservatory, this will help it to avoid overheating. Thus the conservatory should enhance the fine tuning of the mechanical ventilation to internal rooms. The cooling effect of the heat pump should assist its capability to supply quite short bursts of reasonably cool fresh air, even in relatively adverse warm conditions.

At the end of the day, it is probably the attitudes of the occupants that will resolve potential conflict between the quality of air and the underlying manifesto of 'seal tight, ventilate right'. If interpreted in an over-disciplined way, quality may indeed suffer. On the other hand, if interpreted too casually, with respect to natural ventilation overlaid on to the mechanical system, the intended efficiency could suffer at the expense of perceived quality. The post-occupancy inclusion of log burning stoves within the conservatories implies not only valuing the psycho-social potential of these spaces, but also the users trusting themselves not to light them too frequently. Normally, in the UK at least, heating such spaces in winter is considered to compromise their energy-saving role. At Hockerton, the stoves, acknowledged as an afterthought, were apparently for specific seasonal social gatherings such as at Halloween, and definitely not to be used for heating on a regular basis.

Over and above the issue of opening windows, their size relative to their particular context is important in terms of how occupants feel. The same issue of quantity versus quality or energy efficiency versus well-being is relevant. The area of the inner windows at Hockerton has already been mentioned. Given the 6m depth of the adjacent dining kitchen and living areas, it can be convincingly argued that the size was essential for daylight. The windows to dwellings at Gravinnehof were also generous, typically around 75 per cent of their host façade, but then some of these were shielded by the timber and glass screen, or located at low level in a fairly confined courtyard. A quantity surveyor might well have argued for smaller windows in the interests of life-cycle costs, including those of energy. But a convincing rebuttal would be that the quality of life of the occupants would have suffered in terms of prospect and daylight. In the Edwards house, the conservatory and the glazed screen between it and the hallway compensated for the modestly sized Georgian windows of the original house. Moreover, the very cheap specification for the outer glazed skin also complemented the architect's intentions with regard to its quasi-outdoor character. This includes the stimulating experiential contrast between primitive and sophisticated shelter, the former quality taken to a greater extreme here than at Hockerton. Such a sensually justified strategy could well offer an economically viable route to uptake of glazed buffer spaces in publicly funded social housing.

However, the reality is that conservatories on rented housing schemes are relatively rare. Also the direct glazing of rooms tends toward dimensional meanness and does not relate strongly enough to orientation. For example, the windows of the new-build homes in Castlemilk, Glasgow, which were discussed above, defer more closely to the minimum statutory requirement. The net glazed area for bedrooms are about 10 per cent of floor area, living rooms, 13–15 per cent and kitchens, 25 per cent. In Scotland, the minimum was lowered from one tenth of the floor area to one fifteenth back in 1986. By the time such small, if compliant, windows are cluttered with curtains, blinds or both, rooms can be very gloomy. Although the standards adopted for the Glasgow houses are comfortably above this miserly limit, only their kitchens come close to Hockerton's 30 per cent, and unfortunately most of the kitchens face north. At Hockerton all windows face south and are approximately four and a half times the area of the legal nadir. Although it has been elicited that Hockerton's lack of direct contact with the outside and its single-aspect plan justifies such a differential, that is only part of the story. Minimum standards tend to reflect simple economics, which in turn lead to a lack of altruism towards reasonable lifestyle aspirations of occupants. Energy-efficient windows are likely to remain much more expensive than the same area of energy-efficient wall. But narrow, short-term attitudes to building costs, which may or may not result in energy efficiency, should be countered with the wider long-term costs of poor health, well-being and comfort. We must take more notice of 'physiological psychology'. This is a concept that Richard Neutra asserts (Neutra, 1954, p315) dates back to Wilhelm Max Wundt (1832–1920), a German physiologist and psychologist, who employed introspective methods and 'studied sensation, perception of space and time, and reaction times.' (Upshall, 1990).

REFERENCES

Etlin, R. A. (1994) 'The Architectural System', in *Frank Lloyd Wright and Le Corbusier: The Romantic Legacy,* Manchester University Press, Manchester and New York, pp33, 73.

Howieson, S. G., Lawson, A., McSharry, C., Morris, G., McKenzie, E. and Jackson, J. (2003) 'Domestic ventilation rates, indoor humidity and dust mite allergens: Are our homes causing the asthma pandemic?', *Building Services Engineering Research & Technology,* vol 24, no 3, pp137–147.

Kondratenko, I., Porteous, C. D. A. and Sharpe, T. R. (2004) 'Why are new 'Direct Gain' dwellings underperforming in Scotland?', in *Eurosun 2004 Sonnenforum,* proceedings of conference (20–26 June, Freiburg, Germany) PSE GmbH, vol 2, pp370–375.

Neutra, R. (1954) *Survival Through Design,* Oxford University Press, New York.

Sharpe, T. and Porteous, C. (2001) 'New energy efficient public housing in Glasgow – the Priesthill Project', in van der Leun, K. and van der Ree, B. (eds), *North Sun 2001: A Solar Odyssey, Technology Meets Market in the Solar Age,* proceedings of conference (6–8 May), Ecofys, Leiden, the Netherlands.

Tong, D. and Wilson, S. (1990) 'Building Related Sickness', in Curwell, S., March C. and Venables R. (eds) *Buildings and Health: The Rosehaugh Guide to the Design, Construction, Use and Management of Buildings,* RIBA Publications, London, pp261–275.

Upshall, M. (ed) (1990) *The Hutchinson Encyclopedia,* 9th edition, Random Century Ltd., London, p1221.

Vale, B. and Vale, R. (2000) *The New Autonomous House: Design and Planning for Sustainability,* Thames & Hudson Ltd., London.

Wilson, S. and Hedge, A. (1987) *The Office Environment Survey: A Study of Building Sickness,* Building Use Studies Ltd., London.

Chapter 4 Adaptive Control

Having engaged with microclimatic opportunities and key environmental conflicts with regard to the comfort and well-being of occupants, this chapter looks further into the interface between the intended and actual control of the indoor environment. The participatory role of the user/client gains further emphasis, but of course with the means and adaptability of control still constrained or enabled by what the designers have provided. What has to be recognized at the outset is that expectations of performance are rarely met, and the main reason for this is that designers are not realistically predicting or addressing the actions of lay users. Also, although most if not all their interference can in theory be designed out by smart technology, even in this circumstance professional experts are quite capable of setting the main parameters of electronic control inappropriately. However, the agenda here continues to be on projects where there is significant scope for intervention by the individuals who live in buildings or use them, rather than institutional or corporate owners or managers.

For some time now, the concept of 'adaptive opportunities' has been postulated relative to environmental comfort (Baker and Standeven, 1995). Essentially, the hypothesis is that variable, but non-random, actions by users will naturally tend to generate more leeway with comfort than was previously held to be the case. This is the 'loosening up' to which the introduction to the previous chapter referred. Such opportunities often relate to the position and movement of a person in a particular space relative to purpose (functional, cultural, etc.). The opportunities may be consciously taken or, equally, they may be instinctive.

Adaptive opportunities may be enacted in any built environment, whether controlled, as Dean Hawkes puts it, in 'exclusive' or 'selective' mode (Hawkes, 1988). He defines the key characteristics of the former as having predominantly artificial systems with automatic control whereas the latter has a mix of natural and artificial systems and a combination of automatic and manual controls. The selective mode also deliberately engages with the ambient environment more positively than the exclusive mode, the aim being both to exploit free solar energy and to provide a more sympathetic environment for users. It can then be argued that selective mode provides greater scope for adaptive opportunity than its exclusive counterpart. The term 'adaptive control' used here is slightly different, and clearly falls within the realm of the selective mode as defined by Hawkes. It again implies an opportunity, but one which is made available by means of a system or mechanism, for an occupant to modify his or her immediate environment. It implies adjustable controls that are in place because the designers of the building have made them so. Also there is an expectation, or at least a hope, that they will be used logically. Whether or not energy-efficient performance is compromised becomes the prime issue, but the desire for well-being and thermal comfort naturally remains the prime motivation.

Having broadly defined 'adaptive control' to include actions which may interfere with other forms of control, set aside for the following two chapters, three main linked areas will now be explored in depth. Each has specific relevance to solar performance. The first concerns ownership of the means to adapt, while the second applies this to a specific technique, that of domestic sunspaces, and the third considers various socio-demographic influences.

Owning the means of proaction

Controls cannot exist without ownership and the ability to activate them. The prefix 'pro' used with 'action' may be taken as either for, as opposed to against, or as before. For accentuates the positive characteristics of an activity. In any building, the occupants who are in a position to do something to alter their environment are advantageously endowed by the designers. Before implies thinking in advance of taking action. For example, before going to bed on a windy night in winter, one might well weigh up whether the trickle ventilation might provide an adequate supply of fresh air for comfortable sleeping, or whether the window might be left slightly ajar. It is a matter of being able to make decisions about fine-tuning the environment with the benefit of some advance knowledge. The decision would also be very dependent on previous decisions by the designer of the building that may or may not have been subject to input from the occupant or owner. In particular the specification of the window, and the choice and manner of opening can vary widely. Traditional vertical sliding sash and case windows permit great flexibility. A mix of small hoppers and larger casements permit some flexibility. But single opening lights, say of the 'tilt and turn' variety, are much more limiting in terms of adjustability. There are also other considerations that may inhibit occupants from being proactive. People may feel insecure in urban ground floor locations or, if a room is small, the placement of furniture may restrict access to windows.

Dictionary definitions of the word 'proactive' (Allen, 1993), which use the sense of pro as before, also imbue a sense of the positive: 'tending actively to instigate changes in anticipation of future developments, as opposed to merely reacting to events as they occur; ready to take the initiative, acting without being prompted by others'. Such attributes are generally viewed enthusiastically, but when it comes to buildings, there is a risk attached to the proactive behaviour of occupants. Unpredictable or apparently irrational control by them is likely to affect energy efficiency adversely. On the other hand, as has already been mentioned, a building that inhibits a proactive approach may well stress them to a point of affecting their health and well-being adversely. Again, such tensions are best explored by means of case studies.

participatory bilateralism

The proactive ownership of a youth club in Möglingen, on the northern outskirts of Stuttgart in Germany involves an interesting paradox. The architect, Peter Hübner, was anxious from the outset to treat the young users as participatory stakeholders. Asked what kind of building they wanted, a flying saucer or UFO emerged strongly on their wish-list. Hübner responded to this in a very literal way (Figure 4.1). In fact the name of the centre became 'JUFO' an acronym for JUgend FOrum. He then had the idea of a tilted, rotating roof, effectively the base of the inverted saucer, in order to admit or exclude sunlight according to season and time of day (Figure 4.2). This could be classified as an electronically adjustable, direct solar gain technique.

4.1 General view of the JUgend FOrum

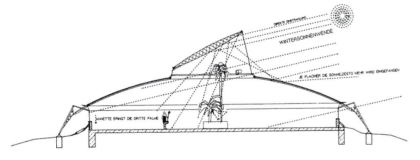

winter section

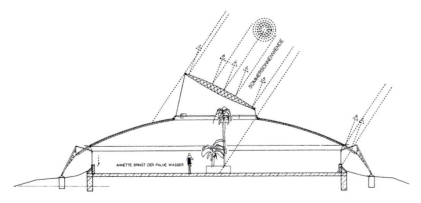

summer section

4.2 Schematics for the rotating roof

In order to keep it as light as possible, but without sacrificing energy efficiency, the convex lens-shaped opaque component comprised: 'a rigid sandwich formed of two paper-thin (0.23mm) sheets of stainless steel inflated and filled with polystyrene granules.' (Blundell Jones, 1996). The shiny surface had the added advantage of being able to reflect about 95 per cent of solar radiation in both long and short wavelength. This again limits solar overheating in hot weather and conserves in cold weather, the thermal emissivity or emittance of the surface to a clear night sky in winter being only of the order of 5 per cent. This specification is naturally outside the principle of users enjoying 'adaptive control'. Also, the mechanism to make movement possible, a cogged base-ring enabling a very low gearing ratio, is automated.

Nevertheless, one may conclude that the concept of a UFO, which still had the capability of moving a major part of its structure while landed, would be very appealing to the young clientèle. After all, it arose from their idea. It moved at least a couple of times during a relatively short visit on a summer evening, and the clicking movement was certainly intriguing to the visitor. Moreover, the users were left with one simple manual control that involved the rotating section of roof. This was a pole to open two sections of window, some 2m high by 0.9m wide, in the high-level clerestory circle of fenestration above the movable base-ring.

In reality this had unfortunately proved unworkable, awkward or inconvenient. Whatever the reason, the windows remained closed at the time of the visit. This was problematic because stratified warm air was then unable to escape. Despite the roof rotating to reduce direct solar gain and French doors to the outside being wide open, the interior was uncomfortably warm. The perceived paradox is that although the automated device worked, the primitive one, which was within the control of the users, did not. This seems to run contrary to normal expectation that if smart mechanisms fail, we can always rely on the basic manual ones to work. It is a view based on the reliability of simple technology. In this case, however, the geared rotational mechanism is as simple as the pole-operated one for opening the windows, and both have a relatively long history. It is only the electronic programmer for moving the ring that is sophisticated. It also raises the question that if automation was good enough for the main movement of the roof, why was it not deemed appropriate for the windows, a much more routine task? An answer might be that it would then tend to more completely exclude the users, the logic being that if they can open and shut low-level windows, they should also be permitted to control high-level ones.

In any event, the sense of ownership among the vibrant members of this club seemed to be undiminished, and the problems of overheating did not appear to concern them unduly. Also, it is important to note that the outer skin is only the outer half of this building's participatory and passive solar identity. As stated in the first chapter, the term 'direct gain' applies to solar systems where irradiation passes through glazing directly into a space. The inner bounding materials, particularly floors and walls, then determine the capability for storing heat. In the case of JUgend FOrum, an alternative concept put forward at the initial brainstorming session between architect and users was 'city of mud'. This idea was also adopted in a rather literal manner for all the interior spaces within the shell of the 'saucer' (Figure 4.3). Anyone who has seen any of the famous BBC Dr Who series on television may note an inverted 'Tardis' connection. The Tardis transmogrified from the small, rather battered old 20th century British police box on the outside into a spacious futuristic interior. The JUgend FOrum reverses this order. The individual spaces defined by the thick earthy materiality inside do support the illusion of 'mud city' within a UFO. Thus ownership through the realization of the two original wishful ideas of the young clients is achieved with due panache.

Of course spatially there is no magic. The interior fits within its given shell. The hobbit-like carving of the internal volume does provide a large amount of thermal storage mass, its logic to stabilize indoor temperature over the daily cycle, just as at Hockerton. However, most importantly relative to proactive ownership, it allowed the original users to participate in the most direct manner by self-building. Whilst the thermal capacitance is outside the scope of day-to-day 'adaptive control' by users, the high-tech/low-tech, transformer characteristic is inherently attractive to the young. Moreover, it is paradoxically the robustly low-tech component of the ensemble, which can be most readily altered. It provides the possibility for a continuing proactive role for any of its young users who wish to be involved. They can physically reshape 'mud city' without discarding the UFO.

4.3   Internal view of 'city of mud'

An earlier project in Scotland again illustrates the bilateral subtleties of automated and manual ownership when it comes to controlling air and, in this case, daylight as well as heat from solar radiation. Methilhill Primary School in Fife, by project architect George Gibson of Fife Council, was included in the 'Building 2000' programme of the Commission of European Communities (CEC). As such, it was subject to intensive dynamic computer modelling at pre-contract stage. Key for the classrooms was the facilitation of natural ventilation and daylight, the aim being to displace electricity. There are two main architectural features to assist in realization – a pair of central atria and large roof windows located between the atria and the perimeter. Sliding–folding screens allow classrooms to extend into the atria, which have background floor heating for cold weather. The sets of roof windows, with opening lights operated by thermostatically controlled actuators – three seconds to open and close – have a manual override. Sets of shading louvres below the glazing are entirely operated by poles, while teachers also control venetian blinds to the vertical windows. Since orientations of classrooms vary from northeast and southeast to southwest and northwest, the issue of glare from the sun will vary considerably over a day, the southerly orientations being the most vulnerable. Also, the southeast façade is twice as long as that facing southwest. Apparently there is a tendency for blinds along this edge to be closed in the morning to prevent solar glare, and thereafter, artificial lighting remains on, and there is seldom a later decision to re-open blinds. Hence, a main objective of the architect has been compromised to some extent. Nevertheless, it would seem that a building such as a primary school does have to provide teachers with the means of individually adjusting their environment, even if sometimes this runs counter to energy-efficiency. This interface between manual and automatic controls will be revisited in Chapter 6 in regard to the detailed design of the adjustable, south-facing and fully glazed façade of another Scottish school with similar architectural ambitions to save electricity by means of daylight and natural ventilation.

early passive solar precedents – bifurcation

Most of the first wave of explicitly passive solar modern buildings, many of which were built in the USA in the 1930s and 1940s, adopted a 'direct gain' strategy, which was more in tune with the pragmatism of the school in Fife than the aesthetic romanticism of JUgend FOrum. Rationalism prevailed, the means of thermal storage conforming to the same utilitarian ideology as the envelope. At the start of this period there were fixed and movable systems to control incoming solar gain, as well as to conserve it once captured. It has already been mentioned that in 1935 the Libby-Owens-Ford glass company marketed its first sealed double-glazed units, which effectively halved the rate at which heat is lost. Even though the organic seals were problematic, with many cases of misting between the two panes, this represented a significant technical advance.

It was also in 1935 that architect George Fred Keck worked with two commercial companies to design and produce external aluminium venetian blinds (Boyce, 1993). These were used in five houses over the course of the following two years. In one of them, the Cahn house, completed in 1936, the movable blinds worked in tandem with a fixed roof overhang. The recognition of architectural geometry and movement to permit appropriate phasing with solar geometry and movement was established for 'direct gain' solutions. In the same year, the Doldertal apartments in Zurich were completed. Designed by Marcel Breuer with Alfred and Emil Roth, they had curtains around the recessed first and second floor terraces, and adjustable awnings and shutters for windows that were flush with the façade. JUgend FOrum undoubtedly takes this principle beyond the pragmatism of flexible shades and fixed overhangs. But the innovation lies in refinement, rather than the principle itself, and, as we have seen, that particular refinement was still susceptible to problems of thermal control.

It was exactly a decade after the technical advances of 1935 relative to direct solar gain, that another architect, Arthur Brown, built the first of many modern 'indirect solar gain' projects (Butti and Perlin, 1980). This marks a radical change of approach, where thermal storage intervenes between solar irradiation that has passed through outer glazing and the internal spaces to be heated. In the case of Brown's design for a house in Tucson, Arizona, a 20cm thick, black-painted concrete wall separated a south-facing conservatory from other accommodation including bedrooms and kitchen. Brown estimated this to delay transfer of solar heat by some eight hours (although one would have expected a shorter period of around five and a half hours for normal dense concrete). However, in cold, overcast weather, considerable amounts of heat would have been lost due to lack of insulation. The combined U-value of this wall and the outer glazing would have been about $2W/m^2K$, approximately ten times as great as a modern energy-efficient wall in a cold nocturnal state.

Hence, for this particular application of indirect solar gain, there are two issues. Firstly, if winters are not predominantly sunny, the net balance of gains and losses of energy will not be favourable. Secondly, the dividing wall respectively constrains prospect and sunlight from and into the rooms that lie behind it. In recognition of these factors, the indirect competitor to a direct passive solar strategy also developed in two directions. One strand retained mass-storage walls, but eliminated the space between transparent envelope and thermal store as an amenity, the gap between glass and wall shrinking to a few centimetres. Although the scope to adaptively control such components may appear to be rather limited, and may be underestimated or misunderstood by both designers and users, it is still present in most case studies. Another strand embraced sunspaces, where the positive transfer of solar energy is not predominantly by conduction through a storage wall. Convection and radiation play stronger parts, and they are inherently much more open to adaptive control

■4.1 Details of the 1967 and 1974 Trombe-Michel wall experiments

4.1(1) The main difference between the two versions was the thickness of the storage wall, reducing from 60cm of very dense concrete (conductivity 1.75W/mK) in 1967 to 37cm in 1974. The time lag for heat to travel through the thick wall was reckoned to be too long at 14–16 hours, while it was too short for the slimmer version at 9–10 hours. The conclusion for this particular climatic location was that 45cm would have been appropriate. Another difference was that since the volumetric heat loss had improved from 1.63W/m³K in the 1967 prototype to 1.00W/m³K in 1974, the area of collector was correspondingly reduced from 0.16 to 0.10m² per cubic metre. Although a British report, compiled not long after the second experiment (Long, 1976), refers to 'a glazed south-facing wall which is insulated from the interior of the house', no insulation was used in these early experiments. This was a later development, as in the use of transparent insulation in the 1980s.

4.1(2) It was also estimated that the later wall provided some 5 per cent more useful heat by convection than the earlier one – 35–40 per cent of the total solar contribution rather than 30–35 per cent.

by occupants. Introduced in the opening chapter and remaining contentious for many reasons, sunspaces will be reviewed at some length in the middle part of this chapter.

Meanwhile, the 'indirect gain' strand of thermal storage walls has been employed and refined in various climatic regions, including some within the scope of this book.

solar thermal storage walls inhibit adaptive control

In terms of research and development applied to indirect solar walls, the first major advances occurred in Odeillo in southern France. Odeillo is home to the Centre National de la Recherche Scientifique (CNRS), within which was established the Laboratoire Energetique Solaire. It is located at 42.5°N latitude and an altitude of 1550 metres, and typically enjoys 204 hours of sunshine in January (Palz and Steemers, 1981). This is nearly 70 per cent of the available period of daylight. At the same time in January the mean temperature is well below 2°C. In other words there is an excellent match between the solar supply and the demand for heat. Moreover, solar geometry at this latitude results in a substantial reduction in transmitted solar energy through vertical glazed surfaces during summer months. As noted previously, once the angle of incidence (that between the solar beam and a line normal to the glass) is over the critical fifty degrees, much of the incident short-wave radiation does not get transmitted through a glass cover. Such a free heating potential during winter, in tandem with an inherent passive overheating regulator in summer, invited innovative exploitation.

It was in 1967 at Odeillo that architect Jacques Michel and scientist Felix Trombe designed and tested the first of their 'indirect gain' experimental solar dwellings. Its south-facing thermal storage wall was patented as ANVAR TROMBE MICHEL. This subsequently became a passive solar champion, and its performance has been well published alongside that of a modified version constructed in 1974 (Trombe et al, 1979; Keable, 1979). ■4.1(1) Of course, issues of detailed design lie in the purely passive realm. There is no scope for adaptive control by occupants. However, the Trombe-Michel wall and its earlier precedents did provide for adjustment by the user with regard to convection.

Both the monitored versions of the Trombe-Michel wall differed relative to that of the 1945 Brown house in that convective exchange between the air behind the outer glazing and the inner rooms was more systematic. In the Brown house, there were connecting louvred doors. In order to exploit thermal buoyancy more effectively, the solar wall at Odeillo incorporated ventilators with hinged flaps at high and low level. These enabled cool air at floor level to be re-circulated past the absorbing face of the wall, picking up any heat from the sun, and re-enter the room at high level, ■4.1(2) with the operation of this left in the hands of occupants.

In relation to hot weather in summer, Trombe and Michel enhanced their advantageous passive starting point by projecting the mono-pitch roof beyond the façade. Further, by opening vents at the top of the south wall to the outside and low level ones inside, together with others in the north wall, the space between glass and wall functions as a 'solar chimney'. Relatively cool, dense air entering the bottom of this sun-heated gap again becomes less dense as it warmed, but this time rising to exit at the top, with the upper vents to the interior closed. Hence the sun assists air to cross-ventilate from the cool north to the warm south.

These devices, rather than the wall itself, provide the possibility for adaptive control. In terms of the monitored performance at Odeillo, the vents were significant. However, it should be acknowledged that perception of irritatingly cool draughts in cool or cold weather might well cause occupants to use them sparingly, assuming that they are to be manually operated. This would especially be the case when the temperature of the surface of the wall was below the desired temperature of the air. The consequent increased radiant loss from occupants to this surface would tend to increase sensitivity to the movement of the air as it executes its convective loop. In particular, the air cooling and descending along the north wall and returning to the lower vents across the occupied part of the floor could result in discomfort. It may also be noted that in terms of technical advancement, the high and low level ventilators associated with a solar collection device were not new. Edward Morse, a notable American botanist and ethnologist, first attached one to his home in Salem, Massachusetts, in 1892, three quarters of a century before the first Trombe-Michel prototype. By coincidence, the location shares almost exactly the same latitude as Odeillo. The solar geometry in both locations is the same even if other climatic parameters are not.

Trombe-Michel principle moves north to Ireland

There were many experimental attempts to exploit the 'indirect gain' Trombe-Michel principle in more northerly latitudes with more temperate and cloudier winters. One of these was a slimmed down version located in rural Ireland. The Oakpath Research Centre at Carlow to the southwest of Dublin at 52.8°N, monitored this project (Figure 4.4) with results reported at the inaugural North Sun '84 in Edinburgh (O'Farrell and Lynskey, 1984). However, most of this information belongs in the next chapter on passive control. In terms of adaptive control by users, the attention focuses on the manually operated bespoke timber vents at the top and bottom of the absorber wall. Although they were fitted with proprietary draught sealers they came in for considerable criticism: 'The adjustable vents to the wall were not satisfactory and these should be precision made and more easily operable... Greater control of the air movement would have increased the performance.'

4.4 Trombe-Michel principle applied to Irish agricultural cottage in Carlow – south façade

4.2 Christopher Taylor Court: variable estimates of U-values

The solar demonstration report for the Commission of European Communities (CEC) and the Energy Performance Appraisal (EPA) report for Energy Technology Support Unit (ETSU) respectively estimated U-values of 1.08W/m^{2}K and 0.65W/m^{2}K. However, it is estimated that the 'cold' or 'dark' nocturnal U-value at 0°C could be as high as 1.30W/m^{2}K. Meanwhile, depending on the precise specification of the shutters, the corresponding nocturnal U-value for the shuttered windows may be about 0.60W/m^{2}K.

Note that, for monitoring purposes, both top and bottom internal vents were fixed in the open position, while the standard 'Greenwood Airvac' vents at the top of the external glazing remained closed. However, having suggested that greater control by occupants of more sophisticated manufactured components could have improved performance, it was also acknowledged that 'the additional operational attention required make it a debatable method for realizing solar gain within normal housing in these climates.'

thermal storage wall in England with movable insulation

A few years later a similar wall in the UK omitted inner vents altogether, but had a different method of potential adaptive control by the occupants. This is the Christopher Taylor Court sheltered housing scheme by architect David Clarke Associates, located in Bourneville 'solar village' in Birmingham at 52.3° north latitude. Sections of solar storage wall in both the living room and the bedroom in each flat have been located next to an equivalent width of fenestration. After a cold sunny day, the idea was that residents could move an insulated sliding shutter from behind the wall to cover the window and French door. This would inhibit loss of heat through glazing, whilst simultaneously allowing the wall to donate its stored heat to the room. Overheating could also be avoided by locating the shutters behind the wall throughout the 24-hour cycle in warm weather, as well as opening windows to increase ventilation. However, according to two monitoring studies (Lewis, 1989; Yannas, 1994 pp98–102), the optimum positioning of the sliding panel was not well understood by all of the residents. Apparently around 35 per cent did not use the shutters at all, while some 60 per cent claimed that they did operate them logically all year round, although not necessarily understanding their insulating role. An additional problem for those that used the shutters as a matter of routine is that on a cold night following an overcast day, while the window would be thermally efficient, the wall would then tend to lose heat outwards quite rapidly. ■4.2 'Thermal mass dilemmas' in Chapter 5 will probe more deeply into this aspect of the passive performance.

Hinged timber awnings were also intended to shade the windows in summer in order to limit overheating, with the warden manually changing their positions in spring and autumn. However, the residents complained that they blocked out too much light and they were reportedly not used after the first summer of occupation. Certainly they were tucked away below balconies and eaves in the spring of 1992. The complaint about poor daylight, particularly within the sitting room is not unreasonable, given that the net glazed area is less than 9 per cent of its floor area. Indeed, including the kitchen, planned as an open recess to the rear of the sitting room, the proportion of glazing appears to be struggling to meet the statutory minimum percentage of the floor area. The irony is that in spite of such misgivings about daylight, curtains are used quite liberally during the hours of daylight, especially on the ground floor. It would appear that the desire for privacy is stronger than the need for daylight (Figure 4.5).

The monitoring also provided evidence that windows were opened to regulate overheating, while thermostats remained set very high. Temperatures in both flats and corridors ranged from 20–25°C and averaged about 23°C daily over the entire year. Furthermore, it was estimated that air was replenished more that twice hourly on average. As a result, the energy consumed for heating the complex was much higher than predicted, representing about three quarters of the total use of energy. However, neither of the two monitoring studies provided definitive answers as to why ventilation was used, rather than thermostats, to regulate indoor thermal comfort. The residents are of course elderly, and older people with a relatively sedentary lifestyle and slow circulation do need higher temperatures than more active younger occupants of housing. Nevertheless, there are striking similarities to the two new housing schemes in Glasgow that were included as case studies in the previous chapter. It may well suit residents of any age that radiators never switch off, and that some fresh air is a welcome complement to a comfortably warm room. This seems to be the most likely, and to some quite logical, rationale for maximum settings of thermostats together with open windows. Unfortunately such a system of control does not sit easily with the aim of conserving energy.

4.5   General view and close-up of south façade of Christopher Taylor Court – note prevalence of curtains for privacy on ground floor

thermal storage wall in Scotland with transparent insulation

Another UK solar demonstration project employing a modified form of the Trombe-Michel wall was also compromised to a significant extent by the actions of users. This is the world's largest application of transparent insulation, commonly abbreviated to TI (see also Chapters 2 and 6), on the southerly façade of a student residence in Glasgow (Figure 4.6). This project was commissioned by the University of Strathclyde (Twidell and Johnstone, 1993),

4.6   Solar TI façade of a student residence in
       Glasgow, facing slightly west of south

with a German company sub-contracted to design and fabricate the TI 'LEGIS' wall, as it was named. The building as a whole was designed by architects Kennedy and Partners, and completed in 1989. The basic principle is to lower outward loss of heat by conduction by inserting the TI between the glazed cover and the solar storage wall. At the same time the TI allows a relatively high rate of solar transmission inwards, thus significantly raising the temperature of the wall in sunny weather. Like Christopher Taylor Court, there are no adjustable vents set into the wall. Here the scope for adaptive control by the occupants lies principally with the windows, their blinds and auxiliary heating appliances. If the passive TI wall under-performs in cool overcast weather, the students are more likely to be tempted to overuse the auxiliary heating, particularly during the evenings and overnight.

Further, if the considerable thermal mass is allowed to cool over a prolonged period, from late December to early January for example, the room might be both cold and stuffy. One can imagine the circumstances of students returning in festive mood, and entertaining a friend or two. The heating would need to be on, in all probability while the window was also open. The final report of monitoring does suggest that such scenarios were prevalent.

A number of critical issues were highlighted with regard to heating. The first was that the consumption of electricity by students is not metered. They pay a flat rate for the accommodation regardless of how much energy is consumed. To make matters worse the 200W electric panel heaters in rooms could not cope with surges in demand. Although students can activate them at any time, they are electronically disabled at regular intervals. The report acknowledges that some of them managed to permanently override this control. It was also found that the intended method of operation and control 'was a mystery for the great majority of occupants, none of whom had been given an explanation of the system.' Similarly the controls for larger 750W heaters in the common rooms had been overridden. One of the reasons in this case was to facilitate drying of clothes. Although there was a communal laundry in one of the blocks, the desire to localize washing and drying of at least small items was strong. It is known that excessive humidity attributable to the drying out of the masonry subsided to a reasonable level after the first winter. However, drying clothes inside the bed-sitting rooms in particular would tend to encourage students to open windows as a means of regulating humidity as well as to facilitate general freshness.

The monitoring came up with several findings regarding the use of windows. One was that the role of trickle ventilators was poorly understood. Alternatively these devices may not have provided sufficient ventilation for some students. It is recorded that although 46 per cent claimed not to open their windows during winter, of the 54 per cent who did more than a third opened them for around two hours daily and nearly a fifth for as long as six hours. From data in the report, it is possible to estimate that the air in the bed-sitting rooms was replenished at an average rate of 0.74 times per hour. ■4.3 This is not in itself excessive, but for the users who admit to opening for several hours at a time, it would lead to a need for auxiliary heat to augment that provided by the solar wall. In other words it would increase the temptation to override the automatic control for the electric heater.

The other aspect that is relevant here is the intensity of occupation. Although a high rate of occupation will increase incidental thermal gain, it will also increase the need for ventilation. Almost half of the students claimed to occupy their flat for 16 hours daily, and a third for 12 hours. Only 5 per cent alleged the lower time of 8 hours, while the balance claimed 20 hours. In other words, the flats were rather intensively occupied, with an average of nearly 14 hours daily.

thermal storage wall in Sweden with isolated solar supply

Another notable variant on the thermal storage wall was the refurbishment in 1986 of a three-storey block of flats in Göteborg, Sweden, by architects Christer and Kirsten Nordström. This project has already been cited in Chapter 2 in terms of its integrated multi-functionality. It may be difficult to imagine how such a closed and hidden system can be subject to the adaptive control of users. It is true that heat from the wall itself is only likely to be affected by the placing of furniture and furnishings, and it was reported after initial monitoring in the early part of 1987 that the solar installation had worked very well (Nordström and Nordström, 1987). However, it was also reported that the auxiliary district heating system was not readily adjusted. In spring, some residents opened windows in order to avoid overheating. To address this waste of energy, the central heating was reconfigured during the summer of 1987 so that it could be 'balanced and adjusted to the solar system.' Nevertheless, anxiety was expressed that since the residents paid a flat rate for heating together with their rent, they lacked motivation to be frugal with regard to consumption of energy. In this regard it is a similar situation to that of the students at the solar residence of the University of Strathclyde in Glasgow.

Christer Nordström explains the situation with regard to the pattern of opening windows and the subsequent action taken in more depth:

> Yes, we had problems with the control system because the whole building was controlled by one central unit. The tenants tended to open their windows when the solar system was activated and the indoor temperature went up. In order to save energy, we had to find a way to manipulate the control system and adjust it to the new 'solar situation'. After monitoring (= looking) which windows were opened, we found an old lady who never opened her windows and we put the temperature detector in her flat. After this, the energy used for space heating went down from 80 per cent (compared to the situation before renovation) to 40 per cent... yes, it was

■4.3 Strathclyde student residence: air change rate from monitored data

The corridor, common room, kitchen, toilets and showers were served by a mechanical heat recovery system. The net load per student week is given as 11kWh. The balance attributable to ventilation or 'air leakage' is given as 15kWh. This may be redefined as a flow of heat averaging 89.3 watts daily (15 divided by 7 days, divided by 0.024). Since the mean differential in temperature between inside and outside is given as 18.3K, the rate of loss due to ventilation is 4.88W/K. The net average volume of a bed-sitting room is 20m^3. The hourly rate of air change is then given by 4.88 divided by 20 and also by a coefficient of approximately 0.33 representing the density and specific heat capacity of air.

very successful. When the tenants opened their windows in winter, their flats became cold and as a result they closed them. But, of course, it all depended on the old lady... I do not know what happened and if she is still living there. But the energy manager of the public housing company told me one month ago that they made a check on the energy consumption in the late 1990s and that the system was still working and the energy consumption was very low.

He also adds: 'During the 1980s there were a lot of experiments with advanced equipment which turned off the heat when the tenants opened the windows – but without success.' (Quotations are from email correspondence, 19 February 2004.)

In any case it is evident that it was not simply the random and intermittent opening of the windows that was critical. These flats had a great deal of insulated thermal capacitance after their renovation in 1986. This would have ameliorated the thermal penalty of open windows, providing they did not remain open for lengthy periods. In this instance it was the arbitrary location of the master thermostat in a single flat that was the influential wild card.

Nordström goes on to talk about a carrot and stick monitoring system applied to a recent housing retrofit:

In our latest multi family solar renovation (255 flats from the late 1960s) a system for individual monitoring of space heating consumption + domestic hot water (DHW) + water + electricity was introduced. It has saved about 15–17 per cent of the energy. As you know, in Sweden all heating is normally included in the rent, which means that the tenants have no reason to save. With this system they will get a reduction of the rent if they have a low indoor temperature and have to pay more if their flat is very warm. It is a simple technology – the indoor temperature is monitored in each apartment.

Although this level of management was not available for the 1986 project, there were other efforts to influence the occupants towards more energy-conscious behaviour. It was apparently the social engineering in the form of the communal greenhouse that allowed the architects to proactively wield some propaganda, if not 'adaptive control', in this regard.

the case for an unexpected 'human interaction factor' in predictions

What the above projects indicate is that even where passive, active or hybrid solar strategies and mechanisms are designed to be self-controlling, the system as a whole may still be vulnerable to unexpected adjustment by users. This means that when the primary solar set-up is found to work as well as predicted, there remains scope for the consumption of energy to be well above the anticipated level. When the design deliberately allows for participatory control, the possibilities widen. There is therefore an argument for building in a more credible human interaction factor into simulations – a pragmatic recognition that occupants will use whatever means are at their disposal in order to meet their particular needs or desires, whether driven by thermal comfort, security, functional convenience, amenity and so on.

A relatively extreme example, which would have been difficult to predict, was that of a taxi driver. He lived on the uppermost floor of a block of flats in Easthall, Glasgow, which were upgraded as a European Solar Demonstration Project in the early 1990s. His bedroom was located below a fan that transported air from a roof-mounted solar air collector through an air-to-water heat exchanger to a preheat tank. The fan was designed to switch on whenever a certain temperature was reached in the collector. Unfortunately, due to the vagaries of the Scottish weather, this occurred intermittently during the daytime, when the tenant, who worked night shifts, was trying to sleep. In spite of pads below the fan to absorb vibration, the acoustic interference was sufficiently irritating for him to gain access to the attic and disable the system.

There is another Scottish project where a control, deliberately provided for occupants to use, proved problematic. This was the mid-1980s passive solar housing project in Stornoway in the Outer Hebrides or Western Isles, mentioned briefly in Chapter 1. In an effort to provide short-term thermal storage solar air collectors were designed to charge a small rock store – an insulated bin filled with clean stones. Ducts from this led to the northern part of the main living space in each of four or six flats. Although these were designed so that fresh air would always flow from rock store into individual dwellings, the reality was judged to be such that cross-flows of air between dwellings could occur. Allegedly, cooking odours as well as noise could transfer between flats via the rock store, clearly an undesirable situation. In any event, there is anecdotal evidence that the tenants tended to keep their adjustable ventilators closed, thus obviating the delayed distribution of solar heat.

As indicated earlier, the pioneering dwelling built in 1945 by Arthur Brown in Tucson, Arizona, may be held to be the progenitor of two passive solar models. Having dealt with adaptive control relative to mass-storage walls, where interaction with users tends to be indirect like the system itself, attention now turns to unheated sunspaces. Since these are potentially attractive spaces, which also add to the equity of any property, the tendency is for occupants to be able to interact more directly. Principally due to this factor, applications of any sunspaces such as conservatories or atria, which are either unheated or heated to a relatively low level, have tended to be controversial as savers of energy. Interestingly, the air collectors were not the principal solar feature for either of the two Scottish projects just mentioned, but rather small, unheated glazed buffer spaces. Both were also monitored, although the project in Glasgow (55.9°N) was measured and analysed much more intensively than the one in Stornoway (58.2°N). Both provided useful insights, not only in terms of the behaviour of users, but also in terms of certain fundamental aspects of the detailed design.

Conservatories conserving?

This section will confine itself to domestic applications in order to keep the focus on the interaction between occupants and the controls at their disposal. Larger spaces, such as atria, employ the same thermal principles, but environmental adjustment tends to be more centrally managed (Chapter 6). Also, all the sunspaces reviewed are intended to be unheated. They may be considered to have achieved a particular temperature at any given time, or over any given period, due to three categories of free thermal gains. These were brought up at the outset in Chapter 1, but it is as well to set out their respective roles in slightly more depth.

- **Solar greenhouse effect:** the first aim is to capture solar energy through a transparent outer envelope by means of the greenhouse effect. Transparent materials transmit a significant proportion of incoming short-wave radiation from the sun, but re-transmit little of the outgoing long-wave radiation from internal surfaces. Thus there is the potential to utilize free solar heat in daytime. The effectiveness, in terms of keeping the temperature as high as possible for as long as possible after sunset, is partly regulated by the specification of the thermal storage surfaces, including their insulating jacket. This means building in heavy absorbers with a slow response. They will be slow to heat up initially, but they will also be slow to lose heat. In terms of more immediate comfort, which would enable intermittent use of a sunspace during brief spells of sunshine during winter, some lighter lining materials may also be advisable. Effectiveness is also partly controlled by the glazing specification, bearing in mind that thin single glazing will maximize radiated gains, but also losses, mainly by conduction. This tends to suggest either some form of double-glazing, which will also reduce surface condensation, or a convenient type of movable insulation, or both.

- **Heat donated by host space:** the second category of free heat to a sunspace is outgoing thermal energy from the interior. In this sense a sunspace may be viewed as part of a multi-layer thermal resistance, in the same way as the air inside a cavity wall. Also, if the air in the sunspace is then taken into the house as all or part of the ventilating requirement, we have a very basic form of passive heat recovery. Again the specification of glazing is relevant as well as that of the opaque outer surfaces. Apart from the thickness and type of insulation, reflective surfaces could reduce outward loss of long-wave radiation, whether attributable to previously admitted solar heat or that in transit from the interior.

- **Shelter effect and other solar gain:** the third free input comes by virtue of the climatic sheltering effect due to the presence of the sunspace, coupled with solar gain through any opaque components. The dividing surface between sunspace and interior is no longer subject to evaporative cooling, or to the conductivity of saturated material and the adjacent layer of air increasing. This effect would occur in the absence of any glazing on the outer skin. Solar thermal gain through opaque material, mainly by conduction, may also be significant in autumn and spring, depending on colour and the main thermal properties of the various layers – conductivity, density and capacitance – as well as respective thicknesses, areas, orientation and tilt. These variables will regulate the time-lag for an external solar impact to be registered on the inside as well as the thermal damping factor. (Thermal damping factor is the ratio of the range in temperature on the inside surface to that outside and is known as decrement factor when expressed in heat flux – ie a ratio of watts rather than one of degrees Kelvin.) It will also, of course, influence the rate of heat being lost from the sunspace and the effectiveness of short-term thermal storage as indicated above relative to the first two categories of gains.

new-build Scottish demonstration

Without getting further into scientific detail, it is self-evident that gains and losses will compete, and that both initial and detailed architectural decisions will have a bearing on optimizing the thermal effectiveness of an unheated glazed space. The first chapter gave an introduction into the potential for specific architectural solutions to influence the theoretical outcome in differing climatic contexts within the UK. However, the monitored performance of projects such as that in Stornoway confirms that the influence of occupants on performance can significantly modify differences implied by design and specification.

The most influential controls that occupants have at their disposal are: firstly, windows and similar devices that are capable of being manually opened; secondly, thermostats controlling the temperature in adjacent heated spaces; and thirdly, the ability to heat the sunspace. If outer windows are left ajar for prolonged periods, the tendency will be for the sunspace to equalize its temperature with that outside. On the other hand, if the windows between the sunspace and the heated interior are left wide open on a frequent basis, the tendency will be for the respective temperatures in the sunspace and heated interior to equalize. Ideally one would wish that the temperature within the sunspace averaged significantly above the external or ambient temperature. However, realistically, one can also expect it to be well below that of the rooms inside. ■4.4(1) In a cloudy, temperate climate it would be wishful to imagine that over a winter the sun would be able to raise the temperature of the air in the sunspace above that in the heated spaces other than intermittently on favourable days.

Hence the periodic arithmetic mean temperature inside a sunspace, whether daily, weekly, monthly or seasonally, is likely to be somewhere in between that outside and that inside adjacent heated accommodation. Then, if the thermostats are set high, there will be two consequences. Firstly, the

■4.4 Details of the Stornoway climate, sunspaces and predicted savings

4.4(1) Mean ambient temperature in Stornoway, September 1985 to May 1986, was 6.1°C, while the calculated mean in the sun-porch was 14.8°C, a lift of 8.7K. The maximum monthly mean lift of 12.0K occurred in February 1986, a particularly sunny, but also cold month. Values for 1986–87 were similar – a seasonal mean lift of 8.2K, and a maximum mean monthly lift of 10.4K in March 1987, again a sunny but cold month. Predicted mean internal temperatures varied according to occupancy patterns, but 21°C was used as the demand setting in the main room.

4.4(2) Each sun-porch is 3.2m wide by 1.2m deep by 2.1m high, and externally double-glazed on the south-facing vertical surface only. This fenestration is 3.0m wide by 2.4m high with two small opening sections, together roughly 10 per cent of the total area of glazing. Critically, in terms of gain and loss, the outer glazing is little over a quarter of the total bounding surface of the sun-porch. Of the remainder, about 80 per cent is in contact with either heated rooms or the stairwell. The balance is bounded by the ground or roof-space and insulated in both cases. The net area of glass in the single-glazed dividing screen is a modest 1.95m².

4.4(3) 10kWh/day was predicted to reduce to 7kWh/day, with the same floor area and glazing, but without the screen dividing the sun-porch from the living space. This value excludes the contribution via the solar air collector rock store. Adding this in, the percentage saving was predicted to increase to 36 per cent. In each case, temperatures in the sunspace were considered useful up to 24°C.

4.4(4) The shrinking of the heating season due to any energy-saving measure is dependant on assumptions with regard to intensity of occupation and the heating regime adopted, including the setting of thermostats. It should also be borne in mind, having previously referred to a parity between November and April in terms of mean monthly ambient temperature, that the combination of all climatic variables, including solar radiation, in this modelling study tended towards a heating season with its centre of gravity in mid-January – whether the nine months from September to May or the seven from October to April.

transfer of heat to the sunspace from the interior will also be relatively high, especially if intervening windows or doors are left ajar for significant periods. However, secondly, although this may appear beneficial in enhancing prospects for recovering some energy via incoming supply of air for ventilation, it will inevitably increase loss of energy through the outer skin. If an occupant tends to open both inner and outer windows frequently, regardless of the weather, the net result is bound to be to increase the overall demand for space heating. On the other hand, if the occupants selectively opened up between interior and sunspace only during sunny conditions, the combined spaces could function successfully in a 'direct gain', as opposed to 'direct loss', mode.

There are of course other variables such as use of curtains and blinds that may affect both incoming solar energy and loss of heat. Although predictive modelling suggests that this aspect can be relatively significant, empirical monitoring indicates that the regimes adopted for ventilation and control of temperature are the main drivers. The project in Stornoway was subjected to rigorous dynamic computer simulations in the pre-contract stage (Porteous, 1983), which indicated worthwhile potential savings attributable to the small south-facing sun-porches. These were located one above the other in two and three storey terraces. ■4.4(2) For example, the annual mean daily heating load for a flat in a first floor, end-of-terrace location would be 30 per cent less than an equivalent 'direct gain' flat. ■4.4(3) This predicted saving also effectively shortened the length of the heating season by two months. September and May were respectively included and eliminated in the 'direct gain' reference and 'indirect gain' solar models. ■4.4(4)

Expressing this another way, and excluding the contribution from the air collectors and rock store, the annual saving was predicted to be 22.0kWh/m² heated floor area (101.4 – 79.4). This may be further translated as 3.3kWh/m² heated floor area for each m² of buffered wall. Such figures indicate worthwhile potential, especially since in this case the sunspace has been included as an essential planning element – the entrance lobby.

The project was initiated and supervised by the Western Isles Islands Council (now known as Comhairle nan Eilean Siar). ■4.5(1) One of three 'most purpose' island local authorities in Scotland, it was, in the 1980s, and remains today, anxious to exploit renewable technologies as well as to provide the best standard of rented housing possible within economic limitations. The terrace of 22 small flats, associated with some larger family villas, is notable as the first new-build, passive solar social housing scheme in Scotland. Figure 4.7 illustrates its essential features schematically.

In terms of economics and specification, the logic of double-glazing the outer screen, but not the inner one, was driven partly by necessity. The local building authority did not recognize the validity of the solar buffer space. It was not a 'conservatory' as defined in the statutory standards, and the bureaucratic attitude expressed was simply to ignore the inner screen. The decision to

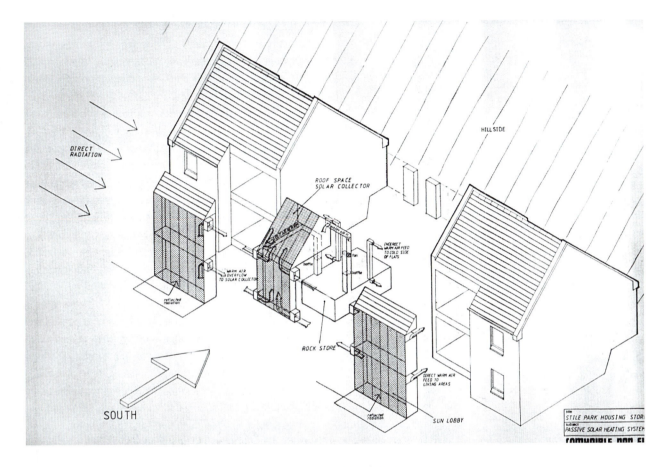

Labels within the figure: DIRECT RADIATION, HILL SIDE, ROOF SPACE SOLAR COLLECTOR, INDIRECT WARM AIR FEED TO COLD SIDE OF FLATS, WARM AIR OVERFLOW TO SOLAR COLLECTOR, reflected radiation, ROCK STORE, DIRECT WARM AIR FEED TO LIVING AREAS, reflected radiation, SOUTH, SUN LOBBY, STILE PARK HOUSING STORE, PASSIVE SOLAR HEATING SYSTEM

single-glaze the latter was taken by the architect for reasons that are now somewhat obscure, but probably to shave costs. The screen was rather rudimentary tectonically, and although it was draught-proofed, there were subsequent complaints of draughts in cold weather. The inevitable gradient in temperature from one side of the screen to the other certainly provides a need for effective seals and for purposeful, rather than accidental, control of ventilation. In this instance, with the screen closed, the tenants could open a large hit-and-miss ventilator above it, the intention being that preheated air could move from sun-porch to living space at high level without being perceived as a cool draught. Nevertheless, when there is a significant difference in temperature between the inside and the outside of the single glazing, it is probable that downdraughts would occur. Air warmed by the heating unit would rise to the ceiling, but cool as it came in contact with the glass. The subsequent increase in density would then cause the air to descend to the floor.

In the post-contract stage, a more basic form of theoretical modelling, which took into account variables due to the specific locations of every flat as well as the intensity of occupation, was compared to quasi-measured ■4.5(2)

4.7 Schematic of Stile Park solar housing in Stornoway – stacked sun-porches

■4.5 Realization of the Stornoway project – energy consumption factors

4.5(1) The Director of Architectural Services was John Paterson, the supervising senior architect who initiated the project was Alan Holling, and the project architect was Fred Courtney-Bennett. 'Most purpose' Scottish island local authorities were established in 1975.

4.5(2) Although there was a split metering system to assist in analysing consumption of energy, reductive estimates had to be made with regard to use of direct electric heating (ie non-storage), allowing for normal use of lighting, cooking and other appliances. This estimate was then added to the measured electric storage units to give a quasi-measured total.

4.5(3) The maximum gust in March 1986 exceeded 32m/s and yet the consumption was just less than 100kWh or 3kWh daily per flat lower than anticipated post-contract.

consumption over two years from 1985–87 (Saluja, Porteous and Holling, 1987; Porteous, 1990). Taking 16 out of 22 flats as not having a misleading characteristic, such as part-time occupancy or use of bottled gas in addition to the measured electric heating, the comparison between prediction and reality was encouraging. In the first season from September to May, the average swing in consumption was 3.3 per cent higher than predicted. In the second year it was 6.8 per cent lower.

However, these percentages are somewhat misleading in that the absolute values of consumption will vary considerably during shorter time steps. For example, a small percentage swing in February could represent a larger number of energy units compared with a larger percentage swing in September. Also the predictions for similar flats took into account varying occupancy factors. As a consequence someone staying in all day, perhaps with a young child, would have had a higher predicted load compared with another person who worked all day. In fact, the average absolute consumption over both years was less than predicted, respectively by somewhat more and less than 400kWh.

Looked at more closely, it was apparent that the amount of the saving relative to prediction reflected certain aspects of the weather. For example, the saving in February 1986 was significantly greater than in February 1987, with the former having sunnier weather and little rain compared to the latter. Then the saving in March 1987 was much greater than in March 1986, when there was less sun, more rain and more wind. The variations below what was estimated might therefore seem perfectly logical, if it were not for the fact that the monitored climatic data were used for these post-contract predictions.

The explanation is likely to lie in the assumptions that were made with respect to demand for heat and ventilation in the post-contract, predictive algorithms, compared with what actually happened (bearing in mind that there is also an element of uncertainty embedded within metered data). It would seem that the theoretical analysis underplayed the potential for the sun-porch to preheat air for ventilation and gives some comfort with respect to infiltration of cool air due to the pressure of wind. ■4.5(3) There also appeared to be a trend for higher than expected heating at the beginning and end of the heating season. This is most likely to be due to an increase in the opening of windows in response to the ambience of autumn and spring, but with heating still switched on.

Taken over the entire period from September to May, there was a mean average reduction of about 12 per cent in the 1985–86 heating season compared with the theoretical value for the same period. This may be regarded as a relatively unusual occurrence, indicating that assumed variables were on the pessimistic side. On the other hand, the measured load for space heating is not only high relative to current standards and practice, but also higher than pre-contract predictions. Expressed relative to the heated area, the quasi-measured arithmetic mean for space heating in 1985–86 was 97kWh/m². If the sun-porch is included as useful area, which it is, the figure looks somewhat better at 86kWh/m².

There are a number of factors to take into account when considering such calculations. The average annual wind speed in the Western Isles is the highest in the UK, with the mean monthly values often reaching 8m/s and rarely falling below 4m/s. Correspondingly, the driving rain index is in the severe category. The pre-contract predictions used a climate-file that represented a less aggressive Scottish location. The dwellings are also not insulated particularly well and therefore more vulnerable to extreme weather. A pragmatic decision was taken by the client not to improve on the statutory standards of the time. ■4.6(1)

From the viewpoint of occupants, the sunspaces provide choice. In closed mode, they define defensible space between the private interior and the stairwell. This includes its role as a draught lobby, enabling arrival and departure without much cool air coming inside the flats. In open mode, the threshold remains in terms of finish – quarry tiles before carpet – but both thermal lobby and privacy are compromised. From a sample of 14 householders who completed questionnaires, it was apparent that varying choice was exerted. ■4.6(2) Overall, it would appear that the different regimes adopted with respect to opening windows and control of temperature were not far off the mark compared with the theoretical values used. ■4.6(3) In terms of the latter, it is perhaps worth noting that the only fixed provision for heating was an electric storage unit in the living room and an infrared heater in the bathroom. This made use of other direct appliances inevitable, electric or otherwise. In the same group of 16, only one claimed not to use any auxiliary means of heating, and out of the entire 22 householders, 4 admitted to using bottled gas. The use of such appliances introduces some additional fuzziness in terms of the monitoring. It would also have been relatively expensive for the tenants, peak-time units being around three times as much as the off-peak units in the case of electricity. On the other hand, it would at least have provided a degree of responsiveness in relation to intermittent passive solar gains.

Also, given the potency of interventions by users, highlighted by a factor of nearly five between the highest and lowest consumer in the first year, it is surprising that the average differences between theory and practice were not greater. All forecasts endeavour to make assumptions on the basis of some known variables and others that are subject to what might be considered likely or reasonable actions by users. Lowest and highest values are by definition extremes. By way of contrast, 'likely or reasonable' might be expected to come close to some kind of statistical average, whether the arithmetic mean or median in the case of a small sample such as this. ■4.6(4)

Returning to the question of whether conservatories conserve, the answer indicated by the project in Stornoway is affirmative, at least on average, with an expectation to save some 30 per cent compared with the equivalent 'direct

■4.6 More details of the Stornoway project and monitoring

4.6(1) The U-value of external walls was just within a maximum limit of 0.6W/m²K, subject to increases in conditions of driving rain. Normal double-glazing was used, with a U-value estimated to be 4.1W/m²K for the outer aluminium windows to the sun-porches. As the inner sliding-folding glazed screen between the porch and the living room was single-glazed, its timber frame and sheltered location yields a similar U-value to the outer glazing, implying a composite U-value for inner and outer glazing of about 2.1W/m²K. Ignoring the potential for preheating the supply of fresh air, the U-value for both layers of fenestration is similar to that of a double-glazed timber window with a low-emissivity coating.

4.6(2) Six householders claimed to have the dividing screen mainly open in summer, at least during the day. Another five claimed the opposite, while the remaining three opted for intermittent opening and closing. During winter, all but two asserted that the screen was kept closed, while those two opened intermittently, presumably responding to fine weather. Significantly, most occupiers admitted to opening other windows regularly during winter – kitchen, bathroom, bedroom and outer ones in the sun-porch. This may have partly reflected the apparent efficacy of the 'passive stack' system of ventilation. This method of exhausting contaminated air was also intended as the main instrument to draw fresh air from the sun-porch into the main living space, rather than the reverse and the expectation to save energy by means of passively preheated air was reliant on it.

4.6(3) The average daily rates of air change every hour assumed for the living room and the rest of the flat were 1.0 and 1.25 respectively while the temperature setting in the living room for a range of occupancy regimes, such as 'in all day' or 'evening only', was taken as 21°C.

4.6(4) The low consumers appeared to be more dominant here. The median value was lower by 15 per cent compared with expectation, and the median heating load from September 1985 to May 1986 was 3kWh/m² lower than the equivalent mean value.

■4.7 'Heatfest' and its organizers: Easthall, Glasgow

'Heatfest', held over a weekend in late January 1987, was a community ideas competition. It was hosted by Easthall Residents Association who organized it in association with a community technical aid centre, Technical Services Agency, and was also sponsored by the Scottish Solar Energy Group and the West of Scotland Energy Working Group.

utility conservatory extension ▽

recessed veranda glazed in △

4.8   Plan view of model of passive solar flats at Easthall, with original chimney breast in key location – stacked glazed-in balconies face southeast or west in demonstration

gain' model. The experience here also seems to provide some degree of confidence that, in spite of widely varying consumption, forecasting reasonable middle ground still has validity, providing an 'unexpected' factor is built in.

further insights from Scottish urban retrofit

Indeed, the experience with Stornoway provided confidence to employ similar small glazed spaces as components of a comprehensive refurbishment package at Easthall, a housing estate dating from the late 1950s and early 1960s on the eastern periphery of Glasgow. The essential difference here was that the existing blocks were randomly oriented. Obvious targets for conversion to unheated glazed spaces were the recessed balconies, or verandas as they are called in Glasgow. However, these could be oriented from due south to due north or any variant between those extremes. A solution that presented itself during an intensive, community-led, brainstorming event ■4.7 was to construct two glazed spaces for each apartment (Ho, 1995). The kitchens were always located on the opposite façade to the balconies and living rooms. They were also very small relative to modern expectations. Therefore, there seemed to be a justification for a small glazed extension to function as a utility room. This would free up space for dining, as well as removing a principal source of moisture from the heated kitchen. Admittedly, if the extension were to function as a source of preheated air, some of this moisture would be invited back into the kitchen. However, provided there was an efficient means of exhaust from it, this would not be problematic. Moist air would not be able to circulate throughout the flat. The glazed balcony on the opposite façade, which completely buffered the main bedroom and was also accessible directly from the living room, could then function as a source of preheated air for these primary spaces. Movement of air in this case could be regulated by the continuous extraction via passive vents into the existing chimney stack, or mechanically from the bathroom, that is, sunspace to living room or bedroom, and possibly on to hallway to bathroom. Thus, in winter, the only room which would require direct external ventilation, as opposed to being supplied via a preheated buffer, would be the small second bedroom (Figure 4.8).

The critical controls available to users in the Easthall project were almost identical to those in Stornoway – adjusting levels of heat and ventilation. However, since there were two unheated glazed spaces per flat, there were more windows to affect performance, and variable orientation was an added factor. Since one of these buffers was designed to be a wet utility space, it was also anticipated that its outer windows would be opened quite frequently. The other main difference between the Stornoway and Easthall projects was constructional. Although Easthall's starting point was extremely poor in terms of energy efficiency, it was to be improved to a better standard than the new-build in Stornoway. On the other hand, at the pre-contract, predictive stage, the proposed specification for the outer glazing of the buffer spaces was more austere at Easthall. It seemed important to prove that a basic single-glazed unheated space, buffering part of a rather poorly insulated wall, could make significantly greater savings than a well-insulated envelope without such an addition. ■4.8(1) In other words, it was a relatively harsh comparison. The extra insulation shortened the heating season, thereby reducing the solar role, while the specification for the sunspace could not be leaner. Nevertheless, the saving predicted (Porteous, 1988) bore up well compared with Stornoway. ■4.8(2) Whether further improvements to general energy efficiency would take the realization of complementary solar savings to a critically low point is a key question. The logical answer is that it could, since some of the winter months are very poor in terms of solar supply. In mitigation, the opportunity for passive or hybrid heat recovery afforded by the sunspace remains on the most overcast day, as well as during the hours of darkness.

Pursuing this further and returning to the issue of the duality of the orientation of the glazed spaces at Easthall, the predictive work held a surprise. The mean predicted September to May temperature in the north-facing, glazed balcony was almost identical to that of the south-facing utility space. ■4.8(3) The former is of course recessed. It is also slightly smaller compared to the latter and it has as one of its heated neighbours the main living room, albeit bordering one of its short edges. Overall it serves to highlight the importance of energy, initially donated from heated spaces, being partly recovered by supplying air via the buffers. It also indicates the advantage inherent in limiting the external envelope of sunspaces. A favourable orientation is only one component of the 'gain to loss' scenario.

When the project was eventually realized as a European solar demonstration, ■4.9 it was decided to improve the specification by double-glazing both the outer and inner screens. Neither of the two blocks of 18 flats that were upgraded in this programme had such an extreme orientation as that of the original predictive model (living rooms facing north). One had living rooms facing southeast, while the other had living rooms facing west. Since one might expect reasonable parity in the case of the east–west block, it is interesting to compare the measured temperatures in the two equivalent second floor, gable-end flats. In each of these flats and in each of two monitored heating seasons, there was less than one degree of a temperature difference between the respective buffer spaces:

Flat a	balcony	1st year	15.06°C	balcony	2nd year	15.95°C
	utility	1st year	15.93°C	utility	2nd year	15.91°C
Flat b	balcony	1st year	16.88°C	balcony	2nd year	17.36°C
	utility	1st year	17.08°C	utility	2nd year	16.66°C

■4.8 Initial predictions for the Easthall project compared to Stornoway

4.8(1) Easthall's original proprietary block walls had a U-value of 2.70W/m²K, which were improved tenfold to 0.25W/m²K, partly by insulating an integral cavity and partly by external insulation. The predictive comparison was between: (i) upgrading all external walls to the 0.25W/m²K standard along with double-glazed windows, but no sunspaces; and (ii) single-glazed sunspaces buffering the wall, having only its cavity insulated and buffered windows single-glazed, and with the remaining areas of wall and windows upgraded to the new standard.

4.8(2) The predicted saving of 30 per cent in Stornoway corresponded to 22.0kWh/m² heated floor area (101.4 – 79.4). In Easthall it was 25 per cent or 19.8kWh/m² heated floor area (79.5 – 59.7). This was for an upper floor, gable-end flat in each case, the significance being that it is one where there are losses through the roof and three walls, but not the floor, since it is assumed that the flat below is heated to the same temperature. Quantitatively, a coincidence is that Easthall's theoretical standard upgrade without sunspaces matches the space heating load of the solar one in Stornoway: 79.5 compared to 79.4kWh/m². The equivalent predicted saving for a first floor flat at Easthall, with no losses via either roof or floor, was proportionately slightly greater at 28 per cent. However, expressed relative to floor area it drops slightly to 18.7kWh/m² (66.2 – 47.5).

4.8(3) the north-facing balcony was predicted to be 13.42°C compared to 13.67°C for the projecting utility space in a second floor flat, and similarly close for other locations.

■4.9 Political birth pangs of the Easthall European solar demonstration project

Although submitted to Brussels in 1988 and approved in 1989, the contract between all parties was not signed until November 1991. Local politics was influential in this delay. The first proposer was Easthall Residents' Association, the second Glasgow City Council and the third Technical Services Agency. The architect was Community Architecture Scotland, the contract was supervized by Stuart Goldie.

Comparing one flat with the other, there were somewhat more significant differences, which corresponded with respective internal temperatures. In broad terms, differences of some three to nearly four degrees in the influential heated spaces corresponded to a range from less than one to nearly two in adjacent unheated glazed spaces. It was also evident in the case of these particular two flats that it was the bedroom that was the driver for the glazed balconies, rather than the living room.

However, two specific flats cannot be deemed representative of a larger sample. Looking at all 18 flats in the east–west block, there is a discernable gap between the glazed balcony and the utility extension:

E–W mean	balcony 1st year 14.5°C	balcony 2nd year 14.7°C
	utility 1st year 13.7°C	utility 2nd year 13.5°C

This may be due to several factors, including the respective functions of the spaces as well as their physical differences. In the other block, where balconies face southeast while utility spaces face northwest, a rather larger gap in temperature opens up. It is reasonable to assume that this reflects the disparity in orientations:

SE–NW mean	balcony 1st year 15.5°C	balcony 2nd year 15.3°C
	utility 1st year 12.3°C	utility 2nd year 12.1°C

It is then evident that the average for all flats is close to 15°C for the balconies and 13°C for the utility spaces. Indeed it was precisely these values for the first year when the mean indoor temperature was just less than 20°C and that outside just over 7°C. Thus the average temperatures for both buffer spaces appear to be well situated relative to heated spaces and ambient conditions. Nonetheless, around the average lay a wide range responding to the variable controls as outlined. Although not actually the case, it would be theoretically possible to have an average where one group tended towards the ambient temperature and another towards the internal temperature, but with few halfway between the two. In fact, only three of the new utility spaces came close to the ambient temperature and none of the former balconies. However, quite a significant number of balconies as well as a few utility spaces came rather close to the internal temperatures, signalling a weakening of their indirect passive solar attributes. The higher the internal temperature, the worse this would be… that is unless the equalization of sunspace and internal temperatures was attributable predominantly to solar gain rather than purchased heat.

Taking first the issue of indoor temperature, there were dwellings where the temperature from September to May averaged about 17.5°C, or even slightly lower. Conversely there were several scoring over 22°C and one of almost 24°C.

Also, the median average virtually coincides with that of the mean, with the seventeenth and eighteenth highest at 19.98°C and 20.1°C respectively in the first monitored heating season. These 24-hour seasonal averages were significantly higher than anticipated. The mean value predicted for all flat locations, assuming about twice as many would be in an 'all-day' occupancy as would be out regularly during the day, was lower by almost two degrees at 18.3°C. It was assumed that the higher reality reflected a certain degree of luxuriating in affordable warmth after years of suffering the cold conditions attributable to fuel poverty.

Although there will always be some exceptions, there was a definite tendency for those with the highest temperatures to have a high rate of ventilation and so also high consumption. ■4.10(1) This again indicates the temptation to overheat, and then resolve consequent feelings of stuffiness by opening windows, although there are other social factors at work here to be discussed in the final part of this chapter. Conversely, although they were in the minority, low ventilators, low temperatures and low consumption corresponded. It is tempting to conclude that if people can be persuaded to accept relatively modest, although still quite adequate, temperatures, then the fuel saving is likely to be boosted due to a correspondingly modest regime of ventilation.

Thus the gap between desired or realized rates of ventilation and those envisaged, or generated, in predictive tools, is again evident. It is not a matter of improving air-tightness. That was not an issue after this comprehensive refurbishment. The crux is what people do in terms of attempting to control their environment to their satisfaction. Balancing energy efficiency with air quality and freedom from condensation, a normal expectation is that hourly rates of air change (ac/h) should be from 1.0 to 1.5 (Baker and McEvoy, 1999). ■4.10(2) At Easthall, analysis of measurements indicated that one third of the households fell below this benchmark, with a mean value just below 1.0ac/h. The following summary is revealing:

mean for lowest ventilator 0.6ac/h	mean for lowest 8 ventilators 0.8ac/h
mean for highest ventilator 4.0ac/h	mean for highest 8 ventilators 3.0ac/h

The second set of values predictably had a very serious effect on consumption of fuel for space heating. The following takes key values from the first year of monitoring ■4.11(1):

lowest consumer 26.1kWh/m^2	mean for lowest 8 consumers 38.1kWh/m^2
highest consumer 193.3kWh/m^2	mean for highest 8 consumers 154.0kWh/m^2
mean consumer 90.74kWh/m^2	median consumer 82.5kWh/m^2

■4.10 Easthall: ventilation and temperature as key influences

4.10(1) The highest eight consumers coincided with all but one of the highest eight ventilators and half of the group of eight with the highest temperatures. On the other hand, all but two of the eight with the lowest temperatures, and all but one of the eight lowest ventilators, are also among the eight lowest energy consumers. The eight with the lowest temperatures were estimated to have a ventilation rate some 37 per cent below the mean, while the corresponding group with the highest temperatures only averaged 10 per cent above the mean.

4.10(2) Baker and McEvoy, in exploring appropriate values for controlled trickle ventilation, cite British Standard 5250 together with two standards of air change due to background infiltration – firstly an average value of 0.7ac/h and secondly a lower value of 0.2ac/h for a well sealed construction. Thus, to give a recommended total in the range 1.0–1.5ac/h (to provide adequately low relative humidity and freedom from problems of condensation) in the first case, added controlled ventilation should be in the range 0.3–0.8ac/h, and in the latter case this should increase to 0.8–1.3ac/h. While the low ventilators at Easthall may reflect a lower intensity of occupation, and thus not be a cause for concern in terms of environmental quality, the high ventilators denote poor energy efficiency.

■4.11 Easthall: consumption influenced by distribution of demand for heat

4.11(1) Full measurements could not be made in two out of 36 houses. Thus results are based on 34 households, with the median falling between numbers 17 and 18 when ranking consumption. These were very close, with the 17th at 82.5 and 18th at 82.6kWh/m². They had variations in terms of achieved temperature – 17th at 19.67°C and 18th at 21.45°C – as well as ventilation rates – 17th at 1.44ac/h and 18th at 1.34ac/h.

4.11(2) Flats with similar temperatures, but different heating loads: their respective mean average daily temperatures over the first monitored heating season, September 1992 to May 1993, were 19.33°C and 19.06°C. The space-heating load of the flat with the marginally higher temperature for the same period was over 25kWh/m² higher than the other.

4.11(3) Comparing temperatures in spaces other than the living room, the three-month value was 15.6°C for the lower consumer, compared to 18.2°C for the higher one, even though the living room averages one degree warmer in the former case.

4.11(4) While, in this second comparison, the high consumer heated the living room a degree higher over the entire heating season and over three degrees higher from December to February, the contrast in the rest of the house was more extreme: 20.54°C compared to 14.36°C. The net result was that the high-temperature flat consumed more than 40kWh/m² more than the other one. Out of the eight flats with the lowest temperatures during winter in spaces apart from the living room, six were in the group of the eight lowest consumers. The picture is less clear-cut at the top end, where only three of the group of eight with the highest temperatures in this zone coincided with the eight highest consumers.

The mean consumption is only 6.5 per cent lower than that of the Stornoway project even though the standards of insulation were significantly better. This was disappointing. The predictive methodology had taken a realistic approach to ventilation, making due allowance for opening of windows during the heating season. In fact the rate, again assuming twice as many 'all-day' consumers as opposed to those where the heating need would be restricted to mornings and evenings, was very close to the actual median position at 1.4ac/h. On the other hand, the achieved temperatures in the predictions were more modest, as stated above with a mean of 18.3°C. This corresponded to a space-heating load of 62kWh/m².

From the predictions it also looked as if every degree of increase in temperature would add about 6.5kWh/m² on to consumption. However, the results indicated that a larger penalty is possible. There could be several reasons for this. Installed insulation might not be as effective as it should be. Heating may displace potentially useful solar gains. There was a mix of electric systems (mainly storage) and standard 'wet' gas-heated systems, with all water-filled radiators having thermostatic control valves. The former are inherently unresponsive and, as already indicated, the latter are vulnerable to being set too high so that occupants feel they are working. However, the main complexity would appear to be related to the distribution of heat within respective dwellings. Some occupants chose to heat all spaces, while others did not. For example, two of the flats were estimated to have the same mean rate of ventilation, very similar mean temperatures, but markedly varying annual heating loads. ■4.11(2) Although they were in different blocks, so that solar gain was a variable over the daily cycle, each flat was in a first floor intermediate location. Thus the scope for errors in heat loss through the fabric was fairly limited and, at first sight, the large gap in heating loads looks puzzling.

The explanation for this apparent conundrum was that one tenant was heating the whole flat fairly evenly, while the other appeared to be concentrating solely on heating the living room. Indeed, the contrast between the respective mean temperatures in all spaces except the living room for the December to February period was stark. ■4.11(3) It is clear then that distribution of heat within a home is very important.

Therefore, there is a question as to whether we should design to expect the main living room to be a great deal warmer than bedrooms. The answer might well be affirmative, provided bedrooms are simply used for sleeping, rather than as bed-sitting rooms for teenagers. It at least challenges the concept of full central heating being required, or even desirable, once the envelope of a dwelling has been made energy-efficient. The combination of solar heat gains and incidental heat gains from occupants, appliances and so forth may be enough to heat all but the main space up to a suitable level for comfort relative to purpose.

However, it would be precipitate to advocate such a step before establishing whether the tendency to heat only the main space was at all widespread in this particular sample. Looking at another pair of flats with the same estimated mean rate of air change, but one with a significantly higher heating load than the other, the same conclusion was reached with respect to distribution: low temperatures outside the living room generally corresponded with low consumption. ■4.11(4) Daytime use of bedrooms, say by teenagers, as well as variable heating of kitchens, bathrooms and hallways is clearly influential in this regard.

It is also significant that in this particular project, not only did all the flats have full central heating, they also all had a fixed means of auxiliary heating in the living room. It would certainly have been politically unacceptable at that time to forego the central heating, but the residents also forcefully expressed a wish not to be deprived of a source of visible radiant warmth at the touch of a switch. In the case of two of the flats, one just above the median in terms of consumption and the other the fourth highest consumer, the householders kept detailed diaries not only of the use of auxiliary heating, but also of the opening of windows and other ventilating devices. These were particularly illuminating.

The lower of the two consumers occupied the middle ground. It was also an 'elderly' household, which may have been responsible for the December to February mean living room temperature of 23.5°C. Such a plateau of heat was undoubtedly in part due to the generous use of the auxiliary electric heater, while the regime adopted with respect to opening windows was fairly reasonable. ■4.12(1) The fact that there was approximate parity of hours between autumn and spring suggested it was the perception of weather that drove the decision to open windows, rather than an awareness of the ambient temperature. In reality, opening in spring will be generally more punitive in terms of compromising energy efficiency.

The diary for the house with the fourth highest consumption follows much the same pattern, except that in this instance there is no part of the year when the opening of windows is particularly restricted. The woman of the house had been brought up to keep a house well aired, and that is what she did. ■4.12(2) Having said that, the airing tended to occur in the morning, while the auxiliary heating was switched on later in the afternoons and evenings.

Returning to the question of whether conservatories conserve, the detailed monitoring at Easthall confirmed this to be the case. If one assumes that occupants would have adopted the same regimes with respect to heating and ventilation in an equivalent reference house, insulated to the same level but with no glazed buffers, there is a significant increase in the heating load. Taking the example of the mean average consumer, this is of the order of 2500kWh or 40kWh/m^2 floor area, and in proportional terms, the theoretical saving is over 30 per cent. Since the monitoring indicated clearly that the lower band of consumers tended to ventilate less and were less indiscriminate in their demand

■4.12 Easthall: auxiliary heating and window opening

4.12(1) The annual consumption for space heating of the more energy-efficient of the two households who agreed to keep diaries was more than 6kWh/m^2 less than the mean average, although just less than 2kWh/m^2 above the median. Use of the auxiliary electric heater averaged more than four hours daily during the main three months of winter, and somewhat less in November and March. The opening of windows in winter was mainly confined to the glazed louvres and door between the kitchen and the utility space, with occasional opening of the sliding patio doors between the main bedroom and glazed balcony in February. The opening up of the dividing windows, those that separate heated from unheated space, increased significantly during the autumn and spring. During the same periods, outer windows of the two glazed buffers were also extensively opened during daytime. In March, for example, all available windows were opened for a minimum of two and a half hours daily, while all of the dividing windows were open for more than twice that amount. In the same month it is recorded that the auxiliary heater in the living room was used for three hours daily.

4.12(2) This tenant also started to use her auxiliary gas fire in mid-September for three hours daily, and peaked at ten hours daily during the first week in December. While the heat in the living room was augmented by an average of seven and a quarter hours daily during this month, the opening of its window averaged well over two hours.

■4.13 Easthall: real versus effective rates of ventilation

The mean average ventilation rate estimated for the mean average consumer was 1.8ac/h and 1.6ac/h in first and second monitored years respectively. However, the heat recovery aspect of the glazed spaces reduced these values to 'effective' rates of 1.1ac/h and 1.0ac/h; since the glazed spaces are at a higher temperature than that outside, the real rate of exchange with these spaces may be viewed as a lower 'effective' rate with the outside air. The same principle may be applied to mechanical heat recovery. Looking at the two examples of the flats with consumption on either side of the median line, the effective rates fall to 0.8 and 0.9ac/h, corresponding to real rates in the order of 1.3 to 1.4ac/h.

■4.14 Easthall compared to Stornoway: consumption range – influence of advice?

Easthall's highest to lowest ratio of energy consumed almost doubled from the first year at 7.4 to the second year at 14.2 (the sample where measurement continued dropped by 10 flats in year 2). The size of flat, and therefore differentials in the make-up of the household may be influential, since the equivalent ratio for the sample of 16 one- and two-person flats in the Stornoway project is lower – 4.8 in the first year, falling to 3.75 in the second year.

for heat, one may be optimistic about a larger proportional benefit for them even though the quantitative saving falls. ■4.13

It is always tempting to adopt 'what if?' scenarios. What would have been the consequence of stronger advice about setting of thermostats? Would an additional incentive or reward of some sort for low consumption, or a penalty for high consumption, have improved the results? Could more advice and 'sticks and carrots' have constrained the range within tighter limits? In terms of advice at least, the evidence at Easthall would suggest otherwise. ■4.14 But one should bear in mind that this was after weeding out six flats with some kind of misleading or aberrant characteristic. Overall, it would appear that the adaptive control of the user is likely to be potent and to negate, significantly, average predicted energy efficiency.

Finally, before looking at attached sunspaces in other housing projects, it should be borne in mind that the glazed balcony at Easthall does not compromise daylight to the living rooms. Thus the lack of roof glazing, inherent in a three-storey stacked system, is inconsequential, with the new outer glazed skin only marginally impacting on the status quo for the bedrooms. This was not so in the Stornoway project, an aspect which consciously limited the depth of the sun-porches. Indeed, the use of sunspaces to directly buffer living rooms in particular, and sometimes all the main accommodation, has become dominant in such applications of indirect passive solar gain. Therefore, the tendency is either for roof-glazed sunspaces, which can be of a relatively generous depth, or stacked sunspaces in the case of flats, which are necessarily of shallow depth, conforming to the Stornoway precedent. The other main buffering variable is height. So far this detailed exploration of the way in which occupants control performance has been restricted to small, shallow, single-storey conservatories.

other sunspace paradigms

Firstly, to expand this repertoire, adhering to a small footprint on plan that does not impact on daylight or sunlight into the heated rooms, and extending vertically to two storeys, a 2003 experimental solar house provides an apparently effortless variant on a sun-porch. Designed by Bean and Swan Architects for Berwickshire Housing Association at Ayton in southeast Scotland, the porch is independent of the main living room, but linked to two bedrooms and the main circulation system. Roughly square on plan, it is recessed centrally on the front façade and oriented fifteen degrees east of south (Figure 4.9). It is designed to function as a source of preheated fresh air for ventilation, with high-level hinged flaps to two bedrooms and a small window to an extended landing on the first floor. It is also designed to be connected to an air-to-air heat exchanger, advantageous in cold weather, when the exchanger on its own would not be able to heat up incoming air to a comfortable level for supply. To avoid overheating in warm weather, there is a high level roof-window with an automated actuator powered by a small solar photovoltaic panel. This is

important since the timber walls lining the porch will rapidly emit absorbed solar heat. Not only does excess heat in summer need an efficient escape route, but also the thermal emphasis should be on rapid convective transfer to heated rooms during sunny winter weather.

With respect to adaptive control, since the roof window is operated automatically and the norm for an entrance porch is to close both outer and inner doors on entering and leaving, the focus is on the three upper vents. Normal thermal stratification, with warm air rising within the porch, should ensure a satisfactory preheating effect when the vents are open. When closed, the porch is still an effective thermal buffer, with only two double-glazed surfaces, that of the tilted roof and the outer wall. Thus it is not too vulnerable to ill-judged operation by occupants. Since the porch does not project, the adjacent living room, with windows facing south and west, is not threatened by loss of either daylight or sunlight. The same applies to the bedrooms. On the other hand, unlike the bedrooms, the benefit of preheated air for ventilation to the living room could only occur indirectly via the stairwell. For example, air entering the upper landing from the porch could descend the stairs as it cools and enter the living room via its internal pass door, if left ajar. However, there are too many unknowns in such a scenario and it would be delusory to expect this to happen on a regular basis.

As a generic system, the sun-porch at Ayton seems robust, and any additional solar cost should be modest, providing an entrance lobby is taken as a prerequisite. It is similar to the double-height sun-porches that architect Tegnestuen Vandkunsten has designed for a terrace of maisonettes above flats

4.10 Maisonettes over flats in Ballerup with double-height, corner glazed sun-porch

in Ballerup outside Copenhagen in Denmark. This was part of the eclectic Egebjerggard 'boiby' Housing Exhibition of 1996 (Figure 4.10). Here the porches are vertically glazed only, and over two storeys high. The living room is located at the upper level and a small window to the sun-porch provides the possibility for a preheated supply of fresh air. Apart from the two doors and the remotely opened light at the top of the external skin, this is the only variable control. Thus the scope for compromising the designer's intention is again limited. Provided such spaces are spacious enough on plan to accommodate at least one chair, they can also function as an attractive conservatory or winter garden, rather than only as a utilitarian lobby. But in terms of value for money, the question arises as to whether the main living space might not have been the more appropriate recipient of such generous glazing, rather than such a small transitory space.

Thus in these two examples, where the presence or absence of a tilting glazed roof is not paramount, the height adds a literal thermo-circulatory dimension of reliability with regard to performance. The opportunities for inappropriate control by users become more constrained. The solar housing at Zollikofen, outside Berne, has already been cited in Chapter 2. Here, tilted and vertical surfaces have been melded and the height increased by one storey. Undoubtedly the three-storey sectional arrangement, associated with seasonally contra-posed convective regimes, will promote energy saving in winter and avert overheating in summer. However, because the sunspaces now buffer all the heated accommodation, the issue of blinds becomes contentious. Not only will they impede outward views, but they may also occlude daylight to the point where the occupants are tempted to switch on artificial lighting. Effectively, they may become barriers to the enjoyment of good weather.

As an alternative, the more traditional form of a lean-to conservatory should not be lightly dismissed. A mono-pitch glazed roof can be shaded without interrupting views through the vertical windows. However, roof-blinds might still excessively restrict daylight to the interior. Also, if, as is commonly the case, the height is lowered and the depth is increased, there will be a greater risk of overheating together with a greater temptation to use the space as another heated room. This issue was discussed in the previous chapter relative to both the individual solution for Brian Edwards and the Hockerton terrace for five families. Although each of these projects conform to a basic lean-to model, the former belongs in the Ayton camp, with no direct links to living accommodation other than one bedroom, while the latter conforms to Zollikofen by functioning as an intermediary to the entire heated volume.

A relatively early UK example of lean-to glazed buffers to all heated rooms is that of Paxton Court (also known as Netherspring) in Sheffield, designed by architect Cedric Green. Here, the model for procurement relates to the issue of operation by the users. This was a competition-winning, passive solar, self-build, cooperative project. As one might expect, a considerable amount of the final detailing was left up to individuals, and this included the means of conserving and controlling solar energy. Thus there were some ingeniously economic variants when it came to movable insulation and roof-shading devices, as well as general finishes (Figures 4.11a and b). It is also likely, given the degree of participation in the realization of their new solar homes, that the subsequent adaptive control would be sympathetic to optimizing their performance. In particular, it did not seem likely that there would be a temptation to heat the spaces in winter, even though their dimensions were generous. They were utilitarian garden rooms, simply increasing the potential use of a normal back garden: patio, clothes drying and so on.

Even so, some of the initial architectural decisions did present problems. For reasons of economy, the lean-to glazed roofs were fixed directly to rafters, with no opening lights. Exhaust of warm air was restricted to a rather small area of glazed louvres located in the gables of the conservatories. At the time of a visit in 1986, when the project was fairly recently occupied, it was noted that a maximum–minimum thermometer had reached nearly 40°C. Monitoring of one of the two-storey houses was carried out as part of the Energy Performance Appraisal (EPA) by the Energy Technology Support Unit (ETSU), Harwell, UK. In terms of success as a conserver of energy, this monitoring found the heat loss coefficient to be 237W/K – some 25 per cent greater than the predicted value of 190W/K (Yannas, 1994, pp52–59). This was attributed to lack of air-tightness, estimated to be 1.5 changes of air every hour, which was roughly twice the value assumed at design stage. However, it is equally possible that, had the building been more airtight, the occupants would have chosen to ventilate up to such a value.

Most lean-to conservatories fall short of buffering all heated accommodation, generally favouring attachment to the main living space. A good example of this is an earlier project for Berwickshire Housing Association in Scotland by a local architectural practice, Aitken and Turnbull. Located at the edge of the small town of Coldstream, the dwellings are planned in semi-detached pairs, with

4.11 Self-build, cooperative passive solar houses at Paxton Court, Sheffield

a two-storey houses – cloth shades; 'Alreflex' insulating blinds

b single-storey houses – bamboo shades; insulated plywood shutters

each entered from the south through a generous glazed porch. This also buffers the entire south façade of the living rooms and the wall up to the level of windowsills at first floor level (Figure 4.12). It was intended that preheated air from the sun-porch could enter either the living room or a first floor bedroom, pressure-steered by continuous low-flow mechanical extract from kitchen bathroom and toilet. However, in one house visited in 2000, after a year or so of occupation, the tenants had taken radical adaptive action. They had removed the double-glazed doors between the porch and the living room. They had also reduced the intended thermal storage by carpeting over the ceramic tiles in the porch. Thus this particular dwelling was operating in a responsive 'direct solar gain' mode, rather than a less responsive 'indirect' one. From information provided on fuel bills, it was estimated that the annual space heating load, including the area of the sun-porch as part of the heated area, was in the order of 75kWh/m². This is on the high side for an energy-efficient prototype at the turn of the millennium, but not catastrophically so.

Regardless of the prevalence of lean-to conservatories and regardless of the actions of occupants, whether or not in tune with energy efficiency, they are inherently restrictive as a typology. They go together with low-density, suburban housing. Then, unless they are fully recessed within the overall envelope as at Ayton or Egebjerggard, they may shade adjacent parts of the façade. On the other hand, the recessed type is to some extent self-shading, as is a continuous terrace of lean-to conservatories, such as at Hockerton. At the same time, there is an increasing environmental pressure towards more compact urban typologies. This in turn pushes the sunspace agenda towards the precedents of Stornoway and Easthall – hence justifying the space accorded to them here.

4.12 Lean-to sunspaces at Coldstream

A recent rural development in Scotland employs slim, semi-recessed sunspaces, without roof glazing, as part of a passive solar strategy (Figure 4.13). Although the setting is a village, and the dominant housing form is that of a short, two-storey terrace that blended with the local Scottish vernacular, the typology of the sunspace itself is capable of translation to urban flats or maisonettes. Designed by architect Gordon Fleming of ARP Lorimer Associates for Ayrshire Housing Association, the exposed maritime climate of Ballantrae ■4.15(1) was influential in the design. The dominant wind is from the south-west, and it seemed logical to locate small sunspaces on the south or west sides of the houses to partly buffer living rooms, dining-kitchens and bedrooms, and act as intermediaries between house and garden. On plan, over and above the shallow, semi-recessed form, self-shading has been minimized by chamfering the two glazed connecting edges between sunspaces and heated rooms. The spaces are large enough to house a couple of chairs, but are deliberately too small to function as extra rooms. The idea was to inhibit any temptation to heat them.

In this case, the sunspace is also an integral component of a proprietary mechanical system of ventilating the houses. ■4.15(2) A manifold in the attic, when switched by the occupant to the 'warm' position, can search for the warmest air, either from the apex of the attic itself or from the top of the sunspace. Alternatively, when switched to 'cool', the air enters via a vent located in the eaves of the north side of the roof. Air is supplied to the interior through a register in the ceiling at the top of the staircase. The stairwell and hall then act as a plenum, potentially supplying air to all other rooms, when doors are ajar. Due to the particular location, mains gas was not available and it was decided to use electric storage heating units in all the main spaces. This, together with lighting and power for all other electric appliances, operates via a special tri-tariff arrangement known as 'comfort plus' whereby a central controller searches for optimum inputs from either off-peak, peak or an in-between 'shoulder' supply. However, although this process is automated, the occupant can set different regimes for three different zones within their homes.

When visiting the scheme on a sunny spring day in late April 2004, the radiant warmth was tempered by a stiff sea breeze. Several issues emerged concerning the interface between what the architect had provided and what the tenants were doing in terms of environmental control. The observations are based mainly on two of the houses that were visited, but also on information provided by the people involved in their procurement. In the latter category, some of the residents had been switching off their system of mechanical ventilation. In some cases, this may have been due to them not realizing that the controller was switched to the 'cool' position, or vice versa. It should be borne in mind that the first summer of occupation, 2003, was exceptionally warm. However, the other factor with regard to this system is that it is intended to run continuously. This means that when set

4.13 Semi-recessed, double-height sunspaces at Ballantrae

■4.15 Ballantrae rural housing: supplementary information

4.15(1) This village is known chiefly as the setting for Robert Louis Stevenson's novel, *The Master of Ballantrae.*

4.15(2) This is the 'Drimaster 2000' supplied by NuAire Ltd.

4.15(3) The aim of the continuous 24-hour cycle is to avoid risk of stagnant air and excessively high humidity overnight.

4.15(4) The tenant who complained of discomfort reported that his quarterly electricity bill for the hot summer of 2003 had been roughly £300, compared with £70–80 for his neighbours.

to 'warm' on a cold evening, both the sunspace and attic options for supply will be cold. ■4.15(3) The delivered air will then tend to descend through the stairwell to the ground floor and settle close to the floor before joining a convective cycle, promoted mainly by the heating units, and rising again. In other words, it will provide an environment that is likely to be perceived as draughty. One of the tenants specifically confirmed this characteristic during the visit, and also commented that his feet could become uncomfortably cold in such circumstances. The same tenant also commented that his bills seemed to be much higher than that of his neighbours across the road. ■4.15(4) In this regard, it was noted that on the afternoon of the visit, the storage heater in his living room was fully on, discharging a significant amount of heat.

In both of the homes visited at Ballantrae, the occupants had adopted quite a liberal regime with respect to open windows, but the heating was also still on. In one case, there clearly was a different approach to each of three zones, and this was evident even on one floor – 'off' in hall, 'on' at a low level of output in kitchen and fully 'on' in the living room. In the second house, all ground floor units appeared to be on at the same medium level of output. Looking round the entire scheme, there was considerable diversity with regard to the propensity to open windows. Generalizing however, many seemed to favour either almost complete closure, or a significant amount of opening, which included the doors connecting sunspaces with gardens. This may have related to whether people were in or out, given that the visit was not only on a Sunday afternoon, but also the best Sunday afternoon of the spring up till then. What is not known is whether any of the houses with closed windows may have had the heating completely off. However, given the fairly unresponsive nature of the heating, together with the prospect of quite a cool evening following the sunny day, the likelihood of this being the case seems rather remote.

In the case of the dwellings with sunspaces open to the garden, the mechanical supply of air to the stairwell would probably have come from the attic. The grey roof tiles would have absorbed a large proportion of the incoming short-wave radiation, and, in turn, this would have impacted on the attic. However, in the case of closed sunspaces, the air may well have come from this source. Whilst the difference between the two temperatures may have been marginal, there is no doubt that the open houses would have consumed more units of energy over the day. Thus we again have a dilemma between an environment that feels good for the given conditions, and one that is more energy efficient.

further thoughts on options for mechanically assisted ventilation

It is worth comparing this particular 'mixed mode' system of ventilation with another generic one. In Ballantrae, a mechanical supply to a central circulation space is augmented by natural ventilation – opening windows, some directly to the outside and others to the sunspace – as well as by opening internal doors.

The flow of air in and out of windows and their trickle vents will largely be dictated by wind pressure and less so by thermal buoyancy. In the project at Ballantrae, the kitchen windows face south and this may result in cooking odours and moisture circulating into other parts of the house. The more conventional solution is to target mechanical extraction from wet zones, with or without heat recovery, and again augmented by windows, and perhaps also by unheated glazed buffers.

This is the system employed at Easthall. The essential difference between the two tactics is that while the latter automatically gets rid of moist air at source, in the former case, this aspect is very reliant on what the occupant does. For example, if the door from the hallway to the kitchen in the Ballantrae houses is closed, air has to be supplied and exhausted either directly via the normal window, or indirectly via the sunspace, or a combination of the two. If the sunspace is involved, it is quite possible for moist, and possibly smelly, air from cooking to re-circulate through the house. A related issue, which is causing some problems for the tenants, is that the outer fenestration of the sunspaces is single-glazed and surface condensation can be heavy. At least one resident used the sunspace to house a tumble drier, apparently opening the outer doors when the drier was in use. Even so, the risk would be that not only would the windows function as condensers, but also some of the very moist air would migrate within the house.

Despite these issues of manual control by occupants that can impact on energy-efficiency, the basic idea of exploiting the air from sunspaces through integration with a mechanical system is intriguing. In theory, the latter should provide a degree of control that might be lacking in a purely passive set-up. An earlier, more urban variant of double-height sunspaces, with glazing limited to the vertical surfaces and where the circulation of air from them is driven by an active system, is that completed in 1990 by the late Theo Bosch in the provincial town of Deventer in Holland (Figure 4.14). Here, a mechanical heat exchanger recovers thermal energy from outgoing air from all wet spaces, its supply of fresh air being limited to bedrooms on the upper level in the case of maisonettes. One of these opens on to the upper part of the sunspace, and it seems probable that occupants might wish to have such windows open, especially overnight. This assertion acknowledges the difference in attitude towards a normal window on an external wall compared with one like this, which is more removed from the outside world. Without the mechanical system, one would have expected warm air at the top of the sunspace to flow into the bedroom, at least during daytime if the internal window were ajar. Then it might eventually return to the bottom of the sunspace via the stairs and living room. However, the mechanical extract from the kitchen and toilet at the lower level requires a supply of air. This could either come through the north or the south façade. In the latter case, it would either draw air in from the sunspace at low level or directly from the one window,

4.14 Semi-recessed, double-height and single-height stacked sunspaces at Deventer

4.15 Stacked sunspaces at Graham Square in Glasgow – facing 15° north of west

which opens directly to the outside from the living room. This is a similar situation to that at Easthall or Ballantrae, where occupants have a choice. In the interests of energy-efficiency, one would hope that they would ventilate via the sunspace in winter. But that might not be so, and hence, as we have seen above, consumption could vary radically.

However, assuming that occupants conform to reasonable expectations, the mechanical system would counteract natural thermo-circulation during the day by drawing sun-warmed, less dense air from the top of the sunspace back down to the bottom. During the night, with an open window between the main bedroom and the sunspace, the mechanical supply of warm air would tend to enter the upper part of the sunspace and then cool in contact with the outer glass, increasing in density and descending ready for entry into the living room and kitchen. In other words, at night, or on a cold and overcast day in winter, the mechanical system will not have to counteract natural thermo-circulation. Rather than competing with a warming cycle, it will work in harmony with a cooling one. There is also a small heating coil integrated with the exchanger as a failsafe for conditions where the fresh supply would otherwise be too cold.

raising architectural stakes – widening performance gap

Returning to Scotland, a final and more recent case study is difficult to ignore in terms of the matter in hand – 'conservatories conserving?' This is an award-winning design by architects McKeown Alexander for Molendinar Park Housing Association (Platt, 2000) and it is again urban, involving stacked, shallow, single-storey, vertically glazed and recessed sunspaces. The site is known as Graham Square, the former threshold to an abattoir in the East End of Glasgow. Aesthetically, the stakes have been raised higher than at either Stornoway or Easthall. With the completely glazed façades reminiscent of much earlier modernist schemes, such as the 1931 Clarté flats by Le Corbusier in Geneva, this project has an aura of flats only available to a wealthy elite. However, it is predominantly rented social housing, and compared with pioneers such as the solar demonstration at Easthall, the most significant change in terms of performance is the greater height and width. ■4.16(1) In other words, the area of the solar façade has increased while the loss of gain by self-shading is relatively slight (Figure 4.15). Apart from three of the flats, where sunspaces are about two thirds of the more typical width and are in a corner situation, the entire living-dining-kitchen zone is buffered.

Although the sample was small, a mainly qualitative survey (Hayton, 2004) uncovered some interesting aspects of control by the occupants. Ironically, although all local housing associations in Scotland pride themselves on participation in the process of procurement, only one seventh of the tenants here chose to participate in this survey. Altogether only four households took part, two home-owners and two tenants. Whether by coincidence or not, according to the figures provided by Hayton, the two tenants were much more energy-efficient than the two owners. One of the latter spent more than three times as much as the lower of the two tenants.

Once respective differences in floor areas are taken into account, the range is even more extreme. Translating Hayton's figures for expenditure to net energy needed for space heating per unit area, the lower of the two tenants is estimated to be less than 35kWh/m^2, the next at less than 55kWh/m^2. On the other hand, the lower of the two owners at close to 110kWh/m^2 and the profligate owner at just over 300kWh/m^2. One may note that this last estimate is nearly 60 per cent above the highest consumer at Easthall. ■4.16(2)

Then, if we accept that at least three of the four dwellings at Graham Square are representative of the range for all twenty, the results bear comparison to those of Easthall, with the two tenants in the lowest three and ten respectively. However, even when disregarding the aberrantly high owner, there is still a factor of three between the highest and lowest. Such differentials serve to mask improvements in energy efficiency ■4.16(3) at Graham Square compared with Easthall. There is no doubt that the primary reasons for the substantial range in consumption are again the regimes adopted with respect to setting thermostats and opening windows. It may also be significant that the tenants had the benefit of detailed advice from the housing association with respect to the use of both the heating system and the sunspaces, whereas the owners did not.

Sadly, the two tenants with the low consumption appeared to make very little use of the sunspace as an amenity, finding it generally either too warm or too cold. This may have something to do with the orientation. The flats of the two tenants face approximately fifteen degrees north of due west. This means that their opportunities for enjoying direct solar radiation will be very limited in winter, when the sun sets well to the south of due west. It would only come into its own during sunny early evenings in spring, and could then well become too warm if not adequately ventilated. Paradoxically, it would appear that the low level of use resulted in the spaces functioning effectively as thermal buffers. On the other hand, the two owners had flats facing fifteen degrees west of due south. They had more opportunity to enjoy the spaces and it was the case that they opened up the dividing screen much more frequently.

Overall, the performance of a varied typology of unheated sunspaces relative to energy-efficient housing, mainly in the rented sector, has been shown to be sensitive to the vagaries of occupants. This particular architecturally upmarket scheme is no different. It is very difficult to see how the architects could have designed out all the susceptibilities that have been described, although there is clearly scope in terms of heat delivery. In particular, ubiquitous water-filled radiators, with thermostatic valves, have been shown to be very temptingly open to overuse in an affordable context. In any case, if standards of insulation are high enough, and if there is a workable system of controlled ventilation that involves some form of preheating, we have seen that the need

■4.16 Graham Square urban housing: supplementary information

4.16(1) The height is about 2.8m, and the width some 6.5m, while the depth is very similar to that at Easthall at 1.2m.

4.16(2) These values are based on assumptions for gas consumed for cooking and heating water, and 70 per cent efficiency for the combination gas boiler. If actual efficiencies were higher, the net rates per unit area would also rise. With the low U-values, a condensing gas boiler was considered uneconomic. However, this means that the UK's Standard Assessment Procedure (SAP) rating is adversely affected. There is a paradox here. If, a condensing boiler would be inefficient due to high levels of insulation, a rating should not be penalized.

4.16(3) U-values for opaque surfaces at Graham Square are approximately 0.20W/m^{2}K compared with 0.25 and higher at Easthall, while windows at Graham Square all have low-emissivity coatings compared with normal double glazing at Easthall.

for auxiliary or purchased heat can be very low. On the other hand, it has been shown that any group is likely to contain a wide range from what might be perceived as sensibly low, to irrationally high, consumption. It also has to be accepted that the lowest group is probably more likely to correspond with predictions or expectations for energy-efficiency than that in the middle. A case is evident for predictive modelling to acknowledge a more realistic standard based on a higher level of middle ground, which has been derived from measurement. Also, using the word 'vagaries' relative to a whole range of tactics adopted to provide comfort is perhaps unfair. The word should be more fairly aimed at the high end, where erratic whimsies are perceived as a factor. Then again, one person's whimsy may be another's rationale.

Socio-demography in focus

Up until now, there has been little attempt to provide further meaning or reason to explain what causes one household to be a high consumer as opposed to a low one. However, certain behavioural patterns, which could be categorized as having a social or demographic bias, are relevant here. Some are so prevalent that they are difficult to isolate. For example, all of Glasgow's peripheral housing schemes, and areas to the near east of the centre, are characterized by social ills such as high unemployment, drug dependency and crime, as well as a relatively high incidence of disability. Although social and economic disadvantage may be very pronounced in Glasgow, such symptoms can be found in many of the cities located within the climatic scope of this book, and they also have a direct relationship to issues such as demand for heat and air in homes.

It should also be recognized that floor areas for social housing tend to be close to the statutory minimum. Whilst this might indicate that they may be more economic to heat than a larger house, when small houses are intensively occupied, they need to replenish their air at a significantly higher rate than a larger counterpart. As we have seen, as soon as a large demand for air prevails, the result is a larger consumption of fuel, already recognized as a 'chicken and egg' situation. The demand for air, to at least some extent, appears to be driven by the demand for heat. Further, despite a modern, middle-income tendency for more work to be done in the home, it is indisputable that dwellings in the low-income sector will be occupied for more hours every day compared with those higher up the social scale.

Another factor that has already been mentioned is that poor people, in Scotland at least, are now in transition from years of suffering the additional burdens of fuel poverty – cold, damp, mouldy homes – to affordable warmth. The tide is turning in this regard. Thermally sub-standard stock is gradually being upgraded (Communities Scotland, 2004) and new dwellings have to conform to increasingly tighter thermal standards. Therefore, it is not surprising to find people wishing to enjoy this novel wealth of comfort to the hilt. Over and above a reactive attitude to the affordability of heat, we have a more generic aspiration towards whole-house comfort. This is a characteristic that is difficult to pin down further. However, there are specific socio-economic influences that were apparent to some extent in Graham Square, which also correlate with some of the earlier findings of the Easthall solar demonstration.

Having gone into aspects of performance that are inextricably tied to the habits and aspirations of occupants, the scene is now set for an appraisal of particular 'lifestyle' or socio-demographical influences, some more readily identified than others. It also means that such influences are not likely to be tied particularly to sunspaces or to any one country. Having made this point, there are nevertheless certain social housing models that are associated with some countries more than others.

Scottish experience

In the case of Scotland, it is the 'housing association' model that has gained prominence over the last two decades. Hence it is convenient to continue with the four households in Graham Square in Glasgow, who cooperated with interviews and questionnaires.

The owner with the very high consumption provided some clues regarding this phenomenon. Smoking frequently inside the flat had the consequence of windows also being opened frequently to clear the air. Also the second member of the household was a cat, who was given the run of the sunspace as a garden, with the intervening sliding glass door constantly in the open position. Effectively this extended the heated volume to include the sunspace. Consequently, double, rather than quadruple, glazing then bounded the living room. Also, the impact of smoking on the metabolism often results in smokers feeling cold, while non-smokers are comfortable. Feeling cold in the living room was admitted in this case, the implication being that the thermostat would tend to be mainly set to its maximum level.

It was ironically the larger rented flat, which was occupied most intensively and generally all day rather than from evening to morning, that had the lowest consumption. One possible reason for this was that an agoraphobic son often used his computer all day long. Both this and the intensity of occupation itself would add to incidental thermal gains, thus reducing the need for auxiliary heat. It may also be that maintaining a steady diurnal cycle of temperature was inherently more efficient than providing twice-daily surges of heat. Certainly the occupancy during daytime would be able to take more advantage of useful solar gain. The dwellings are lightweight in terms of their construction, so that for those who were regularly out from morning to evening, much of the heat gained from the sun would already be lost by the time when heat was most needed.

A further factor at Graham Square is the relatively generous volume in the larger of the two flats in the Hayton survey. Since each is for a maximum of four people, but, in the case of the lowest consumer, was actually only occupied by two, there was approximately 120m^3 of air available per person. If we compare

■4.17 Easthall: ventilation related to smoking, children and pets

4.17(1) The estimated rate of ventilation went up by 50 per cent comparing 8 dwellings with no smokers to 26 with at least one smoker. It also went up by 50 per cent comparing the 8 dwellings with no smokers to 9 with at least one smoker and a pet. The difference in consumption was even more marked. It went up by 80 per cent comparing non-smoking households to smoking ones and up 96 per cent compared to smoking ones with pets.

4.17(2) The 9 houses with children were estimated to have an average of over 40 per cent greater rate of ventilation and 35 per cent higher consumption compared to those without. Also, of the 9 with children, the 6 smoking households ventilated more than 60 per cent and consumed more than 100 per cent compared with the non-smoking ones.

■4.18 Ottrupgård Fjernewarme rural co-housing: energy efficiency values

4.18(1) During a visit in 1996, the following U-values were reported – roof 0.13W/m²K, walls 0.24W/m²K, floor 0.15W/m²K and argon-filled windows at 1.60W/m²K.

4.18(2) The average annual demand for space and water heating was reportedly about 100kWh/m² or 11,000kWh for a house of 110m². If 3700kWh were deducted for water heating, the balance for space heating would be approximately 66kWh/m².

this to two people occupying an Easthall flat (also capable of taking four people), the figure drops by 37.5 per cent to 75m³ per person. The argument can be made, that far from it being inherently more economic to heat the smaller volume, it conversely leads to more indiscriminate opening of windows, and hence to higher heating loads. The greater consumption of the less extravagant of the two owners in the survey at Graham Square conforms to this hypothesis. It is a much smaller flat than those occupied by the tenants, and the volume of air per occupant is approximately 77m³, quite close to a flat at Easthall occupied by two people.

The issue of smoking and the presence of pets was evident at Easthall, both apparently adding to the need to ventilate. ■4.17(1) The presence of young children also seemed to correlate to ventilation and fuel consumption, and the presence of smoking and children generates an additional bias. ■4.17(2) The thermal influence of pets, particularly dogs, is tied to the temptation to use a glazed space as a kennel, and to ventilate it liberally. Odour is an added factor. With young children, the home tends to be more intensively occupied as well as super-heated. The amount of laundering tends to increase significantly and odour can again be a factor with babies. One mother understandably changed her baby in front of the gas fire with the window open to clear the air. The glazed balconies were also ideal play spaces and, in any case, young children tend to wander from space to space, leaving doors ajar.

Danish and German experiences

The issue of families with young children in a rural setting, as opposed to an urban one, was again perceived as an energy factor in the Ottrupgård Fjernewarme Danish co-housing development mentioned earlier (Chapter 2). This was a scheme with a strong commitment to efficient use of renewable energy, in this case an active solar array together with a bio-fuel boiler to provide low-temperature district heating. It is the same psychological issue concerning ownership of controls, which was addressed in the first main sub-section of this chapter, but set in the context of a particular social group with a common sense of purpose. An important by-product of their communal approach was that much of the activity that generates moisture and requires energy has been taken out of the individual homes.

These were well insulated ■4.18(1). In spite of this, the average annual demand for space heating appeared to be quite high ■4.18(2) – of the order of 66kWh/m². Warm water coils below the flooring should result in comfort being achieved at relatively low air temperatures, while the multiple-thermostat factor is not present. The internal brick leaf of the outer walls together with solid internal walls will also provide good thermal storage. This in turn should enhance the capability to air the houses intermittently without losing too much energy. Although the estimate of 66kWh/m² by no means represents an exorbitant heating load, it does suggest a relatively significant proportion due to ventilation. The system for control was a cord-operated trickle vent as an inlet to each room, with passive stack exhaust from bathrooms and kitchen. However, in the safe country context, it is likely that there would be a lot of movement in and out of houses, especially by the children. This would add to the more general tendency to open windows at times when the ambient temperature is low.

Finally one should bear in mind that these houses are some 75 per cent larger than the meagre volume of the flats at Easthall in Glasgow. Therefore, one could reasonably expect the thermal load for ventilation to be higher, even at fairly low rates. On the other hand, it has already been argued above that more air per person can lead to less opening of windows. Actually both propositions could be valid. Assuming comparison of a family of four in Ottrupgård compared with the same number at Easthall, the estimated mean consumption of the larger Danish home lies at the top of the lowest third of the monitored Scottish group.

Another co-housing project in the Vauban district of Freiburg, Germany, came about as a result of a policy to promote participation by citizens. Priority was further given where it was recognized that groups of citizens had a clear policy for sustainability. Groups were also required to form an association, which would work with research partners. In this case the project was given the title 'Wohnen & Arbeiten' (Living & Working), and the association 'Ökobauverein e.V., Freiburg' (Association for Sustainable Buildings) was founded. All residents were required to be members of Ökobauverein. Architect Michael Gies of id-architektur, together with the Fraunhofer Institut für Solare Energiesysteme and the Fraunhofer Institut für Systemtechnic und Innovationsforschung in Freiburg, then designed the building (Figure 4.16). The aim was that its active and passive solar features, together with its measures for energy conservation, would come

4.16 South façade of the 'Wohnen & Arbeiten' (Living & Working) block in Freiburg

close to eliminating space heating in the normal sense. This means that one of the commonly abused controls already identified, a thermostatic control valve on each radiator in each space, is no longer available. There is actually one radiator for extreme conditions in the dining-kitchen and a small one in the bathroom, but otherwise the flats are kept warm at the same time as they are ventilated by a mechanical heat recovery system.

This is a similar tactic to that adopted by Brenda and Robert Vale in the Hockerton housing in England (Chapter 3). The Vauban flats have ducts to deliver fresh air at 18°C through grilles in the floor. This then leaves rooms at about 20°C from the kitchen and bathroom, having picked up additional heat from the occasional use of the radiator, together with passive solar gain, occupants, appliances and lighting, each of these varying according to time and circumstance. The system is expected to be at least 82 per cent efficient, although claims of 85–90 per cent were made during an initial visit in 1999. Such values imply that the exchanger itself is of very high quality in terms of both design and manufacture. It is also relevant that there is a communal laundry in the basement. None of the dwellings have to deal with the moisture from washing and drying clothes. Therefore, the rate of replenishing fresh air is not as great as it would otherwise have been. Also, the proportion of working space – ateliers and offices – will help to keep the production of moisture relatively low.

Moreover, like Hockerton, there is a considerable amount of thermal mass, mainly in floors, masonry partitions and party walls, and the dining-kitchen area is tiled as a passive solar absorber and heat store. This means, that although there is always a possibility of residents opening windows in cold weather, the capacitance will help to limit the negative impact of such actions. Most importantly, because this is another self-build cooperative development, the occupants all have a stake in responsible energy conservation. This started with the design itself, a no-frills geometrical approach where the quality of construction and services can be prioritized. Although each flat is individually tailored in terms of layout and some finishes, their container is a very straightforward rectilinear block. Thus the high proportion of shared walls and floors are thermally advantageous.

When it came to the external envelope, because unlike Hockerton there are no solar buffer spaces, the glazing specification is extremely high. Sturdy timber windows, including sliding patio doors, are triple-glazed with two low-emissivity coatings and cavities filled with heavy gas to give a U-value of $0.7W/m^2K$ and 75 per cent transmission. All opaque external surfaces have 25cm of insulation, while access decks on one side of the block and verandas on the other are independently supported to avoid any thermal bridging. Each of these zones is capped by a tilted solar array, photovoltaics over the south-facing veranda, and flat-plate solar thermal collectors over the access galleries. By being directly involved in the building process, residents know about the specification and what is expected of them in terms of responsible use. There is a further incentive to be economic with hot water, since this is metered, while the small amount of energy supplied to radiators is included with the rent. In any case, the general socio-political climate in Germany, and particularly in Freiburg, is very attuned to environmental awareness and responsibility.

The project was nearing completion in the summer of 1999, so that only predictions were available with respect to performance. The passive and active solar contribution was estimated to be over 20kWh/m^2 and estimates of residual loads seemed quite optimistic compared to other projects. But in Freiburg, home to the headquarters of the International Solar Energy Society, ISES, and the reputed solar capital of Europe, one gets used to very low forecasts of consumption. A small combined heat and power (CHP) system, burning natural gas, was designed to meet the residual annual load for space and water heating together with the balance of the electrical load. In addition, it was intended that gas for cooking would come from a biogas reactor supplied by so-called 'black water' from a vacuum sanitation system. Although Jörg Lange, resident and 'father' of the project, has not yet given up on it, apparently the biogas reactor never worked satisfactorily and the company assigned to this part of the plant is bankrupt. There is also a 'grey water' recycling system (from showers and so forth) used for flushing toilets and gardening purposes; all rainwater is returned to the ground via ditches and gravel filters.

Revisited five years later, the project has been monitored as part of IEA Task 28/38 'Sustainable Solar Housing' (Voss et al, 2002). The annual net thermal demand for space and water heating is given as just below 40kWh/m^2, having allowed for free solar and incidental gains. ■4.19(1) On top of this, there is the electrical demand, met partly by the photovoltaic array and partly by the CHP system. ■4.19(2)

It is an open question as to what extent socio-demographic factors may have been relevant to the actual consumption. A key value to bear in mind and compare with other projects is the net demand for space heating of roughly 30kWh/m^2. In other words, in this urban block, the loads appear to be less than half that achieved for the Danish rural co-housing. Leaving aside climatic differences, which may in any case not be too significant, the compactness and shared surfaces in Freiburg must play a considerable part in this. But the heat recovery system is also crucial to the comparison. It is likely that it meets most if not all of the thermal demand arising from ventilation. Again, a question arises as to whether other urban versus rural factors had relevance to the differential, in spite of similar environmental aspirations and probably quite a similar socio-demographic mix. Whatever the answers, and for all the apparent success of the urban over the rural model, 30kWh/m^2 is compatible with the figure quoted as a 'passive solar exemplar' by the Fraunhofer Institut in 1999 (assuming the latter excludes the contribution from heat recovery). One may conclude that

■4.19 Vauban, Freiburg: details of monitored energy

4.19(1) Less than a quarter of the 40kWh/m^2 is for water (8.7kWh/m^2). Nearly 18kWh/m^2 of the remainder needed for space heating is met by heat recovery; and in order to address a final heating deficit of about 13kWh/m^2, a thermal supply of some 13.25kWh/m^2 is required from the CHP system to top up that from the flat-plate solar array. The CHP and the 45m^2 of flat-plate collectors together supply 32kWh/m^2 to the thermal store, two thirds of which is usefully used for space and water heating (12.6 + 8.7 = 21.3kWh/m^2). In other words, the efficiency of the thermal store and associated distribution is a modest 66.6 per cent. However, some of the losses will be reclaimed inside apartments as useful incidental gains.

4.19(2) 36.4kWh/m^2 of natural gas is supplied annually to the CHP system. The electrical output is 8.5kWh/m^2, to which 1.8kWh/m^2 (m^2 still refers to floor area) is added from the solar photovoltaic array. After allowing for pumps, fans and electrical controls, there is 6.5kWh/m^2 available for other electrical uses; this amount can be exported to the grid to offset, or even overtake, what has to be bought from it. The combined electrical and thermal efficiency of the CHP plant works out at 85 per cent.

one-off experiments such as the 'solar house' in Freiburg, which is probably around half that value once heat recovery is included, are meant to encourage designers and users to strive towards greater efficiency, rather than to represent a realistic expectation for real multi-unit housing projects.

This German social and environmental paradigm marks an appropriate point to return the spotlight to aspects of design that initially set the scene for the occupants. Chapter 2 discussed strategic architectural positions, specifically with regard to the advantages and constraints of solar features having more than one function. Having now teased out some discernable traits with respect to the manner in which people interact with buildings and the extent to which this affects their ability to conserve energy, it is now time to give some more attention to static aspects of design that have potency in their own right. The contention is that even though the holistic architectonic of a building, as conceived and realized by a design team, is always to some extent vulnerable to interference by users, it should also provide and protect a significant degree of immutability.

REFERENCES

Allen, R. (ed) (1993) *The Chambers Dictionary,* Chambers Harrap Publishers, p1365.

Baker, N. and Standeven, M. (1995) 'Adaptive opportunity as a comfort parameter', in *Workplace Comfort Forum,* proceedings of conference, (22–23 March), RIBA, London.

Baker, P. H. and McEvoy, M. E. (1999) 'An investigation into the use of a supply air window as a heat reclaim device', *Building Services Engineering Research and Technology,* vol 20, no 3, pp105–112.

Bloss, W. H. and Pfisterer, F. (eds) (1987) *Advances in Solar Energy Technology,* proceedings of the Biennial Congress of the International Solar Energy Society, (13–18 September, Hamburg, Germany), vol 4, Pergamon Press, Oxford.

Blundell Jones, P. (1996) 'Space Craft, Youth Club, Möglingen, Germany', *The Architectural Review,* vol 200, no 1195, pp44–47.

Boyce, R. (1993) 'Keck's Art Deco and Art Moderne residences', in *Keck and Keck,* Princeton Architectural Press, New York, p59.

Butti, K. and Perlin, J. (1980) 'An American revival', in *A Golden Thread: 2500 Years of Solar Architecture and Technology,* Cheshire Books, Palo Alto, California, pp192–194.

Communities Scotland (2004) *Scottish House Condition Survey 2002,* Scottish Executive, Edinburgh, pp152–171 and 190–219.

Hawkes, D. (1988) 'Energetic Design: Netley Infants' School', *The Architects' Journal,* vol 7, no 25, pp31–46.

Hayton, I. (2004) 'One size fits all? An investigation into the effects of occupants on environmental performance in mass housing'. Special Subject dissertation, 20 April 2004, Mackintosh School of Architecture, Glasgow, Scotland, pp15–59.

Ho, H. M. (1995) *User-Performance Sensitivity of Small Sunspaces in a Scottish Housing Context,* PhD thesis, Mackintosh School of Architecture, University of Glasgow, pp2.1–2.13.

Keable, J. (1979) 'Understanding the idea of passive Solar Collection: Including the Primary Role of Thermal Storage', in *The Passive Collection of Solar Energy in Buildings,* proceedings of conference, (Royal Institution, London, April) UK-ISES, pp1–3.

Lewis J. O. (ed) (1989) *Project Monitor,* Commission of the European Communities, No 47, July, School of Architecture, University College, Dublin.

Long, G. (1976) *Solar Energy: its Potential Contribution within the United Kingdom,* a report prepared for the Department of Energy by the Energy Technology Support Unit, Harwell, HMSO, London, p37.

Nordström, C. and Nordström, K. (1987) 'A multifamily solar house in Gothenburg, Sweden', in Bloss and Pfisterer, pp3561–3565.

O'Farrell, F. and Lynskey, G. (1984) 'The construction and performance of a Trombe wall in a northern climate', in MacGregor, K. (ed), *North Sun '84: Solar Energy at High Latitudes,* proceedings of conference (4–6 September) Scottish Solar Energy Group, Edinburgh, UK, pp39–46.

Palz, W. and Steemers, T. C. (eds) (1981) *Solar Houses in Europe: How They Have Worked,* Pergamon Press, Oxford, pp163–170.

Platt, C. (2000) 'Market Place: McKeown Alexander at Graham Square', *Architecture Today,* no 112, pp24–30.

Porteous C. (1983) *Passive Solar Space Heating in Housing with Particular Reference to the Scottish Climate,* M. Phil. thesis, Robert Gordon's Institute of Technology (now University), pp81–88.

Porteous, C. D. A. (1988) 'Retrofit of thermally substandard housing in Glasgow as a CEC passive solar demonstration project', in *Annexe 1: Energy Demonstration Project No. SE-167/88-UK,* Mackintosh School of Architecture, Glasgow.

Porteous, C. D. A. (1990) *Performance Characteristics of Solar Buffer Zones for Scottish Housing,* Ph.D. thesis, University of Strathclyde, Glasgow, pp18–51.

Saluja, G. S., Porteous, C. D. A. and Holling, A. (1987) 'Experience of passive solar heating in a Scottish housing scheme at 58°N latitude', in Bloss and Pfisterer, pp3686–3691.

Trombe, F., Robert, J. F., Cabanat, M. and Sesolis, B. (1979) 'Some Performance Characteristics of the CNRS Solar House Collectors', in *The Passive Collection of Solar Energy in Buildings,* proceedings of conference, (Royal Institution, London, April), UK-ISES, pp4–23.

Twidell, J. W. and Johnstone, C. M. (1993) *The University of Strathclyde Solar Residences: Final Report of Monitoring,* Energy Studies Unit, University of Strathclyde, pp8–37.

Voss, K., Engelmann, P., Hube W., Bühring, A., Ufheil, M. and Neumann C. (2002) 'Solarenergie und Energieeffizienz in Geschosswohnungsbau – Ergebnisse, Erfahrungen und Trends aus aktuellen Demonstrationsprojekten', in *Symposium Thermische Solarenergie,* proceedings of symposium, Staffelstein, Germany.

Yannas, S. (1994) *Solar Energy and Housing Design, Vol. 2: Examples,* Architectural Association Publications, London.

Chapter 5   Passive Control

Passive solar architecture is achieved by designing to capture, store and deliver the sun's energy. In its purest sense, there are no moving parts. Therefore, this chapter starts with built form. At a conceptual stage, architects either rely on a specific brief from a known client, ideally the eventual user, or a less specific one, where the project is speculative. In this case the user may be either completely unknown, or unknown apart from a type. It is also normal for a project, whether bespoke or speculative, to be designed for a particular site. In this case, there will be known characteristics that are unlikely to change significantly, such as topography, and others that may well be changed by neighbours, such as shading by obstructions. Having said that, architects often have the scope to intervene both with the topography and shading obstructions within the curtilage of their site. In general, the bigger the site, the greater is their freedom to do this.

Therefore, the site together with the brief will have a considerable bearing on the ability to engage with the free heat of the sun in order to reduce the overall consumption of energy. This applies equally to the thermal loads for heating and cooling, as well as electrical loads for a large range of functions. In the latter case, an active–passive partnership might be for photovoltaic panels to power small appliances and mechanical equipment such as fans and pumps, while passive design directly displaces artificial lighting. In order to do this, the three-dimensional realization of a building is the primary enabler, just as it is for the deliberate acceptance or rejection of solar heat. Initially this involves an overriding strategy for the geometry of spaces, individually and together, then moving into ever increasing detail. Such detail includes fine-tuned form, as well as the thermal and other physical properties of materials. Orientation and tilt has already been discussed to some extent in the second chapter. The opportunities and constraints embedded in a strategy of integrating solar components were compared with those of one of isolation. Here the broad decisions, which are embodied in plan and section, are reintroduced in relation to the passive control they provide. The proposition is that such control may be designed to be either immune, or at least not overly sensitive, to manual interaction with users. Similarly, strategic form and dimensioning should harmonize with more sophisticated forms of active control, which may, for example, be required to control the movement of air or shading. For this reason, whilst the focus in this chapter is on static components, these inevitably may require to be placed in a context of elements that are movable, such as windows, as well as fluids, such as air and water, which may be mechanically assisted.

Plan and section

Whilst some aspects of plan and section have already been covered in earlier chapters, and much of the above introduction could apply to case studies such as the simple urban co-housing block in Freiburg or the rural housing at Hockerton, it may be refreshing to start by looking at another facet of culture. Galleries and museums represent a typology that has the capability of being much more passive in character than is generally the case. We tend to associate galleries with sophisticated air conditioning, and precedents also often dull our expectations for very much in the way of natural light. However, there was a programme funded by the European Union in the late 1990s to explore passive options, including exploitation of daylight, through case studies of museums of antiquity in several countries (Tombazis and Preuss, 1998).

light orchestration – Nordjyllands Kunstmuseum

Following this cue, an older art museum where the topography of the site is particularly relevant to sunlight and daylight is the Nordjyllands Kunstmuseum in Ålborg, Denmark, by Elissa and Alvar Aalto with Jean-Jacques Baruël. Of course, Alvar Aalto is renowned for his imaginative use of daylight, and in the only gallery of his prestigious career it would have been virtually preordained that maximization of natural daylight would be of prime importance. Won by competition in 1958, the building was not finally opened until 1972, after many years of struggling to secure finances and four years of construction. More recently, three years before Alvar Aalto's centenary in 1998, it was blessed with a preservation order.

The input of both Elissa Aalto and Jean Jacques Baruël to the project is of some conjecture. Both were much younger than Alvar, but each worked for him during a significant period. Alvar married Elissa, then a young assistant in his office, in 1952, three years after the death of his first wife. Jean Jacques Baruël worked in Aalto's office in Helsinki from 1948 to 1954. He knew and admired his architectural rationale, as did Elissa, and he stoically defended the design against dilution during a prolonged and difficult period of gestation. The Ålborg museum was also drawn up in Baruël's office in Copenhagen at much the same time as two other projects in which Aalto was not directly involved, but where his influence is evident. (One of these was a college in Sönderborg, Denmark and the other Nyköping Town hall, Sweden. Both are shown with the Ålborg museum in Architectural Review, March 1973.) After Aalto's death in 1976, both his widow and Baruël were involved in subsequent sensitive interventions to provide more storage and working space for staff on the lower floor.

The site, originally a sports ground, is a sausage shaped hollow lying to the southwest of a cemetery and separated from it by an access road. The axis of the long dimension of the hollow is northwest to southeast and the gallery, located towards the southern end of the site, adhered to this. The road is some three metres above grade, while the ground to the southeast, southwest and west is densely wooded and rises steeply. Indeed, the highest southwest edge is nearly thirty metres above the level of the base of the site and the slope is approximately 42 degrees. This means the location chosen for the building will be heavily shaded during winter and it is estimated that the entire built volume, including the highest roof, will be in shade at the time of the winter solstice.

However, this is not a building trying to exploit sunshine in winter to offset the demand for space heating. Rather it is a building that succeeds in exploiting solar energy in the form of daylight to displace electricity for artificial lighting. In appraising this aspect, it should be borne in mind that the brief specifically asked for side views out, as well as overhead daylight. This was in recognition of the natural beauty of the site, including its sunken character embraced by the steeply wooded embankments. The footprint of the gallery is compact and roughly square. On section, the gallery is elevated as a piano nobile, accessible directly from the level of the road and sitting above staff parking and services, as well as public ancillary accommodation such as a seminar room and cafeteria. The last two have an intimate relationship with the immediate external landscape, respectively a stepped amphitheatre set into the slope and a sculpture garden within the northern part of the hollow. The gallery above, as one might expect, is generally introvert in character. The exception to this is the part of the main entrance foyer that connects via a generous cascading stair to the lower level. Here a long stretch of fenestration provides a downward view over the sunken lawn. Other views out are mainly upwards. A deep-plan form was chosen, but where there is no need to have more than one level of gallery, there is naturally some emphasis on the upper parts of the structure, in particular the roof, in terms of a capacity to admit daylight.

Having steered the light inside, adopting various techniques to baffle direct sunlight from paintings, the floor, with its generous grid of pale marble adhering to all possible locations for hanging, is an essential reflective component. Photographer Hélène Binet remarks on this, (Harlang and Bak, 1999): 'The museum's interiors are opaque. Only the marble ground reflects the light in such a way that it shines. The ground thus becomes the source of a floating body of light and the viewer walks between two poles of luminescence.' Actually, her first sentence is not strictly accurate. Glass is visible from many angles in the galleries, and Binet illustrates this in several of her striking black and white photographs. Her last phrase also tends toward hyperbole since the white and

5.1 Cross section of roof monitor at Nordjyllands Kunstmuseum

light beige vertical surfaces that separate the 'two poles' are very much an integral part of the naturally lit backdrop to exhibits.

Two main techniques are used to capture daylight – vertical clerestory windows to the highest gallery, and tilted fenestration bounding raised monitors for the more general gallery space (Figure 5.1). The latter lies to the southeast of the former and is a large orthogonal space punctuated by a regular grid of columns (Figures 5.2a and b). Movable display walls may be located in a variety of ways relative to the columns. The roof over this part is the most prone to shading, and hence some loss of intensity of daylight, but the tilt of the glass in the monitors compensates for this by pointing towards the brighter part of the sky (Figures 5.2a, b). A third variant is a set of smaller bays as a continuation of the main space along the southwest edge. These are naturally lit at the rear, by engaging with the first of a stepped cascade of clerestory windows to the high gallery (Figure 5.2c). They also have generous windows facing the steeply wooded slope, part vertical and part tilted. Although the topography and trees shade the building in the depths of winter, it was a challenge to devise ways of excluding direct sunlight at other times. Of course one might well question the basic idea of full transparency in the first instance. Alternatives might have been to use translucent glazing or some other diffusing membrane. But that was the architectural position adopted in response to the brief, and it is not as perverse as it might seem.

The alignment of the building means that all the main surfaces can receive sunlight at some time of the day for a significant part of the year. On the other hand, it was inevitable that the built geometry should respond to the axiom that sunshine will enter northeast and northwest glazing at much lower angles than those facing southeast and southwest. The basic idea of the raised monitors was to reflect direct sunlight from concave scoops suspended within their volume. The orientational divide meant that the northerly surfaces of glass could be larger than the southerly ones. This was simply achieved by tilting the copper-clad roof of each monitor by 20 degrees from the horizontal. Since the glazing is almost 70 degrees, this means that the opaque roof is nearly at right angles to the high clerestory and at an obtuse angle of some 120 degrees to the low one. Even if other angles could satisfy the lighting criterion, the resultant asymmetry contributes satisfyingly to the aesthetic dynamic (Figure 5.1). A visitor may not, and does not need to, interpret the clues as to the functionality of the geometry, where the dichotomy of orientation is not immediately obvious. However, if the logic is followed, it is evident that it is not necessary to align all the monitors in the same direction. One alignment can have the high side facing northeast, while on another it can face northwest. In fact, five relatively long monitors adopt the former orientation, and three shorter ones the latter. On touring the gallery, the shift of axis heightens the architectural experience. It marks arrival at the southwestern edge and a change of direction, which is in tune with the smaller bays as one moves on clockwise (Figures 5.2a to c).

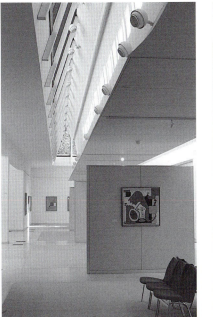  

All monitors are rectilinear on plan and glazed on either three or all four surfaces. This means that if the high glazing is to the northeast, there are short trapezoidal ends facing southeast and northwest. Consequently, the scoops on the sunnier ends have more to cope with in terms of blocking out the sun, and all eight monitors are glazed on their sunny ends. Given the fact that all the glazing is clear, the scoops become paramount as baffles and reflectors. However, being able to glimpse trees and sky as one moves through the gallery is tremendously uplifting, as are the shadows cast by sunlight on to the curved surface of the scoops. The combination of the window frames and spherical artificial lights are the enliveners in this regard (Figure 5.3a). Here, as in many of Aalto's buildings, the lights are placed in such a way as to exploit reflective surfaces, thus mimicking natural light.

Visiting the building during the afternoon of a sunny summer solstice may well have been one of the most severe tests for the monitors and their light scoops, especially at their southern ends where the three concave surfaces intersect. Certainly flashes of sunlight were able to bypass the baffle and directly illuminate walls, as well as floors (Figure 5.3b). In terms of curatorship, one can only assume that this happens relatively infrequently, or to such a slight extent, that it is not considered problematic. The question is whether or not the architects would have known this in advance. Whilst there was no computer software to visualize solar penetration at the time of design or construction, apparatus known as a 'heliodon' was available for physical modelling. Some of the original design sections suggest quite a detailed exploration of solar

5.2 Nordjyllands Kunstmuseum
a gallery approaching from entrance and looking southeast with direction of monitors
b still looking southeast, with monitors at right angles to southwest edge to right
c turning round to northwest: small galleries to left of corridor, which forms the first of a series of steps in the roof form, with high gallery on the far side of the wall on right

5.3 Nordjyllands Kunstmuseum
a shadows of light fittings enliven light-
scoops
b sunlight edits floor and display surfaces on
summer solstice

geometry, but only an accurate three dimensional construct used with a 'heliodon' could have dealt with the level of complexity involved in the interplay between opaque curved surfaces, glazed openings and a moving sun.

The conjunction of design intent and function becomes intriguing here. Had the architects not wished the scoops to appear as suspended islands or peninsulas in a sea of glass, solid ends could have dealt with solar baffling more effectively. Each of the four peninsulas have one solid end, but these face northwest and are close to the first major step-up in a series of five main horizontal roof planes, a plinth from which the high gallery ascends a further three steps. (The corridor in Figure 5.2c forms the southwest edge of this plinth.) But the added aesthetic value of the scoops as inverted islands and peninsulas is undeniable. It almost seems as if they are held up by 'sky hooks'... until one rationalizes! The loads from the roofs of the monitors and their hanging scoops are transferred via slim steel struts, which are lined up with glazing mullions and seem to slide past cantilevered trays of the main concrete roof. One could argue that this is an explicit structure. But in reality, comprehension of the gymnastics takes time and thought. This is a game played to the hilt by very talented players.

Having established a language of curves to tackle the reflection and diffusion of sunlight into the main part of the gallery, this is elaborated by means of a subtle mix of convex, concave and flat surfaces in the more specialized spaces. The high gallery is the spatial crescendo of the building. Its dramatically stepped section (Figure 2.1c, p25) faces southwest and incorporates a series of light shelves, scoops and louvres, the last external. Deep concrete beams provide a further barrier for oblique sunlight. But again it is possible for occasional shafts of sunlight to circumvent the defences, punctuating both floor and walls, and of course any work of art in their path.

Other spaces, such as the small bays behind the southwest wall of the high gallery, have to take more direct action against sunshine in summer. They have internal solar blinds. Even so, a narrow strip of sunlight is able to sneak past and edit paintings, even if ephemerally, on one wall at right angles to the window. However, in spite of any reservations that a curator might have in this regard, the strategy for natural lighting as a displacer of fossil-fuel energy appears to be entirely effective. On that bright afternoon, only a few lights were switched on, and hardly any of these were in the galleries themselves. This may be counted as a considerable success. In many other buildings, where the architects have designed for such displacement, the use in reality is very different.

There is one environmental downside, which is relevant to the passive characteristics of the design, but also relates to the active system for ventilation. As mentioned, the afternoon of that summer solstice was sunny. But it was also quite windy, and the wind, influenced no doubt by the proximity of Ålborg to the sea, was distinctly cold. Therefore, it would have been reasonable to expect that the thermal cooling load for the mechanically supplied air would not have been very intense. However, the subjective perception during a gentle walk through the building, particularly in the lower general gallery space, was of overheating. It was definitely too warm and stuffy.

Two aspects of the design are significant. The first is that the scoops are inherently lightweight. The design idea described above has made this inevitable. They are also clad in an acoustically absorbent ribbed timber lining. Although light in colour, resulting in a fairly high reflection of incoming short-wave radiation, this will still heat up significantly when drenched in sunlight. Subsequent convective and radiant exchanges will result in a layer of warm air near the ceiling. Unless dissipated quite rapidly, it will tend to stratify downwards into the zone occupied by visitors. This is what seems to be happening. Air is delivered through grilles set in the marble flooring, thereafter exiting through slots or grilles located at high level in walls. But these are few and far between, and the only other means of exhaust is by natural leakage through high-level fenestration. From an aesthetic viewpoint, this has been discreetly handled. Some of the walls are hollow, allowing air to return to the plant-room via the network of ducts below the primary floor slab. The problem is simply the scarcity of the exhausts relative to the large floor area. The other apparent potential solution might have been to make use of the generous space within the scoops. But this has been obviated by the concept of the inverted islands and peninsulas.

So we have a building where the passive and active systems are not in complete harmony when it comes to heating and ventilation, but where a deceptively simple strategy for natural lighting appears to have been exceptionally meritorious. Although this was recognized by a commentator shortly after completion, it was also not without serious critique (Brawne, 1973). Michael Brawne refers to the merits of the central high gallery with its 'series of beams and curved terracing, longitudinal shields controlling and diffusing daylight.' The accolade is in the sentence that follows: 'None of these elements, however, eliminates the essential and undefinable quality of daylight; its reality is not destroyed by having to pass through controlling layers: it is only deflected, not filtered.' Later, however, he complains that the architecture, particularly the height, overwhelms the function of this particular space to house temporary exhibitions. He asserts: 'Not even the monumental and vibrant canvases of Rothko could come into their own in such a setting.' He has similar detailed criticism of the general gallery space, alluding to the difficulty that the tartan grid of marble slabs and carpet squares sets up when locating sculptures relative to paintings. He thought that sculpture belonged on the marble, which placed it too close to the movable walls. Thus there is an acceptance of the architectural strength in terms of admitting daylight, but also weakness relative to the briefing requirements: 'What is therefore worrying at Ålborg is to see a level of architectural ingenuity which has few recent parallels but which is not at the same time linked to a conceptual understanding of the inherent problems of the building type.'

light and air – Kuntsbygning in Århus

There is at least one other recent example of a Danish gallery that provides a skilfully muted architectural response to issues of flexibility for visiting exhibitions, while at the same time it cleverly exploits both daylight and natural ventilation, despite constraints. This is the modern art gallery in Århus by architect Mads Møller, also mentioned briefly in the second chapter.

The starting point is particularly relevant. The original gallery, opened in 1917, was small. Vernacular in character, its three main spaces are top-lit and exploit the whole volume enclosed by pitched roofs. What is surprising is that there is no apparent system of either mechanical or natural ventilation. Air appears to enter and exit by fortuitous leakage through fixed skylights, combined with the opening and closing of external doors. The volume of air is also considerable relative to the normal number of visitors to such a gallery, and there is plenty of height to enable beneficial stratification of the warmer air above the occupied zone. Heating pipes, ranged around the splayed surfaces at the base of the pyramids, provide some downward radiant warmth as well as preventing downdraughts from the glass in winter. It would seem that such simplicity was inspirational to Møller.

The main architectural feature of his first extension in 1993 is a long curved wall. Concave to the interior, it effectively blocks out direct sunlight into the new space during the warmest part of the day. At its eastern extremity the wall faces almost due south, while at the other it has curved by about 90 degrees to face west. The wall also continues beyond the ends of the new extension, thus enabling full-height windows that are substantially shaded. The new roof stops short of the wall, allowing a narrow strip of natural light to wash its internal surface. However, at the time of a visit, spotlights shining on to the same surface compromised this effect (Figure 5.4). Finally, additional natural light is provided by a series of three glazed pyramids. Each of these has a horizontal translucent laylight flush with the ceiling. Again, there is no apparent mechanical ventilation, other than a simple extract from a small cafeteria. Although the ceiling is flat and significantly lower than in the original gallery, the extension is open to it. Thus excess heat, which is not caught by the fan, will tend to migrate to the older and higher spaces, while fresh air can enter through the new glazed screens. Indeed, it would appear that a glazed door closest to the serving bar is regularly opened in fine weather so that visitors can consume their fare outside on a sheltered patio.

The next extension, opened in June 2003, posed a more difficult challenge in terms of adherence to natural light and ventilation. The need was significantly to expand the area available for exhibition, without losing the gallery's status as a pavilion set in a relatively constrained, landscaped urban plot. Møller's answer

5.4   Kunstbygning in Århus. Curving
southwesterly wall of 1993 extension –
artificial and natural lighting compete

was to extend down into the ground to the rear of the first extension. The roof of this new space would then be the floor of a new sculpture court. To contain this at the southwest boundary, a linear glazed lantern has been wrapped round the retaining wall, which rises some 2.5m above the level of the sculpture court. A short strip of clerestory glazing sits on top of the wall, and then kicks out by about 2m as a glass roof before descending as a fully glazed screen to the floor of the court. The ensemble, with some help from reflective appliqué material, plunges natural light down the length of this major new display surface and on to the lower floor. Viewed from the level of the court, the blend of transparency, reflectance and opacity provides scintillating ambiguity in terms of enclosure. On descending into the gallery, one is by contrast very aware of the solidity of the bounding walls, their edges forming a deep tray that holds back many tonnes of ground. The wall, which one naturally turns to face at the foot of the stairs, is the one below the linear lantern and its additional luminosity is evident. Of course its source of light is not explicitly revealed until one is close up to works of art displayed on it, and by then the soaring height of the slot above provides a further spatial accent (Figures 5.5a and b).

Possibly influenced by the earlier precedent at Ålborg, Møller has also chosen to use clear glass. Therefore, in terms of curatorship, the issue of direct sunlight must be addressed as well as reflected daylight. Apart from a relatively short time during the morning, when sunlight can illuminate the inside upper part of the rear wall, and very briefly a slot at its base, the structure itself protects the new gallery. However, the long linear light box is one component of a triad. To gain access from the 1993 extension, the curved wall has been pierced. One passes through this into another lantern enclosing the stairs on its convex southwest edge. Although the amount of daylight that passes down through this is relatively restricted, it does receive sunlight. A final glass-sided cube, an off-centre island in the court, sheds daylight between the other two sources. This can also admit sunlight, depending on time of year and day. However, the stair-wall is not used for display, while solar blinds are provided on the two sunny surfaces of the cuboid lantern. Thus the issue of solar heat gain and glare has been dealt with very simply, while daylight does displace a significant amount of artificial lighting... just not so comprehensively as at Ålborg. Additional roof lighting could have been provided, but one has to bear in mind that, unlike Ålborg, visitors have a direct relationship with the lanterns at what is still the natural ground level. To have increased their frequency would have compromised a restrained aesthetic dialogue, and the effectiveness of the court as a singular outdoor room. The architectural response to this dilemma was to provide large square diffusers below arrays of luminaires, which match the laylights of the first extension. The quality of the light coming from these in daytime is of course different from that upstairs, but they are not seen side by side, and the aesthetic reference is valuable.

Compared with Ålborg, the other major difference is that the lanterns provide air as well as light. Given the liberal dimensions of the sunken gallery, this tactic appears surprisingly serendipitous. All three have opening lights, but it does not necessarily follow that an adequate supply will enter and leave, and, more importantly, disperse evenly over the area of the floor. However, although it was admitted that the gallery had overheated during its formal opening, it seems to work well under normal circumstances. In fact, the perception was

5.5 Kuntsbygning in Århus
a   looking southwest from foot of stairs into 2003 extension below sculpture court
b   looking up into glazed lantern above southwest display wall of 2003 extension

5.6   Kunsthaus in Bregenz
a   detail of glass rain-screen at external corner
       on sunny day
b   looking down staircase, with indirect
       daylight through ceiling on sunny day

rather better than for the mechanical system at Ålborg. The fluid dynamics on any given day would be sensitive to wind direction and strength, as well as solar intensity. One could easily imagine a southwest stream of air entering at high level along the long lantern, descending to the floor, since it would be fairly cool, and then leaving by the other lanterns as it heated and became less dense. The thermal mass of the wall behind the stairs would help in such a scenario, especially if warmed by the sun. The means of heating is not for the most part evident and it is probably safe to assume that low temperature coils play a part. Following the precedent of the original building, there are other slim heat emitters visible at the base of the lanterns. Again, these will tackle downdraughts from the glass in cold weather.

relevance of latitude to designing for daylight

What singles out these two Danish case studies within the geographical scope of this book is the fact that clear glass is deliberately used as a passive solar mechanism to displace electricity. Therefore, their particular latitude is relevant to the size, orientation and tilt of fenestration and techniques adopted to intercept direct sunlight. There are several other galleries of note that also exploit daylight imaginatively, but without such direct relevance to latitude and orientation. The use of diffuse glazing is common to all of these, but their overall architectural concept and expression is remarkably varied.

For example, in Barcelona, Spain, well outside the climatic territory of interest here, there is the gallery devoted to the work of Joan Miró. The first phase by Josep Lluis Sert was opened in 1975, and the prominent rooftop light catchers, which face northeast, southeast, southwest and northwest, accentuate the chunky concrete architectural rhetoric of the period. Then, more than six degrees further north at 47.5°N and more than 20 years later, we have Peter Zumthor's ethereal glass tower in Bregenz, Austria, with similar orientations for its four identically dimensioned façades (Figure 5.6a). In this building, the light, which is initially diffused through the vertical surfaces into generous horizontal voids below respective floor slabs, is delivered through diffuse glass ceilings to each gallery. The exception to this is when exhibiting artists, such as Gilbert and George, insist on exclusively lighting the gallery artificially. Then blinds descend and the subtly varying natural luminance and raison d'être of Zumthor's concept is sabotaged, apart from above the staircases (Figure 5.6b). The similarly demure glass-clad gallery by Gigon and Guyer in Davos, Switzerland, not far south of Bregenz, employs very much the same technique (Figure 5.7). This is not, however, a multi-storey gallery, and it does raise the question as to why light should be bent through 90 degrees when roof glazing would have been possible. To the west of Bregenz, back in Switzerland in the northern suburbs of Basel, this is exactly the approach used by the Renzo Piano Building Workshop for the Fondation Beyeler. Here a multi-layer diffusing roof in conjunction with some shaded full-height windows creates an enormously pleasurable and appropriately atmospheric environment through the use of natural light. In aesthetic and tectonic terms, features such as the tilted arrays of absorbing glass embellish the horizontal presence of the building (Figure 5.8a). Indeed, viewed across fields from the west, the gallery is reminiscent of a prairie house by Frank Lloyd Wright (Figure 5.8b).

Such examples reinforce the point that some solar techniques are equally valid for widely varying locations, while others require specific fine tuning. The use of clear glass at Ålborg and Århus implies the latter. However, the use of diffuse glass in the other four examples does not necessarily provide a climatically transferable formula for overall energy efficiency. There is the gain and loss of heat to consider as well as daylight. For example, one would expect the spacing and tilt of fixed devices used to limit the transfer of solar heat in Basel to be optimized relative to 47.5°N. Even so, there may still be a substantial cooling load in summer, which can only be addressed by use of air-conditioning. Such a load would increase, the hotter the climate, while the frequency and tilt of the devices would have to alter. The extensive use of concrete and limited area of glazing by Sert in Barcelona, compared with the galleries in Bregenz, Davos and Basel, also suggests a logic that relates to respective Mediterranean and mid-European climates. So too does the dispersed plan of the former, with its greater self-shading and greater surface area for heat to dissipate. Compare this with the compactness of the latter three, which aligns well with the higher levels of insulation.

daylight and air for utilitarian use – sport, production and transport

Devoting space to a particular end use, inevitably brings up the issue of transferability of concepts and techniques to other building functions. For

5.7   Inside the lighting void over gallery at Davos

5.8   Fondation Beyeler, Basel
a   detail at edge of glass roof – note tilted
       absorbing glass sheets
b   general view from west

5.9 Sports 'factory' – schematic section showing system for natural light and ventilation
Architects: David Morley Architects
Project: National Cricket Academy, Loughborough University

diffuse sky

air out

air in

0   10m

KEY: CROSS-SECTION

1	tension net	3	rooflight	5	steel portal truss	7	lights
2	roof blinds	4	metal roof panels	6	roof net	8	umpire's gallery

5.10 'Showroom' for PV factory in Freiburg – louvres functionally advertise the product

example, the provision of natural lighting and ventilation through roofs over a series of sports buildings in the UK by architect David Morley is on a similar exploratory and developmental path to that of the gallery in Basel (Figure 5.9). However, the differences are just as significant. These buildings by Morley are all essentially large sheds, which have to observe strict economic constraints in comparison with a gallery. They are sports factories rather than cultural beacons. Within their respective architectural territories, however, similar levels of architectural ingenuity are discernable, and investing in visual prestige is now more common in the industrial sector than formerly. The solar photovoltaic factory in Freiburg by architects Rolf + Hotz is an example of this (Figure 5.10). It advertises its products by using them functionally and evocatively as fixed louvres clipped to a tilted south façade. The spacing and tilt of the louvres is such that a significant amount of direct and reflected solar energy is transmitted in winter, while shading is maximized in summer. The effectiveness on a hot day in late June has been described elsewhere (Porteous, 2002, p158), with a drop in temperature from outside to inside of some 10K.

Buildings for all forms of public transport are quite analogous to factories, except in this instance the assembly line is moving people and their baggage through the system. In recent times more attention is being paid to the quality of that process, and although we have been accustomed to bus terminals being the poor cousin of railway stations and airports, this is no longer the case. The one completed in 1996 in Göteborg, Nils Ericsson, designed by architect Niels Torp, is a case in point (Cerver, 2000). It is a structurally economic building, essentially a large shed, but one where the quality of the environment is akin to that of a botanical greenhouse (Figure 5.11a). Torp has used the cross section to good effect in terms of maximizing daylight and ventilation, while avoiding excessive solar heat gain. A clever asymmetric section uses two sets of propped trusses. One set is oriented slightly south of due west and therefore has to deal with considerable solar gain during the warmest part of the day. It also covers the main part of the concourse. The stepped section of the glazing provides the means of integral shading canopies as well as generous natural ventilation (Figure 5.11b). On the other side, facing somewhat north of east, a faceted cascade of glass sits over the curvature of the top booms of the trusses. Small retail units are located at intervals along this side. Much of the solar radiation that passes through the glass in the morning is absorbed by the roofs of the retail units, while later in the day as the ambient temperature rises, the geometry of the section ensures that most of the direct radiation is reflected.

daylight and air for educational buildings

Publicly owned educational buildings also tend to have quite stringent budgets, as well as being required to convey status. The library by the vibrant Dutch architectural practice of Mecanoo for Delft Technical University is an example where a quirky form has a thermal rationale, while at the same time it does not compete with an earlier lecture theatre by the respected partnership of Van den Broek and Bakema. In other words, it respects both its climatic and architectural context. But avoiding confrontation with an earlier presence does not mean that it dumbs down. Essentially, a rhomboid on plan is tilted up from the green sward

5.11 Bus station at Göteborg
a   inside concourse looking north-north-west
     – note asymmetric cross section
b   west-south-west façade, with stepped
     cascade of windows in open position

5.12   The cone sheds daylight deep into the
library at Delft Technical University

to the east of the theatre and is gently fractured by a depressed wedge, which
is the entrance. Additionally, a truncated cone dramatically punctures the raised
lawn. It allows daylight deep into the centre of the new building and
accommodates four reading levels above the main entry concourse (Figure
5.12). The point of the cone is visually completed as a playful frame of struts and
tension cables. Thus viewed from the earlier building, the cone appears as a
large sculptural element in the verdant parkland of the campus, while the main
mass of the rhomboid is largely suffused as landscape. The tilted turf roof
effectively denies a west elevation, otherwise vulnerable to overheating.
Substantial edges become visible as one moves round the building, clockwise
or anti-clockwise, but by then the relationship to the older theatre is not so vital.
The distortion of the north, east and south walls of the library from the vertical
plane is also surprisingly functional. To east and south the tilt is outwards to
protect smaller working spaces from excessive solar heat gain, while to the
north, the fully glazed façade tilts back to maximize daylight to a large computer
hall. Like the factory in Freiburg, other detailed environmental aspects of the
library have previously been fleshed out (Porteous, 2002, pp186–188), the focus
here directed to the passive strengths of plan and section.

Returning to Scotland, a new adult learning centre by architect Richard
Murphy in Kirkintilloch, has a section that follows the rationalist approach of a
linear extrusion. Its straightforward spatial quality evokes the directness of the
factory in Freiburg, as opposed to Mecanoo's oblique and rather hedonistic
expression of a building in the round. The linearity was a simple response to the
site, a relatively narrow strip of ground between an unassuming road and the
Forth and Clyde Canal, recently restored and providing a seductive green link
between Scotland's two main cities. Attention was therefore directed to the
canal, lying to the north of the road and well below it in level. The building is
entered from the east towards a centrally located circulation spine, which
initially heads west. Individual classrooms lie to the south of this route adjacent
to the road, while a slight fall in level defines the main computing concourse
facing the canal. At the west end, a dogleg stair allows the circulation spine to
return to an equivalent first floor position as a gallery. Accessing a second
south-facing tier of classrooms, this overlooks students working at computer
clusters, each of which is marked by a triangular oriel window cantilevered
towards the canal. A second staircase at the east end then provides a link back
to the entrance.

Along the line of the wall between the circulation spine and the classrooms
is a continuous strip of opening windows. The roof projects over this to provide
protection from direct sunlight for much of the year while the low angle sunlight
of winter is reflected off the ceiling that slopes down to the north and terminates
over another band of clerestory glazing above the oriels (Figure 5.13). Although
there is a considerably greater proportion of glass along the northern edge than
the high southern clerestory, the canal is lined with mature trees. Thus the

southern edge has greater potency in terms of daylight than one might imagine, and the combination is successful in rendering artificial lighting unnecessary in this prime space during bright weather. There are two sources of electric light, and both of them exploit the sloping ceiling as a reflector. The first is a series of halogen up-lighters mounted below the upper gallery. The second is a series of fluorescent luminaires. These are hidden in a trough that forms a pelmet to the oriel windows and the sill of the northern clerestory.

However, harping back to the issue of adaptive control, the lighting is not automated. A receptionist is in charge of the switches. During two separate visits, one in summer and one in spring and both on sunny days, she had put the strip of luminaires on. Although she agreed that the daylight was perfectly adequate without them, she appeared to like their added artificial ambience. She also operated the actuators for opening the high-level clerestory, while cost cutting had apparently removed this facility for the lower one. The section implied the potential for cool, moist air to enter from the north, descend until heated by people and computers, and then rise by natural buoyancy and exit at high level to the south. Alternatively, with a strong southerly wind, reverse cross-ventilation would be possible. To a degree, these scenarios were compromised. Opening along the south edge was in the hands of the receptionist, the lower clerestory was effectively limited to its natural lighting function, and opening the oriel windows was in the hands of the users. Moreover, the receptionist was in the line of fire from cold draughts as visitors operated a wide automatic sliding entrance door. Hence she was relatively disinclined to open the upper windows in sunny, but cool, weather.

5.13 Learning Centre, Kirkintilloch – cross section maximises opportunity for natural light

Despite these factors, which were not insuperable, the plan and section conforms to a strong environmental agenda. A final passive attribute is that the slope of the site allowed the heating plant to be located below the computing concourse. Much of the heat lost from the plant in winter is gained by this primary, north-facing space. Together with the incidental gains and insulated outer shell, it should have a very modest demand for auxiliary heating, while the rooms on the south side have greater potential for useful passive solar heat gain. Overall this building supports the claim that, if well designed, the passive attributes of plan and section can fulfil their intended role despite some idiosyncratic control. Within the concourse, the part most vulnerable to overheating due to lack of open windows is the upper access gallery. This is not too critical for a circulation route. The low, north-facing sedentary area should remain adequately cool under such circumstances, and if it does start to overheat, students have openable windows to hand. They can compensate to an extent for any failings of management.

If the building had been organized and shaped less optimally, an active system of energy-conscious control could have struggled to work efficiently. On the other hand, it is inherently threatening to performance if designers grow too complacent in terms of their expectations for plan and section, especially the latter. For example, expectations for thermal buoyancy or 'stack effect' are frequently unrealistic. Schematic arrows on published sections suggest that air will move in a certain way, when there is very little difference in height between openings, and there may be very little difference in temperature between two bodies of air.

A building of a similar size to the Scottish learning centre, but with an explicitly ecological and solar agenda, and a section that appears to rationally assist in this purpose, is that of De Kleine Aarde (The Little Earth), an environmental research and demonstration centre in Boxtel, near Eindhoven in the Netherlands. Designed by Tjerk Reijenga of BEAR Architecten, a single-glazed rectilinear atrium separates a relatively slim two-storey block from a deeper single-storey wedge on plan. The latter houses cafeteria, kitchen and ancillary spaces, while the former has a series of rooms for work and education below overnight accommodation for visitors. The rooms and the mono-pitch roof over the two-storey part face north. The orientation suits offices, which tend to overheat through use of computers, while recesses on plan allow some east and west sunlight into bedrooms above. In juxtaposition, the glazed roof of the atrium has a gentle pitch to the south where it meets the flat roof (Figure 5.14). This in turn overhangs the southerly glazed façade of the cafeteria, allowing it to receive sunshine in winter, while being shaded in summer. The atrium provides a thermal buffer and source of fresh air to both heated parts of the building in winter. It is a quasi-outdoor space, which is solar enhanced and sheltered from bitter Dutch winds. The logic of the design suggests that natural

5.14 De Kleine Aarde, Boxtel – inside the atrium with all south and north windows open

ventilation should occur primarily from south to north. Fresh oxygenated and moistened air can enter via a clerestory ribbon of windows above the flat sedum roof of the single-storey block and exit via a second strip at the top of the glazed mono-pitch. In addition, the glass roof incorporates photovoltaic cells, at the time of building in 1995, the largest building-integrated array in the Netherlands. Its important secondary function for the atrium is to provide dappled shading in warm, sunny weather.

All this seems very plausible. However, one has to keep in mind that the cross section of the atrium is such that its respective banks of opening windows rely heavily on wind, rather than thermal buoyancy. When the direction is southerly, cool air should indeed enter through the vertical clerestory on the south edge, and descend to the floor down this side of the atrium before rising on the northern side to exit. Any solar absorption by the north wall of the atrium will enhance this mode of circulation. If the wind is from the north, it should provide quite strong negative pressure at the high part of the glazed roof, and so the circulation should still work from south to north. If the wind is from the east or west, the circulation of air within the atrium may be different, but one would not expect it to be stagnant. The only potential problem is that on a hot and still day there is not enough height between respective opening sets of windows to induce convection.

This was the situation at the time of a visit on 12th August 2003. That day marked the zenith of a heat wave, with the temperature outside reaching at least 36°C. Inside the atrium, in the shade at floor level, the reading on a maximum-minimum thermometer reached 48°C in the course of that afternoon. A potential solution to such an extreme situation would have been to specify opening windows at the foot of the two glazed gable ends. Although there were double doors in each of these locations, and they could have been wedged open, this was not policy. They were the type of doors that invite being closed. It was also not policy to leave the high-level sets of windows to the atrium open at night in case rain came into the atrium. This in turn raises questions about attitudes to what are intended as protected outdoor spaces, rather than normal indoor ones. The other issue here was that a timber superstructure was specified as a conscious environmental choice. Thus, although the south-facing wall inside the atrium will provide a welcome rapid response to passive solar gain in winter, it will also contribute to overheating on a hot day in summer. The floor constitutes the only significant thermal capacitance capable of damping down swings in temperature.

There are two points to make here. Firstly, it is seldom possible to optimize all aspects of thermal performance through plan and section, and in this case the overheating did not critically affect the operation of the building. Indeed, in spite of the temperature in the atrium in what was an acute test, the rooms facing north remained acceptably cool. However, the second point to make is that design could have improved the situation. Low-level windows in the gables would have helped natural thermo-circulation. This might have made the atrium slightly more tolerable on this unusually hot and windless day. The other seasonal expectation, to enhance passive gain in winter, would have been more difficult to address. The low pitch of 15 degrees or so is not ideal for maximizing transmission of direct gain, which in this case is further inhibited by the presence of solar cells. But if the pitch had been raised, there would have been all sorts of serious architectural implications. As it was, it had an easy visual relationship between the two-storey building and the single-storey one.

sectional consequences of stack-dominated ventilation

Buildings which have made a greater effort to provide effective stack-controlled natural ventilation, invariably have more striking or strident sections. Thurfjell's 'shark's fin' tower (Figure 5.15a) exhausts air from the Wasa City atrium in Gävle, Sweden. In this case, in common with many such spaces in Scandinavia, the atrium is not completely fortuitously heated. It is connected to a district heating system, and warm coils in the floors provide background heating in winter. The aim is to heat it to 18°C during working hours and 10°C out of working hours. Also, according to predictions (Glaumann, 1989), the promenade level should not rise more than 8°C above the outside temperature. The venting of warm air becomes critical in summer, and hence the 'shark's fin', which punctuates the more traditional geometry and has 30m^2 of vertical north-facing opening windows, varying from 23–28m from the lowest floor level. There are also sliding shutters on top of the main part of the glass roof to the atrium, their highest point being about 18m above the floor. In winter, when these are closed, air from the atrium passes through air-to-air heat exchangers located on the flat roofs of the flats. These supply air to the shops at the base, which in turn circulate it back into the atrium. Accepting the need for this active assistance in winter, it is the section in particular that allows the building to passively play the dominant part in handling air movement.

The venting tower for the atrium of the Eco-Centre in Jarrow, near Newcastle in the northeast of England, designed by architect Carole Townsend of Earth Sense, is another example where there is a large differential in height between inlets and outlet (Figure 5.15b). This compact building, triangular on plan, was built to a tight budget, but did not compromise its objectives by economizing on height. In this case, the ventilation is designed as a once-through natural system at all times. Air enters offices via trickle vents or open windows, and is drawn across into the central atrium principally by thermal buoyancy. Wind will also play a part, particularly if the opening vents at the top of the tower are subject to negative pressure.

Another seminal building in the UK, Queens Building at Leicester's De Montfort University, is fully naturally ventilated and daylight optimized (Twidell and Howe, 1994). Designed by architects Short Ford and Associates together with Max Fordham as environmental consultant from 1989 into the early 1990s,

5.15a Looking up 'shark's fin' tower of atrium at Wasa City at Gävle
5.15b Looking up triangular tower of atrium at the Eco-Centre in Jarrow

it is a testament to relatively simple physical and computational modelling. ■5.1 Whilst the rich neo-Gothic flavour of the architectural detailing might not be to everyone's taste, stripped back to the essentials of plan and section, it is spatially impressive (Figure 5.16). It is also equally effective as a boldly pioneering experiment in natural ventilation, executed at a time when mechanical solutions were more in the ascendancy than they are now.

Some architects are undoubtedly more reluctant to engage with the visual consequences of natural ventilation to the extent that is the case in the last three examples. The verticality or simply the bulk and height of devices to exhaust air may run counter to their fundamental aesthetic concepts. If this is the case, and the intention is to exploit natural ventilation as far as reasonably possible, it usually means that there is greater reliance on wind-driven convection… as at Boxtel. Over and above the spatiality of plan and section, the other passive environmental controller is that of thermal mass. Commonly, there is not enough to damp down excessive swings in temperature. At De Kleine Aarde, the green agenda of minimizing energy for production and carbon neutrality took priority over thermal capacitance. It was not that the issue was ignored. However, for at least some architects, the rudimentary science of dynamic thermal behaviour remains mysterious, with the consequence that it tends to be prone to myths and misunderstandings.

Thermal mass dilemmas

Getting to grips with the basics of thermal time lag, damping, capacitance, admittance and response is in reality not too formidable. The first two terms are

■5.1 Predictive methods used for Queens Building in Leicester

Sophisticated 'computational fluid dynamics' (CFD) is now commonly used in advanced convective performance analysis. In this case the computer model ECADAP (Environmental Computer Aided Design and Performance) and the physical model in a saline solution both ignored the effects of wind. The assumption was presumably that if the system worked solely by thermal buoyancy on a calm day, and provided dampers were incorporated to control excessive ventilation due to wind pressure, the tests were adequate. A good match was obtained comparing the two methods. In addition, a dynamic thermal simulation model, ESP (Environmental Systems Performance), was used to predict hourly temperatures in the auditoria. Results indicated only nine hours annually with the temperature exceeding 27°C, and none during the academic period.

■5.2 Open and closed systems for ducting air

5.2(1) An open system is normal for mechanically ventilating and heating/cooling buildings. Rooms become part of the network for circulating and often re-circulating air, but traditional modern metal ducting does not contribute to the passive storage capability of a building.

5.2(2) Closed loops, if embedded in the solid parts of a building, can help to reduce both heating and cooling loads, but are unconnected to the ventilation needs. A body of air simply goes round and round a connecting system of cavities, although it will need some topping up to compensate for leakage. One of the first closed loops to be integrated with passive solar heating accommodated air heated by a furnace. This was the hollow system of 'radian' tiles devised by architect George Keck towards the end of the 2nd World War (Boyce, 1993). We are now also used to closed loops being used to circulate air that has been preheated by the sun. Keck's hollow floor was an updated hypocaust, except, unlike the Roman version, the air did not contain the products of combustion and it returned back to the plant room to be reheated. The duct-tiles were also the main passive solar absorber, and they were an attempt to make auxiliary heating more responsive to solar gain. The supply of warm air could be rapidly turned off, so that the tiles would soon be able to accept the solar gain, but without this being displaced by the purchased fuel. The storage capability would be less than that of a solid slab, but in areas with a relatively small winter supply of sunshine, this would be advantageous. The innovation was also contemporaneous with the 'solar hemi-cycle' designed by Frank Lloyd Wright for Herbert Jacobs and his family. Its closed loop of warm water gave rise to the problem of solar displacement (Chapter 1). It is intrinsically less responsive to solar gain than Keck's solution.

relevant to the entire external envelope from outside to inside, and also connected to the third, as well as to the thermal properties of conductivity and density. The last two are concerned more specifically with exposed parts of the inner linings. However, if air ducts, either for the delivery of air into occupied spaces ■5.2(1) or closed loops, ■5.2(2) are embedded within solid parts of a

5.16   Bridges in the multi-level circulation spine of Queens Building enliven spatial drama

structure, the lining material of such voids also becomes relevant. Indeed, it can add significantly to the admittance and short-term thermal storage capability or capacitance of a building, as can increasing the area of surface in contact with the interior – for example, by coffering or corrugating a concrete ceiling. By moderating temperatures, such tactics reduce the amount of energy required to heat or cool the supply of air. Ultimately, the critical aspect of capacitance (along with conductivity and density) relative to these other four thermal definers of time lag, damping, admittance and response, is its location.

If the focus is specifically on admittance, which may be loosely defined as the ability to store and release heat to a bounding space, the performance is compositely influenced by the location, area and properties of the surface and a limited thickness of material behind. One may think of admittance as a dynamic thermal transmittance or U-value that is concerned with a relevant lining of the construction. Therefore it is conductivity that is fundamental, but of course this also relates to density. Dense materials have a slow response due to fairly high conductivity, capacitance and admittance. Less dense materials have a lower conductivity, capacitance and admittance, and so a faster response. Therefore, high admittance moderates both cooling and heating loads, and a great deal of thickness is not necessary to achieve this. This point was forcibly made at the 'Cool Space' Conference held at the RIBA (Royal Institute of British Architects) in London early in 2001 (Williams, 2001). However, Williams did not emphasize the crucial role that thermal mass plays with regard to time lag and damping, that is its intervention between the environment outside and the one inside.

Unlike admittance, which is only concerned with a few centimetres next to occupied spaces, or air-transport ducts contained within the structure, the entire thickness of the envelope is then of significance, as well as its thermal properties. A 60cm brick wall will behave differently from one that is only 20cm thick, just as it will behave differently from one of stone, which is also 60cm thick. The overall thermal performance of relatively thick masonry walls may be quite acceptable in terms of energy efficiency, even though U-values are high, relative to modern standards. This will of course depend on both the programmatic and climatic context, but it means that thermal mass and dynamic behaviour cannot be ignored.

For the mathematically minded there are of course SI (Standard International) units associated with thermal capacitance – rather too many, one might be forgiven for thinking! But the concept is clear. Capacitance describes the ability of a material to store energy. ■5.3(1)

When it comes to estimating thermal time lag and damping, it is again the basic thermal properties, available from many sources, that control performance. ■5.3(2) They are used to determine other important thermal attributes. It is quite easy to conceive how relatively thick and heavy constructions will influence internal temperatures, but putting values on it is more daunting, especially when

■5.3 Units of thermal capacitance

5.3(1) Thermal storage may be described as 'specific heat capacity' (J/kgK – joules, the basic units of energy, per kilogram, the basic unit of mass, and degree Kelvin or Celsius). Alternatively, it may be described as volumetric thermal capacity (J/m³K, which is the product of density, kg/m³, and specific heat capacity) or simply thermal capacity (J/K, the product of mass, kg, and specific heat capacity). To make matters worse, some textbooks use slightly different units for 'specific heat capacity': kJ/kgK (J/kgK divided by 1000) or Wh/kgK (J/kgK divided by 3600, the number of seconds in an hour). With regard to this last unit the essential relationship to remember is that one joule equals one watt multiplied by one second (or one watt equals one joule divided by one second). A watt is a flow of energy, while a joule is a flow quantified over time.

5.3(2) To estimate time lag and damping, 'specific heat capacity' (J/kgK) is used in conjunction with density (kg/m³) and conductivity (W/mK). The ratio of conductivity to density multiplied by specific heat capacity (so denominator is volumetric thermal capacity) is called thermal 'diffusivity'. The square root of the inverse of thermal diffusivity (seconds per square metre) is then used to determine the time lag and damping factor for single homogeneous materials. That is actually quite easy with the aid of a normal calculator. However, for multi-layer constructions, the mathematics is much more complex. It is not simply the sum of the values for individual layers, and we now rely on computers to make such calculations.

there are several layers of different materials. To acquire this knowledge, which is important in terms of dynamic performance, the mathematical journey from the initial properties in modern multi-layer construction is fairly demanding. Normally, architects require others to do this for them, but they should get to grips with the essential principles, in the same way as with structure and mechanical services.

embedded fluids for heating and cooling

As usual, the easiest way to explain concepts is by means of case studies. One example is the Gleneagles Community Centre to the west of Vancouver in Canada by John and Patricia Patkau (Carter, 2004). They have used large tilt-up concrete sandwich panels, a common system in North America, as structural spine walls that also incorporate the means of both heating and cooling (Figure 5.17). Approximately 30cm thick overall, the inner layer of concrete incorporates a serpentine arrangement of water-filled pipes. Protected by insulation, the filling of the sandwich, the walls present a suitable area of surface for radiant warmth or coolness to the interior. The distance from the pipes to the inner surface is appropriate in terms of thermal admittance and capacitance. In winter, a geothermal heat pump can keep the wall at a steady 21°C, but cool water can circulate in warm summer weather. The network of absorber coils is buried some 1.5m below the car park, where the ground temperature will be fairly stable – cooler than ambient in summer and early autumn, but warmer in winter. Low-grade heat is thus extracted from this source, when the circulating fluid in the coils has expanded and cooled into a vapour. It is then compressed by the pump, thus heating up and returning to a fluid state to exchange its

5.17 View into gymnasium at Gleneagles Community Centre, looking towards thermal wall

thermal energy with water. In this way, static thermal mass is exploited at both the supply and delivery end of an active system, with solar energy passively involved by heating the ground.

The ceiling, formed by cassettes of rough sawn timber spanning between the main laminated timber arches, has other environmental functions. Although it also has a certain amount of useful thermal capacitance, it acts most purposefully as a lung or sponge, absorbing and desorbing considerable quantities of water vapour produced by the athletic activities of the users. It also functions as an acoustic absorber, damping down the reverberation that would have become dominant with another smooth, hard finish. That is not to say that the ceiling could not also have accommodated serpentine heating coils. These are now available as proprietary systems for many types of construction, including timber, and are used in floors, walls and ceilings. It might also be argued that they are less riskily incorporated in non-structural layers.

In principle, the walls of the Gleneagles Community Centre have much in common with the solar retrofit of housing in Göteborg by Christer and Kirsten Nordström. One difference is the system for collecting solar energy, which is more direct, although still isolated from the means of delivery and requires the active assistance of fans. The other is the use of air as the fluid for transporting energy. The apertures are necessarily larger, and the mass separating them from the interior is considerably thicker than the inner leaf of the Patkau wall. It is also inherently less problematic in terms of future maintenance. Although some dirt might bypass filters, this will not impinge on the interior, as might leaking water. Modified walls from outside to inside have a brick skin, 8cm insulation, air ducts, the original solid 'no-fines' concrete wall and plaster. As indicated above, admittance is quantified in the same unit as a U-value. It is also used to calculate a thermal response factor. ■5.4(1) The point here is that although the inside of the construction, and therefore its internal admittance, is unchanged, the response factor for the entire construction is altered by the new additions. Admittance now becomes relevant interstitially, due to warm air circulating in the wall to and from the roof collectors, nearly doubling the area of surface that is of thermal relevance.

The thicker, multilayer construction at Göteborg, compared with that of the Gleneagles Community Centre, suggests a slower response. From a cold start, the heat-up time will be longer. On the other hand, the advantage is that the wall functions as a larger thermal store, ironing out excessive fluctuation in temperature over the daily cycle. The solar-heated ducts lining the far side of the no-fines wall will enhance the storage effect for a large proportion of the opaque wall surface and admittance is relevant for twice as much of the wall's thickness over the affected area. Since it is now being heated from two directions, the thermal response of the wall will be more rapid, with the insulation inhibiting conducted loss outwards.

■5.4 Thermal admittance, response and damping

5.4(1) Admittance may be regarded as dynamic heat flux, concerned only with the first 75mm or so of a bounding surface, and is termed a Y-value. A thermal response factor is defined in terms of the ratio of the Y-value to the U-value, each multiplied by the area of a surface in question, and moderated by the addition of heat loss by ventilation. Before the Göteborg retrofit, this ratio for the solid, 30cm-thick, no-fines wall may have been in the order of 1.5. After the addition of insulation, it would have been significantly greater – at least double the original ratio. By contrast, the admittance to transmittance ratio for a slim construction, such as a 10cm sealed insulated panel, will tend towards 1.0, with a rapid response.

5.4(2) 'Damping factor' is the ratio of the daily range in temperature on the inside surface of the wall relative to that outside. Because ambient conditions fluctuate more than those inside, this ratio is less than 1.0, but the lighter and/or thinner a construction is, the closer to 1.0 it becomes – for example, an uninsulated corrugated metal roof lined with plasterboard. In the Göteborg case, the inner surface of the solar enhanced storage wall will have a smaller range in temperature than if there had been a normal cavity. Therefore the damping ratio will be lower – say of the order of 0.2.

5.4(3) The theoretical 'equivalent outside temperature' (T^{eo}), compared with the measured temperature outside (T^o), have equal respective averages, but the T^{eo} amplitude is less than that of T^o. The greater the thermal damping, the flatter will be the theoretical T^{eo} curve. Not only does this signify thermal stability, it is also likely to decrease the cooling load. Allowing for the unavoidable heating effect of direct solar and incidental gains, it is likely that the respective graphs of the internal 'base temperature' and the 'equivalent outside temperature' will be reasonably close, almost throughout the daily cycle. In other words, the magnitude of any cooling load is likely to be minimal and readily dealt with by opening windows or shading.

Not only that, the higher the temperature of the solar heated air from the roof, the more likely it is that the wall will heat up to the extent that heat will now flow into the interior, rather than simply slow down the rate of loss from it. On a sunny day in winter, the south-facing brick skin could heat up, although not to as high a temperature as the inner leaf. But overall, compared to the equivalent profile without the solar enhanced ducts, the profile of temperature from inside to outside is significantly changed on a sunny day. In other words, the daily period for heat to be steadily lost from the inside to the outside will be considerably shorter than without the solar contribution. The related aspect of thermal damping ■5.4(2) will also be beneficially affected.

Given that the construction now has two heavy layers plus the insulation, it is not likely in winter that much solar energy absorbed by the new skin of brick will directly reach the interior. Rather, the benefit is due to the rapid capture of solar energy indirectly via the roof and transportation to short-term storage. This means that free energy collected during a cold day can usefully address the demand in the evening and overnight, the time lag through the no-fines estimated to be over nine hours. During a hot day in summer, the solar heat from the roof is discarded and the cavity in the wall will remain relatively cool. The time lag for solar heat to travel through the entire wall will be considerable, probably as much as 15 hours. The heating effect through south-facing windows will of course be much more rapid, although slowed to some extent by the thermal mass inside. The delay due to the combined effect of wall and windows should help to avoid overheating. The inside will now read the ambient temperature with its maximum occurring close to the coolest part of the night, and its minimum close to the warmest part of the day. This concept, which takes into account the dynamic effect of thermal mass over a daily cycle, may be plotted graphically as the 'equivalent outside temperature' and used to determine the cooling load. ■5.4(3)

Returning to conditions in winter, another way of looking at the wall is that its effective U-value will lower, even to the extent of becoming a negative value, when it is able to donate heat to the interior. Had the solar air collector been mounted vertically on the wall, the zone immediately behind the transparent cover would become very warm in sunny conditions. As with the actual installation at Göteborg, the internal storage wall would then have heated up after a certain time lag. Now the daytime profile from outside to inside would be nearly all 'downhill'. Put another way, the entire construction would give heat to the interior.

This was essentially the system adopted by architect Gustav Hillman for a new block of flats in Berlin, developed within IEA Task VIII project 'Passive and Hybrid Solar Energy Buildings' and also dating from the late 1980s (Schreck et al, 1987). Vertical solar air collectors took warm air on an internal closed loop through hollow concrete floors and walls. In this case the system is designed to complement passive sunspaces, where exchanges of energy are open and subject to interaction with the occupants (Chapter 4).

solid solar masonry walls

A competing technology, for optimizing the dynamic thermal performance of external walls over daily cycles, is that of transparent insulation (TI). The TI walls for the 'solar house' in Freiburg (Chapter 2) and the Strathclyde student residences (Chapter 4) are useful case studies in this regard. However, it is not that easy to compare weekly data published for Strathclyde with annual values of some 44kWh/m² given for Freiburg. ■5.5(1) The difference in the solar supply may vary significantly from year to year, let alone from Glasgow to Freiburg. There are also differences in ambient temperature, velocity of wind and specification of the complete building envelope that will influence the length of the heating season.

Although a broad-brush comparison is tempting, apparently indicating quite similar values, ■5.5(2) it needs to be remembered that respective floor areas are relatively arbitrary. If we are to rationally compare respective performances, it is much safer to compare values per unit area of TI. In this case 127kWh/m² is estimated for Strathclyde from November to April. ■5.5(3) This is considerably more than the approximate value of 100kWh/m² given for the solar house in Freiburg. However, there is a logical explanation. Given its superior external envelope compared with Strathclyde, the solar house should have a shorter heating season, with fewer good solar months. The convex surface is an advantage within the shorter time frame, but once a heating load has been displaced, energy gained via the TI is not useful.

It is also of interest that in the Glasgow demonstration, it was found that slightly more heat was gained than was lost through the TI wall over a heating season. It was estimated that the effective U-value was minus 0.08W/m²K (Johnstone and Grant, 1994). The length of the heating season is again critical to such a value. If the season shortens, the average incident radiation will drop, and the effective U-value will increase. Since the length of the heating season is also largely determined by the occupants' demand for heat and window-opening habits, one has to treat claims regarding the effective U-value and the amount of useful solar heat transmitted with some caution. Since the project manager, his wife and young toddler occupied the solar house at Freiburg during monitoring, some of the issues attributed to unpredictable behaviour could be discounted. One might also feel justified in being a bit sceptical about round figures like 100kWh/m². But, having established that the value claimed for Strathclyde is 27 per cent higher and identified why this should be so, the scepticism is blunted. Freiburg's figure seems to reflect a more energy-efficient project, where the quantitative opportunities for exploiting free solar energy are correspondingly reduced.

■5.5 TI saving – Freiburg compared to Glasgow

5.5(1) Freiburg's 'solar house' has 64m² TI, 15cm thick and backed by a storage wall of 24cm lime-sand blocks. The information provided during a visit was that this is estimated to save approximately 100kWh/m² wall annually, or a total of 6400kWh (Porteous, 1999). If this is expressed per unit of floor area as elsewhere, the value is approximately 44kWh/m² (145m² heated floor area). At Strathclyde, the thickness of the TI is reduced to 10cm, while the storage wall of dense concrete blocks is 15cm thick (Twidell and Johnstone, 1993). On a sunny day in February 1992, the inner surface of the wall varied between just over 23°C and 29°C, while the temperature of the air in the room remained fairly steady at 22°C. The average weekly thermal contribution of the wall for two monitored weeks that February, which was published in the report to the EU, worked out at 5.4kWh/m² TI or 1.76kWh/m² floor area of each bed-sit. The difference in temperature between inside and outside averaged more than 18K. It was also reported that there had been a negative effective U-value for every month of the year, averaging over monthly intervals.

5.5(2) Predicted average solar radiation for Glasgow on a south-facing vertical surface in February is close to its average from November to April (Page and Lebens, 1986). If the measured February value for Glasgow is multiplied up for these six months, the total is quite close to that of the 44kWh/m² estimated for Freiburg. Whether coincidentally or not, there is a degree of comfort that such apparent compatibility exists for the technique: 1.76kWh/m² floor x 26 weeks x 0.90625 = 41.5kWh/m². (Predicted incident solar radiation on a south-facing vertical surface: November–April mean = 0.90625 February 1992 mean.)

5.5(3) 5.4kWh/m² wall x 26 weeks x 0.90625 = 127kWh/m².

■5.6 Impact of TI on length of heating season: Freiburg compared to Glasgow

5.6(1) The length of a heating season depends on the period of time that the internal base temperature is higher than the ambient temperature. The base temperature (and hence the length of the heating season) will reduce as the U-value and/or rate of ventilation reduces – i.e. becomes more energy-efficient. At Freiburg, the cold U-value for the opaque northern wall is 0.16W/m²K; the cold U-value of the TI wall is higher at 0.51W/m²K without the blinds and 0.40W/m²K with blinds (Wiggington and Harris, 2002, pp143–148). The values given by Wiggington and Harris correspond with 10cm TI and 30cm sand-lime brickwork. These compare with 15cm and 24cm, the thicknesses noted during a visit in 1999. If the latter figures are correct, U-values would fall to 0.42 and 0.36, respectively assuming a conductivity of 0.61W/mK for brick and 0.09W/mK for TI (the second value based on a U-value of 0.79W/m²K for a 10cm thickness, and capillary diameter of 1.7mm) (Wittwer, 1988).

5.6(2) In the case at Strathclyde, the cold U-value for the TI wall without the blind drawn up is given as 0.60W/m²K, and 0.48W/m²K with the blind up. This compares with an estimated value of 0.22W/m²K for the opaque construction. The 0.60W/m²K U-value in Strathclyde's report to the EU also corresponds with a conductivity of 0.09W/mK for the TI (10cm polycarbonate capillary).

5.6(3) It was established that staining at Strathclyde was attributable to diesel particulates suspended in the air, the site being quite close to a busy road. The fenestration covering the TI was not airtight and the five-storey height of the cavity behind the glass, coupled with the manner in which the TI was attached, caused a 'bellows effect'. Although the open-ended TI structure is intended to inhibit any convective cross-flow, it appears that air did tend to get sucked partially into the small capillary voids. This occurred in patches distributed in a random manner over the entire TI surface. The apparent randomness and nature of contamination caused more post-contract surprise than its presence, which was predicted pre-contract: '… here electrostatic properties affecting adhesion of dirt/dust may be a critical factor.' (Porteous, 1988)

In a sense this highlights the complexities of the 'north is best' assertion aired in Chapter 1. Freiburg is approximately eight degrees of latitude further south than Glasgow. But it is in a continental location, where temperatures in winter will be several degrees lower than its marine-influenced TI counterpart. Thus one would expect the heating demand in Freiburg to be greater than Glasgow. When it comes to solar supply, Freiburg also has a significant edge on Glasgow. From November until April its global radiation on a horizontal plane is approximately 50 per cent greater. However, the designers have stepped in to lower the energy load as near to zero as possible in the German case, thereby lowering the potential for one of the techniques that is itself critical to achieving that goal. One can assume that the TI wall has shortened the heating season by more than an opaque alternative. ■5.6(1) Therefore, in estimating the effective length of the heating season, it would be helpful to know how many days would be added if the TI wall were replaced by opaque insulation.

Unlike the Freiburg solar house, where virtually every aspect is experimental, the Strathclyde demonstration was financially constrained by a conventional budget, other than for the specifically untried features such as the TI. This is reflected in ambitions for energy efficiency, in turn affecting the length of the heating season. Again, theoretical substitution of TI with the opaque specification ■5.6(2) legitimately allows extra days relative to the TI performance. However, the more erratic actions of students, compared to the Freiburg situation, are able to lengthen the period of apparent demand. Even though this chapter is exploring passive architectural aims, the limits of these can be distorted by perversity of use. A resultant longer period of demand gives the impression of better performance than should be the case, because it includes more favourable solar weather, particularly in spring.

Setting aside the unanticipated intervention of students, the concept of the TI mass wall was not undermined. Even black staining ■5.6(3) on the polycarbonate 'honeycomb' did not overturn the storage function of the wall, with its average negative effective U-value. The only caveat is that the results are skewed by the length of heating season assumed in the analysis of measured data. Regardless of such fine-tuning, the principle of the TI wall has been proved for a northerly location with rather wet winters. It is then interesting to compare this technique with a glazed mass wall, which does not have the benefit of the insulation.

The experimental Irish Trombe-Michel wall at Carlow in Ireland is an example. The storage wall consisted of 20cm dense concrete blocks, plastered internally and painted black externally with 'permaroof', which proved less resistant to solar bleaching than expected. The time lag between the respective maximum temperatures on the outside and inside faces of the wall was almost exactly four hours, and there was a further period of about two hours between maximum solar irradiance and the maximum temperature on the outer black surface. This meant that when the ambient temperature peaked at three in the afternoon, the inside surface did not reach its maximum until seven in the evening. On a sunny day in April the wall had a strong steadying effect on the internal temperatures over a whole day (O'Farrell and Lynskey, 1984). The influence of direct solar gain was clearly dominant in terms of when the maximum was reached, while the minimum followed that of the wall. This was because the profile of air temperature indoors on a sunny day is always strongly influenced by the direct solar irradiation through windows, with the delayed effect of heat transmitted through the wall less immediately apparent. On a dull, cool day the temperature of the air indoors and that of the wall tend to be quite close, because there is very little gain through windows and the wall will be losing any heat left over from a previous sunnier day. However, in the example given here, as windows were kept closed during monitoring, the rooms did overheat somewhat on sunny days, reaching almost 30°C with the ambient maximum 10K lower in spring. The difference between respective minima on such a day was considerably greater than this value, with rooms staying above 20°C while the ambient temperature plunged to less than 5°C.

Nevertheless, assuming relatively warm temperatures could be tolerated or moderated, the short-term thermal storage could last overnight after a sunny day. Had the house been occupied, some of the stored heat would have been lost to ventilation. But this would have been countered by useful incidental heat gains. Overall it is safe to say, that in sunny spring weather, the house could function without auxiliary heating since there was none employed during monitoring, and neither were there any incidental gains from occupancy. It was a different story on a cold overcast day during the same month. The internal face of the wall reached only two or three degrees above ambient, and was very close to the recorded temperatures of air in the rooms. This left a differential in terms of comfort ranging from about eight to ten degrees over the entire daily cycle. With a cold U-value of 1.8W/m²K for the Trombe-Michel wall, a high heating load was inevitable during any prolonged overcast periods during winter. Without much of a solar charge during the day, the wall would simply lose heat rapidly – say ten times as fast as a modern insulated wall.

Transparent insulation therefore presents itself as the perfect solution. Provided that overheating can be effectively tackled, we can reap all the advantages of the short-term thermal storage while not suffering from excessively high cold U-values. A possibility, which lies between the simple Irish Trombe-Michel wall and the TI walls of Strathclyde and elsewhere, is that of Christopher Taylor Court in Birmingham. The construction is exactly the same as the Irish one apart from the glazing being vertical and closer to the wall, the outer surface of which is covered in 'Maxorb'. This is a relatively costly material, which selectively absorbs a very high proportion of incoming shortwave solar radiation, but emits a correspondingly small amount of energy outwards in long

5.7 Influence of selective coating on mass wall

5.7(1) Maxorb is generally assumed to absorb in the range 0.95–0.99 or 95–99 per cent, while it only emits in the range 0.08–0.11 or 8–11 per cent.

5.7(2) By increasing the thermal resistance of the air gap behind the glass from about $0.18m^2K/W$ in the case of Carlow to about $0.40m^2/W$ with 'Maxorb', the cold U-value will improve to about $1.3W/m^2K$. This is still very high relative to modern standards for normal opaque walls; but, according to the monitoring, the break-even point for a zero effective U-value is a mean solar irradiance of approximately $80W/m^2$ (Yannas, 1994). The predicted mean daily value for Birmingham, incident on the absorber and averaged over all weather conditions from November to April, is $53W/m^2$ (Page and Lebens, 1986). This corresponds to an effective U-value of $0.08W/m^2K$. In other words it is $0.16W/m^2K$ higher than the negative value estimated for the solar residences in Glasgow.

wave. 5.7(1) The effect of this selectivity is both to increase the amount of solar heat stored within the wall and to reduce the amount that is lost outwards from it. The net result is an effective U-value close to zero. 5.7(2) It is not as efficient as the TI, but it still outperforms typical traditionally insulated construction. It is also a construction that would transfer well to regions with a more favourable ratio of solar supply to demand – for example, a mountainous part of southern Europe or the USA.

One should remember that the time lag of four hours is advantageous relative to the maximum demand for heat in the domestic sector. The inner surface will reach its maximum temperature at around seven in the evening and continue to deliver heat for some hours after that. The other advantage is that the higher radiant temperature of the surface, compared with a normal wall, should mean comfort is attainable at lower air temperatures. Any tactic that reduces radiant loss from occupants, whether a Roman hypocaust or a 20th century 'muracaust' as in the case of Göteborg, will enable fresh thermal comfort as well as displacing auxiliary heating. In turn, it has been shown in the previous chapter that such freshness tends to be accompanied by lower rates of ventilation. It should become a win–win–win scenario. However, as reported in connection with the project in Birmingham, expectations are frequently not met. Thermostats were not set down and loads for space heating were much higher than expected. It would appear that more sophisticated thermostatic controls are required, such as ones that recognize the heat stored in the wall as well as the temperature of its surface and respond accordingly.

thermal mass and timber construction

In general one can say that adequate thermal capacitance is important for any building with a regular occupancy cycle. For commercial or institutional buildings with a large quantity of incidental gains from lighting, equipment and appliances, high thermal storage will tend to bring profiles of internal 'base temperature' reasonably close to those of 'equivalent outside temperature' profiles (see 5.4(3)). Thus cooling loads can be minimized. There are few building types where thermal storage is not advantageous. The ability to make buildings, especially housing, more immune to intermittent opening of windows in winter has already been flagged. It is therefore frustrating that the building industry, in many of the climatic zones of interest here, has opted for light prefabricated construction. However, there are significant differences from country to country. Much of the housing in Germany and Austria uses prefabricated timber components with an increasing application of solid, as opposed to framed, floors and walls. 'Stacked plank' is one such technique, which will provide a considerable amount of thermal mass, as well as the ability to absorb and transmit water vapour. Because timber has a larger specific heat capacity than dense concrete, the difference in respective thermal capacities is less than one might imagine. 5.8(1)

Austria is also host to some intriguing solar experiments with timber walls. A novel light construction used by architect Walter Unterrainer for a house in Bregenz is somewhat analogous with the Freiburg TI wall. ▪5.8(2) The aim is to keep the surface of the stacked cardboard and the adjacent capillary air cavities warm during daytime, again with the result of lowering the effective U-value. According to Unterrainer, the effective value often reaches zero or less. ▪5.8(3) In winter the effectiveness of the system is helped by snow cover, which significantly increases the amount of reflected solar heat transmitted through the glass cover and absorbed by the cardboard honeycomb. Unterrainer is dubious about how well the technique would transfer to regions with much cloudier winters, such as Scotland. But there is little doubt that it would work in other mountainous areas to the south.

composite construction

Prefabrication of such components in Austria is of a very high standard, and this factor is undoubtedly an important part of its effectiveness. In any case, there is no reason why a construction that is predominantly of prefabricated or site-fabricated timber, should not incorporate heavier masonry components as well. The work of Brian MacKay-Lyons in Nova Scotia exploits a high standard of carefully detailed Canadian timber construction, but not necessarily with quite the precision of Unterrainer. Roughness is often deliberately contrasted with a smooth and exact material. He is also not reticent to use concrete as part of his palette. A common formula for his houses is the use of a timber superstructure, often reinforced or stabilized where required by steel, together with polished concrete floors incorporating warm-water heating coils. It is the same construction technique adopted by many American passive solar houses in the 1940s, and although the issue of purchased heat displacing some of the solar heat is still there, such floors do make very economic short-term solar stores. It is also interesting just how much some clients empathize with the system. For example, in the Howard house in West Pennant, Vivian Howard recognizes that the primary living accommodation on the ground floor and mezzanine benefits hugely from solar gain compared with the children's rooms on the lower ground floor – but without overheating and without any shading devices (Figure 5.18a). The heavy floors, coupled with opening windows at low and high level, and the maritime location, are sufficient to maintain comfortably low temperatures in warm and sunny weather. She also does not mind that the original concept of a timber floor, returning slightly up the walls as a reference to the inside of traditional clinker boats, was abandoned in favour of the polished concrete. Cost was an issue as well as thermal performance.

In another MacKay-Lyons dwelling know as Coastal House No. 22, located close to the mouth of the historic LaHave river estuary (LaHave, meaning the haven, was the name given to the estuary by the French explorer Samuel de Chaplain in 1604), the owners find comfort with the thermostat set to about

▪5.8 Timber versus concrete and an innovative Austrian solar wall

5.8(1) If we compare a solid timber floor with that of dense concrete, in each case 15cm thick and with an area of 75m², the respective masses differ by a factor of 4.0 (the mass of timber at 530kg/m³ x 11.25m³ = less than 6000kg, compared to 2100kg/m³ x 11.25m³ = close to 24,000kg). But comparing respective thermal capacitances, the factor reduces to 2.4. (Specific heat capacity of softwood at 1.38J/kgK x 5962.5kg = 8228kJ/K compared to specific heat capacity of dense concrete at 0.84J/kgK x 23,625kg = 19,845kJ/K; 19,845 ÷ 8228 = 2.4.)

5.8(2) Unterrainer's construction from outside to inside is: 7mm translucent wired glass; 40mm air space; 160mm corrugated cardboard, configured in a similar manner to capillary TI (capillaries at right angles to glass); two layers of 40mm solid timber; vapour control layer; 40mm cork between timber battens; 18mm cement-bonded wood chipboard. The main difference compared with the Freiburg TI wall is of course that the cardboard is opaque and solar penetration of the material is estimated to be of the order of 12mm.

5.8(3) Unterrainer provided technical information in a lecture at the Mackintosh School of Architecture, Glasgow on the 21st January 2004, confirming cold U-value of the construction of 0.20W/m²K and mean effective U-value of approximately 0.13W/m²K.

5.18a Main living space of Howard House, West Pennant, with polished concrete floor
5.18b Living space of guest wing, Coastal House 22, with polished concrete floor

18°C. They are completely committed to the design and construction, and appreciate the value of relatively high radiant warmth complementing relatively cool air (Figure5.18b). Such understanding of, and enthusiasm for, material physics seems to be inseparable from a corresponding passion for the aesthetic moves made by MacKay-Lyons. It is a stunningly skilful and beautiful composition, which is rendered in an equally moving landscape.

cladding, colour and other storage media

In many of the projects by MacKay-Lyons, the use of external timber cladding, whether in the form of shingles or boarding, can have a beneficial impact on the dynamic performance of the lightweight enclosing walls. Here, the ability to heat quickly in conditions of intermittent direct sunlight, or cloudier diffuse conditions, will help to keep the average temperature of the external surface, as well as any trapped layer of air behind it, relatively high during daytime. Thus it will tend to lower the mean effective U-value in a way similar to the Unterrainer wall. For favourably oriented surfaces, the darker the colour, the more beneficial it will be, even though the majority of the thermal work is done by the hidden insulation. In regional terms, Nova Scotia is host to many varieties and grades of timber. In coastal areas, the shingles were traditionally immersed in a mix of cod liver oil and red ochre to prolong their life. The resultant dark red colour should absorb about 70 per cent of the sun's heat. However, even western red cedar or other timber such as larch, which weather to a silvery grey and normally require no further preservative, will absorb a reasonable amount. Such simple vernacular techniques fall within the modern terminology of rain-screens. However, they are more than that, since they can also contribute positively to thermal performance. In presenting a case for 'folk-tech' principles of building, MacKay-Lyons makes a telling natural analogy: 'Shingles act like feathers of a duck, repelling moisture while responding to the wet-dry and freeze-thaw cycle like a living skin.' (MacKay-Lyons, 1996).

The same principle with respect to colour (if not to feathers) applies to masonry walls such as those of the Nordström project in Göteborg, although increasing thermal movement with greater darkness of colour will require careful use of control joints. Experiments carried out at Napier University in Edinburgh in order to ascertain the influence of dark relative to light have indicated a significant difference in older buildings, especially those with solid walls. ■5.9(1) It has been estimated that for a whole building, the colour of the external walls can alter the annual heating load by as much as 20 per cent. A black wall, with a transparent cover, will save even more. ■5.9(2) It follows that, although the stock of buildings such as housing with solid walls is reducing, the effect on the external skin of a modern, well-insulated, multi-layer wall would still be valuable. In scientific terms, a white surface behaves selectively in that it absorbs shortwave radiation poorly, yet emits longer wave radiation well. The darker the colour, the greater the tendency to equalize absorption and emission.

Once inside the external envelope and after initial insolation of materials in direct view of the sun, colour ceases to be relevant. Materials may be light in colour without affecting long-wave radiant exchanges, but they may also be light in terms of their mass, which will inhibit thermal storage. An alternative to a dense solid material, such as concrete, is a much less dense phase-change material. ■5.9(3) These can be placed to receive as much benefit as possible from passive solar gain, and the colour of the contained material is again relevant relative to initial short-wave radiant gain. Even a limited heat-store will help to reduce loss of solar gains by early evening. Also, where there is a 'direct gain' passive solar strategy, and the heating season is shortened by high standards of insulation, too much thermal mass can be a handicap. There will not be enough heat transmitted from the sun to charge it. This inevitably depends to a significant extent on the detailed glazing specification as well as sizes, orientations and tilts, and would be the case whatever the solar availability in winter.

Optimizing heat and light balance through glazing

The development of advanced glazing products is essential to a review of modern solar architecture, particularly in relation to optimizing the balance of transmitted heat and light. This is a very specialized area, and one that is quite widely published elsewhere (Jesch, 1987, 1988, 1989; Compagno, 1995, pp57–75 and 77–120; Daniels, 1997, pp135–162). On the other hand it is also an area where the penetration of the market has been slower than the scientific and technical advances. The specification of expensive products must go hand in hand with life-cycle costing, one of the long-term benefits being that the products have no moving parts. However, the potential drawback is lack of flexibility. For example, basic reflective or heat-absorbing glass may help to reduce cooling loads, but that means the opportunity for useful solar gain in winter is also reduced. The coatings and tints of early types of such glazing also significantly compromised views out of buildings, as well as the external appearance of the façades. Hence there has been a lot of research and development associated with clearer 'variable transmission glazing'. The essential tactic is to reject solar heat gain during some parts of the year, whilst accepting it at others. Parallel to this, there has been considerable progress made with related products, including transparent insulation or TI (see also Chapters 2 and 4), where the emphasis is on maximizing radiant gain and minimizing conducted loss. These are sometimes associated solely with glazing, when not unduly reducing incoming light is a factor, and sometimes integrated with opaque surfaces.

mirror-optics and other progress in variable transmission

One line of development with variable transmission was that of 'mirror-optics' (Köster, 1988, 1989) (Figure 5.19a). Bespoke mirror-optics or glass prisms located in the cavity of double-glazing can take account of any solar geometry. These devices then have two functions. The first is to admit and deflect solar

■5.9 Colour, mass and phase-change materials

5.9(1) A solid 220mm brick wall (U-value = 2.3W/ m^2K), facing south in Scotland, has an annual heat loss of about 150kWh/m^2 if painted white and with an indoor temperature averaging around 18°C. The same wall painted black will have a heat loss of only about 70kWh/m^2 due to the additional absorptance of solar gain, saving over 50 per cent. The effective U-value of the wall is reduced to approximately 1.0W/m^2K.

5.9(2) Measurements in Edinburgh (MacGregor, 1979), comparing a white 15cm thick concrete wall with a black one with a glass cover, gave a saving of 25kWh/m^2 in late autumn.

5.9(3) Phase-change materials such as Glauber salts were introduced to the solar community in the 1950s. They can be integrated with internal components like tiles, colour then being initially important. Heat is absorbed and stored at the first change of state when heated by the sun; and then the stored heat is released as it cools in the evening. The advantages are compactness, similar to water compared to solid masonry, and the relatively large amount of energy stored within a relatively low mass. However, although interest is currently reviving, economics, longevity and stability were probably the issues that have resulted in relatively low uptake of this technology.

heat gain on to suitable surfaces within a space. Köster calls this 'optical energy transport'. The second is to optimize diffusion and spread of daylight within the space. Köster calls this 'automatic optical daylight modulation'. In the closing lines of his paper to the 3rd International Workshop 'Transparent Insulation Technology' held in Freiburg in 1989 he is eloquently enthusiastic about the future for his mirror-optics:

> *Do less and accomplish more – do nothing and accomplish everything.*
> *The promise of solar-architecture becomes true: a passive building*
> *completely in harmony with the outer climate – no computer and no*
> *tracking, just using the sun itself as software control – an architecture*
> *in harmony with nature!*

The statement has echoes of at least two famous architects, the 'less is more' of Ludwig Mies van der Rohe, and 'harmony with nature' cannot fail to evoke Frank Lloyd Wright. In any case, Köster seems to have mounted a good sales pitch. His technique quickly became commercialized in Germany as 'Ökasolar'. Architects Eble and Sambeth used 'Ökasolar' for part of the fenestration in the atrium of Frankfurt's 'Ökohuis', 1992 (Figure 5.19b). The practice of Percy Thomas also used it in the UK for a comprehensive secondary school at Swanlea in London, 1993.

Since the German example is associated with the voluntary sector and the British one with cost-conscious public sector, this kind of application is encouraging. However, in these particular buildings, the opportunity to displace electricity for lighting is limited since the glazing is not used in the windows of workspaces. The role is mainly one of heat balance, capturing useful gain in winter and reducing overheating in summer. The argument for this material as opposed to normal glass plus blinds or adjustable louvres, is just as Köster made it – no moving parts.

A related development by Lichtplanung Christian Bartenbach was used in a seminal environmental building. This is the Brundtland Centre in Toftlund, Denmark, by KHR Architects in association with Esbensen Consulting Engineers, which was built between 1992 and 1994 at 55.11°N latitude (Wiggington and Harris, 2002, pp103–108) (Figure 5.20). Here a fixed interstitial array of specular louvred blades is used in the upper section of double-glazing to divert light onto a highly reflective ceiling. The middle section at eye level contains inverted venetian blinds, which can be adjusted by a central control system. They too can throw light onto the ceiling, while also allowing visual contact with the outside to be maintained. A specially designed linear asymmetric fluorescent light fitting is located along the line of the transom at the bottom of the middle section. Following in the footsteps of Alvar Aalto, the idea is that artificial light is in harmony with natural light, while using surfaces of the building as reflectors. But we should not forget that where there is light, there is also heat. Therefore both the blinds and the reflectors of the luminaires

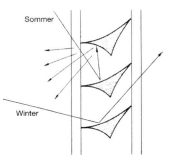

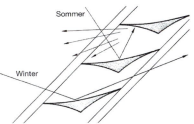

5.19a Köster's mirror-optics – typical sections

5.19b 'Ökasolar' used at Ökohuis, Frankfurt –
visually less intrusive than venetian blinds

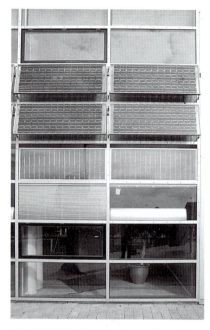

5.20 Detail of south façade of Brundtland Centre in Toftlund with glazing hierarchy, noting the twin array of PV panels between floors

constitute part of the energy balance. A bottom section, corresponding to seated eye level, has a further interstitial venetian blind, but this time the occupants can manually adjust the tilt of the blades. In terms of the thermal balance, it is the middle and lower layers that provide for short-term variable transmission of solar heat as well as light, by moving the blades of the blinds according to the weather and time of day. By contrast, the fixed upper blades allow the amount of solar radiation that enters the rooms to vary with season. More will be reflected out in summer than in winter. Also, when adjustable blinds are closed overnight, the U-value will improve significantly, say from 25 to 35 per cent, depending on the emissivity of the blades.

Other rather simpler variants of Köster's mirror-optics and Bartenbach's specular blades are prismatic louvres and laser-cut panels or LCPs (Brandi, 2004). The former can be designed for variable transmission of solar heat, reflecting mainly in summer and transmitting more in winter. They are also devices to diffuse light. The latter is generally more geared to inward deflection and diffusion of both heat and light. Prismatic louvres usually have a flat upper surface and prismatic lower surface, which is practical in terms of accumulation of dirt. However, prismatic glass for variable transmission can also be incorporated vertically within multiple glazing systems, where dirt is not a concern, while the incisions of LCPs in flat Perspex sheets are inherently easier to keep clean and are also commonly incorporated within glazing cavities. When used independently from the glazing, there may be an option for fixed or movable prismatic louvres or LCPs.

A more sophisticated device that can also be used to achieve variable transmission of solar heat is the holographic diffractive film or HDF (Daniels, 1997·pp143–147). This was applied to external solar tracking louvres mounted over the roof of a building at the Stuttgart International Garden Exhibition, 1993. The design was developed by architect Manfred Hegger in association with two scientists from the Polytechnic University of Cologne. (Professor Hegger is partner in the practice Hegger, Hegger-Luhnen and Schleiff who were also architects for the Academie Mont Cenis in Herne, in association with Jourda and Perraudin, which is discussed in Chapter 2.) In essence, the HDFs accept low-angle winter irradiation but reject solar gain at other times. The louvres were effectively double-glazed components, with the holographic grid within an outer glazing sandwich focusing light on to silkscreen strips mounted on the inner surface of the inner glass. These reflected the heat back out through the upper glass. It was also possible to mount photovoltaic cells on the silkscreen strips, and this was done in one of the arrays.

Possibly the ultimate concept for smart or intelligent glazing is the 'polyvalent wall' proposed by Mike Davis of the Richard Rogers Partnership London (Daniels, 1997, pp160–161). However, such concepts are still some way from the regular marketplace. Hutchins reports that much more pragmatic innovation, such as electro-chromatic, variable-transmission glass, has difficulty in moving rapidly from successful research, development and demonstration into the commercial world (Porteous, 2000). The fundamental objective with such glass is again to be able to block solar heat in warm weather, but without unduly reducing daylight. This can be achieved with coatings, such as amorphous tungsten oxide, applied in much the same way as a standard low-emissivity coating. While the latter works entirely passively to enhance the greenhouse effect in winter, the former will provide a reversible colour change when a low-voltage current is applied, and with transmission of light reduced by as little as 5 per cent. Other particle coatings can give 'angular selectivity' designed to maximize passive gain in winter, but reject it in summer; and this has only a slight effect on outward visibility as the inward radiation angles differ from the outward viewing angles. An alternative method of electrically altering transparency is by means of a liquid crystal interlayer within a glass laminate. However, in this case an electrical current is required to achieve transparency. Further options are thermo-chromatic layers such as vanadium dioxide. As the temperature increases, this coating proceeds to a metallic state causing infrared reflectivity. Yet another development is self-adjusting photo-chromatic glass where the transmission decreases automatically in response to ultraviolet and shortwave visible light. This does, however, have the disadvantage of darkening and consequently heating the glass. Hutchins believes that electro-chromatic coatings and those with angular selectivity are the most promising.

alternative integrated innovations

Returning to the strategic objective of regulating solar heat and dispersing light, the light-grid developed by Lichtplanung Christian Bartenbach and Siemens AG is placed interstitially within double-glazing in the same way as mirror-optics. The renowned solar architect from Munich, Thomas Herzog used it, for example, in 1993 in the roof of the Congress and Exhibition Hall in Linz, Austria. It is not visually transparent and its primary aim is not to give variable transmission, but rather to reflect direct solar radiation and to diffuse light. Thus it is more akin to an interstitial venetian blind, except the blades are not adjustable. It might also be regarded as a refined integrated brise-soleil (Daniels, 1997, p151). ■5.10 It is designed for specific geographical locations, orientations and tilts in such a way that the goal of excluding direct sunlight is achieved throughout the year. It consists of 'specially shaped plastic louvres coated with highly reflective pure aluminium; the louvres are arranged in a regular grid pattern to create light shafts sat next to each other in tight rows.' (Compagno, 1995, pp72–73)

An innovative transparent glazing system, which tackled increased thermal comfort in winter, particularly for north-facing windows, was that of Visi Heat, marketed for a relatively short period in the late 1980s and 1990s by Solaglas Ltd. The product was initially developed in Finland, arising from the need to maintain vision for trawlers in Arctic seas. A low-voltage current is applied to an

■5.10 Light-grid: vital statistics for solar versus light transmission

The total solar transmission factor of the light-grid is given as only 0.2 or 20 per cent, while the direct light transmission varies from 5 to 65 per cent and the diffuse light transmission varies between 5 to 22 per cent. The shading factor also varies through quite a large range from 0.75 to 0.20.

invisible low-emissivity coating on the glass. In the commercialized Visi Heat double-glazing, the inner pane was heated slightly higher than the adjacent air, thus enhancing the mean radiant temperature within a room as well as avoiding uncomfortable downdraughts. Moreover, the selective nature of the coating was such that it was claimed that only about 15 per cent of the heat generated in the glass would be lost to the outside (Porteous, 1989). This was used in at least one Scottish case study, a courtyard house in Dollar, a few miles to the north of the Forth Estuary, for the parents of architect Andrew Whalley (Figure 5.21). The design solution, on a fairly restricted site, demanded a significant proportion of northerly glazing – hence the decision to use heated glass. However, although the technology was not overly demanding, the tariff structure applied to non-storage electrical systems in Scotland does not particularly favour this technique. Whether for this reason or due to general lack of interest, Solaglas withdrew this product after a relatively short period.

Such an example highlights the complexities of uptake. We are moving into a time when the control of the supply of electricity relative to its demand will be much more sophisticated, as well as responsive to the vagaries of multiple renewable generation and storage sources. This could completely alter the future economic climate for products such as Visi Heat. Similarly, if a fiscal structure was introduced that significantly penalized commercial organizations and large public institutions for lack of energy efficiency, the necessary boost might be given to advanced glazing. This would of course favour climatic areas with relatively high heating loads in winter, as well as the possibility of cooling loads in summer.

Whatever new economic incentives may emerge, it is still incumbent on architects and other specialist designers to devise systems that are innovative

5.21 'Visi Heat' (clear) and 'Thermascrene' (translucent) glazing by Solaglas at Whalley house, under construction, June 1989 – note electric cable at extreme top of photograph

and effective, without being overly complex or vulnerable. In Chapter 2, mention was made of a 19th century patent application for what was effectively an intelligent wall. The chemistry was not difficult. A potassium solution got darker as it got hotter. Instantaneous direct solar gain would thus have been delayed, whilst the fluid would give up part of its stored heat to the interior during the evening. On the other hand in cold weather, the transmitted thermal losses would have been very high, and there were practical issues around containment. Over 110 years later, a house at Ebnat-Kappel in Switzerland by Dietrich Schwarz (Schittich, 2002) attempts to address these issues. Small paraffin-filled plastic containers (rather like green glass blocks) provide a thermo-chromatic, phase-change storage wall. This sits behind triple glazing, the central glazing element being a variable-transmission prismatic sheet. The entire thickness is 105mm and the system is purely passive, with no electricity involved and a low level of technology. It should cost a lot less and be more reliable than an electronically programmed polyvalent wall. On the other hand, it will of course still cost a lot more than an opaque alternative or a simpler screening device without the thermal storage capability.

external screens – competition for advanced glazing?

In tandem with work on advanced glazing, there has been marked progress refining basic fixed louvres, designed to be located outside windows. Since the early days of the static brise-soleil promoted by Le Corbusier, there have been innumerable variations in terms of both dimensions and materials. Furthermore, there is a tendency for some architects to apply these as a shallow cliché to over-glazed buildings, with dubious functionality relative to orientation. Reference was made to this ubiquity (some might also consider an iniquity) in Chapter 2. The practical challenge is to cut out unwanted direct sunshine and heat at different times of the day and year, while at the same time having a minimal impact on daylight. A new product, designed to be fixed outside glazing, has been christened KoolShade (Williams, 2004a). It consists of woven bronze micro-louvres (1.27mm wide, 0.18mm thick and set about 1.33mm apart at a nominal angle of 30° to the horizontal). Although they do not have the variable optical attributes of Ökasolar, heat gain is estimated to be only 14 per cent of incident irradiation. The close-set structure blocks virtually all direct sunlight for different orientations and times of year, while transmission of daylight significantly outperforms that for opaque venetian blinds. Since it also baffles wind and rain, it has a potential to moderate natural ventilation through inward opening or sliding windows.

The other benefit of KoolShade, as for Ökasolar, is that the interruption to visibility is relatively slight compared with competing movable devices, or other fixed ones. The effect is different in each case. Some visual distortion is inevitable with the transparent louvres of Ökasolar, while the KoolShade operates as a veil, with vision dependent on a brighter source of light on one side of the screen or veil than the other. The well-known Danish architects, Henning Larsen, used a perforated veil of stainless steel panels on the westerly façade of a relatively small vertical extension to the headquarters of Berlingske Tidene or BT, one of Copenhagen's newspapers (Figure 5.22). Since this occupies a corner site and there is a completely transparent façade to the north, the issue of blocking daylight is not as acute as the need to prevent glare and overheating during the afternoon, as well as damping down noise from the busy street to the west. Occupants can also still see out through the unscreened

5.22   Berlingske Tidene extension in Copenhagen
        at night

glass at night, whilst to the person on the street, the new corner appeared as a potent showcase, the visual editing of the perforated panels evocative of newspapers. Peter Davey, as editor of *The Architectural Review*, describes the screen as 'both veil and carapace' and refers to 'shadow play' on to the screen at night (Davey, 1995).

transparent insulation

Such external screens, which may be considered accessories affecting the balance of heat and light through windows, were, by definition, not included in the series of TI Workshops in the late 1980s. Not only is the materiality intrinsically opaque if not the product, but also the thermal resistance is negligible. While they can insulate buildings against overheating, the term 'insulation' in TI implies an ability to inhibit heat loss as well as permit useful gains – at times and places, and in buildings, when they can displace demand for energy. Thus the TI workshops included all forms of high performance glazing as well as many variants of TI as used in the solar house in Freiburg and the Strathclyde student residence. For example, there is a sister product of Ökasolar called Ökalux, which is simply a sandwich of acrylic TI, with the capillary structure at right angles between two sheets of glass. If the glass is clear, there may be limited visual transparency, depending on the position of occupants relative to the glazing. However, an extra layer of a material such as fibreglass may be introduced deliberately to give a greater level of opacity. There are other similar commercial products such as Ultrawarm Thermascrene by Solaglas, which do this. Kalwall (see ■5.11(5)) does much the same by varying the density of its fibreglass fill. However, for all of these, the capability to diffuse incoming solar radiation and light is not the same as varying transmission with changing solar geometry.

The ability of such materials to limit loss of heat overnight or during cold and sunless days is inevitably sensitive to their thickness. ■5.11(1) If 75–100mm is specified, there is tough competition from transparent, energy-efficient glazing, especially if the aim is not to diffuse daylight. A fully transparent retrofitted glazing system employed in Switzerland (Pinna/Schwarzenbach/Süsstrunk Architekten, 1989) achieved an average U-value, including the frame, as low as 0.6W/m²K. Two layers of selectively coated polyester foils ■5.11(2) were inserted between outer and inner float glass set 90mm apart. In this case, the depth of the frame has practical and economic consequences for opening windows, which were included to provide occupants with the means of supplementing low rates of ventilation by mechanical displacement. However, slimmer alternatives developed at much the same time, such as the 'LBL' three-pane krypton window ■5.11(3), have a very similar performance (Fricke, 1989).

If diffusing systems are acceptable, there are alternative TI materials with significantly lower rates of conductivity than capillary polycarbonate. ■5.11(4) In the case of aerogel, there is a long history of development dating back to the

■5.11 Transparent insulation variants

5.11(1) The U-value of a glazing unit, where capillary TI replaces a normal air gap of 20mm is approximately 2.4W/m²K. Any advantage compared with a fairly routine specification for transparent double-glazing is limited to its diffusing characteristic. However, if the thickness of the TI is increased to 75mm, the U-value drops significantly to just below 1.0W/m²K.

5.11(2) A selective coating permits high transmission of shortwave radiation, but inhibits loss in long-wave, as in low-emissivity glass. It is visually completely transparent.

5.11(3) LBL window: a third pane is inserted symmetrically into a normal double-glazed unit with a 20mm gap, resulting in triple-glazing with two 8mm krypton-filled gaps, and the two inner sheets of glass having low-emissivity coatings. The estimated U-value is 0.7W/m²K.

5.11(4) Other TI materials: acrylic foam has a conductivity value of the order of 0.04W/mK (Jbach, 1987) One acrylic foam is Imacryl foam, a foamed acrylic sheet material (PMMA) consisting of irregularly gas-filled bubbles. Aerogel (a highly porous material consisting either of silica, alumina, zirconia, stannic or tungsten oxides, or mixtures of these oxides) has a conductivity of about half that – 0.02W/mK at ambient air pressure, or as low as 0.01W/mK if evacuated (Caps et al, 1987; Kistler, 1942). The conductivity also varies with temperature and it is reported that measurements, using a hot-wire method, found values approximating to 0.01W/mK at 20°C and 0.02W/mK at 50°C (Hanna, 1994; Nilsson et al, 1983).

5.11(5) Normal Kalwall panels provide a large range of U-values for a single thickness. This is achieved by varying the density of the translucent fibreglass filling. U-values for thermally broken panels vary from 2.57 down to 0.56W/m²K. This implies conductivity values for the fibreglass of about 0.4W/mK down to below 0.05W/mK. A U-value of 0.28W/m²K for the equivalent 70mm panel filled with Nanogel implies its conductivity is 0.02W/mK. This is estimated to provide 13 per cent light transmission. That this product is now to be marketed (panels are presently sized at a maximum of 1.2m wide by 3.6m high) indicates a confidence that aerogel technology has moved beyond vulnerability to moisture and slumping.

early 1930s (Caps et al, 1987; Kistler, 1931). By the late 1980s, work was ongoing with regard to thermo-chromatic gels, which enhance scattering or diffusion once a certain critical temperature is reached (Beck, Link and Fricke, 1989). However, one practical problem with aerogel has been associated with the difficulty in achieving long-term chemical stability. For example, monolithic silica aerogel is vulnerable to attack by water. Another problem has been the slumping over time of the gel, whether between the stiff bounding layers of glass or alternatives such as glass-reinforced polyester.

Experiments in the late 1980s to encapsulate a layer between two sheets of glass, while maintaining the efficacy of the seals and avoiding excessive thermal bridging, highlighted the issues needing to be tackled before such a product could be sold (Jensen, 1989). Nevertheless, in the long-term the prospects looked promising. Today, the Cabot Corporation in Boston has produced Nanogel. Pores of 20 nanometres give a product that is claimed to be 99.9 per cent air and 0.1 per cent silica dioxide by volume (Williams, 2004b). It would also appear that Nanogel is going to be available as an alternative to the special white fibreglass in the Kalwall panels. ■5.11(5) The combined product is to be known as Kalwall + Nanogel, having a remarkably low U-value of less than 0.3W/m²K.

However, while single static products such as Nanogel might be held up as epitomizing the energy-efficient balance of heat gain and light, there will always be a competing desire for greater flexibility... the kind of flexibility that implies moving parts.

REFERENCES

Beck, A., Link, A. and Fricke, J. (1989) 'Light scattering thermochromatic gels', in Jesch, L. F. (1989) pp17–20.

Boyce, R. (1993) 'Development in a passive solar house', in *Keck and Keck,* Princeton Architectural Press, New York, p75.

Brandi, U. (2004) 'Daylight Control', *Detail*, vol 2004, no 4, pp368–373.

Brawne, M. (1973) 'North Jutland Museum of Arts, Aalborg, Denmark', *The Architectural Review,* vol 153, no 913, pp162–164.

Caps, R., Büttner, D., Fricke, J., Heinemann, U. and Löffler, G. (1987) 'Thermal properties of monolithic, granulated and segmented aerogel', in Jesch, L. F. (1987) pp28–30.

Carter, B. (2004) 'Lighting the Community', *The Architectural Review,* vol 216, no 1292, pp67–75.

Cerver, F. A. (2000) 'Urban transport: Nils Ericson Bus Station', in *The World of Architecture,* Könemann, Cologne, pp80–81.

Compagno, A. (1995) *Intelligent Glass Façades,* Birkhauser, Basel.

Daniels, K. (1997) *The Technology of Ecological Building,* Birkhauser, Basel.

Davey, P. (1995) 'Danish Detail', *The Architectural Review,* vol 197, no 1180, pp52–53.

Fricke, J. (1989) 'The LBL three-pane krypton window', in Jesch, L. F. (1989) pp62–65.

Glaumann, M. (1989) 'Basic Case Studies', in Hildon, A. and Seager, A. (1989) pp205–208.

Hanna, R. (1994) 'Aerogels and their future role in buildings', in MacGregor, K. and Porteous, C. (1994) pp341–346.

Harlang, C. and Bak, A. (1999) *Aalto & Baruël – Nordjyllands Kunstmuseum,* Fonden til Udgivelse af Arkitecturvaeker, Copenhagen.

Hildon, A. and Seager, A. (eds) (1989) *International Energy Agency Task XI, Passive and Hybrid Solar Commercial Buildings,* The New and Renewable Energy Promotion Group (REPG), Energy Technology Support Unit, Harwell, UK.

Jbach, H. W. (1987) 'Application of acrylic foam for improvement of single pane glazing', in Jesch, L. F. (1987) pp33–35.

Jensen, K. I. (1989) 'Transparent cover with evacuated monolithic silica aerogel', in Jesch, L. F. (1989) pp58–61.

Jesch, L. F. (ed) (1987) *Transparent Insulation Materials for Passive Solar Energy Utilisation,* proceedings of the 1st International Workshop (27–28 November 1986, Freiburg, Germany), The Franklin Company Consultants Ltd., Birmingham, UK.

Jesch, L. F. (ed) (1988) *Transparent Insulation in Solar Energy Conversion for Buildings and Other Applications,* proceedings of the 2nd International Workshop (24–25 March, Freiburg, Germany), The Franklin Company Consultants Ltd., Birmingham, UK.

Jesch, L. F. (ed) (1989) *Transparent Insulation Technology for Solar Energy Conversion,* proceedings of the 3rd International Workshop (18–19 September, Titisee/Freiburg, Germany), The Franklin Company Consultants Ltd., Birmingham, UK.

Johnstone, C. M. and Grant, A. D. (1994) 'Strathclyde University's Low Energy Passive Solar Residences: Conclusions of the Monitoring Programme', in MacGregor, K. and Porteous, C. (1994) pp217–222.

Kistler, S. S. (1931) *Nature,* vol 127, p742 (cited Caps et al, 1987).

Kistler, S. S. (1942) *Journal of Physics and Chemistry,* vol 46, p19 (cited Caps et al, 1987).

Köster, H. (1988) 'Future solar architecture: a new role for glass', *Sun at Work in Europe,* no 5, April, pp5–6.

Köster, H. (1989) 'Automatic heat control with mirror optics', in Jesch, L. F. (1989) pp66–69.

MacGregor, A. W. K. (1979) 'A solar skin for solid walls', in *The Passive Collection of Solar Energy in Buildings,* proceedings of conference, (Royal Institution, London, April), UK-ISES, London, pp39–43.

MacGregor, K. and Porteous, C. (eds) (1994) *North Sun 94, Solar Energy at High Latitudes,* proceedings of the 6th Biennial International Conference, (7–9 September, Glasgow, Scotland), James & James (Science Publishers) Ltd., London.

MacKay-Lyons, B. (1996) 'Seven stories from a village architect', *Design Quarterly,* no 165, Summer, p12.

Nilsson, O. et al (1985) 'Thermal Properties of Silica Aerogel', in proceedings 1st International Symposium, (Wurzburg, Germany, September). (cited in Hanna, 1994).

O'Farrell, F. and Lynskey, G. (1984) 'The construction and performance of a Trombe wall in a northern climate', in MacGregor, K. (ed), *North Sun '84, Solar Energy at High Latitudes,* proceedings of conference, (4–6 September) Scottish Solar Energy Group, Edinburgh, pp39–46.

Page, J. and Lebens R. (1986) 'Hourly incident solar radiation averaged over all weather conditions', in *Climate in the United Kingdom: A Handbook of Solar Radiation, Temperature and Other Data for Thirteen Principal Cities and Towns,* for the Energy Technology Support Unit, Harwell, HMSO, London, p166.

Pinna/Schwarzenbach/ Süsstrunk Architekten (1989) 'Basic Case Studies', in Hildon, A. and Seager, A. (1989) pp43–48.

Porteous, C. (1988) 'A window wall to watch', *Scottish Energy News,* August, West of Scotland Energy Working Group (c/o RIAS, Rutland Sq., Edinburgh), p6.

Porteous, C. (1989) 'A low energy atrium house in Scotland', *Sun at Work in Europe,* no 8, October, p31.

Porteous, C. (1999) 'Summer Rhineland Tour', *Sun at Work in Europe,* vol 14, no 4, December, pp2–5.

Porteous, C. (2000) 'Oxford Accent on Smart Glass', *SunTimes,* Scottish Solar Energy Group Newsletter, Issue no. 20, January, Mackintosh School of Architecture, Glasgow, p4.

Porteous, C. (2002) *THE NEW eco-ARCHITECTURE,* Alternatives from the Modern movement, Spon Press, London.

Schittich, C. (2002) 'Solar House in Ebnat-Kappel', *Detail,* vol 2002, no 6, pp736–737.

Schreck, H, Hillman, G. and Nagel J. (1987) 'Integrated passive and hybrid solar design in multifamily housing, Berlin', in Bloss, W. H. and Pfisterer, F. (eds), *Advances in Solar Energy Technology,* proceedings of the Biennial Congress of the International Solar Energy Society, (Hamburg, Germany, 13–18 September), Pergamon Press, Oxford, vol 4, pp3555–3560.

Tombazis, A. N. and Preuss, S. A. (1998) 'European Commission DG XII, Joule programme retrofitting of museums for antiquities in the Mediterranean countries. Case Study: The Archaeological Museum of Delphi', in Goetzberger, A. and Krainer, A. (eds), *Proceedings of the Second International ISES Europe Solar Congress,* (Portoroz, Slovenia, 14–17 September), The Franklin Company Consultants Ltd., Birmingham, UK, section II.I.18, pp1–6.

Twidell, J. W. and Johnstone, C. M. (1993) *The University of Strathclyde Solar Residences: Final Report of Monitoring,* April 1993, Energy Studies Unit (Environmental Systems Research Unit), University of Strathclyde, Glasgow.

Twidell, J. W. and Howe, B. (1994) 'Passive ventilated, daylight optimized, low energy Engineering Building, De Montfort University', in MacGregor, K. and Porteous, C. (1994) pp243–250.

Wiggington, M. and Harris, J. (2002) *Intelligent Skins,* Architectural Press, London.

Williams, A. (2001) 'Surface airier', *The Architects' Journal,* vol 213, no 9, pp42–43.

Williams, A. (2004a) 'Made in the shade', *The Architects' journal,* vol 219, no 23, p42.

Williams, A. (2004b) 'Out of this world', *The Architects' Journal,* vol 219, no 24, p56.

Wittwer, V. (1988) 'Transparent insulation materials', in Jesch L. F. (1988) pp2–4.

Yannas, S. (1994) 'Flats', in *Solar Energy and Housing Design, Vol. 2: Examples,* Architectural Association Publications, London, pp98–102.

Chapter 6   Machine Control

The term machine is used here to embrace active systems with moving parts, where controls may take full advantage of electronic technology, but may still vary from automatic to manual. Inevitably, some of the issues around 'machine control' have already come up, for example, in relation to intervention by users. Indeed, there is a distinct mirroring of aspects covered in Chapter 4. Here however, as with the previous chapter, the emphasis is directed more strongly towards the intentions of the designers, and in particular where the performance of the system appears to be subject to dilemmas, limitations or shortcomings. This slant, with technology sometimes in the dock together with dubious decisions made by professionals, has again been subdivided into three main topics: movable controls attached to glazing, solar air collectors, and issues associated with interactive control and management.

Diffusing, shading and opening – glazing controls

Movable devices to control sunlight, sky glare and solar heat gain appear to have obvious advantages compared with fixed ones. However, there are numerous pitfalls. Both shading and opening devices complement the preceding section on completely passive optimization of transparent and translucent envelopes. Again, the responsiveness of control systems can be critical, especially when there are rapidly changing climatic characteristics over the course of a day. The balance between wind, rain and sunshine may be difficult to reconcile. Controls may compete, and be too finely or too coarsely tuned, with negative consequences in either case. Similarly there are pros and cons for external, interstitial and internal systems.

wear and tear

Firstly, there is the matter of longevity and robustness. This is more readily overcome for mechanisms to open windows, or other adjustable ventilators, than it is for diffusing or shading components, especially when these are located externally. Wind, rain, sunshine and biodiversity will all take their toll on the shading material itself, as well as the mechanism for moving it. The external blinds used on sections of the glass roof of the Burrell Museum in Glasgow,

6.1 External shading mechanisms, Burrell Museum, Glasgow – these only operated for a short period relative to the life of the building (photographed November 2004)

designed by architect Barry Gasson, testify to the ravages of nature and, reportedly, did not function for long after completion (Figure 6.1). The relatively shallow slope over the restaurant and cafeteria would have been an additional factor relative to the build-up of dirt on the fabric. Even where external blinds have been used vertically or at a much steeper pitch, and in a less windy context, they will remain vulnerable.

An example is the array for the long west-facing glazed arcade of the research and development building in the Rheinelbe Science Park at Gelsenkirchen, Germany (51.6°N), completed by architects Kiessler + Partner in the mid-1990s, with the involvement of both the Fraunhofer Institut and Ingenieurburo Trumpp. Setting aside the advisability of constructing a tilted west-facing wall of glass in the first place, it seems ironic that the seemingly uncomplicated solution of external shading appears to be more at risk than the daunting task of lifting large sections of the façade upwards (Figure 6.2). Both are evidently specified to limit solar overheating, and both are powered, as this demand for cooling occurs, by solar photovoltaic (PV) arrays on the roof. Thus, having provided the problem of excessive passive solar gain at the hottest part of the day, Kiessler has apparently neatly solved it with active solar measures. However, while both the small electric motors for moving the blinds, and the much larger ones for moving the glass, are safely protected inside, the blinds and their rollers and guides remain outside as a recurring item for maintenance and replacement.

This in turn raises the question as to whether the environmental solution to the given problem was over-egged. Given the area of the openings, evaporative cooling of incoming air by an artificial lake, and the height between inlets and outlets together with the active assistance from fans at high level, one could have expected the entire cooling load to be met by ventilation. After all, the highly glazed living space of the Howard house by Brian Mackay-Lyons (Chapter 5) had no means of shading and the clients found that it never became unbearably warm. In the much larger concourse by Kiessler, localized shading inside is also possible by means of planting or parasols.

In another European project, blinds posed the question of necessity as well as operation. This is the student residence at Strathclyde University in Glasgow, already discussed relative to adaptive opportunity and thermal mass. The reflective blinds, which were pulled up to shield five storeys between the outer glass and the TI, frequently jammed. Part of the problem was that they were initially programmed to pull up if there was too much radiation as well as too little radiation. This meant a minimum of two operations daily, but possibly much more on intermittently sunny and cloudy days. Even so, it is likely that the problem of jamming indicated either poor quality of the lifting mechanism or poor supervision of the installation. To make matters worse, the slope of the site meant that 'cherry-picking' plant could not gain access. It has been necessary

6.2   View looking north past west façade of R &
      D building in the Rheinelbe Science Park

to laboriously erect scaffolding in order to free stuck blinds. This enables fixed panes of glass to be removed and replaced. To resolve this onerous burden of maintenance, far less frequent movement of blinds was enforced, moving only twice annually – up in summer and down in winter. Having significantly coarsened the strategy for avoidance of overheating, as well as that of conserving heat, it is then fair to challenge their necessity.

   Indeed a much smaller European demonstration project, with TI retrofitted over south and east walls at the home of Dr Leslie Jesch ■6.1 in Birmingham, UK, relied on opening windows to avoid overheating. Although not the answer given by predictive modelling at Strathclyde, it is probable that opening windows together with passive stack ventilation would have avoided overheating. This then leaves the issue of conserving heat more effectively than with the TI on its own. Pre-contract, it would have been interesting to compare the performance of the blind with a static option, such as a low-emissivity

■6.1 Leslie Jesch: a solar champion

Dr Jesch edited the TI workshop proceedings referenced in the previous chapter. He also launched and edited Sun at Work in Great Britain, which later became Sun at Work In Europe, running successfully for many years; not to mention editing Sun World and initiating the establishment of ISES Europe, the first large regional component of the International Solar Energy Society.

6.3   South façade of junior school in Glasgow, showing glass louvres and glazing with integral venetian blinds – note pupils' work attached to glass

coating on the inside of the glass along with a selective coating on the outer face of the storage wall. Without exploring the maths or modelling in depth, it is certain to be a marginal difference.

optimizing control

The first matter of longevity and robustness is inextricably linked to the second one of control. If it is automatic, how finely set should be the switches? Does there need to be more than one environmental parameter to activate switches? If so, will they compete? Should there be a manual override? If so, who should be able to use it? These are all questions that could well arise relative to the adjustment of blinds, louvres, windows and other ventilators. The last returns us forcibly to the issue of adaptive control addressed in Chapter 4. As a reminder of this, but with a further case study, a new block of classrooms for a junior school in Glasgow by architects Elder and Cannon (Figure 6.3), illustrates the risks of leaving power in the hands of teachers. The architectural aim was to use daylight to displace electricity for lighting, and natural ventilation to displace electricity for fans. It has a south-facing façade and, where adjustable external diffusing glass louvres do not shield windows, there are interstitial venetian blinds. Therefore, four critical controls are available to the teachers – lights, windows, louvres and venetian blinds. The first are nearly always on in all classrooms; the second are seldom opened in any classroom; the third are occasionally adjusted; and the fourth almost never move from the fully closed position in any of the classrooms. The reason behind the last and least expected inaction is that the teachers find the windows to be useful extra wall space for displaying the work of pupils. With the blinds open, there would be too much 'glare contrast' to see the work. Overall, it is a remarkably similar story to that raised in Chapter 4 with regard to the solar school in Fife. Teachers require control, but do not tend to use it as designers hope.

Another institutional building in Glasgow, the main administrative headquarters of the Strathclyde Police Traffic Division, has adopted the same aims, but a different solution, to a south-facing façade. Smith McEwan Architects also wanted to displace electricity for artificial lighting and ventilation. In this case, machine control has been purposefully minimized, but is nevertheless an essential component. In order to passively avoid excessive solar gain, the façade has been tilted outwards by 7.5°. This means that the critical angle of incidence of about 50° (see Chapters 1 and 2) will be exceeded for a reasonable amount of time around the centre of the day in the warmest part of summer. Green-tinted 'anti-sun' was also specified for the external pane of glass, and manually operated solar blinds were provided internally. The design of the façade, including the proportion of transparent to opaque surface, was assisted by the LT method (Steemers and Baker, 1994). However, the concept of allowing occupants to fine-tune light by means of the blinds, and ventilation by opening windows, has been compromised by the detailed specification. The blinds are lowered and raised by means of a fixed handle attached to their rigid spars, which means that they cannot go higher than an average human reach. This reduces the amount of available daylight. There are also no effective friction-stays on opening windows to enable fine-tuning of natural ventilation. As a consequence, especially in windy conditions, there is a disincentive to open up. The allocation of a desk fan to every workstation would appear to confirm a tendency to seek comfort by agitating the air already inside the space, rather than introducing fresh air. Thus the intention of achieving satisfactory environmental control, including cross-ventilation, by very limited use of automation has not been realized. While a basic building management system satisfactorily operates high-level windows at each side of a central atrium, reliance on the common sense of occupants to open windows along the perimeter has proved shaky. Moreover, the artificial lights are also manually operated, and the occupants appear to be switching these on, regardless of the adequacy of daylight.

Returning to the more mechanized building in Gelsenkirchen, the system for both blinds and windows in the arcade or concourse is automated, but security staff have access to a manual override. Thus it is possible to have the sliding 'portcullis' windows open with the blinds remaining up on a warm day. The awnings on the south-facing edges of offices and laboratories are also beyond the control of individual occupants. As the sun moves in and out of formations of cloud, the awnings move up and down. In other words the parameters for control are so finely tuned that they can be visually aggravating. Perhaps to combat such irritation from the central control, the occupants all have vertical adjustable blinds within their offices, as well as the ability to open French doors and opaque ventilation panels. (Baird, 2001). However, while the latter two are practical, and the ventilation panel wisely includes an insect mesh, vertical blinds of the type used have a tendency to deaden any space aesthetically, as well as to significantly reduce daylight. The lesson so far from Gelsenkirchen, as well as from Glasgow, is that it is not easy to achieve an appropriate balance between central electronic management and local intervention by users.

For another building, Rijkswaterstaat at Ijmuiden, the Dutch headquarters for looking after the North Sea Canal, the climate is strongly influenced by the maritime location at 52.5°N. Designed by architects Atelier Z and completed in 1999, a different approach from that at Gelsenkirchen has been taken regarding control of external blinds for open-plan workspaces. In the middle of a sunny day in August, the external blinds remained down for a considerable period after the sun had left a particular façade. The consequence of this was that automatically dimmed fluorescent fittings were not operating at such a low level of illumination as they should have been. The blinds effectively 'robbed Peter to pay Paul'. Some of the electrical load associated with cooling may have been

6.4   Atrium of Rijkswaterstaat – windows closed with weather sunny but windy

saved, but at the cost of additional lighting. Also, although each fluorescent fitting measured the level of light on desk-tops, the dimming could not turn them completely off, no matter how bright the natural light. There is a manual switch, but it turns all the lights off, thus defeating the aim of individual control. Although such a system avoids periodic start-up surges over a working day, it results in a visually and psychologically unsatisfactory situation. It gives a dull lustre to the interior, while the outside looks sparklingly inviting and, having made people more environmentally aware, it must be frustrating that the lights should remain on when not required.

The same building seemed to have a switching dilemma when it came to opening and closing windows in the atrium (Figure 6.4), which functions as a concourse for entry, reception and circulation between the two main parts of the working accommodation. It is partially shaded by PV cells set into the glass roof, while façades are not shaded. Openable windows further regulate the temperature and thermal comfort. These are located close to the bottom and top of the atrium and are opened by a thermostat once a preset temperature is reached, but may also be closed by an anemometer, according to the velocity of the wind. Therefore, there can be competition between the microclimatic parameters, especially on a sunny and windy day. If the thermostat has initial priority over the anemometer, one can imagine that the expectation would be that once excessively warm air has been exhausted, the wishes of both controls would coincide. However, the issue of time lag between respective automated instructions is again relevant. During a relatively brief visit in such weather, the atrium varied from pleasantly fresh, with windows open, to rather too warm, with them closed. In the latter condition, the space was a great deal warmer than the adjacent working spaces with their mechanical control. It is also worth remarking that the atrium is bounded on the two sides adjacent to the offices by two massive rammed earth walls, as well as having a heavy floor. The nature of admittance and response (Chapter 5) means that only a part of the thickness of the walls is relevant in terms of modifying swings in temperature inside the atrium, while the whole thickness helps to regulate time-lag and damping between the atrium and offices. Overall, as a transitory space, this aspect does not seem critical. Rather, it is worth noting that, had a similar system been applied to natural ventilation of the working areas, the impact of overheating would have been considerably more serious.

Rijkswaterstaat's atrium is relatively small in area. Therefore the prospect of supporting a glass roof with integral PV as fixed partial shading is not too challenging. In tandem with the control of ventilation, this canopy has a useful role in the avoidance of overheating. In a very large atrium, where the spans are considerably greater, the issues are different. The weight of such a roof is a serious concern, and, without resorting to very elaborate ventilating measures, shading will be more central to thermal control.

A good example is the new roof over the internal court of Kingsdale School in Dulwich, south London, at about 51.5°N (Figure 6.5). Here De Rijke Marsh Morgan Architects have taken ETFE ■6.2 technology on an interesting adventure with the help of services consultant Fulcrum and commercial firm Vector Special Projects (VSP). The dimensions are approximately 85.5m by 37.5m, covering some 3200m². VSP developed a technique so that triple layer cushions can respond to changing levels of sunlight. In other words it is a 'variable transmission' version of standard ETFE (Littlefield, 2002), which relies on some active assistance. Littlefield describes it thus:

> The system works by fixing an internal layer into the cushion, which can be moved up and down pneumatically; by printing graphics on both the outer and internal layers, the amount of daylight admitted can be adjusted by controlling the distance between the overlapping patterns... The new lightweight structure will be capable of blocking out 50–95 per cent of sunlight.

Littlefield also mentions work by VSP's main competitor, the aptly named Skyspan, to chemically coat a film of aluminium on to one of the layers of the cushion. This is moving away from variable transmission and also to a more passive solution, although the help of a machine is of course still required to keep the cushions pressurized.

However, such techniques need to be treated with some caution. During a visit on a sunny afternoon, one day after the equinox in September, it was noted that the canopy produced quite an overcast effect – rather as if rain were imminent, belying the real weather. This is not surprising, given that at least half the direct sunlight is obstructed, while virtually full shade is attainable. It suggests that applications might be more suited to spaces such as lecture theatres, where this range would be useful, and presumably the technique could be adapted to a different range – say 35–80 per cent sunlight transmission. At the time of the visit to Kingsdale School, the level of shading induced by the new canopy was automatically controlled, while artificial lights were manually operated. Whatever percentage of daylight was transmitted, large overhead lights within the space were switched on, as was the lighting in bounding spaces. On the other hand, the space had certainly not overheated due to solar gain. The environment within the atrium seemed comfortable, as well as fresh. It was explained that the lighting inside the atrium was to facilitate cleaning, and that it was also desired to have the school brightly lit for an impending visit by parents just after school hours. This raises issues of operation and competing priorities for utility, comfort and energy efficiency. A thermal advantage may simultaneously incur an electrical handicap, a theme to be developed further in the final part of this chapter in relation to other case studies.

■6.2 The chemistry of ETFE

ETFE is ethylene-tetrafluoroethylene, the basic ingredients being ethylene (C_2H_4), a colourless inflammable gas, and fluorine, a non-metallic chemical element in the same group as the halogens, which occurs normally as an inflammable and toxic gas.

6.5   ETFE canopy at Kingsdale School – note artificial lights inside while outside is sunlit

shading with heat as a useful by-product

Remaining with innovative variable shading control for transparent roofs, but bringing the scale right back to that of a domestic conservatory, two earlier experimental projects at Napier University in Edinburgh are notable for attempting simultaneously to shade and to divert the incident solar energy to heating water. The principle is to solve a problem without having to dump potentially useful free energy.

The first is titled 'fluid shades'. A fluid, with dark coloured particles in suspension is pumped through a translucent double-skin panel, which is located under the roof of the sunspace. The particles absorb solar radiation and the circulating fluid transfers the heat to a thermal store. Depending on the dimensions of the roof, this could be used either for space heating or for domestic hot water. The concentration of the suspended particles, and thus the absorptivity and transmissivity of the panel, may be varied to provide variable shading.

The second system is called 'fin shades'. Several rows of 'pipe and fin' or 'clip fin' absorber strips, based on solar water heating technology, are located under the glass roof. The fins may be rotated to provide shading and collect solar heat, without severely diminishing the amount of daylight entering the space. Also the low-emissivity surface of the fins inhibits downward transfer of heat during the day and upward radiant loss at night. Water is circulated by a pump through the fins and again transfers heat to a thermal store.

shading with heat as a useless by-product

The ability of any shading fins or louvres to function as a solar absorber may lead to unintended problems. Staying in Scotland, the new Wolfson Medical School Building for the University of Glasgow (55.9°N) provides a controversial example of a fully transparent, double-skin façade. This project, designed by Reiach and Hall Architects and completed in 2002, takes the topic of 'diffusing, shading and opening' into a third area of concern. Here the solution applied to the design and detailed specification, coupled with that applied to control, defies any environmentally conscious rationale – all the more surprising because, in terms of 'machine control', there is only one movable component. This is a venetian blind, which is constructed of cedar slats and located between the fixed outer skin of unframed glass and the fixed inner screen of framed glass. Its function is indeed to shade and diffuse daylight entering the area lying immediately behind, known as the 'study landscape'. More explicitly this is the zone for 'information technology' or IT plus a library, with banks of computers aligned at right angles to the windows and bookshelves located further back. Because the façade is curved from southeast to due south, it is important to prevent direct sunlight from shining on to monitors (although the position of books and computers could have been reversed).

As one might expect for a building of this nature, the cedar blind is controlled electronically by a building management system (BMS). When fully down, which is where it has inexplicably been for almost all of its life to date, the slats appear to have three positions – almost fully closed, open at about 30° to the horizontal and fully open (horizontal). The artificial lighting is similar to that described for Rijkswaterstaat at Ijmuiden. When the slats are closed, it is quite dark and gloomy in the 'study landscape' and lights appear to be fully on. When they are set at 30°, the space is somewhat lighter, but the lights are still on, although potentially dimmed. When they are horizontal, there is enough light to see monitors, but the adequacy of daylight for reading could be contentious, depending on weather, time of day and proximity to the window. At any rate, even though parts of the screen of cedar slats may be at different settings according to their position on the curve, the lights are never off; and no matter how dull and uniformly overcast the sky is, the blinds remain down.

It is legitimate to ask 'why have a fully glazed wall if it cannot displace electricity for lighting, let alone provide a decent view?' Moreover, since students may enter the 'study landscape' having first experienced a gloriously day-lit triangular atrium (Figure 6.6a), the subdued combination of artificial and natural light comes as a depressing anticlimax (Figure 6.6b), especially when associated with permanently closed windows and air conditioning. This then touches on the need for, and function of, the outer skin of glass. The missed opportunity is for the inner screen to open without disturbance from traffic noise. Providing that there were adjustable and adequately sized vents at the top, inlets at the bottom and free passage for air at each floor level, the void between the two skins could function as a 'solar chimney'.

6.6a The structural glass roof over the atrium of the Wolfson Building

6.6b The inside of the 'study landscape' with cedar-slatted blinds occluding daylight

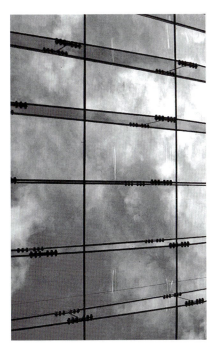

■6.3 Examples of earth cooling

Examples of such passive earth cooling coupled to a mechanical system of distribution vary significantly in latitude and climate (from continental to maritime). One is the exhibition building by Fielden, Clegg, Bradley Architects at the Doncaster Earth Centre in northern England (53.5°N). Another is the nocturnal air supply to the atrium of the PV factory in Freiburg by architects Rolf & Hotz (48°N). The technique has also been used at a domestic level – the Solar House in Freiburg and the 'Ecobuild' experimental houses at the Dutch government's ECN Research Centre in Petten on the northwest coast of Holland (52.8°N) are examples.

Not only could this have exhausted air from inside by natural thermo-circulation, but it would have also helped to prevent the façade from overheating in hot weather. In this last regard, one may note that dynamic modelling has shown that a double-skin façade will inherently tend to overheat more than a single-skin one (Kondratenko, 2003). Nevertheless, the advantage of having an outer fixed skin lies with the opportunity for reducing both ventilating and heating costs. For example, in summer, if fresh air had been led into the atrium through an underground labyrinth of ducts ■6.3 and provided with a route into the 'study landscape', the system for ventilation would have needed minimal active assistance. Furthermore, in winter, the air exhausted from the top of the solar chimney could have been passed through a heat exchanger to reduce the energy required to heat incoming fresh air. In her theoretical study for a similar double-skin façade, Kondratenko has shown that the combination of recovered heat together with the solar-preheating effect will substantially reduce demand for space heating in winter.

Unfortunately none of this has happened. Not only is the inner skin fixed apart from service access at each end, but also there is no means of controlling the upward passage of air between the two skins. There are fixed slots at top and bottom, as well as at each floor level, where toughened glass sheets enable maintenance. This means that the flow of air within the void will be seriously interrupted on its journey to the top, while the cedar slats function as a solar absorber. Indeed, the sunnier the weather, the more the tilt of the slats will increase the area for absorptance in radiant view of the sun. Also, their hue has of course darkened noticeably over the two years since the building was first occupied. The façade is effectively a solar air collector, but cannot be usefully used in cold weather, nor can the hot air rapidly escape in warm weather. Instead it increases the burden for the air conditioning. Thus the only practical function, which can be attributed to the outer glazing, is that it protects the cedar slats from the harshest aspects of the local climate – wind and rain. Had there been an alternative specification of an efficient solar venetian blind, or any of several completely passive diffusing and reflecting options of the kind described in the previous chapter, worthwhile displacement of artificial lighting could have been achieved.

selective versus exclusive modes

The commentary on the above case study may seem harsh. But it does serve to emphasize the risks associated with cliché and inappropriate use of material in a particular context. In doing so, it flags a need for a more environmentally sympathetic and holistic approach to mixed or selective mode heating, ventilating and lighting systems (passive/active 'selective' compared to 'exclusive' control as used by Hawkes – Chapter 4). If architects are better briefed on the essential principles and concepts, they will be in a more persuasive position. Full air conditioning in the exclusive mode may be easy to design and control, but it is an energy guzzler and seldom enjoyed by occupants. Specialist consultants must take this on board and challenge their own traditionally tight certainties. The Wolfson Building also highlights the fact that a sophisticated BMS is only as good as the parameters that humans give it. The computing truism 'rubbish in, rubbish out' holds good. The prohibition of blinds being open in overcast conditions could only be justified if the movements are too frequent, as with the science building in Gelsenkirchen. Then the result may be irritating, and even counterproductive in terms of motorized energy required. But such an argument should be weighed against the potential benefits of the initial decision to fully glaze. The cedar 'veil' is too extreme to be functional. Looking through glass darkly is not uplifting.

More positively, the critique has shown that relatively small adjustments to the design and specification could have made a substantial improvement to performance. A double-skin façade, which inadvertently and negatively functions as a solar air collector, provides a cue for turning this technique to advantage. More generally it indicates a potential role for solar energy in mixed-mode systems of ventilation. Indeed, the more we insulate and the more energy-efficient we make glazing, the more pressing becomes the need to tackle ventilation. We are back at the 'quality versus quantity tensions' of Chapter 3, but now from the perspective of the detailed design and performance of systems.

Harvesting hot air – integrated collectors

Moving air seems to have more appeal to architects than other fluids such as water or an antifreeze solution. It is more within the domain of constructional integration, with not so much necessarily devolved to the expertise of specialist consultants. Using solar energy to heat air, as well as to move it, is possible through a fairly large range of temperatures. In terms of the initial collection, the cool or low end of this spectrum involves spaces that may nevertheless be occupied. These are normally unheated, or heated to a lower level than the main accommodation, and include the whole panoply of small and large sunspaces. A lift of 5–10K above ambient can make a significant difference to the demand for energy in adjacent heated spaces. Because of the relatively low level of temperature, the saving in energy is principally confined to preheating air for ventilation coupled with an enhanced buffering effect. More complex issues of 'machine control' applied to larger sunspaces are left to the final part of this chapter, while Chapter 4 covered this quite fully for the domestic sector, posing the question 'do conservatories conserve?'. The emphasis at that stage of the discourse was on the scope that users had to affect the efficiency of the system. Here, it is the aims of the architectural team that are to come under closer scrutiny.

At the high end of solar-induced hikes in temperature, a transparent air collector has no other use, apart from possibly forming part of the outer skin of

■6.4 George Löf's breathing solar air collector in Colorado

In the mid-1940s, after a gap of just over 60 years since the 19th century wall-mounted solar air collectors of Professor Edward Morse in Salem, Massachusetts, Professor George Löf fitted a transpired (breathing) solar air collector of some 43m² on to the southern slope of his own house in Boulder, Colorado. The cover was a double layer of glass, while the absorber was overlapping sheets of glass, each successive layer covering two-thirds of the one below. The bottom sheet was fully painted black, and thereafter the top third, so that the sun's view was of a fully black absorber. Air from the room below was ducted into the bottom of the collector above the overlapping plates, and out at the top below the plates. Thus 'upward flowing air passes between plates, picking up heat stored in them and becoming very hot'. On a sunny day Löf estimated that air entering at about 21°C would leave at about 82°C, a lift of over 60K. The heated air was then connected to his gas-fired warm air heating system, and was estimated to save 25 per cent in the first winter of operation. To further improve its performance he added an insulated thermal store of 6 tons of crushed rock. This was estimated to increase the solar contribution to about 33 per cent. The main problem with the system seemed to be that some of the absorber plates cracked due to heat stress. It may be noted that its continental location at 40°N made this ideal territory for solar heating, with cold and sunny winters.

a building. Designers may more easily predict its performance. It is solely intended to raise the temperature of air as high as possible using the free energy of the sun. Hence, it has a transparent cover and dark absorber of some kind in the same way as a flat-plate collector, which uses a liquid as the medium for transferring energy. The objective may still be to lower energy loss by ventilation, but other options are also available. Heat may be transferred to the fabric of the building, or to the hot water system, or become an integral part of a warm-air heating system.

early development and general principles of solar air collectors

Solar air collectors, as opposed to sunspaces, have a respectable history of over 120 years. Having said that, and acknowledging the work of mid-20th Century pioneers such as George Löf ■6.4 in America (Butti and Perlin, 1980), their more common usage did not gain momentum until the 1980s. Importantly, the technique in its various guises is viable for cool, cloudy climates. The low thermal mass of the collector itself assists in this regard. Transparent solar air collectors of different types have now been extensively tested in various parts of northern Europe, including Scotland. Indeed, there has not been a single North Sun conference, since its inauguration in 1984, which has not included reportage of dedicated solar air collectors. In the 1990s a parallel effort took hold with opaque solar air collectors, the lift in temperature fulfilling a preheating objective similar to sunspaces. This section confines itself to the scope for using glazed and unglazed solar air collectors to conserve energy, as well as to improve the quality of air and reduce the risk of condensation and mould.

Having established that the term 'solar air collector' does not include spaces designed for human occupation, it is nevertheless still reasonable to regard a sunspace at 27–30°C as being in the mode of a collector. The warmer upper part certainly provides a favourable site for an array of air collectors, for example, as in the project at Paxton Court in Sheffield by Cedric Green (Chapter 4). The temperature of air entering the bottom of the collectors has a head start, and can therefore be readily boosted to charge a short-term thermal store. Although most people can tolerate up to 30°C indoors for short periods, temperatures within a glazed solar air collector can rise as high as 80 or 100°C. Not only is this untenable for human occupancy, but it is also necessary to check the melting point of some insulating materials, as well as to detail for thermal expansion.

Low thermal capacitance is important within air collectors. This is quite different from a sunspace, where the most important attribute for users is as an amenity, and capacitance is needed to avoid overheating as well as extending the period of comfort. In a collector the aim is for solar radiation to be absorbed but not stored. The layer of air close to the absorber becomes quickly warmed, and the more tangling air has with the absorber the better. To avoid much of this heat being lost outwards, the air is transported rapidly away. It may either be taken directly into a usable part of a building or into a medium for thermal storage, and sometimes both. The effectiveness of the collector will depend initially on the nature of the outer cover, the absorber and the control mechanism for moving the air, and thereafter on the design of any heat exchangers and stores.

development of glazed solar air collectors in Scotland

Given that there are so many examples of solar air collectors, especially in northern parts of Europe, there is some value in focusing on research, development and demonstration in one climatic region. Two air collectors in Scotland were introduced earlier (Chapter 4), because they had been compromised to an extent by the actions of users. These are now considered in terms of their unhampered performance in a wider Scottish context.

Air collectors serving the 22 flats at Stile Park in Stornoway (58.2°N) were not monitored. However, there were predictive calculations, which of course assumed that the occupants would make use of the adjustable vents provided. The specification for the entire system was kept as simple as possible. ■6.5 The single-glazed collectors are lined with slabs of mineral wool, which are spray-painted black. Air is ducted from the top of the attic to the top of the short-term thermal store, and returns to the eaves of the attic from the bottom of the store. The store comprises clean stones. These are contained in an insulated concrete box below the first half-landing of the access stairs, and are treated with a benign chemical to prevent any fungal growth. Stub ducts deliver air from the store to the living spaces.

It was calculated that the omission of the rock store would add 10 per cent to the electrical heating load of a typical first floor, gable-end flat (Porteous, 1983). Although this corresponds to a drop of 22 per cent in the solar contribution, the first value is the important one in terms of fuel consumption and one has to ask what such a percentage means in units of energy. In this case it is just over 250kWh annually or about 5kWh weekly per flat, which is marginal relative to the cost of the provision. On the other hand, useful lessons were learnt. Setting aside the issue of transference of noise and odour between dwellings, which was serious, the physics of the set-up did work. In the absence of continuous measurements, spot-readings indicated that the collector performed as expected.

The next Scottish project to be completed was also relatively far north, but close to the sunnier east coast. It is a set of five houses for Ross and Cromarty District Council in the small market town of Dingwall at 57.6°N. They are sited adjacent to near-identical ones, which are heated by natural gas. Architect David Somerville initiated the idea of solar air collectors for both space and water heating in 1989, and the houses were occupied, including by him, in the autumn of 1990. An Irish company, ETI, marketed the system under the trade name 'Trisol'. (This collector is now marketed by another company, NuAire, as part of a smaller system to enhance the supply of pre-warmed air for ventilation, with an

■6.5 Simple solar air collectors in Stornoway

The collector is part 'black attic', with 42° tilted glazing, and part vertical. Each has a single-glazed transparent cover, an air space and the black mineral wool absorber. The total area of each collector is 14.4m² and the rock store is 6.4m³, giving a volume to area ratio of 0.45. Taking monthly mean averages of solar radiation, the rock store was estimated to take 4–14 hours to charge up. Typical mean monthly lifts in temperature within it would be just over 4K in December and January, going up to 10K in March and 12K in May (Saluja, Porteous and Holling, 1987).

6.7   Close-up of the solar absorber in the 'Trisol' system used at Dingwall

option for solar water heating, but without the large thermal store and heat pump.) 'Trisol' signified three components: the collector, which covers approximately half of the south-facing surface of the roof; an energy processing unit with brine store; and the heat pump. The latter two elements are both located in the attic. The absorber in the collector is officially a trade secret, but appears to be a loose non-metallic equivalent of steel wool (Figure 6.7), which fills the cavity between glazed cover and backing insulation and offers an appropriate amount of resistance to the upward flow of air.

In sunny weather, warm air can be supplied directly from collector into the dwelling. Once it has reached a satisfactory level of comfort, spare heat can then go into the store, where an indirect coil heats domestic hot water in a standard cylinder with an electric immersion heater as back-up. On an overcast day, air from the top of the collector is routed through the cold (evaporator) side of the heat pump, cool air returning to the bottom of the collector. Air from the dwelling is at the same time passed through the hot (condenser) side of the heat pump, returning to the dwelling at 30°C or more. To deal with very cold and overcast days in winter, a 6kW electric auxiliary electric heater was fitted. However, due to the speed of delivery, this led to uncomfortable stratification of temperature. Somerville describes how the situation was resolved (Somerville, 1992):

Following discussions with the electricity supply company a 6kW immersion heater was installed in the hot water cylinder within the house.
In winter conditions this delivered heat by indirect circuit to the heat store in the roof space thus reversing the summer time heat transfer.

The utility company also agreed to an economic 'total control tariff', which acknowledges the storage characteristic of the system.

There were other teething problems associated with the electronic controller. Initially it was very sensitive to surges or spikes in the supply, apparently caused by a nearby dairy. The controller then gave incorrect instructions to the occupants and also burnt out several heat pumps. However, the manufacturer was able to suppress the effect of the spikes on the microprocessor, and the problem was solved. Given the variables introduced by occupants, it was not really possible to compare the performance of the 'Trisol' dwellings with their gas-heated neighbours (whose tariff per kWh of delivered heat was lower than that of the 'total control'). It had also been decided to insulate the solar houses to a somewhat better standard than the traditional ones, introducing yet another difference.

Monitoring of the air collectors on the roofs of the Easthall demonstration project in Glasgow at 55.9°N in 1992 provided yet more useful information, as well as further problems to be overcome (Porteous and Ho, 1994). Since the aim here was primarily to preheat water for domestic use, the efficiency of the air-to-water heat exchanger is important. It was also decided to use a perforated aluminium absorber, which was anodized black (Figure 6.8). Air is breathed

6.8   A roof-integrated solar air collector at Easthall, aligned with the glazed-in balcony

through the metal (thus termed 'transpired-plate'), providing a similar dynamic effect on the flow of air to that of the 'Trisol' collector. The initially installed heat exchangers were radiators for standard 'Transit' vans, since laboratory tests had shown that these mass-produced components were very efficient. Before this decision, there had been consideration of bubbling air directly through the preheat tank, but the idea was discarded to avoid any risk of supporting the legionella pneumophila bacterium. Lifts in temperature vary significantly, depending on the time interval examined and the juxtaposition of key climatic parameters. ■6.6(1)

Even though the 'Transit' radiators worked as expected, and there was a large drop in temperature either side of them, there was enough warmth left in the air to use it usefully to refresh and warm the stairwell. ■6.6(2) Here, the existing heavy construction of the bounding walls and stairs function as thermal storage, which helps to maintain a fairly steady level of warmth. The overall performance seemed quite satisfactory. Then it was noticed that the heat exchangers were made of aluminium and would not make very good neighbours to the copper plumbing! All were subsequently replaced with bespoke copper units, but these proved rather less efficient. Nevertheless, what was lost to the water was gained to the stairwell. An advantage of this was, that on a bright and cold day, the thresholds to the flats are noticeably warm. It gives the occupants something tangible to associate with their solar panels, as opposed to their hot water, which can only be taken on trust. Another problem was achieving a satisfactory seal to the collectors and ducting. The former were constructed on site and constituted part of the weatherproof envelope, but the process would have been better had the components been prefabricated in the controlled environment of a factory.

The transpired-plate collectors at Easthall may be compared to those designed for the earlier retrofit of the flats in Göteborg (see also Chapters 2 and 5). There are two key differences. Firstly, the air does not pass through the Göteborg absorber. Secondly, its absorber is corrugated rather than flat. This provides a greater area of surface with air passing through the trapezoidal voids between the metal and the insulation below it. The respective characteristics would tend to cancel each other in terms of performance. In other words, a better specification in each case would have been for a perforated and corrugated absorber. At any rate we know that the Swedish collector worked well enough to have a significant impact on the temperature of the original 'no-fines' concrete wall. At much the same time Methilhill Primary School in Fife (see also Chapter 4) included a 'black attic' collector, which was very similar to that employed for the flats in Stornoway. A visit in 1993 elicited that the air collector, which is dedicated as a reservoir of preheated air for mechanically ventilating the internally located main hall, works well. Temperatures are regularly in the range 50–60°C and the collector contributes to overall energy efficiency, which is 25 per cent less than the norm.

■6.6 Breathing solar air collectors in Easthall

6.6(1) The access stairwell is part of the thermal loop. Its pre-warmed air is ducted at eaves level to enter the collector below the aluminium absorber. It is then drawn through the perforations, leaves the collector via a manifold at the top, passes through the air-to-water heat exchanger and is ducted back to the foot of the stairwell. Water from the heat exchanger is taken to a preheat tank, which feeds individual hot water cylinders in a set of six flats. On a single day in October 1992, the lift in temperature between the cold feed and the top of the preheat tank peaked at 12K and averaged 6.7K. Taken over the whole week including that day, the average lift more than halved to 3.3K. The equivalent lifts, subtracting the temperature of the cold feed from that measured at the inlet from the collector to the heat exchanger, were respectively 28.0K (with the temperature leaving the collector reaching 40.5°C), 14.6K and 8.5K. Earlier that year, in May, the temperature at the outlet from the collector had reached 73°C, but at that time an unsealed section of ducting had resulted in a large drop before air entered the heat exchanger – almost 30K. The preheating of water was thus compromised until the problem was rectified. The other lift in temperature of note is that between the inlet and outlet of the collector. In May this averaged 26.5K over one day, with a high of 42.5K, and an average for a whole week of 20K. In the week in October the lower equivalent values were 10.5K, 23K and 5.5K. Thus the collector was shown to work well, as was the preheating system.

6.6(2) On the day in October which yielded nearly 7K to the preheat tank, the average temperature of the air leaving the heat exchanger was just below 20°C, which helped to bring the temperature in the stairwell up to over 16°C. This was more than 9K above that outside.

■6.7 Unglazed air collectors: details of tests

6.7(1) The area of the test rig in Edinburgh was 2.3m² set at a 45° tilt, and absorptance of slates approximately 0.85. More than six months of measurements indicated a collector efficiency varying from about 30 to 60 per cent, according to increasing 'mass flow rate' of air (kg/sm²). For a period of one month (27th April to 25th May 1989) this corresponded to a daily output from 0.75 to 3.00kWh/m² for incident solar radiation within a range of 1.25–6.50kWh/m². Some scatter in measurements was assumed to be due to variable flow of wind over the slates.

6.7(2) The area measured was 4.7m². The boarding, called 'sarking' in Scotland, was not in this case covered in roofing felt. Later 'solar slate' roofs had to penetrate felt at exit points.

6.7(3) The initial efficiency was calculated to be approximately 10 per cent, but after adjustments the figure increased to 21 per cent.

6.7(4) One household spent £130 on electricity over 27 days in January 1996, equivalent to some 1,800kWh.

6.7(5) Four sections of flexible plastic pipe, 60cm long and 2.5cm in diameter, are inserted into the space between the steel sheet and membrane. These are connected to a manifold, a plastic pipe of 15cm diameter. A depression is created by an 80W fan, which induces a flow of about 40l/s. The fan either operates by time clock (say from 8.00am to 6.00pm) or by thermostatic switching based on the temperature of the steel roof sheet.

6.7(6) The area of influence was found to be small at 2.8m². On a sunny spring day in March 1996, with a solar intensity of 900W/m², efficiency was estimated to be 47 per cent – within the range of the original test at Napier. Delivery temperature peaked at 35°C, equivalent to harvesting about 1200W from the ambient air. The temperature in the hallway increased by about 10K, from 12°C at 9.00am to 22°C at 2.30pm, and dropped to 17–18°C during the evening.

development of unglazed solar air collectors in Scotland

Prior to an involvement with the solar air collectors at Easthall, Napier University had undertaken initial experimental work with respect to unglazed, transpiring systems (MacGregor, 1992). Results from a small test rig at Napier were very encouraging. ■6.7(1) Slim synthetic slates were fixed to a perforated board. A plenum formed behind the board with a variable speed fan located at the highest point drew ambient air up through the slates, through the perforations, and finally back out via a length of flexible ducting. This is exactly the same principle described in ■6.4 above for Löf's experimental absorber, except with a different material and without the glass cover.

This initial experiment led to measuring a larger slated area on a real house, where plywood behind the rafters formed a multi-channel plenum, and gaps between butt-jointed boarding directly below the slates ■6.7(2) substituted for the previous perforations. In this case the pre-warmed air was delivered into a north-facing bedroom via an old chimney. A differential thermostat switched a 60W centrifugal fan on and off, with one sensor located immediately under the slates and the other in the bedroom. The efficiency was initially disappointingly low. However, after attempting to seal the plenum more thoroughly, as well as redesigning the manifold at the top of the plenum to give more uniform flow, it more than doubled. ■6.7(3) This is still well below the performance of the preliminary test. Although the pitch of the roof was similar at 40° and the orientation close to due south, the slates were much thicker and more uneven in quality. Also, it seems likely that the cracks between the boards provided more resistance to flow than the previous drilled holes. Together with problems of achieving a satisfactory seal within the plenum, this combination of factors had considerable impact. One also has to bear in mind the absence of roofing felt below the absorber, since the presence of such a material would have further inhibited flow of outside air into the plenum. Nevertheless, at this stage, the technique was thought to hold promise, two key advantages being invisibility and low cost.

The next significant step regarding 'solar slates' was embedded within a research project with the title 'Breathing Sunshine into Scottish Housing' (MacGregor, Taylor and Currie, 1996). Napier University was commissioned to undertake this work by Scottish Homes, a public sector housing quango. It involved comparative monitoring of ten dwellings in Edinburgh that had a track record of condensation and mould attributed to innate thermal inefficiency. ■6.7(4) Four of the houses had a variant of the system described above and three were fitted with a proprietary 'Drimaster' system of ventilation by the company NuAire Ltd. Three others functioned as control houses. Dating from the late 1940s, the homes used a construction devised by the British Iron and Steel Federation. In particular, the roof is unusual compared with traditional Scottish methods. The outer skin has a low pitch of 25° and comprises steel sheeting, now lined internally with a plastic membrane. Insulation has been added to the underside of this in order to enhance its role as a solar air collector. Bearing in mind the position of the steel and plastic on the 'cold' side of the insulation, it is important that the loft space is well ventilated. Otherwise, the collector would also function as a condenser, especially at night.

The means of extracting warm air from under the steel, to be delivered into the upstairs part of the hallway, is relatively simple. ■6.7(5) The area of influence of the collector on the steel roofing was determined through the use of thermal imaging. In good weather, the performance proved to be very satisfactory. ■6.7(6) However on overcast days, the performance was understandably less impressive. It was comparable with that of the 'Drimaster' system, which simply draws air into the house from the loft. The respective controls proved somewhat controversial. The fans in the solar houses were restricted either by time or thermostat, in particular to prevent them running overnight. Even then, it was apparent that residents did not welcome cool draughts. NuAire, on the other hand, believes that 24-hour operation is essential to combat condensation. In fact, both the solar and the 'Drimaster' groups observed an improvement in terms of condensation, whilst the control group experienced problems with surface condensation on windows and the return of mould in bathrooms, as well as mildewed clothing and musty smells.

NuAire now market the 'solar slates' concept as 'Drimaster Ecosmart'. This provides the option of air through a plenum below rafters, as in the first two experiments by Napier University, air from the top of the attic, or cooler air through the eaves on the least sunny side of dwellings. The system may also be adapted to include sunspaces as an alternative to the plenum, as described for the houses at Ballantrae (Chapter 4). An option with a glazed air collector is another more costly variant. It has greater solar potential, but is not invisible. Even though the 24-hour operation remains a debatable decision, it is a step forward that such techniques are now commercially available.

As such systems begin to be replicated, more experimental work on opaque, transpired solar air collectors has been demonstrated, this time in the village of Duns in the Scottish Borders (MacGregor, 2001). Four PV cells were carefully matched to a 10W direct current fan, the objective being that the fan will only operate when there is enough solar energy to activate it. This draws air from an indeterminate area of roof below the tiles via a single outlet. The air then passes through a short length of flexible ducting and is delivered into a utility space. This was a retrofit to existing dwellings owned by Berwickshire Housing Association, and the space to which pre-warmed air is now delivered was previously vulnerable to mould. Lifts in temperature of up to 20K are predicted, ■6.7(7) with an annual energy saving of around 1,500kWh. Given the capital cost of approximately £500 per dwelling and negligible running costs, it seems to be a sound investment.

6.7(7) At the time of a visit in the spring of 2000, the ambient temperature in the afternoon dropped to 7°C and sunshine was intermittent. The fan came on during this time due to a sudden burst of sun. The temperature at the outlet to the space measured 24°C. The lift of 17K was impressive, suggesting that concrete roofing tiles contributed stored solar heat.

■6.8 Airing windows – details of PASSYS tests

6.8(1) PASSYS test cells were distributed to several European countries in the 1980s to enable a single standard for testing different solar components in different climates.

6.8(2) WISACs: In mild and sunny weather, lifts reduced to around 25K, while on cool days with sunny intervals, lifts were between 35 and 40K. On cold and dull days, the lifts were much more modest at about 4K, while on mild overcast days they could be as little as 1.5K. Even on a very sunny day, the daily average is naturally significantly reduced – to approximately 6.5K. Nevertheless, this represents a daily gain of 1.6kWh/m^2, and in the most unfavourable condition, there was a small positive gain. During the night, the collector would recover some heat being lost from the interior, provided a positive flow from outside to inside was ensured.

6.8(3) Supply Air Windows: This technique was apparently first tried in the 1940s and then researched in Finland in the 1970s and 1980s. Bart Jan van den Brink also used it, for example, in Holland in his house in Almere (see Chapter 2), although he reversed the glazing order with the double layer to the outside. The first series of tests at the Scottish Laboratory of the Building Research Establishment (BRE) were carried out without the mechanical control of a fan. The phenomenon of 'flow reversal' was observed on particularly sunny days.

small window-integrated options

In parallel with this work on developing opaque air collectors for tilted roof surfaces, there has been progress on vertical 'window integrated solar air collectors' or WISACs. An experimental rig was initially attached to a west-facing window at the Mackintosh School of Architecture (Porteous, Ho and Kilmartin, 1994). Then a more elaborate full-size mock-up was installed facing due south on a PASSYS ■6.8(1) test cell at the Building Research Establishment's Scottish Laboratory in East Kilbride, just outside Glasgow (Figure 6.9) (Porteous and Baker, 1997). Essentially the aim is to enhance controlled trickle ventilation into rooms using glazed collectors. The flow of air in the tests was actively controlled and the transpiring absorber was a non-metallic fabric. In sunny weather, quite substantial instantaneous lifts of 50–60K were measured on collectors of 1.3m height, but again dropped significantly over longer periods and in other conditions. ■6.8(2) It was estimated that over a heating season, the daily input would average just below 1.0kWh/m^2, or about 250kWh/m^2 from September through to May. It was also found that, similar to the unglazed collectors, increasing the rate of flow increased efficiency. These findings complemented other work at East Kilbride testing 'supply air windows' (Baker and McEvoy, 1999). Fresh air is introduced through a slot at the bottom of a single outer sheet of glass, entering the test cell at the top of the inner double-glazing. ■6.8(3)

further work on absorbers and dynamic insulation

During much the same period, other experimental work in Scotland compared the respective performances of selective and non-selective absorbers with small glazed and unglazed vertical, transpired-plate collectors (MacGregor and Kennedy, 1994). It was found that the selective coating of 'Maxorb' foil had only a marginal influence, whilst the addition of the transparent cover, in this case twin-wall polycarbonate, roughly doubled the efficiency. A few years later, further tests were carried out on other full-scale mock-ups attached to a PASSYS cell at East Kilbride. These measured the performance of a 'dynamically insulated' wall, but this could equally be termed 'unglazed transpired solar air collector'. Again, a series of measurements were made with the flow of air controlled by a variable-speed fan (Baker, Porteous and Sharpe, 2001). ■6.9(1) Results were encouraging. The effective U-value came close to zero, while there was also a useful preheating effect. This raised the temperature by 12 to 15K depending on the rate of airflow, although it was recognized that part of this was due to the exchange of heat behind the plasterboard, as well as within the insulation. An extension of this work explored the potential for wind assisted 'passive stack ventilation', augmented by a small PV array (Baker, Porteous and Sharpe, 2002). ■6.9(2) However, due to several factors the performance of the wall did not match the results of the earlier test. A final successful phase was then undertaken (Baker, Porteous and Kondratenko, 2003). ■6.9(3)

large-scale, multi-faceted proposal

A bold Scottish proposal, which involves retrofitting with both glazed and unglazed transpired air collectors has unfortunately not yet been realized. This is the Solar Towers in Glasgow or STinG project (see Chapter 2). Here a large multi-storey opaque transpired collector, with a glazed accelerator at the top, was intended to move air up seven storeys, across a roof and down seven storeys (Sharpe, Porteous and MacGregor, 1998). The project would also have served as an excellent demonstration for smaller window integrated solar air collectors. It is frustrating that such ambitious projects can fall by the wayside, perhaps due to technical caution, perhaps due to financial constraint, and perhaps simply due to lack of effort and will by the owner of the building or buildings in question. Viewed objectively, it is evident that solar-warmed air can play a multi-faceted role in cool climates. Even though the units of energy contributed may, in terms of cost and benefit, sometimes appear to be too close to call, there can be other important spin-offs, albeit harder to quantify.

Fuelling competition – interactive control and management

'Fuelling competition' may be read in at least two ways. One distinct meaning alludes to the competition between solar displacement of fuels for space heating, commonly gas or oil, and that for lighting and appliances, which, other than for cooking, is mainly electricity. Although natural gas and oil may be used to generate electricity, they can be used much more efficiently to heat buildings directly. Thus, when expressed in units of 'primary energy' (which include the energy used in production and distribution), they significantly outperform inefficiently generated electricity. The caveats to this are that some areas may not be served by mains gas, and for both liquefied petroleum gas (LPG) ■6.10 and oil, energy for transport will reduce overall efficiency. Methods adopted to save energy may be flawed, and actually add to consumption. Some devices, such as heat exchangers, save oil or gas, but add in electricity (Chapter 3). Absence of a passive provision can result in heavy use of electricity. For example, lack of suitable provision for passively drying clothes inside and outside dwellings places reliance on tumble dryers, which are usually subject to the most expensive tariffs. However, such conveniences may be deemed essential for users. Although incidental gains from lights and equipment may displace solar gains, the design of buildings can help by reducing the need for artificial lighting and locating appliances in spaces that face north. There may be dilemmas with regard to continuous versus intermittent operational cycles. Instruments to regulate one component such as the façade, with the aim of saving thermal energy, may or may not work as intended, and will always have a consequent influence on related servicing systems, usually involving electrical loads. There is a complex interdependency of all moving components in a building, which relates broadly to the functionality and appropriateness of

6.9   Mock-up of window integrated solar air collectors on PASSYS test cell, with detail of fabric absorber and air inlet slot

6.9 Airing walls: details of PASSYS tests

6.9(1) Air was initially drawn in through joints and voids at the foot of corrugated steel cladding. It then had to pass through 17.5cm-thick cellulose insulation, contained by fairly fine-mesh netting, and into a slim void behind the internal lining of plasterboard. It was finally collected into a manifold at the top of the wall and delivered via a flow meter.

6.9(2) A nine-cell polycrystalline-Si module powered a small DC fan. It was found that both the diameter of the stack (5cm) and the fan (from a hair drier) were somewhat undersized. Also, the PV and fan impeded the flow of air, as did the flow meter at the entry point.

6.9(3) This test increased the diameter of the 3m-high exhaust pipe to 10cm and fitted a back-draught device to the distribution manifold. Results indicated viability, providing 0.6 air changes per hour and an estimated saving of 32 per cent over a period of 24 days, mainly in February. A perforated inner lining (as for an acoustic ceiling) was also tested in lieu of the plasterboard and found to give satisfactory results. A 25W fan and 12-cell monocrystalline array was modelled as a remote system (so as not to impede air flow at the top of the stack). It was found to be adequate to compensate for warm and calm periods, when wind pressure and thermal buoyancy might struggle to give an adequate rate of ventilation.

6.10 LPG family

Liquefied petroleum gas is the liquid form of butane, propane or pentane, produced by the distillation of petroleum during oil refining. The product used for heating and cooking is generally known as 'propane' in North America, as opposed to LPG in the UK.

6.11 Netley Abbey design team

The project architect, under Sir Colin Stansfield-Smith as Hampshire County Architect, was Dennis Goodwin. Nick Baker of the Martin Centre was consultant for the passive solar design and Fuller and Partners provided building services engineering.

electronic instructions. Even if every aspect of 'machine control' is optimized, there remains an issue of how well it is geared to the passive criteria and how well it is managed over time. The issue of spaces, designed to be passively heated, being compromised by active heating is serious for all sunspaces. But there is a scaling factor in that larger spaces such as atria affect competing fuels more consequentially than smaller ones such as domestic conservatories (Chapter 4).

Leading on from this, a second, and less hard-edged, implied meaning of 'fuelling competition' is that between passive and active solutions, with a tendency for architects to champion the former while their service consultants lean to the latter. It might be conjectured, for example, that the nature of mechanical components and performance data may not be very appealing for architects. They also might be prejudiced against the appearance of glazed collectors, and they might lose interest in the technical refinements of unglazed ones, even though they do not present an aesthetic threat or challenge. It is the same 'out of sight, out of mind' issue as with any servicing system. Pursuing this further, an adjunct to the active side of passive–active tension could be the competition between different technical options available for using a single fuel. In an area where electricity seems to be the simplest choice for all purposes, an electric boiler could compete with a heat pump on the basis of reliability or life-cycle cost. Again, such decisions would seem to move more into the domain of the specialist consultant. It is of course essential to recognize and devolve influence to the refined knowledge and skill of individuals within teams. Nobody would argue with that assertion. But teamwork can be greatly synergized when understanding and respect for different areas of expertise is unreservedly mutual. The techno-experts must opt into aesthetic ambitions, and architects must opt into engineering realities. Unfortunately such reciprocity is still relatively rare, even in multi-disciplinary architectural offices.

lessons from a solar primary school

An alternative or a supplementary method of tackling this issue is to link up with academic institutions, especially schools of architecture with a track record of energy modelling. A case study from the mid-1980s is that of Netley Abbey Infants' School in Hampshire. The partnership between Hampshire County Architect's Department and the Martin Centre in Cambridge ■6.11 was essential to the process of design. Close to the south coast of England at 50.9°N, the project continues the theme of air as a dominant part of the environmental strategy and has lessons for 'fuelling competition' as defined above.

The timetabled structure of schooldays and standard size of classes means that there are known quantities of incidental thermal gains. Problems of environmental control relative to two Scottish schools have already been brought up. Both of these operate in selective mode with a mix of automatic and manual controls. This was again the strategy adopted at Netley. Here the majority of the classrooms face northwest, with a relatively narrow series of bays aligned at right angles to a one-sided circulation arcade facing southeast. In other words, these classrooms do not have to cope with significant solar heat on top of that from the pupils. This means that, theoretically, both sources of free energy can be usefully exploited in cold weather. The two exceptions, a music room and one classroom that both face southeast, are passively protected from direct sunlight by means of overhanging roofs and projecting flank walls.

The circulation space is deliberately designed as a linear sunspace (Figure 6.10), with both tilted and vertical glazing. Not only does this make it a cheerful breakout adjunct to the classrooms, but also it forms the source of fresh air supplied to them in winter. Air from outside initially enters the sunspace through adjustable glass louvres and rises to small air-handling units combined with gas boilers. These are discretely located on a high-level mezzanine, which covers the thresholds to teaching bays, as well as activity bases within the bays and toilets. The boilers boost the temperature as required, and the air is delivered through relatively short lengths of duct at the same level and centred on each bay. An outer sleeve to the ducts allows them to double as conduits for extracting used air and also to host low energy fluorescent light fittings.

In cold weather, the two main thermal donors to the entry corridor are the sun and the heated spaces. The air-handling units will also pick up some heat from lights, although the aim is that it should be as naturally lit as possible. Having delivered the air, most should then circulate back to the starting point, either through a tilted set of louvres above the class-bases or through a ceiling vent to the service mezzanine. Thus the freshness of the supply is very dependent on the amount of new air entering via the external louvres. A controller is intended to allow the teachers to adjust the proportion of fresh air (Department for Education, 1994):

6.10 View within linear sunspace at Netley Abbey Infants' School

> An objective of the design was to give the users control over their environment. Classroom temperature is controlled by a knob marked 'warmer/cooler' and mechanical ventilation is achieved by a button marked 'fresh air', which switches from a full recirculation mode to a mix of preheated fresh air and recirculated air, which reverts to recirculation after a time delay of about 30 minutes.

In reality, the knob relies on 'warmer' and 'cooler' symbols, while the button is not marked 'fresh air', simply relying on its green colour for identification. In rather warmer weather, say in spring and autumn, the aim was to increase the proportion of new air, with used air leaving by natural thermo-circulation via automatic ridge-vents. In summer, with the air-handling units switched off, the idea was that cool fresh air would enter via the northwest façade, and leave via the same vents along with air in the corridor.

However, air has a tendency not to perform as anticipated, especially when several control variables are available. To eliminate one of these, heated air returning

■6.12 Details of monitoring at Netley

6.12(1) Overall, the values Yannas gives for 1986–1987 (Yannas, 1994) do not quite correspond with those given by Hawkes (1988), who adds an extra for the kitchen. Yannas reports that in 1986–1987 (noted as the first of three years of monitoring), gas for space heating accounted for 70kWh/m² (delivered energy); total energy consumption, including hot water, lighting and appliances was 97kWh/m², a primary energy equivalent of 150kWh/m². Hawkes gives 1986–1997 as the second year of monitoring after a year of teething problems in 1985–1986. The problems were 'traced to malfunctions in the control systems which were rectified in the summer of 1986.' The values Hawkes gives for 1986–1987 are 91kWh/m² for delivered energy and 143kWh/m² for primary energy. When the energy consumed in the kitchen is added, this rises to 108kWh/m². Yannas reported that electricity for lighting and appliances 'accounted for some 50 per cent of the total primary energy consumption, CO_2 emission and fuel cost.'

6.12(2) The buffer averaged 8K higher than ambient at times when heating was required and was above 10°C for 94 per cent of the occupied hours and above 15°C for 50 per cent of the time.

in an uncontrolled fashion from classroom to the entry buffer, closers were fitted to intervening doors. However, it is thought that the teachers did not operate their 'fresh air' button frequently enough. It was reported that the quality of the air in winter was poor, with rates of ventilation only achieving one quarter of the required standard of 30m³ per person hourly. A response to perceived stuffiness was to open external windows or doors, rather than operate the mechanical system; and, perversely, some teachers used the mechanical system in summer, thereby supplying excessively warm air into classrooms (Yannas, 1994).

There are slight variations in reports of the school's performance ■6.12(1), but there is no doubt that electricity for lighting and appliances was a significant part of the load. One reason for overuse of artificial lighting related to a design decision. Although secondary daylight reaches the southeast end of the classrooms from the glazed corridor and the service mezzanine, the fenestration on the northwest side includes an opaque panel, which accommodates the blackboard. Glare from the surrounding windows makes this difficult to see without the constant aid of electric lights, and additional roof windows were subsequently fitted to augment daylight from above.

In general, although the monitored temperature within the buffer corridor was much as expected ■6.12(2) (Yannas, 1994) and shading was introduced to limit overheating in summer, teachers complained that it was too cold in winter. To address this complaint, supplementary heating units were eventually added in both classrooms and the glazed arcade. In spite of its laudable aspirations, it would seem that the mixed, passive–active, selective mode of operation is quite daunting. Nevertheless, during an ISES tour on a sunny afternoon in the summer of 1988, the perceived atmosphere in teaching areas was pleasantly fresh, and that in the sunspaces perfectly tolerable. Both teachers and students seemed to be content with their lot, or, at least, did not wish to complain to the visitors. As a post-script, entering the school, one passes by an internal atrium. This space, now converted into a heated library, was intended as a passive thermal regulator to the main hall, and also provided a more substantial indoor–outdoor activity space than that of the solar corridor. Although teachers had apparently been irked that the latter is too narrow for extended use, one has also to bear in mind that users often want 'icing on their cake'. On the other hand, it is also evident from a recent study that, despite the changes made in response to complaints by the teachers, control of the internal environment remains problematic (Keren, 2005). Compared with opening a window or door, there is no explicit and immediate connection between pushing a button or turning a knob and achieving a desired environmental change.

tutorials at a university campus

Moving from primary to higher education, the Jubilee Campus at the University of Nottingham in the East Midlands of England (just below 53°N) is a notable example of large atria associated with workspaces and an innovative means of mechanical ventilation (Figure 6.11). Designed by architect Michael Hopkins and Partners with Ove Arup and Partners as structural and service engineers, there was again a specialist academic consultative role, this time with the in-house School of the Built Environment at the university. Although it was more specifically in connection with a large array of glass-integrated PV cells on the roofs of atria, a principal end-use for the electricity generated is to run the ventilating fans. Therefore the academic interest extended to ventilation, which is claimed to be 'super efficient' (Hicks and Riffat, 2001; Berry and Thornton, 2002). The basic idea is to minimize the drop in pressure across the system by pushing large volumes of air at low velocity. ■6.13(1) Thermal wheels located at the top of stair towers recover heat from outgoing used air ■6.13(2) and supply floor voids in working spaces via large vertical ducts flanking the threshold to the stairwell. A small boiler tops up the temperature in winter as required, while indirect evaporative cooling is used in hot weather. ■6.13(3) Used air is thus displaced from below, entering through low-pressure floor diffusers. It then leaves offices via a manifold located at the top of partitions, feeding into central corridors that are in turn connected back to the stairwell. One problem with this system is, of course, that the fans are still required during the winter, when solar collection is low. In summer, on the other hand, doors are quite often left open, which would tend to interfere with the intended flow. Rooms also overlook the atria and windows may also open on to them. Air then joins the main exhaust at high level, moved by a combination of thermal buoyancy and cross-ventilation, and slightly assisted by large conical rotating cowls with attached wind vanes.

6.11 Inside atrium at Jubilee Campus looking east towards service stack

There are retractable awnings to shade windows in rooms facing outwards along the westerly edge of blocks, as well as a deliberate effort to minimize loss of daylight. For example, the PV arrays are kept well back from the fenestration to workspaces, windows amounting to more than half the area of the façades. Artificial lighting is designed to be very efficient with automatic dimming geared to natural light levels and occupancy sensors. The U-values are significantly lower than was required by building regulations at that time. ■6.13(4)

However, the achieved energy load in the monitored year was 88 per cent higher than predicted (Hicks and Riffat, 2001). ■6.13(5) The consumption for lighting and appliances accounted for nearly a quarter of this at about 20kWh/m^2. If it is assumed that the prediction for lighting was fairly accurate, a conclusion might reasonably be that computers are largely responsible for this addition. Alternatively, the excessive use of internal blinds could result in a much higher lighting load. It is also understood that the automatic sensors were not popular and that desktop fans are used to increase air movement. Whatever the reasons for the electrical increase, there is still over 50kWh/m^2 to be explained. This leads to an examination of why heating loads should have been significantly higher than anticipated.

A minor factor may have been the timing of the monitoring before the buildings had completely dried out. The campus was occupied in late 1999.

■6.13 Details of monitoring at Jubilee Campus

6.13(1) The pressure drop is estimated to be 280–340 pascals (or Newtons per square metre), less than a quarter of what is deemed to be normal.

6.13(2) Each wheel is 2.4m diameter, 40cm deep, weighs 0.58 tonnes, and has a surface area of $2300m^2$. The pressure loss across the wheel is estimated to be 60 pascals and low velocities through it provide an exchange efficiency of 84 per cent (Berry and Thornton, 2002).

6.13(3) As the air passes back through the plant tower (above the stairs at the end of each atrium) on the way out, it passes through an evaporative cooler and then through a heat exchange wheel. Heat is thus removed from the incoming air via the wheel.

6.13(4) U-values (W/m^2K) are 0.29 for external walls, 0.22 for flat roofs; 0.39 for the ground floor and 2.4 for windows, respectively compared with elemental maximums of 0.45, 0.45, 0.45 and 3.3.

6.13(5) The predicted target for energy loads was $83.6kWh/m^2$, but the achieved level in the monitored year $157kWh/m^2$. Of that, the figure of $33kWh/m^2$ for lighting and appliances is two and a half times the predicted $13.1kWh/m^2$.

6.13(6) John Berry of Ove Arup and Partners, as well as Special Professor in Building Technology, University of Nottingham, related this scenario in email correspondence of 13th September 2004. He is co-author of papers describing the project in some depth (Taylor and Berry, 2000; Berry and Thornton, 2002).

6.13(7) BP Saturn monocrystalline PV arrays generated around $76.5kWh/m^2$ cell area (approximately 30 per cent less than predicted) during the monitored year reported (Hicks and Riffatt, 2001).

Monitoring for a year commenced six months later with the results reported in the spring of 2001. Concrete floor slabs are deliberately exposed to assist in damping swings in temperature. Driving out their initially embedded moisture will inevitably add to winter heating loads. Then, if higher rates of ventilation during winter caused temperatures in the atrium to be lower than expected, the heating demand in adjacent rooms would increase. What is thought to be a more authoritative explanation is that the management of a particular servicing arrangement reduced the effectiveness of heat recovery. The doors at the foot of the service tower were frequently left open to allow goods in and out. ■6.13(6) This meant that the outgoing air through the thermal wheel would have been cooler than predicted. In addition, the rooms may have been heated to higher levels than modelled pre-contract. Assuming that some combination of these four possible explanations was responsible, it needs to be borne in mind that the extra heating implies fewer units of primary energy than extra lighting and appliances. However, the electrical load will be offset in this case, since part of it is met by renewable energy.

Having said that, another disappointment was the performance of the PV arrays. ■6.13(7) The low pitch and less than ideal westerly orientation are likely to have been factors here, given the large amount of reflection that will occur once the angle of incidence goes beyond 50 degrees. Moreover, the cells steadily reduce in efficiency with increasing temperature, and their surface was reported as being frequently rather hot. Finally, the air handling towers, with their prominent conical cowls and the cleaning gantry, which is necessary at such a low pitch (Figure 6.12), will provide a certain amount of shading in mornings. This can knock out 'strings' of cells for a period, whilst the malfunctioning of inverters (converting from direct to alternating current) may have had further negative influence.

On the credit side, as with the primary school at Netley, the overall architectural ambience is laudable, and happy occupants may constitute an economic benefit that is at least as great as energy savings that could otherwise have been made. According to a major new study, the initial findings of which were announced at the RIBA Conference in Dublin in 2004 (Arnold, 2004), 'there was a clear link between high productivity and good air, light and acoustic quality.' The quality of air and light in particular will tend to be higher in atria than in more confined adjacent working spaces. Therefore it is no surprise that such spaces attract activities related to both work and leisure. During a visit to the Jubilee Campus at the end of April, one atrium was being used as an attractive semi-outdoor setting for a group tutorial, while part of another is now permanently used as a cafeteria. This may be regarded as a beneficial by-product of the design. However, such benefits also entail risks for the consumption of fuel. Although the atria were designed to be completely unheated other than by the sun and by adjacent workspaces, the introduction of tables and chairs has resulted in the use of patio-type gas heaters.

risks of partially heating buffer spaces

In a similar building in Trondheim in Norway, at 63.3°N, the popularity of such airy sunlit spaces ultimately signalled a more significant penalty. Per Knudsen headed a design team that linked a series of naturally ventilated atria to existing buildings on the campus of the Norwegian Institute of Technology. Three were on an east–west axis so that the original blocks of accommodation looked north and south into them. The fourth was on a north–south axis and connected a teaching block to the west with two new lecture theatres, which filled in an existing courtyard, to the east. Thus the external perimeter of the existing campus was dramatically reduced, but the buffered accommodation now had to be mechanically ventilated. Given the harsh winters and the intended use as transitory meeting places, it was initially thought that the atria should be heated up to a minimum of 15°C, while offices had a design temperature of 20°C that could be easily met by small radiators (SINTEF, 1989). All the pre-contract predictions of energy savings were based on these assumptions. ■6.14(1) To achieve 15°C in the atria, radiant panels were fitted to a fairly narrow horizontal section at the apex of symmetrically pitched double-glazed roofs (Figure 6.13), while convectors were fitted to glass walls to prevent down-draughts.

The strategy also allowed the atria to house services such as the ventilating ducts required for the heated spaces. However, these are sited above windows and result in some diminution of natural light to the offices. Thus a system to control the thermal environment penalizes the lighting one. Although it might be argued that much of Norway's electricity is generated by renewable hydropower, which serves both artificial ventilation and lighting, it is difficult to condone a principle of one facility putting an extra burden on another. However, this is a relatively minor matter

6.12 Conical cowls and cleaning gantry at east end of atrium at Jubilee Campus

6.13 Looking west down an atrium at the Technical University Campus, with radiant heating at apex of roof

■6.14 Monitoring and predictions at Trondheim

6.14(1) The annual space heating load for the chosen glazing specification double, low-emissivity for roof and gable walls, single for internal façades – was predicted to be 114kWh/m², a reduction of about 20 per cent compared with the existing situation. Measured values for five months of the first heating season (i.e. an incomplete season) gave somewhat lower values as one might expect – 97kWh/m² for the offices only and 78kWh/m² for the offices and atria combined. An autumn or spring bias may be inferred from this data – if a ratio of 4:1 in terms of floor area is assumed, the load for heating the atria up to 15°C would have been very small at around 2kWh/m² ... (97 x 0.8) + (2 x 0.2) = 78.

6.14(2) Thyholt used a G value, the ratio of heat loss from the atria to the outside ($\Sigma U_o A_o$ W/K) to that from the primary heated spaces to the atria ($\Sigma U_i A_i$ W/K). She found that this needed to be as low as 0.2 in order that an atrium could be heated up to 20°C for a reasonable amount of energy (in a 50–100kWh/m² range). She examined real buildings with atria, where the G values ranged from almost 10 for an attached atrium down to 0.85 and 0.64 for linear and 'core' (internal) atria. Although there is a linear relationship for G values over 1.0, with the temperature to which the atrium could be economically heated dropping steadily, the graph steps up below G values of 1.0, and particularly below 0.2. From the information provided (SINTEF, 1989) it appears that a typical atrium at Trondheim could have a G value as low as 0.5. Even so, to heat up to 20°C was well outside the range assumed to be acceptable. Thyholt also stated that 'some buildings with glazed atria have reported energy use in the 500kWh/m² range'!

compared with the consequence of a change in thermal management policy within the atria. In order to make them comfortable for teaching, it was subsequently decided to heat these spaces to much the same level as the offices. This means that instead of the atria functioning as solar enhanced edge-insulation to a large proportion of the footprint, we now have a single, deep-plan, thermal environment, where both overheating and a demand for heat may occur simultaneously in certain weather. For instance, upper south-facing offices could overheat on a sunny day in winter, while the floor of the atrium is shaded and requires heat to boost it to comfort level for seated learning. An effort was then made to predict the consequence of raising the mean minimum temperature within such atria, essentially by using a simple ratio as an indicator (Thyholt et al, 1998). ■6.14(2)

free heat to buffers and related energy-efficiency measures

A method of providing more free heat to atria or sunspaces is to site them on top of other heated spaces. One example of a large atrium of this kind is that of a new building for ECN, the Dutch Government's research centre in Petten, on the northwest coast of the Netherlands at 52.8°N. It is code-named No. 42 and designed by Tjerk Reijenga of BEAR Architecten, the same architect as for De Kleine Aarde in Boxtel (Chapter 5). Essentially the floor and most of two walls are bounded by regular accommodation. The decision was taken to single-glaze the atrium and to incorporate PV cells in the roof to provide partial shading. However, this raises another fuelling dilemma, as the cells will curtail the amount of daylight available for offices. Having visited the building on a sunny afternoon in summer, it was noted that the entire floor-plate of the upper level of offices was adequately illuminated without artificial lighting. However, this was simply a qualitative observation, because the floor was unoccupied at that time. The occupied floor below told a different story. It must have received only slightly lower levels of daylight, but had all of its artificial lights switched on. This may have been partly associated with varying use of venetian blinds to combat glare, but the issue remains – artificial lighting is being used when it would appear to be unnecessary and the underlying cause and subsequent effect is not being adequately addressed.

The adjacent 1960s building, designated No. 31, connects with the atrium only at its western end, and so is not strongly influenced by it. It has nevertheless been retrofitted in order to address cooling loads and glare. Its south façade has been fitted with an array of opaque PV shading lamellas. ■6.15 Although their performance is being closely monitored, including aspects such as the build-up of dirt in the marine location, there appear to be no plans to assess the impact of the new brise-soleil on occupants. Even though there had been an expectation that the lamellas might to some extent act as light shelves, they will also block out daylight. Consequently the effect on the use of artificial lighting is likely to be complex. The same focus on the performance of the PV arrays had also obscured the fact that the windows of Building 42's atrium were closed on a sunny afternoon. This might have been due either to a control malfunction, or to wind sensors competing with those for temperature as at Rijkswaterstaat in Ijmuiden. The essential matter is that this kind of situation will increase the load on the mechanical system for cooling. Again, the programme of monitoring is not yet holistic enough to evaluate such glitches.

A theoretical project in Glasgow (Chapter 2) was envisaged as an exemplar for solar retrofit of a large institutional building, building-integrated photovoltaics (BIPV) playing a large part in this case (Kondratenko, 2003). As at the Technical University at Trondheim, it was proposed to fill in existing spaces between buildings, but in this case there was the added advantage of a base of deep-plan accommodation similar to the new building No. 42 at Petten. Courtyards located above this podium had the potential for conversion into attractive atria. In one case the host accommodation would lose heat to the atrium through five surfaces, and four in the other, where the courtyard opened up to the south. However, the main thrust of this work concerned double-skin façades – over-cladding the existing south façades with a new BIPV glass wall. This immediately solves one problem. It enables windows to open without subjecting occupants to excessive noise from traffic. It also enables the original façade to be economically insulated. However, as noted above in relation to the Wolfson Medical School Building for the University of Glasgow, it will cause more overheating than had the extra skin not been there. Therefore, a simple mechanical ventilation system was proposed, with some cooling capability provided by ground water. In summer this would supply air into the central corridors and thence into rooms, which it could then leave via windows into the new 'solar chimney' and be exhausted to the environment at the top. Thus thermal buoyancy in the 'chimney' would augment the mechanical process, while occupants are part of the control system. In other words it is a selective mode of control, which solves two other critical problems. Both the corridors and the rooms presently suffer from stagnation and poor air quality. In winter, the supply of air at the top of the solar chimney would be connected to the same dispersed air-handling units, this time supplying warm air to the offices via the corridors, where a significant part of the warming is attributable to the double-skin system. ■6.16(1)

This leaves one potentially problematic question. Can relatively simple and economic means compensate for the loss in daylight due to the presence of the new skin? The answer is yes. A reflective maintenance grid at sill level and a slightly reshaped and reflective suspended ceiling was predicted to give marginally superior distribution of daylight than at present. Not only does the multi-tasking approach dramatically improve the thermal environment, with impressive attendant savings in energy, it does it without increasing electrical demand, which it then offsets by generating electricity on site. ■6.16(2)

Reducing the scale and focusing back on atria located above heated accommodation, there are two domestic case studies where the seasonal

■6.15 PV performance at Petten

Each PV lamella is 3.0m long by 0.84m wide, set at about 37° tilt and using Siemens polycrystalline cells. In spite of ventilation holes in the underside, cells tend to overheat – 35K above ambient at 1000W/m^2 irradiance, with efficiencies dropping by about 0.4 per cent per degree of overheat. One row of lamellas in line with occupants' vision above sill level is manually adjustable, but at the time of a visit in 2003, the building was still empty. There is an additional polycrystalline PV canopy forming a cornice at roof level. The area of the lamellas and canopy is approximately 440m^2, and this generated 22,276kWh in 2002: 50.6kWh/m^2 of PV. There is a further 260m^2 of BP Solar frameless monocrystalline modules on the roof itself, with a shallow convex tilt to the south. This collected 29,271kWh in 2002, or 112.6kWh/m^2 of PV. The total collected was 8 per cent less than predicted, but, over and above the problems of dirt and overheating, nearly one third of the roof inverters and more than one third of the lamella inverters failed at least once.

■6.16 PV predictions in Glasgow

6.16(1) During the modelling process, Kondratenko evaluated the PV cell thermal contribution in contrast to second and third thermal considerations – that transmitted through the clear parts of the glass and that lost from the offices to the 'solar chimney'. She found that the last was significant and the second would have been greater had the PV not been there at all. Although the thermal difference between a solar chimney with PV and one without is marginal, her work dispels the myth that hybrid electrical-thermal PV systems owe a great deal to the capture of heat generated by the cells. Most hybrid BIPV applications are attached to heated spaces, so that heat recovery from them tends to dominate in cold weather. She found that the saving on a fairly typical day in January was likely to exceed 1.0kWh/m^2 of floor area. Omission of the cells, to leave a fully transparent second skin, would result in a very minor increase in saving of approximately 0.02kWh/m^2.

6.16(2) It was predicted that the double-skin façade would generate about 73kWh/m^2 of PV area annually. This rather low value for monocrystalline PV confirms that a vertical surface is not ideal. A saving of nearly 11kWh/m^2 floor area annually was also estimated if BIPV opportunities were realized over the entire complex.

6.14 Winter garden located on top of boiler house at Kilwinning

balance of thermal donations works well. One functions as a winter garden for a group of dwellings for the elderly. This is located in the small town of Kilwinning to the west of Glasgow, and was designed by architect Roan Rutherford while working for the Irvine New Town Development Corporation. There is a communal heating system, with the boiler house opportunistically sited in a basement below the winter garden. Its flue also functions as a structural pivot for the space (Figure 6.14). When the demand for heat in the dwellings is at its highest, the incidental gains donated from the boilers to the winter garden are at their greatest. Periods with little or no demand for heat correspond to the sun playing a strong passive role, the boilers often being on stand-by.

A very similar project in this regard is the single Norwegian dwelling in Stokkan, Trondheim, at 63.3°N (Jacobsen et al, 1992) (Figure 6.15a, b). Here a generous double-height atrium or winter garden is located above a basement plant-room containing a heat pump and thermal store. The sunspace buffers the south face of all the living accommodation, while it is also partly protected to the south by a single-storey garage. One might query the specification of an electric heat pump, but in this case it exploits the atrium as its ambient source, with a bypass directly to the outside for warmer weather. It is integrated with the system for mechanical ventilation and heat recovery, and supplies low-temperature radiant floor coils as well as domestic hot water. The bathrooms proved to be a slight complication in terms of energy efficiency. The exhaust air from the heat pump passes through these spaces and tends to overheat them. Nevertheless, there is a good partnership between the passive solar contribution and fortuitous gains from the heating system, the latter falling off naturally as the former increase. Other incidental gains, for example, appliances in the kitchen, are located towards the north of the plan and so do not compete with the atrium.

heat pumps versus boilers

Another project that uses heat pumps in association with a thermal store is that for new housing in Shettleston in the east end of Glasgow by architect John Gilbert in association with engineering services consultant Enconsult (Figure 6.16) (Gilbert, 1999). In this instance any heat escaping from the store is of benefit to a generously glazed access stairwell, in effect, a triple-height atrium. In contrast to the store, also charged by an array of flat-plate solar collectors, ■6.17(1) the two pumps are compact, each weighing only 7kg. These exploit an unusual post-industrial ambient source – water at about 12 or 15°C lying at the bottom of a disused coalmine 130m below the site. At the time of a visit, which coincided with the autumnal equinox during the first year of occupation in 1999, the subterranean resource was yet to kick in. The active solar panels were able to meet the domestic hot water needs, while passive solar gains and high levels of insulation were keeping autumnal space heating loads at bay. Once again a specialist servicing system is of benefit to a purely architectural one. Because this is an electric heating system in a city where natural gas is the dominant fuel, the utility company was motivated to allow a special tariff ■6.17(2), and to sponsor the capital cost of both the solar panels and 'solar slate' ventilating systems (as described in 'harvesting hot air' earlier in this chapter) to four of the dwellings.

Two years later, on the east side of Scotland in the county of Fife (slightly further north than Glasgow at 56.1°N), the same architect used the same consultant and very much the same heating technique. This was the solar retrofit of 1960s housing in Lumphinnans near Cowdenbeath, a locale resonant with industrial political history and known as 'Little Moscow'. The site is approached via Gagarin Way, named after the first Russian cosmonaut. Again a defunct coalmine was a useful ambient source for heat pumps. Here the ground water had a temperature averaging around 14.5°C at a depth of 170m, while the thermal store and twin heat pumps are located in former stores within a stairwell. ■6.18(1)

In this case passive sunspaces are independent of the thermal stores. These are slightly extended recessed balconies (similar to those used in the Easthall solar demonstration project), angled out from the façade to increase solar capture and enlarge usable space (Figure 6.17). They are single-glazed using a Danish system called 'Vitrol'. Frameless tempered sheets of glass may

■6.17 Shettleston housing, Glasgow: thermal storage

6.17(1) A 10,000 litre thermal store has a small footprint on plan, housed in a two-storey high stack. A Scottish company, AES (Appropriate Energy Systems), manufactured the 32m² collectors, while another Scottish firm, Solar Energy Systems, carried out the installation. Therefore, the energy embodied in transport for a specialized component was relatively low.

6.17(2) The thermostats in individual hot water cylinders are set at 45°C, 10K lower than the supply from the heat pumps to the main store. If the residents want it hotter, they must use an electric immersion heater. However, this is on a special 'Economy 2000' tariff.

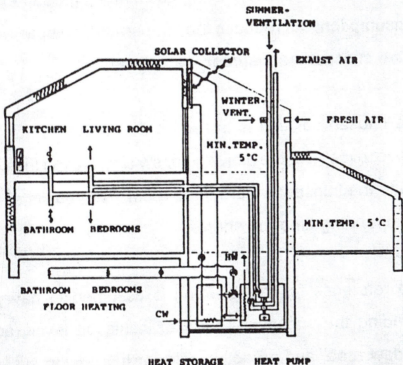

6.15 Solar house at Stokkan: a) cross section showing mechanical servicing; b) double-height winter garden above plant room

6.16   The combined geothermal heat pump and
       solar system for Shettleston

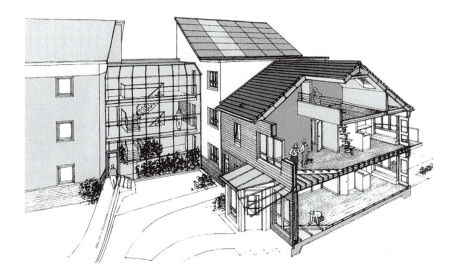

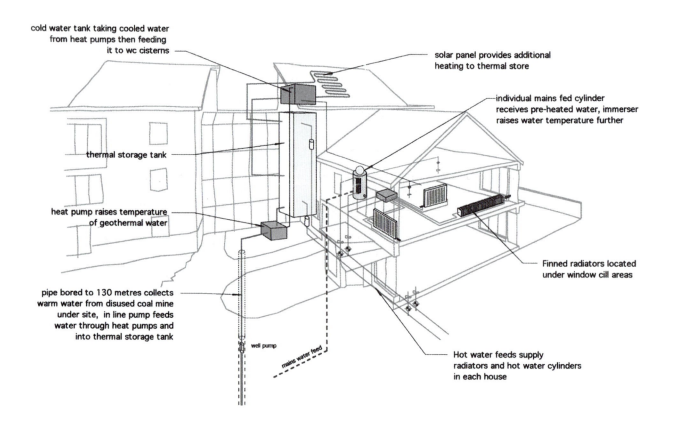

cold water tank taking cooled water
from heat pumps then feeding
it to wc cisterns

solar panel provides additional
heating to thermal store

individual mains fed cylinder
receives pre-heated water, immerser
raises water temperature further

thermal storage tank

heat pump raises temperature
of geothermal water

Finned radiators located
under window cill areas

pipe bored to 130 metres collects
warm water from disused coal mine
under site, in line pump feeds
water through heat pumps and
into thermal storage tank

well pump

mains water feed

Hot water feeds supply
radiators and hot water cylinders
in each house

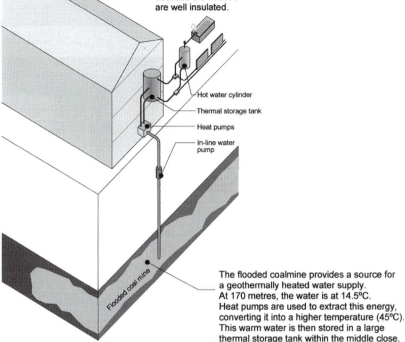

Geothermal Heating System

Warm water is pumped to radiators and a hot water cylinder in each house. Low temperature heating is effective because the houses are well insulated.

Hot water cylinder
Thermal storage tank
Heat pumps
In-line water pump

Flooded coal mine

The flooded coalmine provides a source for a geothermally heated water supply. At 170 metres, the water is at 14.5ºC. Heat pumps are used to extract this energy, converting it into a higher temperature (45ºC). This warm water is then stored in a large thermal storage tank within the middle close, before being circulated to the houses.

6.17 Solar-geothermal retrofit at Lumphinnans: a) schematic; b) sunspaces

be opened singly, as normal casement windows. Alternatively, by employing a folding-sliding mechanism, the sunspaces may be opened up to the extent of becoming open balconies once again. The simple engineered sophistication of this ironmongery perhaps pushes it into the realm of 'machine control' even though it is operated entirely by minimal human energy. Most importantly, it is part of an integrated strategy, which allows small heat pumps to operate in tandem with compact thermal storage, to give a commendably low value for energy consumption ■6.18(2) – predicted to be less than 40kWh/m². In an area where miners used to receive free coal, and so did not have to worry about lack of thermal comfort or hot water, the 21st century energy solution in a post-coal era of high local unemployment seems socially appropriate and compensatory.

A particular attraction of heat pumps is that they can operate in fairly isolated situations, where the supply of alternative fuels can be problematic. They are also relatively flexible when it comes to available ambient sources. An example is the one used to heat the 205m² Murphy house designed by Bo Helliwell and Kim Smith on Gambier Island in British Columbia at 49.5°N (outdoor room described in Chapter 3). Technically, this is described in the same way as those used at Lumphinnans and Shettleston in Scotland. Its geothermal heat pump, instead of water from old coalmines, simply uses the sea with some

■6.18 Lumphinnans housing, Fife: thermal storage and performance

6.18(1) The capacity of 1500 litres is much smaller than that used at Shettleston partly due to its higher temperature of 55°C and partly due to the high thermal storage mass of the dwellings with cavity brickwork insulated externally with 70mm of CFC-free polystyrene.

6.18(2) In 2001, the 'economy 2000' tariff was approximately 4.2p/kWh, and the predicted annual fuel bill for heating and hot water using the dynamic simulation programme ESPr was around £105, representing 2500kWh. The coefficient of performance (COP) of the heat pumps was estimated to be up to 4.5, and the pumps have hermetically sealed compressors with R22 fluid, the least damaging of the CFCs.

■6.19 Background to Helliwell + Smith's home and studio

Barry Downs worked for the architect Fred Hollinsworth at an early stage in his career. Hollinsworth was renowned as a pioneering West Coast modernist of the 'First Vancouver School' , of the same mould as Arthur Erickson, and apparently inspired by a visit to Vancouver by Richard Neutra. Downs won an award for the house in West Vancouver in the 1960s, and its recent refurbishment and studio extension by Helliwell + Smith, Blue Sky Architecture has now also been recognized in this way.

600m of plastic pipe held in a wire cube anchored at a depth of 18m. This works in conjunction with low-temperature heating coils embedded in a screed below the floor, as well as a mechanical system of ventilating and adjusting thermal comfort, which uses an air-to-air heat exchanger. This plant is housed below bedrooms in a small basement, which respects a dip in the natural level of the ground at the west end of the building.

Helliwell and Smith are pragmatic with respect to heating systems in particular situations. Their own house and studio since 1998 in West Vancouver is a refurbishment of, and extension to, a 1960s house by Barry Downs. ■6.19 It is in a suburban location and the original oil-fired boiler serving a warm-air heating system has been replaced by one fuelled by natural gas. However, the registers to deliver warm air in the ceilings of the lower floor of bedrooms did not provide adequate comfort. Therefore, a limited amount of electric under-floor heating has been added.

In coastal locations where electricity is the only readily available fuel for heating, a small electric boiler may be more practical than a heat pump. The sea may be too far away, the ground may be solid rock, and salt-laden air may not be a very suitable source in terms of maintenance and longevity. Brian MacKay-Lyons took this decision for several on-grid seaboard houses in Nova Scotia, the boilers supplying warm-water coils embedded in polished concrete slabs. Alternatively, there may be no mains supply of electricity. Faced with this situation in the remote interior, he designed the Gibson-Livingston house, 1990, with a combination of flat-plate collectors, a PV array and a back-up propane generator. He has also used a heat pump for his own new office in Halifax, where this proved a pragmatic choice.

A visit to a passive solar community school on the island of Benbecula in Scotland's Outer Hebrides in 1993 reinforces the point about vulnerability of heat pumps on particular sites. Two large air-to-water units were relegated to an auxiliary, rather than a leading, role. This was partly due to them not standing up well to the onslaught of salty air, and partly to the fall in oil prices at that time. Oil-fired boilers, originally intended as a back-up facility, met 60 per cent of the thermal load. Another machine, a 60kW 'Wind Harvester', was intended to contribute significantly to the electrical demand, but had also been prone to teething problems – after several years most of these problems (including power cuts due to gales and seabirds) seemed to have been resolved, with over 500kWh being generated daily. Also, the energy management system had recently addressed peaks in demand such as better control of light to save 80kW when the cooking load was highest.

An alternative strategy for heat pumps is to use them in conjunction with an active solar system. This was the method used to resolve the expensive heating shortfall in the ambitious project by Bart Jan van den Brink to accommodate a seasonal thermal store within a single dwelling (Chapter 2). Electricity was the only available top-up fuel and the demand for it proved to be considerable. In 1999 the original 'pump dry' system was modified to one with anti-freeze in the collector, heat exchangers and a heat pump. This means that a much smaller amount of electricity can now raise the temperature of the thermal store to the required level in winter. Thereafter, the original water-to-air heat exchangers supply adequate warm-air heating to the interior. It is also noteworthy that this was not van den Brink's last attempt to utilize long-term thermal storage with an active solar system for one dwelling. His millennium house sited in the ecological village of EVA Lanxmeer in Culemborg also has such a store, this time with 40cm of insulation. However, this again loses its heat too rapidly. Van den Brink now considers short-term storage of a few days to be a more pragmatic approach. In a recent project for floating dwellings ▪6.20, he is using vertical thermal solar collectors for space and water heating together with storage in ice and a heat pump. He also proposes integrating PV with the roof and collecting rainwater.

small-scale CHP and heat exchangers

The message here is that advanced technology still has to respect specific local conditions. Having devoted some considerable space to heat pumps, the progress with small-scale combined heat and power (CHP) systems should not be ignored, particularly in terms of their ability to burn renewable, or other freely available, fuels. While the example of the 'Wohnen & Arbeiten' solar housing in the Vauban district of Freiburg (Chapter 4) burns natural gas, the solar PV factory in Freiburg by Rolf and Hotz (Chapter 5) has adopted rapeseed oil as a solar alternative. Plenty of this crop is grown by local farmers. The Akademie Mont-Cenis in Herne-Sodingen, Germany (Chapter 2) also uses a CHP system to meet the balance of thermal and electrical loads. In this case the physical heritage of a former coalmine is again key. Firedamp gas (mainly methane) fuels the CHP plant, its pressure fortuitously being higher when atmospheric pressure is down. Thus in overcast weather, when the output from the building's PV arrays is low, the methane should be able to meet the shortfall.

Apart from lighting, one of the main end-uses for electricity in this campus is to power mechanical heat recovery units for the buildings within the main glass envelope. Air-to-air heat exchangers have come up in several preceding chapters as well as this one, the objective being to recover as much heat as possible from outgoing air. When taking ambient air from the upper part of an atrium, the possibility exists that the 'fresh' supply might be warmer than desired inside individual buildings. In this case the exchange would be reversed and the possibility of overheating could occur. For that reason it is necessary to have some alternative method of admitting cooler ambient air, or to have another way to cool the incoming air. A reversible heat pump would be one method of achieving this. However, during very cold weather, taking the fresh air from an already pre-warmed ambient source has a distinct advantage. It may not be necessary to heat the air up any further before delivering it.

▪6.20 Proposed floating dwellings in the Netherlands: quantitative detail

A two-storey dwelling sits atop a partially submerged basement. This has 70m³ or 80 tonnes of ballast. The floor between the main floor and upper floor is also of concrete to increase thermal mass within the dwelling, and is heated by low-temperature water coils. There is 35m² flat-plate collector and 40m² PV, estimated to supply 2000kWh annually.

■6.21 Task XIII apartments, Amstelveen: performance detail and comparison

6.21(1) U-values are less than 0.2W/m²K for all opaque surfaces and 0.7 for windows.

6.21(2) The value of 12kWh/m² given for space heating may be compared with the final heating deficit of about 13kWh/m², having deducted 18kWh/m² for heat recovery, measured at the co-housing project in the Vauban district of Freiburg (Chapter 4).

For example, Theo Bosch's solar dwellings at Deventer in the Netherlands (Chapter 4) have roof-mounted heat exchangers with an associated coil from the boiler in order to be able to top up the already pre-warmed incoming air to a comfortable level. By contrast the International Energy Agency (IEA) Task XIII 'Advanced Solar Low Energy Buildings' solar apartment block in Amstelveen, just south of Amsterdam (Figure 6.18), follows the example of the Akademie Mont-Cenis with heat exchangers sited within a generous atrium. Atelier Z designed this scheme with the mechanical engineering department of Delft Technical University as part of the architectural team. Here, although U-values are commendably efficient ■6.21(1), the very low predictions of space heating are, as in other projects, reliant on heat recovery ■6.21(2) and negligible opening of windows during the heating season (ed. Hastings, 1995). External shading blinds are also programmed to come down when internal temperatures go above 22°C, although there is a manual override as well.

wider questions

Stepping back from the detail of energy-efficiency, there are wider questions to ask. For instance, is the provision of a large atrium as at Amstelveen sustainable for housing, even allowing for the generous subsidy the building received? The areas of individual flats seem generous at about 90m² for three persons. Is this too generous? To put this in perspective, this is 35 per cent greater than the heated area of the Easthall solar flats in Glasgow. Is this area too frugal? Is Amstelveen's frontage width of 8.6m viable in terms of land use and the

6.18   General view of south façade of Task XIII solar apartment block in Amstelveen

attendant length of infrastructural services? On the other hand, having decided to afford this space, with all the extra building cost and embedded energy this entails, the gain in social amenity is surely valuable, and the added volume will allow rates of ventilation to be correspondingly lower. Such questions invite a range of opinion, which steers solar buildings and components into the more amorphous arena of 'sustainability' and green architecture.

REFERENCES

Andresen, I. and Hestnes, A. G. (eds) (1992) *North Sun 92, Solar Energy at High Latitudes,* proceedings of conference (Trondheim, Norway, 24–26 June), SINTEF Architecture and Building Technology, Trondheim.

Arnold, D. (2004) 'Airy offices create 15% work boost', *Building Design,* 16/07/04, Issue 1634, p5.

Baird, G. (2001) Ch. 5: 'The Science Park, Gelsenkirchen, Germany', in *The Architectural Expression of Environmental Control Systems,* Spon Press, London, pp68–79.

Baker, P. H. and McEvoy, M. E. (1999) 'An investigation into the use of a supply air window as a heat reclaim device', *Building Services Engineering Research and Technology,* vol 20, no 3, pp105–112.

Baker, P. H., Porteous, C. D. A. and Kondratenko, I. (2003) 'Further progress on PV-assisted dynamic insulation walls in Scotland, in *ISES Solar World Congress 2003: Solar Energy for a Sustainable Future,* proceedings of conference (Göteborg, Sweden, 14–19 June), Solar Energy Association of Sweden.

Baker, P. H., Porteous, C. D. A. and Sharpe, T. R. (2001) 'Hybrid PV dynamic insulation wall in Scotland: early test results', in van der Leun, K. and van der Ree, B. (2001).

Baker, P. H., Porteous, C. D. A. and Sharpe, T. R. (2002) 'Progress on PV-assisted dynamic insulation wall in Scotland', in *Eurosun 2002,* proceedings of the 4th ISES Europe Solar Congress (Bologna, Italy, 23–26 June), ISES Italia, Rome.

Berry, J. and Thornton, J. (2002) 'Design for Green, Jubilee Campus, Nottingham', *Ingenia,* no 13, pp35–40.

Butti, K. and Perlin, J. (1980) 'An American revival' in *A Golden Thread: 2500 Years of Solar Architecture and Technology,* Cheshire Books, Palo Alto, California, pp202–206.

Department for Education (1994) *Passive Solar Schools: A Design Guide,* Building Bulletin 19, Architects and Building Division, Department for Education, HMSO, London, pp72–75.

Gilbert, J. (1999) 'Geothermal Energy in Glasgow', *Sun at Work in Europe,* vol 14, no. 3, p13.

Hastings, R. (1995) *Solar Low Energy Houses of IEA Task 13,* James & James (Science Publishers) Ltd., London, pp33–34.

Hawkes, D. (1988) 'Energetic Design: Netley Infants' School', *The Architects' Journal,* vol 187, no 25, pp31–46.

Hicks, W. and Riffat, S. B. (2001) 'Monitoring of the Jubilee campus building – An example of building integrated renewable energy systems', in van der Leun, K. and van der Ree, B. (2001).

Jacobsen, T., Hestnes, A. G. and Raaen, H. (1992) 'The solar dwelling at Stokkan, final results', in Andresen, I. and Hestnes, A. G. (1992), pp72–78.

Keren, H. (2005) *The Environmental Interface in the Architecture of School Buildings,* MA (Architecture: Sustainability) dissertation, University of East London, pp 29–43.

Kondratenko, I. (2003) *Urban Retrofit Building Integrated Photovoltaics (BIPV) in Scotland, with Particular Reference to Double Skin Façades,* PhD thesis, Mackintosh School of Architecture, Glasgow School of Art, University of Glasgow, pp134–164.

van der Leun, K. and van der Ree, B. (eds) (2001) *North Sun 2001: A Solar Odyssey, Technology Meets Market in the Solar Age,* proceedings of conference (Ecofys, Leiden, the Netherlands, 6–8 May), Leiden, The Netherlands.

Littlefield, D. (2002) 'Blow up', *Building Design Envelope,* October, pp7–9.

MacGregor, K. (1992) 'Solar Slates' in Andresen, I. and Hestnes, A. G. (1992) pp147–152.

MacGregor, K. (2001) 'Field Trials of Solar Ventilation Systems in the Scottish Borders', in van der Leun, K. and van der Ree, B. (2001).

MacGregor, K. and Kennedy, D. (1994) 'Experiments with transpired plate solar air heating collectors', in MacGregor, K. and Porteous, C. (1994), pp329–333.

MacGregor, K. and Porteous, C. (eds) (1994) *North Sun 94: Solar Energy at High Latitudes,* proceedings of the 6th Biennial International Conference (7–9 September, Glasgow, Scotland), James & James (Science Publishers) Ltd., London.

MacGregor, K., Taylor, A. and Currie, J. (1996) 'Breathing Sunshine into Scottish Housing', in *Eurosun 1996,* proceedings of the 1st ISES Europe Solar Congress (Freiburg, Germany, September), Fraunhofer Institut, Freiburg.

Porteous C. (1983) *Passive Solar Space Heating in Housing with Particular Reference to the Scottish Climate,* MPhil thesis, Robert Gordon's Institute of Technology (now University), pp111–129.

Porteous, C. D. A. and Ho, H. M. (1994) 'Performance of a solar air collector at a CEC Demonstration Project, Easthall, Glasgow', in MacGregor, K. and Porteous, C. (1994), pp317–322.

Porteous, C. D. A., Ho, H. M. and Kilmartin, L. (1994) 'Thermally efficient window design for the Scottish housing market', in MacGregor, K. and Porteous, C. (1994), pp383–388.

Porteous, C. D. A. and Baker, P. H. (1997) 'Performance of a thermally efficient timber window with integral solar air collector', in Konttinen, P. and Lund, P. D. (eds) *North Sun 97,* proceedings of the 7th International Conference on Solar Energy at High Latitudes, (9–11 June, Espoo-Otaniemi, Finland), Helsinki University of Technology, pp790–796.

Saluja, G, S., Porteous, C. D. A. and Holling, A. (1987) 'Experience of passive solar heating in a Scottish Housing scheme at 58°N latitude', in Bloss, W. H. and Pfisterer, F. (eds), *Advances in Solar Energy Technology,* proceedings of the biennial Congress of the International Solar Energy Society (Hamburg, Germany, 13–18 September), Pergamon Press, Oxford, vol 4, pp3686–3691.

Sharpe, T. R., Porteous, C. D. A. and MacGregor, A. W. K. (1998) 'Integrated solar thermal upgrading of multi-storey housing blocks in Glasgow', in Muldonado, E. and Yannas, S. (eds), *PLEA 98: Environmentally Friendly Cities,* proceedings of the conference, (June, Lisbon, Portugal), James & James (Science Publishers) Ltd., London, pp287–290.

Somerville, D. (1992) 'Application of the Trisol heating system in northern Scotland', in Andresen, I. and Hestnes, A. G. (1992), pp111–114.

SINTEF (1989) 'Basic Case Studies', in *International Energy Agency Task 11, Passive and Hybrid Solar Commercial Buildings,* The New and Renewable Energy Promotion Group (REPG), Energy Technology Support Unit, Harwell, UK, pp181–186.

Steemers, K. and Baker, N. (1994) 'Informing Strategic Design, The LT Method', in MacGregor, K. and Porteous, C. (1994), pp191–196.

Taylor, W and Berry, J. (2000) 'The Greening of Nottingham: Jubilee Campus, University of Nottingham', in Steemers, K. and Yannas, S. (eds), *Architecture, City, Environment,* proceedings of the PLEA 2000 conference (July, Cambridge, UK), James & James (Science Publishers) Ltd., London, pp100–107.

Yannas, S. (1994) *Design of Educational Buildings,* Environment & Energy Studies Programme, Architectural Association Graduate School, London, pp9–15.

Chapter 7   Green Solar Future

The reason for contemplating a green or eco-sensitive solar future lies with the inexorable growth of environmental concerns on a global scale. While acid rain may have been tackled to some extent, depletion of tropical rain forests continues apace, fluctuating holes in the ozone layer remain worrying and, according to US government scientists, global warming has recently 'jumped abruptly' (Lean, 2004). ■7.1(1) It has been reported that even the White House, in the run up to a presidential election, has now 'conceded that emissions of carbon dioxide and other heat-trapping gases are the only likely explanation for global warming' (Younge, 2004). Unfortunately, while Russia has now signed up to the Kyoto protocol of 1997 after a gap of seven years (Walsh, 2004), the USA has not, having rejected the protocol in 2001. Even if the primary Kyoto target ■7.1(2) is met, many would argue that the impact will not be nearly sufficient. The change to patterns of weather is also now being taken seriously by UK government studies, with stricter building standards in the offing based on carbon-emission tests (Gates, 2004). ■7.1(3) However, dissidents again argue that the impact of this will be negligible. In 2004, the chairperson of Shell, Lord Oxburgh, has publicly stated that burning oil and gas threatens the planet, but sees CO_2 sequestration below ground or seabed as the solution rather than reliance on renewable energy (Leggett, 2004). Leggett goes on to remind us that Tony Blair acknowledges that solar energy alone can meet the energy demand of the world. But we should not assume that Blair has suddenly become a solar champion. The entire context of this assertion is not given. It may be possible, but that does not mean that he would recommend it. Sir David King, scientific adviser to the UK government, also stresses the urgency of tackling climate change and asserts that Blair sees it as a priority for the UK (King, 2004). However, although King states that CO_2 is higher than at any time for at least the last 740,000 years and is explicit about the need to move towards a low carbon economy, he is vague about the means he would recommend to achieve it. The reality appears to be that the UK supports the strategy of Lord Oxburgh, despite strong opposition from environmental organizations such as Greenpeace (Carrell, 2004). Another reality is that the British Prime Minister has approved a recalculation upwards of the amount of CO_2 that can be emitted by industry and

■7.1 Global warming: Mauna Loa, Keeling curve, Vostok ice core, Kyoto etc.

7.1(1) Measurements by US government scientists report that the increase in CO_2 during 2003 was the highest yet, marking a three-year surge. Measurements on top of Hawai's Mauna Loa summit (approximately 3500m) in March 2004 showed CO_2 had reached 379ppm (parts per million), as opposed to 376 in 2003, 373 in 2002 and 371 in 2001. These are three of the four largest increases on record, the other being in 1998. The increase up to 379ppm is 64 per cent above the average over the last decade. This is not strictly an abrupt jump. Rather it is the inexorably increasing, although up until recently very shallow, exponential gradient known as the Keeling curve (Christianson, 1999), derived from the Mauna Loa data. Depressingly, the more recent extension of the curve confirms that action taken by all countries since the 1980s to reduce emissions of greenhouse gases has made no global impact. In the case of the USA, it is now estimated that buildings account for two-thirds of the electricity demand annually, three-quarters of which is generated through the combustion of fossil fuels (Olgyay and Herdt, 2004). The highest previous levels of CO_2, estimated from the Vostok ice core from Antarctica, were just below 300ppm 130,000 and 320,000 years ago, and circa 280ppm 230,000 and 410,000 years ago (Guldberg and Sammonds, 2001). The latest Antarctic core (3270m) will extend this knowledge by a further half million years (Brown, 2005).

7.1(2) A fundamental target of the Kyoto accord is that 55 countries, responsible for 55 per cent of greenhouse gas emissions, reduce these by 5.2 per cent compared with 1990 levels by 2012. For countries such as the UK, the enforceable target is CO_2 down by 12.5 per cent from 1990–2012.

7.1(3) The new Part L to building regulations in England and Wales aims to improve energy efficiency by at least 25 per cent; but unless such standards are applied retrospectively, the rate of renewal of building stock means that the impact of such changes will be felt very slowly.

power plants in the UK (Milner, 2004). The announcement of this laid the ground for an admission that the UK target of 20 per cent reduction in CO_2 by 2010 compared with 1990 levels is now reduced by 6 per cent (Radford, 2004). Without delving further into his or any other leading politician's position on solar energy as a part of the solution, there are certainly governmental, scientific and industrial sceptics with respect to the seriousness of changes to all environmental phenomena, but particularly global warming.

Conflicting views on global warming and environmental sustainability

There are those who do not accept that human activities, as opposed to natural phenomena, are principally responsible for any significant alteration to the upper atmosphere, and those who accept the evidence that this is the case, but do not think it is of serious concern. In the first case, most doubters accept that human activities result in emissions of gases, which contribute to the greenhouse effect. They just do not believe or do not want to think, say, for economic reasons, that the artificial impacts on the biosphere are, or have been proved to be, more influential than variable volcanic and solar forces. This is important because it means that, for this type of sceptic, there is still a case for being more energy-efficient and reducing the output of CO_2 and other greenhouse gases – to err on the side of caution.

Then the second category of sceptic includes those who accept that the rise in temperature in recent centuries, and the present highest level of CO_2 for over 400,000 years, is primarily due to human intervention. But they point out that this does not correspond with the highest average temperatures over recent millennia (Guldberg and Sammonds, 2001). CO_2 and temperature can move in opposite directions over historical periods of a few thousand years. In the much longer term of over several hundred millennia, it is also evident that in some 40 per cent of strong surges in insolation, associated maxima of CO_2 follow by as much as twenty millennia. In other words it would appear that in these ancient incidences (230,000–400,000 years ago), the climate was slowly driving up CO_2, rather than the other way round. Furthermore, many of the second type of sceptic are suspicious that either the modelled forecasts of rise in temperature, or the consequences of this, and sometimes both, are incompetent or inaccurate, with a bias to doom-laden exaggeration.

Bjørn Lomborg belongs to this tendency, and repeatedly argues that money could be more fruitfully spent on improving social conditions. However, an environmentalist, Tom Burke, rejects Lomborg's posture as being founded neither on science nor scepticism, but asserts that it is simply nonsense (Burke, 2004). Again, the principle of erring on the side of caution should mean that people such as Lomborg should at least not oppose a green solar future. Why should there not be reductions in the production of greenhouse gases as well as other socio-economic reforms at a global level? Thus, in theory, the only active opposition to positive green action should come from people who are militantly against effective, long-term eco-husbandry, rather than those who have doubts about the damage to the status quo of the biosphere.

dimensions of sustainable architecture

The issue of global warming has now become bound in with the terms 'sustainability' and 'sustainable development'. These have become so politically charged, so widely used, so ambiguous and so loosely applied, it is necessary to give a definition here within the context of solar architecture, especially since both are now established as architectural currency. Unfortunately, the semantics are open to interpretation and manipulation by sectors with widely differing political objectives, including neo-liberals who have no difficulty in finding a gloss for the worst kinds of global exploitation. However, taking the alternative, benign, socio-environmental stance, it is generally accepted that both terms are relative, rather than absolute. It is also accepted by most people that they involve enabling the healthy and thriving continuity of life on Earth. In short, they signify providing positively for posterity. It is also generally recognized that such an interpretation embraces a process with three main overlapping dimensions. One might continue with the alliteration and call these people, place and prosperity. These correspond respectively to the terms social organization, environmental resources and economic growth of the World Commission on Environment and Development (led by Gro Harlem Brundtland), when defining sustainable development and also acknowledging that there are limits imposed by technology at any given time (World Commission on Environment and Development, 1987).

Unsurprisingly, either semantic set, wittily illustrated in Figure 7.1 compared with the usual interlocked schematic bubbles of text, carries a significant caveat if it is to signify sustainability People must adopt a responsible and ecologically ethical stance to place and prosperity. Human ecology has to respect and work with all living organisms and their environments, and not allow narrower facets of prosperity or economics to undermine this fundamental aim. There is nothing wrong with the concept of anthropogenic ecosystems, provided some pragmatic guidelines are observed. For eco-altruism to prevail, there must be some regulation. One can draw analogies to the abuse of human rights such as slavery, or torture and imprisonment without legal representation. There has to be accountability. Unfortunately there is a long history of significant gaps between what is needed and what is delivered. This is where politics intervene, and why definitions of sustainability tend to be politically loose in their language. However, the adage of 'where there is a will, there is a way' seems apposite here. One can think of countries that have remarkable records of achievement, despite overwhelming obstacles strewn in the path of their sustainability. For instance, Cuba's record in relation to education, health and green agriculture is exemplary, the last born out of necessity in the post-USSR era.

Quite rightly, this book has widely and deeply excavated the interaction between people and buildings in their context, particularly the means of

7.1 The concept of three overlapping dimensions of sustainability – people, place and prosperity – per William Heath Robinson.

controlling their internal environment and embracing both physical and psychological responses. Using the term people also implies an interaction with technology as an integral part of culture. The tensions that exist between people as the creators, as opposed to the users, of the built environment have been acknowledged in the structure of successive chapters. Place is also central and embraces natural resources, topography, ecology and climate. However, all of these terms are constrained in this book by the word 'cool' in the title. Prosperity implies economic limits, including an awareness of cost over the life of buildings. But it also contains a wider sense of thriving or feeling good in a particular setting, which implies enhancement over time rather than just maintaining a less than satisfactory equilibrium.

solar-green, green-solar interface

One can then reasonably argue that green or environmental architecture is the product of the parameters of an ethically driven process of sustainability and that solar architecture belongs in such a classification – that is, all solar buildings should by definition also be green buildings. This is where matters become more slippery. As we have seen with regard to passive design, an initial decision in terms of glazing quantity, orientation and tilt may result in relatively expensive or complex solutions to mitigate overheating and glare. Alternatively, the reverse may occur. The rate of heat loss may be excessive, but still with too much glare at times. In relation to active solutions, there is a considerable degree of scepticism about aspects of pollution, payback and so on. It is easier to claim that all green buildings are to some extent solar buildings. If placing and sizing of windows relative to the cyclical movement of the sun has not been considered, then one can argue that the building is not green, regardless of all other concomitant eco-sensitive characteristics. The same argument holds for energy-efficiency and, by and large, the case studies in this book show that energy-efficient buildings and solar-efficient buildings are in partnership, not in competition. Therefore, green buildings must first and foremost be energy-efficient, solar buildings. That does not necessarily include or exclude active solar components, the use of which should be free from irrational prejudice by environmental architects.

A recent international symposium held in Scotland ■7.2(1) tackled disputed territory for both solar PV and active thermal systems. Bart Jan van den Brink's story of initially pushing practical boundaries somewhat too far in an attempt to bring the solar supply in summer and the demand for heat in winter closer together, leading eventually to a more pragmatic position, reminds us that green buildings in the developed world rely to some extent on sophisticated technology. Since the developing world may lack expensive infrastructure while also reasonably aspiring to a similar level of modern convenience, active solar technology deserves to be considered. This includes both PV and thermal arrays, and similar climatic environments to those explored here may be found in poorer countries. For example, southern Chile is weak in terms of both food power and industrial power, while cold oceanic currents and topology moderate the climate over a large range in latitude. However, it was stated at the outset that particular case studies would be drawn from northern parts of Europe and North America, including countries with a surplus of energy like Canada and Norway. The enemy of solar or any renewable, clean energy is cheap and often 'dirty' energy from other sources, and neither of these two countries is exempt in spite of their hydroelectric power. The incentives to generate and save energy based on principles of altruistic ecology are still vulnerable to the competing laissez-faire of economic greed. Even in countries where positive fiscal structures are in place to promulgate renewable generation of electricity in tandem with energy-efficient buildings ■7.2(2), there remains a tangible degree of public reluctance, cynicism, scepticism and ignorance.

For instance, one commonly held myth is that PV can never generate enough to pay its cost back economically, and uses more energy in its manufacture than it generates over its life. In response, we have the current figure of six or seven years payback in the UK (corresponding to about three years in southern Europe) and recycling lifting the electrical generation per cell into a range of five to ten times the energy used to make it. ■7.2(3) Another contention is that PV is more damaging to the environment than other technologies. Although its 'additional environmental impact costs' are currently estimated to be about 20 per cent more than for electricity generated by gas in EU countries, we have to remember that using gas in this way has a downside. It means using up a diminishing fossil fuel nearly twice as fast as if it were used to heat buildings directly. Also the cost of PV is mitigated by it doubling as a cladding or shading component, and it gives off no emissions and no noise during operation. ■7.2(4) The pro-PV lobby could go on. Active solar thermal technology can be similarly defended, particularly since it normally displaces at least part of some other less benign mechanical installation, usually with a non-renewable fuel. Active systems should also be inherently easier to control than passive ones, even though various case studies have demonstrated the scope for interrelated complexities to cause glitches.

eco-footprint, ambitions and constraints

An emerging mechanism for evaluating sustainability in general, and the sustainability of buildings in particular, is that of eco-footprint. For example this may be defined as the area of forest needed to produce a certain quantity of timber for a building, and the additional area of forest to absorb CO_2 produced by burning fossil fuel in that building. ■7.3(1) Although it is recognized that this is not an exact science, there have been recent efforts to embed earlier work by Wackernagel and Rees (1996) in a method for green building assessment (Olgyay and Herdt, 2004), as well as attempts to quantify all consumable products in this way (Desai and Riddlestone, 2002). However, the discipline at

■7.2 Active thermal and electrical systems: barriers challenged

7.2(1) Active Solar Myth Busting Symposium, 29th January 2004, Dundee, organized by the Scottish Ecological Design Association, Scottish Solar Energy Group and Dundee Sun City.

7.2(2) A good example is the Waterkwartier scheme in Amersfoort (Chapter 2). Here, not only is the tariff the same whether buying or selling electricity generated by the PV arrays, but also 20 per cent of the selling value goes to the occupants. The utility company retains ownership of the installation and carries out any necessary repairs, including to the roofs.

7.2(3) Figures were given at Active Solar Myth Busting Symposium by Tim Bruton, who was then BP's Executive Director for Crystalline Solar Technology. Additional environmental impact costs in €/kWh are 0.41 for PV and 0.34 for gas. They are also 0.99 for hard coal and 0.73 for lignite.

7.2(4) Prof. Nicola Pearsall, Director of the Northumbria Photovoltaics Applications Centre at the School of Engineering and Technology, University of Northumbria, addressed many such issues at Active Solar Myth Busting Symposium under the heading 'Photovoltaics in Practice'. She also included useful guides to size PV arrays in the UK: one kWp (kilowatt peak output in clear sky conditions) = $10m^2$ modules (depending on type of PV, orientation, tilt etc.); and a UK expectation is an annual output of 750–800kWh/kWp (75–80kWh/m^2 PV area).

■7.3 Eco-footprint numbers

7.3(1) It is estimated that we need some 1.3ha of forest for each m^3 of timber produced and 0.35ha to absorb each tonne of CO_2 produced from burning fossil fuels (Desai and Riddlestone , 2002). Quantifying entire industries would be very complex, but the underlying principle is valid.

7.3(2) The World Wildlife Fund (WWF) *Living Planet Report 2000* (Desai and Riddlestone, 2002) estimates that the total bio-capacity of the earth amounts to about 25 per cent of its surface or 12.6 thousand million ha (126 million km^2). This assumes that deserts, high mountains and deep oceans are of 'low biological productivity', but the rejected 75 per cent begs the question of suitability for forms of renewable power generation. WWF argues that once a further 10 per cent is set aside for wildlife conservation, there is a balance of some 11.3 thousand million ha available to meet human needs. Divided by the global population of 6 thousand million, a target figure of 1.9 ha per capita is obtained. Predictably, estimates for all the developed countries significantly exceed this value. To redress this situation, two questions present themselves – firstly, is the 11.3 thousand million estimate realistic and, secondly, should the target vary to take account of varying regional factors?

7.3(3) The estimated eco-footprint for Canada is 7.66 ha per capita (Desai and Riddlestone , 2002), less than 25 per cent of the area of land available. In the Netherlands, the corresponding eco-footprint is given as 5.75 ha per capita, reflecting somewhat greater efficiency, but this is over 27 times greater than the area of land available. Even though the Netherlands makes much more intensive use of its land, both agriculturally and for industry, the respective differences are immense. There may also be significant variations within the regions of one country. The eco-footprint of the UK is given as 6.29 ha per capita, which is 15.5 times greater than the area of land for each person. But if the same value is used for Scotland alone, it is now only 4 times the area of land, and like Canada, some of this could be classified as biologically marginal. If one added in the recognized territory of surrounding sea and ocean in each case, such regional differences would be magnified.

present only goes so far in terms of recognizing both practical and political realities. By comparing an average area of ecological footprint in one country with that of another, there has so far been little acknowledgement of the differences wrought by different scales and natures of territory. Instead the case is made for global equity, where each country brings its average eco-footprint per capita within a limit representing the available bio-capacity of the planet. ■7.3(2) However, playing devil's advocate, one could argue that a small intensively populated country like the Netherlands requires different infrastructural solutions to a large sparsely populated country like Canada. Accordingly, these should be reflected in varying eco-footprint targets. ■7.3(3)

Similarly, choices for active electrical or thermal solar applications, or purely passive green applications, will inevitably reflect particular ambitions and constraints. These will vary with relevant local and regional characteristics, which are usually dominated by the prevailing economic and political climate. A particular region developing an industry around active solar components could be one such influence, which would have a direct bearing on the eco-footprint. However, as the topic of this last chapter implies a much wider field in terms of potential case studies, these have been consciously confined mainly to the work of two practices, whose names have already been introduced, plus some brief references to others.

Ambitions and constraints might also be perceived as opportunities and threats, but if this signifies a scale of freedom for architects, innovation is possible at all points along it. Whichever semantics are used, a good example is the overriding aim of the rural micro-community of five families at Hockerton (Chapter 3) to be as fully autonomous as possible, as well as to be materially green and achieve a zero CO_2 balance, all within a very tight budget. Besides the design and construction of the super-efficient dwellings, the realization of these aims involves a wind generator, recently complemented by a linear PV array, two methods of water collection, one for drinking and one for other uses, a reed-bed drainage system, growing food and bee keeping. However, an active solar thermal system was not deemed necessary. Instead a heat pump works in tandem with the passive solar conservatories to provide hot water. On the other hand, in the case of the similarly deep green EVA-Lanxmeer eco-village, active solar thermal, as well as electrical arrays, are very much in evidence. The same can be said of the 'Wohnen & Arbeiten' urban co-housing project in the Vauban district of Freiburg (Chapter 4). Both solar thermal and PV are included as dual-purpose canopies, although there is still a residual reliance on natural gas. One could also draw parallels between the Vauban project and the widely published Beddington Zero Energy Development (BedZED) by architect Bill Dunster in south London for the Peabody Trust (Figure 7.2) (Hawkes and Forster, 2002; Gregory, 2003). Here PV arrays complement passive solar thermal gain and very low rates of heat loss, while the balance of thermal and electrical needs are met indirectly by solar energy in the wood-chip combined heat and power plant.

All four developments require commitment on the part of the residents, although the extent of this varies and one might question the level of participation in BedZED by the wider local community. There is some contrast between BedZED and the fully participatory model of Vauban in its area of sustainable regeneration from military to civilian use in a small city, which has a firmly established reputation for solar architecture. BedZED's context is that of any suburb in London, its nearest new neighbours to the south and east being typical examples of retrogressive private development. One might counter-argue that BedZED represents a more comprehensive and radical 'compact city' model compared with the Vauban project. It has demonstrable strengths, which are considerable as a green oasis with a remarkable range of enclosure and prospect, as well as excellent solar access. For all that, its 'zero energy' titular objective is not met. One occupant of a two-apartment flat acknowledged a bill from July to September 2004 that averaged £27 per month. This implies a significant number of units of energy billed in a period when there should have been no space heating and a reasonable amount of electricity generated by the PV arrays. Water heating and use of electrical appliances must be mainly responsible for this.

7.2   Part of south façade of BedZED terrace

In other projects the green agenda may be much more focused. The work of Shigeru Ban in Japan on structures that are reliant on cardboard tubes is driven more by the risk of earthquakes than climate – a tangible threat motivates one innovation. These constructions are inherently green in terms of their CO_2-neutral materiality with very low embodied energy, ratio of mass to enclosed volume, and the ease with which they can be fabricated, constructed, deconstructed and recycled. Embodied energy in its fullest sense normally means the energy used in extraction of raw materials, in transport to a place or places of manufacture and/or processing, in manufacture and/or processing, in transport to a building site and finally in construction or assembly. It follows that energy used in demolition or disassembly for re-use or recycling should be taken in lieu of the extraction of raw materials stage.

Inevitably, the relativity that is implicit in sustainability and 'green' does not necessarily imply an absolute for anything, including embodied energy or autonomy. On the other hand, one aspect may be weighted inappropriately relative to another. It is quite possible to achieve renewable autonomy in an architectural context that lacks green aspiration. A bio-CHP plant, as used at BedZED or the PV factory in Freiburg, could have provided heat and power to any building – possibly one with very high embodied energy. Indeed, in contrast to BedZED where great care was taken to reduce embodied energy and to recycle materials as far as possible, one might query whether the choice of structural steel at that solar factory is as green as timber might have been.

merit and diversity in environmental architecture

The argument here is that sustainability as a process and greenness as a product should still inclusively align with architectural merit and diversity, as well as accepting certain pragmatic, often economic, realities. It is just that the diversity should work with the possibilities and limitations implied by sustainably addressing people, place and prosperity. That should result in an aesthetic that has reacted to particular natural or cultural characteristics of place, but not necessarily in an obvious, demonstrative way. It has been shown that solar collection is not as geometrically confined as one might think. Techniques for cool climates with a high proportion of diffuse solar irradiation can transfer to ones with a much higher direct contribution, but also with temperatures that generate a significant demand for heat. Therefore, we have a situation where aesthetic expression may be legitimately diverse within a single climatic context. The response to the existing cultural, natural and artificial locus is likely to be more influential in determining visual outcomes; and in the first case, historical precedent cannot and should not be ignored.

Susannah Hagan (2001) poses three criteria to be considered relative to environmental architecture – symbiosis, differentiation and visibility. Briefly, she posits that the first is essential, a mutually beneficial relationship between building and its natural context, more often than not already subject to human change. The second is more problematic to pin down. Can there be different symbiotic solutions, given the same place, and should different places engender distinct visual language? The third criterion questions the extent to which new forms, directly related to the environmental functioning of a building, may define the aesthetics. For example, the ventilating cowls of BedZED are visually vociferous, as are the ventilating towers at the Queens Building in Leicester (Chapter 5). However, both devices are very different in appearance. It is interesting that the first, which caps a passive stack ventilation system with heat recovery, is a modernized version of a 19th century invention, the 'McKinnel double tube', while the second has a neo-Gothic syntax, similarly evoking 19th century technology. Hagan suggests that environmental architects divide into two camps – an arcadian minority who are essentially pre-industrial in spirit, and a rationalist majority who are more inclined to new techniques and technologies. However, such classification provokes paradox. If arcadia implies a rural idyll or rustic simplicity, projects such as that of Hockerton are surely arcadian. Even so, its terrace of houses could not be more rational. Rustic simplicity also aligns with the 'organic simplicity' of Frank Lloyd Wright. But Wright was certainly not pre-industrial in spirit.

It is clear that any study of green or environmental architecture should investigate both the rural and the urban condition, and both 'green-field' and 'brown-field' sites. Many of the case studies, which have been included here as relevant in a solar context, have also been examples of brown-field regeneration.

Some, such as Dolf Floors's Gravinnehof and Theo Bosch's housing in Deventer, have also had to address solar accessibility on restricted and historically sensitive urban sites. To an extent, the constraint of space disappears in rural schemes, whether arcadian, rational or both, but these can at least partly be 'brown-field' in nature. The Ottrupgård Fjernewarme project in Denmark was built within a former farm. Not only were its outbuildings refurbished for new communal purposes, but also the project as a whole brought in new life, with more young people and children, and more intensive horticulture. The Earth Balance project to the north of Newcastle in Northumbria, UK, has a very similar agenda (Porteous, 1997). It is no surprise to find that one of its initiators is Malcolm Newton, the author of the ingenious back-to-back solar housing discussed in the first chapter. As at Ottrupgård, new buildings were needed. This then introduces a 'green-field' challenge integral to an essentially 'brown-field' concept. But building anew on green land is not a blank canvas. Both Fjernewarme and Earth Balance had to accommodate intensive horticulture as well as facilitating renewable energy – wind and water power for Earth Balance, active solar collection and storage for Fjernewarme. Ecological treatment of sewage, such as a reed bed, also takes up space, and must observe certain conditions. It is then perfectly reasonable to explore new-build on rural sites in a quest for a green solar future. All it does is increase the required level of architectural sensitivity and skill, including the application of the science needed to produce solar buildings in cool and cloudy climates.

The work of two North American practices

Aspects of the work by two practices in Canada, one in British Columbia and one in Nova Scotia, have already been brought up in preceding chapters. As it happens, their buildings are more often than not located on green-field sites. Both portfolios also belong in the green or environmental genre. However, Brian MacKay-Lyons in the east is justifiably reluctant to accept such a simple categorization. Similarly, the work of Bo Helliwell and Kim Smith in the west has been published in the wider terms of picturesque, tectonic and romantic qualities (Boddy, 1999, pp8–15). One might also argue that the western practice leans more to the arcadian and the eastern one more to the rationalist approach, but it will be shown that both have a strong contemporary rationale. What is incontrovertible is that each has carved out distinct architectural territory that ascribes to people, place and prosperity. Partly for this reason, and partly because case studies in northern European countries have already had a good airing, some of their work has been chosen as the principal focus for this final chapter. The choice is also connected to interesting commonalities and contrasts of ambition and precedent, acknowledging that the demographic and socio-economic climate in Canada differs significantly from its European counterparts.

contextual commonalities and differences

Helliwell + Smith: Blue Sky Architecture sets out its stall for an architectural programme as a response to place, climate, materials and structure. This methodology is distinctly environmental and regional. A programme, of course, addresses the needs of people – their clients, usually also the occupants. Place defers to the detailed topography of the site, land and water, as well as its eco-systems supported by the nature of its climate. They carefully research the microclimate of sites as well as acknowledging regional characteristics, which in turn relate to resources. They strive to use local materials as much as possible, and also exploit local skills to achieve desired results. The structures they use are a manifest expression of the primary material in British Columbia – timber. But there is more to it than that. For example, the formal language of post and beam is rooted in first nation architecture. This was adopted by architects such as Arthur Erickson and melded with Pacific Coast modernism. Bo Helliwell worked from 1968–72 in the office of Erickson-Massey, and the impact those four years had on him is still evident. Architectural historian Trevor Boddy asserts (rightly, it would seem) that a house Helliwell designed during this period, the 1970 Rothstein house in Whistler, was also strongly influenced by the 1964–65 Sea Ranch Condominium in California by MLTW (Boddy,1999, pp8–15). MLTW is Charles Moore, Donlyn Lyndon, William Turnbull and Richard Whittaker. Boddy further compares Helliwell and Smith's work with that of Glenn Murcutt and others in Australia.

This immediately defines mutual connections with Brian MacKay-Lyons in Nova Scotia (the practice now named MacKay-Lyons Sweetapple Architects Ltd.). His former tutor and mentor was Charles Moore of MLTW and Glenn Murcutt is a good friend. It is perhaps too easily forgotten that Moore's early Californian work in the 1960s had an evident regional and climatically sensitive flavour. In addition, it was one that more often than not had an inner sequence of spatial and structural order, which set up a different grammar to that of the external skin. For example, there are the two roof-lit, load-bearing 'temples' within the small house for himself at Orinda in 1962 (Allen, 1980, pp24–29). These define the main sitting area and a sunken bath, and their asymmetric placing has some interesting consequences. Since the raised lantern is symmetrically centred over the ridge of a hipped roof, the vaults over the 'temples' have a skewed geometry that influences the channelling of light. The outer envelope then has a layer of opaque sliding panels that can open up corners directly to the outside. In the main sitting zone, the column of the larger 'temple' nearest the corner allows eaves beams to cantilever over a considerable distance. Thus the opening up can be dramatic. Apparently Moore described this as placing his piano into 'a kind of exhilarating jeopardy' (Allen, 1980, pp24–29). At the same time the sliding doors offer the alternative of shading and containment. Thus the apparent simplicity of the building belies a very rich formal resolution.

The Sea Ranch Condominium again plays with rooms within rooms, as well as expressing a vigorous articulation of a diagonally braced post and beam structure (Allen, 1980, pp30–37). The Sea Ranch Swim Club, 1966 and also by MLTW, uses both accommodation and earth berms to provide a wind-sheltered microclimate (Allen, 1980, pp39–41). The Budge house built in 1967 near Healdsburg had counterbalanced screen walls, which folded up to the ceiling in order to open the house out to the landscape (Allen, 1980, pp48–53).

While Moore's work grew ever more playfully exuberant, humorously engaging with post-modernism, there is a spare quality to most of MacKay-Lyons's work that aligns with the cultural history of Nova Scotia (see the quotation on page 31 of this book). His trick of using 'saddle-bags' to maximize spatial opportunities and flexibility within a main space is not only a reference to one of Moore's first realized projects, the Bonham house in the Santa Cruz Mountains (Allen , 1980, pp16–19), but it is also immensely practical. That said, an early example of his own work overlays a disciplined idea of core and skin with humorous overtones of Moore's rather later work. This is the 1985 conversion of a 200-year old house at Kingsburg, in itself a green act, where all the original partitions were stripped out and replaced with his version of a local lighthouse. A central tower, its girth reducing with height, contains a wilful stack of sleeping shelves, lofts and belvedere, as well as plumbing and hearth (Figure 7.3). Brian MacKay-Lyons describes it with poetry, passion and commitment:

The House on the Nova Scotia Coast is symbolically
the center of our universe as family.
It is an archetypal one-room 'House', wrapping around a massive 'Hearth',
and wrapped by a 'Grove' of optimistic fruit trees, inside an archetypal
*   village.*
It is a utopian project that is a built argument
for preservation of the agrarian cultural landscape.
The restored shell, contrasting the modern interior, is a metaphor
for the social contract between the individual and society.
My family climbs into the safety of the hearth to sleep.
(MacKay-Lyons, 1995, p25)

It can be argued that the complex rationalism of the Sea Ranch Condominium has prevailed for Brian MacKay-Lyons as a line of more quietly restrained enquiry. His work has been recognized as research through practice (Carter, 2001), with qualities that are very particularly associated with place: 'Both extremely rational and highly idiosyncratic, MacKay-Lyons' work shows how rootedness in a place, however geographically isolated, can result in architecture as rigorous as that produced anywhere.' Although Sea Ranch was also one of several early influences for Bo Helliwell, he has increasingly moved towards a subtly vibrant and romantically extrovert vocabulary of angled and undulating walls and roofs, especially after his partnership with Kim Smith. In order to

7.3   Inside and outside the 1985 conversion of
      the MacKay-Lyons house at Kingsburg

understand this progression, one has to return to respective architectural roots. The Gulf Island of Hornby became their shared working arena during the 1980s. Helliwell moved there in the 1970s, after completing a post-graduate course at the Architectural Association in London, and set up Blue Sky Design with Michael McNamara as partner. The Graham house, designed in 1976 and completed seven years later in 1983 remains a remarkable example of their work together (Figure 7.4). Not only was it their first major collaboration in terms of its design, but also they were both involved in self-building the 620m² complex. This provided first hand skills with respect to constructional techniques, and established the idea of a structure where heavy post and beam elements internally are complemented by a load-bearing skin of fenestration. The mullions of the latter are simply slim posts at closer intervals than the primary ones inside.

Meanwhile, before her career as an architect, Kim Smith had designed and helped to self-build a large boatshed, as a prelude to self-building a 12m ocean-going catamaran. This was followed by more self-building with fellow architectural students in Vancouver from 1980–82. Later in the 1980s, she bought a house on Hornby Island, which became a test-bed of pragmatic architectural subtraction and addition. The bold cliff-side creation of an architectural technician, it offered scope for a linear studio slung below two floors of existing accommodation, which was also extended and opened up. Still the Hornby studio of Helliwell + Smith, this building touches its verdant cliff very lightly, and makes the most of its commanding position, whether in terms of arrival, activity or repose (Figure 7.5).

coastal Pacific projects

Much the same tactic of subtraction and addition has been used for their house and main studio of Blue Sky Architecture in West Vancouver. The original upper ground floor has been opened up to provide a generous linear, living-dining-kitchen-study space. A cascade of extra terraces has been added overlooking the steeply sloping garden to the southeast. Their new studio projects out on the other side towards the access road, with a curved glass wall addressing a dense temperate rain forest to the west. A tilted roof in the form of a hyperbolic paraboloid dramatically tops the space. There is a remarkable green discipline about this extension. Although it is at the same level as the main floor and the site slopes up steeply at this side, it is a diagonal slope, with the floor level well above grade at the east end. Thus no retaining walls were required and the load of the timber structure could be taken into the ground at relatively few selective points. This meant that the new extension could be built very close to existing trees. In fact only one tree had to be felled, while all the growth beyond the westerly screen of glass shades the interior (Figure 7.6a). The upward sweep of the roof towards the northwest corner not only recognizes the position of the public entrance to the studio, it also acknowledges the rising ground. Each rafter coincides with a mullion along this edge while at the other, easterly side the rafters come to rest on a chunky horizontal beam.

One might ask why a beam and not the wall, and why horizontal, when the other side slopes? At one level it might be perceived as a wilful architectural move, but it involves more than the aesthetics of the space. The horizontal beam rests on piers, which internally buttress the slim timber-framed wall, located parallel and close to the boundary. It is a counterpoint to the structurally effective curve of the load-bearing screen on the other side. Each pier supports the load of three rafters via the beams, which are located close to the inner edge of the piers. In turn this construction permits a tilted clerestory strip of windows to face the sky and shed daylight down the eastern wall of the studio above bays of bookshelves (Figure 7.6b). The fact that the beam is parallel to the bookshelves provides a sense of anchored stability to the ensemble. This is the architectural and green synergy of place, climate, materials and structure relative to the programme.

In terms of solar design, the objective was to avoid overheating in a room occupied by several people and computers. At the same time the eastern clerestory and the full-height western facets of glass help to maintain an awareness of the external environment and the daily cycle of the sun. The extension does not compromise access to sun and view from all the main rooms of the house, where roof overhangs, and the projecting decks in the case of the lower floor of bedrooms, provide fixed shading. This solution has great clarity, but was not reached without polemics. Two earlier ideas were systematically and mutually assessed, before being discarded – a 'Bo-idea' for

7.4 Inside the main living space of the Graham house – note the sectional device for providing daylight and ventilation deep within the floor plate

7.5 Helliwell + Smith's cliff-side home and studio on Hornby Island – looking into main living space from upper entry level

7.6 The West Vancouver studio of Blue Sky
Architecture
a curved west facade
b straight façade opposite, facing to the north
of due east

the studio at low level on the southern side; and a 'Kim-idea' for a high-level, northwest solution, using the car port as a starting point.

Another ordering mechanism, which is clearly present in much of Helliwell + Smith's work is that of front and back. Historically, we are used to a formal front, always facing the street or other public approach, while the back can be more informal and offers privacy. In the case of Helliwell + Smith, the front sometimes coincides with access. Arrival at the Murphy house on Gambier Island by boat is such an example. Their own studio and house in West Vancouver is more complex, but entirely logical. The studio is entered from the public edge, as is the house. The path from carport to door is romantic and informal, down steps and across a bridge, which spans a pool. Meanwhile the real front of the house is private, with fantastic views across the bay to the city centre. Even though the entrance is not always located on the front, it is nonetheless adopted as a formal device – one which relates to orientation and aspect, as well as to programmatic function, and therefore to relative areas of glazing. The concept of front and back may translate to fluid and solid, flexible and specific, served and servant and so on. In their studio, the front is the curved wall of glass, with the entrance occupying the corner, while its back is the straight wall close to the boundary. The back of the house on the other hand adopts the same informal functionalism as the entrance, with the projecting stairs to the lower level clearly expressed. In the Murphy house, the front is an undulating wall, mainly glazed from floor to roof in order to capture the ocean view through pine trees. It was important to the clients that the house should intrude minimally on the natural landscape of the island. Viewed from the sea, the gentle form of the front is virtually invisible. By contrast, the back is a series of juxtaposed flat planes, more solid than transparent, that enclose the utility spaces (Figure 7.7). The unifying curved roof follows the geometry of the plan, with the exception of the outdoor room (see Chapter 3), which it oversails. The whole nestles elegantly within its sylvan nirvana.

The Greenwood or 'Fishbones' house on Galiano Island also has a long and predominantly glazed scalloped wall facing the ocean and a jetty for arrival by boat. This means that it is a relatively private front, while in this case the house is more usually accessed from the rear. A public road bounds the site on the northeast, several metres above the entrance and garage. Hence even this side is secluded, with a limited glimpse from the top of the driveway into the forecourt and over a turf and glass roof. The careful placing on the site, with a minimum amount of excavation to secure a southwest-facing ledge on the restricted and steeply sloping interface between forest and rocky shore, is evocative of Frank Lloyd Wright. However, if such a precedent has relevance, it is not the whole story.

The highly disciplined juxtaposition of curved and orthogonal form has become a signature of Blue Sky Architecture. Here the flowing façade to the ocean terminates in a substantial cedar post set out from a massive stone chimneystack at the southern end (Figure 7.8). At right angles to this and parallel to the eastern boundary, a flat wall then turns through 45° and moves in and out as required to enclose the garage and provide a recess for the entrance, with children's bedrooms jutting out beyond. The 45° move relative to the eastern boundary is formally and structurally important. A long horizontal ridge, also at

7.7 The curvaceous front and angular back of the Murphy house

45° to the eastern wall is the spine of the plan and section. Programmatically, in the diurnal core of the dwelling, the spine is a demarcation between leisure and work. In the nocturnal part, it separates the adult zone from that for children and guests. Where it intersects with the eastern wall at its southernmost post, the ridge beam turns horizontally at right angles to connect with the post that marks the south end of the scalloped façade. It then turns at right angles again, but this time slopes down towards the southeast to connect with a final post on the line of the eastern wall, and simultaneously defines a small triangular outdoor space. To the southwest of the spine, parallel cylindrical cedar rafters drop down at varying angles to provide a flowing form for the roof in harmony with that of the wall. However, to the northeast there are simple mono-pitches and flat roofs respecting the predominantly rectilinear forms, which accommodate utilitarian spaces. A long stretch of this is a lean-to clerestory similar to that used in their studio. This window to the encircling forest allows morning sunshine to penetrate the heart of the house and enables stack-assisted cross ventilation (Figure 7.8).

If Frank Lloyd Wright was possibly a subliminal influence in terms of topographical placement, there is at least one late 20th century building in Europe that has formal similarities. The technique of a horizontal spine or backbone acting as a launch pad for curvilinear gymnastics on plan and section is reminiscent of the Japanese cultural centre in Kraków, Poland, by Arata Izozaki & Associates (Cerver, 2000). Completed in 1994, its sinuous accents suit the location on the west bank of the River Wisła, a small enclave of green between the flowing water and the busy main road that bypasses the old city centre. However, within its voluptuous envelope, Izozaki uses a series of regularly spaced, and identically dimensioned, hollow brick piers as an orthogonal ordering device. From these, diagonal struts support his roof, which undulates on plan and section in two separate halves (Figure 7.9). The piers, each with a generous rectilinear opening, also define a primary circulation route for visitors, as well as forming ducts for controlled circulation of air. Izozaki's synthesis of programme, structure and services undoubtedly has green resonance. The rationale is one of multiple added value, as well as being formalistically analogous to some of Helliwell + Smith's buildings.

Returning to British Columbia and the Murphy house, a similar spine is used as a spatial and structural delineator between curvilinear front and angular back. A large rectangular Douglas fir beam, the underside of which is at the level of the top of doors, is aligned to coincide with the sliding screen of the outdoor room. It again mediates between work and leisure in the principal diurnal space (Figure 7.10) where a substantial circular post, a former tree from the site, breaks the span. The beam runs right through the centre of the post, which carries on to the roof and thus helps to stabilize the structure, as do other elements such as the massive masonry chimneystack. Thereafter, relatively slim

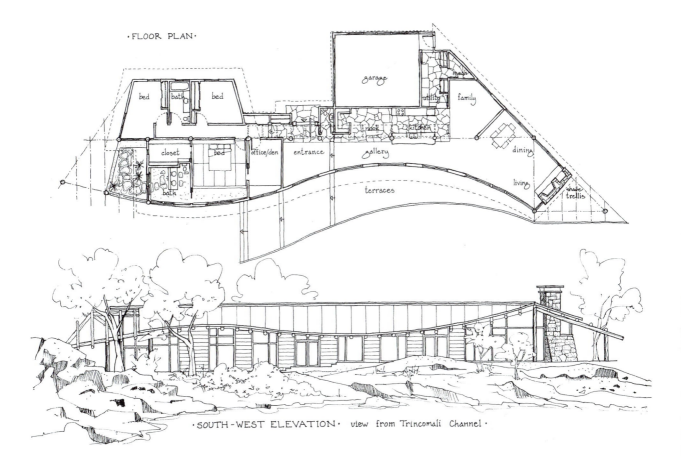

·FLOOR PLAN·

·SOUTH-WEST ELEVATION· view from Trincomali Channel·

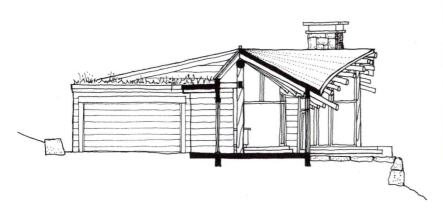

· CROSS SECTION · through entrance ·

7.8 The Greenwood or 'Fishbones' house on Galiano Island:

a plan

b elevation

c cross section

d interior view

7.9   Japanese Centre for Art and Technology in Kracow: a) external and b) internal view

rectangular posts on the top of this beam provide intermediate support for each rafter, which can then span a fairly moderate distance to either load-bearing mullions or timber-framed sections of the outer wall. Douglas fir is used throughout for structural timber, including tongued and grooved roof-decking and windows, while the unglazed parts of the exterior are clad in flush-jointed, tongued and grooved cedar siding. On the south side rafters also cantilever beyond the face of the wall, providing a visual cornice and additional shading to that of the trees. To accommodate the roof's changing curvature, the posts simply have to alter their length. At least the principle is simple, but since virtually every junction is visible, successful realization depends on predictive accuracy at the pre-contract stage, as well as high standards of carpentry in execution. Dimensional stability of the structural timber plays an important part, and to help in this regard it was all radio-frequency (microwave), vacuum kiln-dried. The process of building also recognizes the isolated location. As soon as the roof was on, the building crew lived in, the house temporarily used as their finishing workshop.

A similar degree of accuracy was demanded for 'Fishbones' on Galiano Island. Here, visible junctions had to be accommodated between circular posts, eaves-beams and rafters. As a client, Barry Greenwood was strongly against metal connections and practicalities made other demands relative to aesthetics. For example, the main bedroom required a degree of acoustic isolation from the main space, while visual continuity down the length of the building was equally important. The constructionally demanding solution, frameless glass set into horizontal rectangular beam, circular rafter and post, is beautifully executed.

Somewhat easier, but with the same meticulous attention to detail, is the copper gargoyle from the roof. This is functionally seated on one of the projecting cedar rafters and also celebrates the purpose of the roof at a pivotal position on plan. It not only axiomatically coincides with the roof's concave centre-point, but also that of the façade, which in turn aligns with one of the primary columns to the north of the island unit of the kitchen. Although one might talk about the ecological benefit of a copper roof and spout relative to rockery plants on the terrace below, the architectural panache of this small component relative to a bigger whole moves beyond the realm of green qualities.

Trevor Boddy (1999, p14) emphasizes the picturesque and romantic nature of these designs, 'treating nature more as a visual system than one where energy concerns dominate'. He suggests that '"green" or "organic" architecture seems to offer some parallels to their work.' Peter Davey, in his preface to the same book in which Boddy writes (1999, pp5–6), accepts that ecological consciousness is deeply embedded in their work. This view is positively qualified: 'Helliwell and Smith are inheritors and interpreters of the Organic tradition of Modernism. But they are free of its often claustrophobic tendencies.' However, because there are picturesque and romantic layers embedded in the aesthetic and tectonic ambition and resolution of each programme in terms of place, climate, materials and structure, it does not mean that these metaphoric planks of their methodology are subsidiary. They are fundamental, and they are essentially bound up with a process of sustainability that carries a particular Helliwell + Smith hallmark. It is a hallmark that, from the outset, recognized value in precedence as well as always looking forwards in terms of refinement.

The Gadsby house, 1988–92, bears examination as the outcome of the first formal partnership between the two while still with Blue Sky Design (that is, just before setting up Blue Sky Architecture). As with the Greenwood house, there is a front facing out to the ocean. This is backed by all the utility spaces along the public side of the plot. Entry is again through paired sets of this ancillary accommodation. The long façade of the main living-dining space faces virtually due east and, on this occasion, front and back meet on the south edge. Here a triangular section of roof glazing covers part of the kitchen and a loggia facing into a walled sun court. This is complemented by another section of glass over the west-facing entrance threshold and lobby (Figure 7.11). A third roof-glazed triangular extension to the rectilinear master bedroom juts out to claim the view and morning sun. Thus the daily cycle of the sun is carefully considered. Inside, the roof glazing over the kitchen and entrance porch allows sunlight deep into the main space throughout the day, without compromising the paramount nature of the views north and east to the sea. Moreover, large ceramic floor tiles over the areas that receive most sunshine provide useful thermal mass. External spaces allow migratory scope for sun or shade from dawn to dusk. The decks along the east side can receive some sunshine until midday, while a generous

7.10 The spinal beam of the Murphy house, looking west into the main room (Bo Helliwell in background)

7.11 The Gadsby house looking into main living
area west towards entrance porch

triangular roof overhang also provides the opportunity for shade and shelter. The sun court is both more secluded and sheltered, while a second garden court with a hot tub is functionally located on the northwest corner next to internal plumbing.

On plan, there is one major directional shift of about 25°, while on section, siting the dwelling over a natural hollow allows the living space to drop by two steps and still to gain some extra bedrooms below. The change of angle is essentially taken up in the main space, allowing the convenience and functionality of an orthogonal discipline in the smaller rooms and closets. As in the Greenwood house, there is a primary ridge beam. However, here it soars diagonally across the main space, tilting upwards towards the northeast. At each extremity it is supported on slim corner posts, with only one additional central support. This is a chunky circular timber post, around which the spiral stair to the lower floor pivots. Thus the structure, plan and section are synergic. In particular the position and tilt of the beam skilfully regulates the volume, with maximum height and openness over the main living space contrasting with the lower volume of the kitchen with its internalized view from the sink on to the sun court. Whilst the dynamics of the geometry are probably more attributable to the influence of Kim Smith, the single central support is reminiscent of an earlier Hornby precedent, that of the Lloyd house 'leaf retreat'. Bo Helliwell included this in his 1974 historical dissertation and as a special issue of *Architectural Design* (Helliwell and McNamara, 1978).

ubiquitous environmental concerns

It almost goes without saying that Helliwell + Smith use good standards of insulation and glazing, as well as ecologically sensitive finishes. For example, low-emissivity, argon-filled, triple glazing is used in the Greenwood house to complement the insulated and untreated cedar-clad walls. The roof is similarly well insulated above the structural cedar decking, as is the heated screed below the cherry-wood flooring. As a matter of policy, the timber is sourced as locally as possible, with fabrication by local contractors. In its natural state, timber is of course an innately benign ecological material. It is carbon neutral, non-toxic, acts as an absorber for moisture and, as stated previously, it is a surprisingly good thermal store, given adequate thickness. However, one might still question the green credentials of individual dwellings in isolated places, especially when they sometimes seem luxuriously large. This could challenge the output of many practices that rely substantially on one-off domestic commissions. Although a well-known British architectural commentator, Martin Pawley (2001), seems not to have a problem with this in the UK, others do, particularly the environmentalists who are concerned about the inbuilt reliance on personal transport. This brings us back to the debate about the relativity of eco-footprints in varying contexts. There is no reason why the intensive European context cannot have an efficient and fine-grained system of public transport to serve built-up areas. But this is difficult to justify or achieve as populations reduce and distances expand.

In a country as large and as sparsely populated as Canada, detached houses on reasonably large plots, as well as cars to get to them, are hard to argue against. Also, by and large, wealth or relative wealth does not generally seem to be perceived as having been aggressively acquired at the expense of the less fortunate; and dwellings in a beautiful landscape are not automatically regarded as threatening or despoiling – as they are now in Scotland, unless grouped in corporate estates. Throughout the UK and other densely populated European countries, such apparently haphazard and unrestrained growth continues to burgeon around existing villages, towns and cities. Unfortunately, more often than not it also continues to display monotonous anonymity, not to mention the visual impact of regurgitated goulash. Most (in the UK at least) are stuck in some dreadful pseudo reflection of the past. Speculative developers in particular, but also housing associations and lenders, insist this is what people want. Having said that, the public sector remains the one area of occasional enlightenment compared with the private one, where the profit incentive always seems to be contradictory to aesthetic quality. One might argue whether people are seduced or traduced to open their wallets to such regressive pastiche as the least line of resistance, rather than actively seeking it. But if 'my home is my castle' is the main incentive, the plots are simply too small to provide that aspirant degree of seclusion. On the other hand, the model runs counter to a cohesive sense of community.

In Canada there is still room for the culture of the pioneer, the culture of possibility; and given a big enough plot, the character of a housing cluster becomes much more diffuse, with controlled nature asserting its dominance. Ironically, a diffuse community also seems to be a realistic goal. For example, Helliwell + Smith's house and studio is on a 0.2 hectare (half-acre) plot with virtually no visual awareness of neighbouring houses. Yet there is a tangible sense of 'West Van' togetherness. Settlements in more remote rural areas are not so different. The less dense vegetation surrounding the Gadsby house on Hornby Island means that neighbours are rather more in evidence, while the aura of village life throughout the island could hardly be more robust. Key social hubs are a co-operative shop and gas station, a recycling and re-using centre, a community hall and a local pub with cool jazz of a Friday – all vibrantly thriving. The size of plots tends to be somewhat smaller than 0.2 hectare and is about 0.15 in the case of Gadsby. Even so, they are still very generous by typical northern European standards for populous suburban areas, or the equivalent expansion of smaller towns and villages. In the UK one would expect to find four or five dwellings crammed into a fifth of a hectare. Exceptions to this are older models. For example, the crofting 'townships' to be found in the Highlands and Islands of Scotland have an equivalent generosity in terms of land. There is calm and privacy in open landscapes, but there is also a sense of collective, interactive purpose. In Canada, where a higher density of more than 15 or so dwellings per hectare is economically dictated, low-rise condominiums are a pragmatic solution, especially when in, or close to, a town or city. There is a fine 20th century demonstration of such a development on the steeply forested slopes of West Vancouver by Arthur Erickson, which might be regarded as a timber equivalent of the 1961 Siedlung Halen by Atelier 5 just outside Berne in Switzerland. High-rise housing is also now being built at a great rate in the centre of Vancouver. The demand is huge, reflecting the current price of land.

Therefore, individual dwellings, sometimes on relatively isolated virginal sites, but more often in clusters, cannot just be shunted out of sustainable sight. The Pacific Coast region of North America has developed a seminal reputation for radical domestic experimentation that dates back to the arrival of Rudolph Schindler at the outbreak of the First World War and Richard Neutra in the 1920s. Much of the innovation would today be regarded as ecologically aware (Porteous, 2002). Much of it has also now been absorbed into suburbia. Once accepted, such locations may also throw up some quite tricky environmental issues. For example, there is understandably a minimum distance stipulated between a septic tank and a well for fresh water. Due to this constraint, the Gadsby House has a large cistern in its basement to store rainwater collected from the roof. In the case of the Greenwood House, the client chose not to do this, but to install a desalination plant in an outhouse. He was familiar with the technology, felt comfortable with it and could afford it.

coastal Atlantic projects

Exactly the same issues occur in Nova Scotia although, as indicated earlier, its climate is in some respects harsher than that in British Columbia. Consequently, there is less dense afforestation and smaller trees. There is still plenty of space and there seems to be a tendency for minimal landscaping around dwellings, perhaps more referential to the prevailing and austere agrarian and fishing culture than the climate. Hence we have Brian MacKay-Lyons (1995, p12) referring to buildings 'perched on the land like brightly coloured dice.' In fact, despite the name of this province, the built forms, materials and colours are much more redolent of Scandinavia than Scotland. The cost of land is presently a good deal cheaper in Nova Scotia than British Columbia and so building plots in rural locations tend to be less constrained. More ground can be afforded with fewer natural obstructions such as trees. This provides the possibility of pavilions in the round, rather than the more bipolar arrangement with public and private edges, which are common to several of Helliwell + Smith's commissions. A corollary to the vernacular heritage is that MacKay-Lyons has no compunction about building on the top of hills, rather than on the side. His sculptural regional aesthetic, with his simple forms vigorously editing the anthropogenic landscape, defers more to Europe and Le Corbusier than Frank Lloyd Wright and Usonia. ■7.4

A good illustration of these issues alongside the fundamental ethos of MacKay-Lyons is the 1999 dwelling known as Coastal House No. 22 (Carter, 2001). Near the mouth of the historic LaHave estuary at 44.2°N, the way in which the programme has been interpreted and then positioned on the landscape is key. Initially the site being considered was a single drumlin. This is one of a pair, roughly 150m apart, and in an elevated position relative to other houses in the vicinity. MacKay-Lyons, in any case fascinated by duality and reciprocity, saw a golden opportunity. He persuaded his client to purchase both grassy drumlins. He then aligned two perfect pavilions on their respective summits. The approach is dramatic. Once seen in their elevated purity, the road spirals round and up, eventually arriving at the opposite side of the larger of the two. This is the main house, volumetrically a double cuboid, while the second is the guest wing, a reflection of the first in terms of the facing elevation, but shorter in length. Effectively it is simply a smaller second house, which is approached on foot via a bridge across the low-lying and sometimes wet ground between the two drumlins.

Although there are panoramic views in all directions, compass orientation was also a major consideration. Having made the decision for respective living spaces to face each other, the main house has been given solar priority. Thus it is situated on the northerly drumlin, with its double-height living room facing south to the guesthouse, as well as west. To include the superb view north to the LaHave estuary, the living space extends under the main bedroom into the dining space (Figure7.12). The same happens in reverse in the guesthouse. It

■7.4 Frank Lloyd Wright and Usonia

Usonia and Usonian were terms used by Frank Lloyd Wright in a philosophical, political and practical sense applied to the USA. In his autobiography (Wright, 1977) we find him referring to a 'new sense of Architecture' to 'awaken the United States to fresh beauty and the Usonian horizon of the individual', which he claims to be enhanced by 'this great lever, the machine'. He also refers to 'the great Usonian Life, the universal life of our own true democracy' and 'the road to Freedom in Usonia'. The association of USA and utopia is inescapable, and Wright used Usonian as a paradigm for houses in the 1930s and 1940s.

7.12 Coastal House 22: view south to the guesthouse and north to the LaHave estuary

has a large window facing south to the Atlantic below the bedroom and a more constrained double volume facing north and west. Each building also has a wing wall, stretched adherence to the aligned reciprocity, forming an eastern windbreak to respective patios. Although it means that guests will not receive much sunshine on theirs until late afternoon, there is another outdoor element, a deck to the south of the guesthouse close to the edge of the cliffs.

Referring back to the influence of Charles Moore, there are no rooms within rooms as such, but a spine of stairs and storage has a strong identity, critical to a parti of served and servant spaces (parti is defined as 'choice, means or method; … the choice of approach when realizing the scheme' (Curl, 1999)). This is evident from the architect's drawings (Figure 7.13). Forming the demarcation between the main living spaces and all the east-facing single-height utility spaces together with double-height porte cochère, the spine is an internal manifestation of the external wing walls. The staircase descends on to a striking stainless steel shelf, which continues the alignment of the storage out into the landscape. The served/servant parti is similar to that employed by Helliwell + Smith, but a difference lies in the relative suppression of it externally. Only one freestanding element breaks out of the main double cuboid, but it too conforms to the essence of the parti.

7.13 Coastal House 22: architect's drawings – plans (north to right) and elevations, the plan clearly showing the parti of 'served and servant'

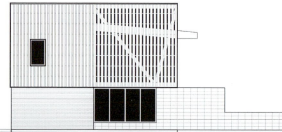

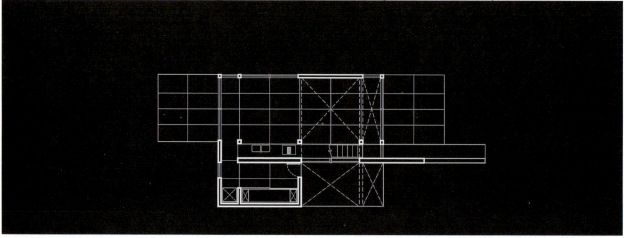

Lying to the west of the living space in the main house, it contains an open hearth and bookshelves, beefed up by the plant room behind. It is known as the 'bump'. What the stair-storage-shelf and the 'bump' achieve is to leave an uncluttered, but economic, width for the primary spaces. The 'bump' is a version of Moore's 'saddlebags', while the spinal feature again manages to be completely practical while lifting architecture on to another aesthetic plane. Thus the resolution is bound in with pragmatic green aspects, such as conveniently concentrating the expensive wet and warming services, as well as poetic symbolism – the fixed but pivotal hearth, and the vertical movement along the line of transition. It also allows flexible use of the main spaces. The bedroom doubles as the working space for one partner, while the living room fulfils the same function for the other. This is green strategy in action.

The other striking Moore precedent is the exposure of diagonal timber struts. It is particularly bold in this instance because two of them embrace the bed (Figure 7.14). As with the work of Helliwell + Smith, the tectonics are essential to the whole. A light timber building with so many openings requires to be well braced. Even though the external visual expression is of a pair of timber boxes on top of metal and glass ones, each building is in reality all one coherent

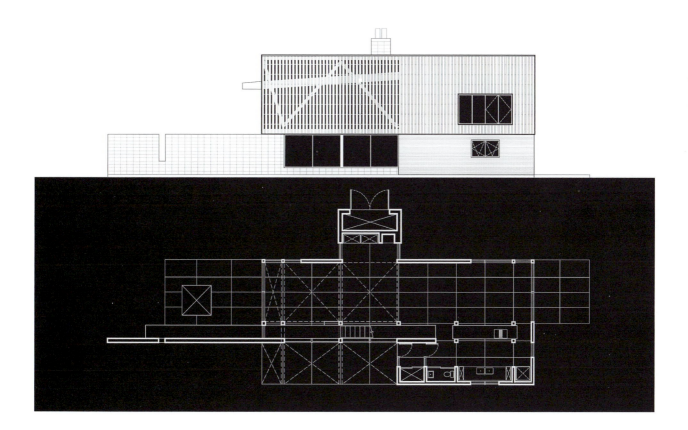

7.14 Coastal House 22: structure integrated in the main bedroom, looking north

construction. Just as the polished concrete floors are not an issue for the owners, neither is the structural and material rationale. They love it, and it is all value for money – another reason why this project deserves to be credited as green.

Internally, there is absolutely no wasted space. The planning is faultless in this regard. This is partly attributable to the decision to separate the two components. It takes slightly more in the way of materials, but there are no conflicting circulatory demands. The only elements that might be challenged as being too generous are the double-height portes cochères. But they celebrate entrance as well as providing practical shelter while loading and unloading cars at the main house. Moreover, they were absolutely essential to the cuboid composition, and the extra cedar siding for the upper rain screen is hardly extravagant.

A similar kind of reciprocity between main house and guest wing is employed at the 2004 Hill house (see also Chapter 3) on the South Shore of Nova Scotia (*Architectural Review*, 2004). In this case, the two elements of accommodation are just either side of a single summit, allowing both a minimally excavated lower ground floor. In the main house, this accommodates studio, utility and exercise space. In the other part, which also has a generous garage-playroom at ground level, the bedrooms are at the lower level. The main part of the house has slight solar dominance, with the bedroom facing east and main space receiving sunlight from dawn to dusk. However, in this case the guest wing does not face back to the main house, but out to the south, and so is not exactly disadvantaged in terms of sunlight. Similarly, there is no wasted space in the planning: built-in storage plays a significant role and the palette of materials is restrained – the usual heated polished concrete floors, hemlock ceiling, maple fitments and an external skin of cedar shingles. This house also collects rainwater from both of its mono-pitched roofs, which slope gently down towards the central court. This supplements the supply from a borehole, with the facility to switch from one to the other.

An equivalent elegant clarity exists for non-domestic buildings by the practice. The new community theatre in Parsboro has only three programmatic components, all below a single unifying mono-pitch roof – a large flexible theatre space, a narrow two-storey strip of ancillary accommodation through which the theatre is entered, and a covered portico-foyer. This last houses the remains of the small ship around which the theatre has until now revolved, making use of temporary tented structures for each production. There are actually three materials used on façades, but each has a very distinct role. Hemlock lines solid parts of the sheltered ancillary spine, cedar shingles clad the two flanking gables of the theatre, and galvanized corrugated steel protects the tilted wall on the seaward face. The roof is finished in the same material, with sections of corrugated plastic integrated above the portico. The structure is mainly a combination of steel and timber, with concrete playing a very minor role. Steel columns bring their load on to concrete pile caps, which are in turn supported on pairs of timber piles descending through the artificially built-up ground of the site.

The computing technology centre for Dalhousie University in Halifax also reduces quite an elaborate programme to a few simple elements. All the teaching spaces face northward to the street, while a vertiginous linear atrium, housing a muscular cascading stair and with a social area at its foot, faces southward (Figure 7.15). It is also bridged at intervals over its height by cul-de-sac retreats. These allow students to take short breaks from their closed world of computers into spectacular sunlit vantage points. Indeed, a slight eastward bias will allow students to enjoy sunshine here well before midday, while the corresponding westward bias of the IT areas should not cause overheating. The large angle of incidence in late afternoon will mean that most of the solar heat will be reflected and a mainly exposed structure of concrete provides plenty of thermal mass, which absorbs heat from computers in the northern section and solar heat gain in the southern one. There are selective areas of lightweight linings for acoustic absorbency, and these may be regarded as an internal reflection of the external skin, held off from the grid of concrete. Entry into the atrium from the street-level foyer is one floor up from its base. The sense of looking down as well as up at this arrival point adds to the legibility as well as the drama of the space, which also functions passively as part of the return circulatory system for mechanically supplied air. Servicing is stacked conveniently at east and west extremities. Overall, this building may not immediately display green or solar characteristics, but these issues have been considered in a practical and coherent manner within an undemonstrative rectilinear shell.

The need for a 'value system of complexity'

It was the absence of such order and legibility that architect and academic, Professor Isi Metzstein, criticized when interviewed about the controversial new Scottish Parliament building at Holyrood in Edinburgh:

It lacks some kind of logic that could offer some clues to de-coding the forms … I think architecture needs some kind of narrative, not exactly a hierarchy, in which some parts of a building are more important than others. In other words, a value system of complexity in materials, construction and form.

Queried as to why this approach is so important, he goes on:

It is important because you read a building. The building tells you what it is. At Holyrood, every bit of the building is equally elaborate, there is no clear way through it. There is no way to recognize when you have come to something important; you don't know what to look at first. All buildings need an unfolding sequence. (Lewis and Metzstein, 2004)

7.15 The atrium of the computing technology centre at Dalhousie University, looking west

As just one example, the random distribution of superfluous screens over windows and other parts of the façades contributes to the external obfuscation and 'look at me' and 'look at this' to which Metzstein refers (Figure 7.16). Asked whether the building should be more functional and formal, Metzstein comments: 'It is not about formality it is about orchestration. Like a piece of music, a building has a structure, it tells you where the next piece of the composition is going to come from and where it is going.' (The transcription of excerpts from the interview of Isi Metzstein by Penny Lewis has been reproduced here without any amendment to punctuation.) This sentiment echoes the words of Louis Kahn (1962): 'At some point there must be a place of maximum intensity.'

Although Isi Metzstein was not talking 'green', the essence of both how a building reads and a value system of complexity seems to be fundamental to sustainable, environmental design. That is not to say that the last work of an eminent architect such as Enric Miralles, together with the significant contribution of his widow, Benedetta Tagliabue (the other half of EMBT), and RMJM (Robert Matthew Johnson Marshall), does not have strengths, but simply that it does not seem to have the strength of canonical, logical clarity.

Taking up his critique from a solar perspective, Metzstein complains of too much daylight in the main chamber, implying that it is over-glazed. Actually, he was questioning the need for any daylight in such a space. While it may be legitimate to posit a 'black-box' solution, the counter-position that daylight is desirable, even if only because we tend to feel deprived over time in its absence, can be justified. In this regard, it could be argued that the chamber is a qualified success. The direct vertical fenestration on the east and west sides of the chamber has necessitated anti-glare shields. These are not very skilfully handled on the east side to the rear of the visitors' gallery. Gravity is exerting its

7.16 The 'look at me' and 'look at this' of the new Scottish Parliament's exterior

influence over the internal solar blinds, which, perversely, are horizontally drawn. Unsurprisingly, they are not adequately tensioned and are sagging. By contrast, in the case of the west façade, a thin layer of sycamore is securely sandwiched between two sheets of glass to form a light-filtering mural. MSPs and visitors view this as they face towards the presiding officer. Miralles clearly expresses his fascination with translucence and multiple layering, and in this case the screen is practical in editing the relatively confined view beyond the windows, as well as preventing glare. In terms of admitting daylight, it is the reflected light from east-sloping roof glazing, in particular via glass 'guillotines' suspended above the west side of the chamber, that is paramount. On a dull day the consequence is that the chamber appears subtly lit rather than over-glazed. Indeed it is a tribute to the architectural resolution that, even in such weather, it is still possible to appreciate the space without artificial lighting, which appears to be over-provided in the extreme and is now left on regardless of ambient brightness. A veritable forest of lights hang from the roof structure and one can contrast the intrusiveness of these fittings relative to daylight with the elegant symbiosis achieved at the museum in Ålborg (Chapter 5).

If the main chamber can be praised with a faint damn, it has to be said overall that there is neither a convincing strategy for orientation and natural lighting, nor for natural ventilation. For example, there have been justifiable complaints from MSPs that their offices are under lit, requiring the lights to be on, not to mention too warm with an inadequate area of opening windows (Tait, 2004). This is not surprising, given the design of the projecting oriel windows on the west façade. Their extruded shape makes airing awkward and excessive 'glare contrast' inevitable, with the area of glass very small relative to the depth of offices. Hence there is a need for more or less permanent artificial lighting in the workspace. Perhaps MSPs should be grateful that at least this is handled reasonably, with the ceiling acting as a reflector for background illumination, complemented by task lighting on their desks.

An assertion was made near the beginning of this chapter that while a solar building is not necessarily green, a green one should always be to some extent solar. The Scottish Parliament does not get to the starting block on either basis. Orientation does not seem to have influenced any of the fenestration. For example, accepting the logic of the decision to align the MSPs along the western boundary to enclose a private court, there is a thermal argument for the offices to face east rather than west. The temperature of the air is cooler during periods of morning sunshine than in the afternoon. Hence there would have been justification for larger windows facing in this direction. But if that is put down to dubious judgement, orientation appears to be otherwise a matter of happenstance. The plan of the main complex still defers to the collage of leaves and twigs presented at the time of the first stage of the competition. Inevitably, this results in a considerable amount of mutual obstruction to daylight as well as sunlight. Apart from this, the tight collision of the four buildings immediately west of the debating chamber, with their pointed forms causing some external spaces to terminate in extremely acute angles, implies great future difficulty in terms of maintenance. The architects seem to have become fixated on the dense and often awkwardly claustrophobic, not to mention unhealthy, grain of medieval Edinburgh, rather than its spatially generous and environmentally reforming Georgian counterpart.

Finally, although there was a considerable amount of hype at an early stage concerning environmentally sensitive materiality, such aspirations fell by the wayside. Excessive use of concrete threatens the environment both in terms of finding sources of aggregate and in terms of the production of cement. The sourcing of all the other main materials outside Scotland not only betrays a laissez-faire approach to sustainability (Dorrell, 2004), but also confirms the lack of a value system other than that of hard cash. The cost has of course been a major political bone of contention. But setting aside specification, sourcing and the hikes attributable to the type of contract, bomb proofing and so forth, there is no escaping the amount of material that can be laid at the door of the planning concept. The number of discrete components of accommodation and the excessive circulation, at least partly driven by placing the offices of MSPs at the opposite end of the site from the main debating chamber, equate to a very large area of external surface relative to usable space.

By way of contrast, it can be argued that all the case studies, described and discussed previously in this chapter, conform to the premise of logically respecting and optimizing sunlight and daylight, as well as the principle of pragmatic planning and bioregionalism in terms of materials. Orientation, position, size and specification of fenestration have all been carefully determined relative to the topographical and climatic locus. Each project also has Metzstein's value system of complexity as well as Kahn's places of maximum intensity – crescendos, according to the former's musical analogy. Moreover, the economically low surface to volume ratios implied by the simple forms of MacKay-Lyons, compared with the rather more elaborated ones of Helliwell + Smith, may be interpreted as a logical response to differing climates and cultures.

Similarly the lack of active solar thermal and electrical systems in both sets of work, can be understood in contrast to more committed and interventionist political climates or cultures in countries such as Holland and Germany. Nevertheless, since it exploits a solar-heated ambient source, one may consider a heat pump to be an active solar thermal variant. As the one chosen in a number of the Canadian and European case studies cited, the advantage of out-of-sight compactness is self-evident. There is a credible argument that architects should not be force-fed solar panels, which are bound in with tricky aesthetic decisions. Essentially, over-regulation is riskier than a policy of tempting incentives. If they do opt in, then panels can be discreetly handled, as several of the case studies in Chapter 2 demonstrate. Successive chapters have also shown that the performance of any building is sensitive to systems of control through a wide passive–active and participatory–automatic (or selective–exclusive) range, and not necessarily in the same respective order. Although this principle applies to all systems in all climates, there is a point made in the preface that seems to hold true. Just as a green building should be a solar building, but the reverse is a harder proposition, a solar building will find it easier to transfer from an area with a poor supply–demand ratio to one with a more favourable balance than vice versa. The original Trombe-Michel wall is a case in point. Substantial modification is required to make the principle work in a less favourable climate, but such a modification might still be advantageous moving in the other direction. The ability for occupants to compromise heating performance also seems to be more sensitive to situations where the solar supply is relatively small compared to demand. The opposite is likely to be true of cooling. The wills and perceptions, both rational and apparently irrational, of occupants have been shown to be a factor in this regard, and there seems to be a case for instituting tangible incentives.

Thus it is clear that performance relative to climate, and particularly a cool climate, requires a value system of complexity not only in materials, construction and form, but also in control systems and psychology. One might still be tempted to seek the comfort of an established value system of complexity such as 'commodity, firmness and delight' (Wotton, 1624; Wilkes, 1988) or one could simply refer to the original Latin version of Vitruvius – 'venustas, utilitas, firmitas' (Morgan, 1914; Wilkes, 1988). ■7.5 Austin Williams, technical and practice editor of the *Architects' Journal*, recently advocated such adherence, whilst railing against having to subject ourselves to 'mundane tick-box criteria' embodied in phrases such as 'positive impact on the local community and environment' (Williams, 2004). One can certainly sympathize with his frustration over current bureaucratic and political 'speak', whilst acknowledging that utilitas and commodity address prosperity in a manner that would still appeal to modern politicians and economists. It has also been made very clear in this book that engendering delight is of strategic importance to architecture. However, unless the semantics were to be significantly stretched, either triad would tend to leave aspects of people and place under-explored relative to meaningful characteristics of sustainability tackled here. Also, in whatever way a value system is termed and while much can be achieved logically and intuitively by architects, it should be accepted that some systematic number-crunching is still required – both pre-start and post-completion. Peter Davey (Boddy, 1999, p6) says of Helliwell + Smith's designs: 'The buildings are kindly, and tender to humankind and nature, which are both enriched by their existence.' This is so, but it is a calculated enrichment. It does not happen by chance, but because their iteratively adjusted methodology, which is based on principles of sustainability, has made it so.

■7.5 Vitruvian triad: sense and sensibility?

Cassel's Latin Dictionary (undated) defines venustas as 'loveliness, beauty, charm, attractiveness', utilitas as 'usefulness, utility, advantageousness, profitableness, use, profit, advantage' and firmitas as 'firmness, durability'. This does match Wotton's later version quite closely. For example, a dictionary definition of commodity (Allen, 1993) is 'profit, expediency, advantage, convenience or privilege'. Morgan (1914) also uses 'durability' for firmitas and 'beauty' for venustas, but reduces utilitas to simple 'convenience'. According to his translation, convenience is achieved 'when the arrangement of the apartments is faultless and presents no hindrance to use, and when each class of building is assigned to its suitable and appropriate exposure'. In this last regard, Vitruvius was clearly concerned with prevailing winds, and their impact on health and comfort, as well as gaining solar warmth in winter while avoiding solar overheating in summer.

Brian MacKay-Lyons (1995, p24) also says: 'The human urge to build is a fundamentally optimistic act. Architects have no business with cynicism, pessimism or distopias [sic]. We are in the business of optimism.' Isi Metzstein (Lewis and Metzstein, 2004) expresses this only slightly differently when responding to a question about changing things through process: 'Building is a fantastically confident process, in the sense that somebody knows that something can be done.' While not dissenting from these abstract sentiments, a question to be asked is whether their sense can be numerically valued? If the answer is yes, then the psychologically charged dimensions of contentment, happiness or delight remain very under-researched. If a feel-good factor arising from solar architecture, and ideally green solar architecture, is a reliable indicator of better health and better productivity, it must be tangibly counted in together with any non-renewable energy saved or renewable energy generated.

Then we can have a green solar future.

REFERENCES

Abley, I. and Heartfield, J. (eds) (2001) *Sustaining Architecture in the Anti-Machine Age,* Wiley Academy, Chichester.

Allen, G. (1980) 'Projects', in *Charles Moore,* Whitney Library of Design, New York.

Allen, R. (ed) (1993) *The Chambers Dictionary,* Chambers Harrap Publishers Ltd.

Architectural Review (2004) 'House on the hill', *The Architectural Review,* vol 216, no 1292, pp89–91.

Boddy, T. (1999) *Picturesque, Tectonic, Romantic House Design: Helliwell + Smith, Blue Sky Architecture,* The Images Publishing Group Pty. Ltd., Australia.

Brown, P. (2005) '900,000-year-old ice may destroy US case on Kyoto', *The Guardian,* London, 23 April, p18.

Burke, T. (2004) 'This is neither scepticism nor science – simply nonsense', *The Guardian,* London, 23 October, p24.

Carrell, S. (2004) 'Britain to push greenhouse gas plan', *The Independent on Sunday,* London, 31 October, p4.

Carter, B. (2001) 'Architecture at a threshold: three houses by Brian Mackay-Lyons', *Arq,* vol 5, no 1, pp39–52.

Cerver, F. A. (2000) *The World of Architecture,* Könemann, Cologne, pp312–313.

Christianson, G. E. (1999) *Greenhouse: The 200-year Story of Global Warming,* Constable, London, pp166–168.

Curl, J. S. (1999) *A Dictionary of Architecture,* Oxford University Press, Oxford, p484.

Desai, P. and Riddlestone, S. (2002) *Bioregional Solutions for Living on One Planet,* Green Books, Dartington, UK (for the Schumacher Society, Bristol), pp24–31.

Dorrell, E. (2004) 'Scots shunned in timber row as Holyrood bosses turn to Europe', *The Architects' Journal,* vol 220, no 8, p5.

Gates, C. (2004) 'Extreme weather warning', *Building Design,* July 30, no 1636, p4.

Gregory, R. (2003) 'Wake up call', *The Architectural Review,* vol 214, no 1281, pp44–48.

Guldberg, H. and Sammonds, P. (2001) 'Design tokenism and global warming', in Abley, I. and Heartfield, J. (2001), pp72–83.

Hagan, S. (2001) 'Introduction', in *Taking Shape: A New Contract between Architecture and Nature,* Architectural Press, Oxford, pp x–xix.

Hawkes, D. and Forster, W. (2002) 'Review of BedZED: Sustainable Development, Bill Dunster, London, 2002', in *Architecture Engineering and Environment,* Laurence King Publishing in association with Arup, London, pp86–95.

Helliwell, B. and McNamara, M. (1978) 'Handbuilt Houses of Hornby Island', *Architectural Design,* vol 48, no 7, pp451–479.

Kahn, L. (1962) 'Team 10 Primer 1953–62', *Architectural Design,* December, p582.

King, D. (2004) 'Clean air act', *The Guardian,* London, 24 November, Society section, p15.

Lean, G. (2004) 'Global warming spirals upwards', *The Independent on Sunday,* London, 28 March, Home section, p9.

Leggett, J. (2004) 'Are we ready for when the oil runs out?', *The Guardian,* London, 18 June, p1.

Lewis, P. and Metzstein, I. (2004) 'Complexity, a conversation', *Prospect,* September, pp31–33.

MacKay-Lyons, B. (1995) 'Seven stories from a village architect', *Design Quarterly,* Summer, no 165.

Milner, M. (2004) 'Revised emissions regime comes under fire', *The Guardian,* London, 28 October, p22.

Morgan, M. H. (trans) (1914) *Marcus Vitruvius Pollio, De Archtectura, The Ten Books on Architecture,* Cambridge, Mass., USA.

Olgyay, V. and Herdt, J. (2004) 'The application of ecosystems services criteria for green building assessment', *Solar Energy,* vol 77, no 4, pp389–398.

Pawley, M. (2001), 'The sand-heap urbanism of the twenty-first century', in Abley, I. and Heartfield, J. (2001) pp142–161.

Porteous, C. (1997) *SunTimes, Scottish Solar Energy Group Newsletter,* no 18, September, Mackintosh School of Architecture, Glasgow, p10.

Porteous, C. (2002) *THE NEW eco-ARCHITECTURE,* alternatives from the modern movement, Spon Press, London, pp13–16, 74–78, 88–90, 94–97.

Radford, R. (2004) 'Beckett admits defeat on climate change target', *The Guardian,* London, 9 December, p4.

Tait, M. (2004) 'MSPs: New Parliament is shoddy and unfinished', *Metro,* Edinburgh, 31 August, p2.

Wackernagel, M. and Rees, W. (1996) Our Ecological Footprint, *New Society Publishers,* Canada.

Walsh, N. P. (2004) 'Russian vote saves Kyoto protocol', *The Guardian,* London, 23 October, p20.

Wilkes, J. A. (ed) (1988) *Encyclopaedia of Architecture, Engineering and Construction,* John Wiley and Sons, vol 2, p172 and vol 3, p312.

Williams, A. (2004) 'Ticking the right boxes', *The Architects' Journal,* vol 220, no 7, pp14–15.

World Commission on Environment and Development (1987) 'From One Earth to One World: An Overview by the World Commission on Environment and Development', in *Our Common Future,* Oxford University Press, Oxford, pp8–9.

Wotton, H. (1624) *The Elements of Architecture,* London.

Wright, F. L. (1977) 'Freedom', 'Usonian', 'Who looks and sees' and 'Journeyman preacher' in Book 4 of *An Autobiography: Frank Lloyd Wright,* Quartet Books, London, pp374–377.

Younge, G. (2004) 'Bush U-turn on climate change wins few friends', *The Guardian,* London, 27 August, p18.

PICTURE CREDITS

Note: all photographs by Colin Porteous unless otherwise stated

Chapter 1 North Sun Context

1.1 Plan of 'direct gain' passive solar house by Stillman and Eastwick-Field
© David Stephens and with permission of John Stillman; drawing reproduced from International Journal of Ambient Energy, Vol 6, No 3, 1985, Ambient Press Ltd

1.2 3-dimensional 'cutaway' of 'indirect gain' solar house by Malcolm Newton
© Malcolm Newton, Newton Architects; drawing reproduced from International Journal of Ambient Energy, Vol 6, No 3, 1985, Ambient Press Ltd

Chapter 2 Multiple and Added Solar Value

2.12 Solar house in Freiburg – plan, section and detail of façade
© Dieter Hölken; drawings reproduced from Sun at Work in Europe, Vol 7 No 4, 1992

2.15a John Darling Mall at Eastleigh in Hampshire, plan
© Hampshire County Council; drawing reproduced from 'Schools of Thought, Hampshire Architecture 1974-1991, by Richard Weston, 1991

2.17 Images from proposed BIPV retrofit project for Strathclyde University
© Dr Irena Kondratenko; reproduced from PhD thesis, Mackintosh School of Architecture, Glasgow, 2003

2.1 The solar cladding features of the STinG project in Glasgow
© Dr Tim Sharpe; reproduced from draft Thermie bid, Mackintosh School of Architecture, Glasgow, 1998

Chapter 3 Environmental Comfort and Well-being

3.1b Cross section through access promenades, detailing glass and timber screen
© Dolf Floors – architekt iva, Amersfoort

Chapter 4 Adaptive Control

4.1 General view of the JUgend FOrum

4.2 Schematics for the rotating roof
© Peter Hübner; drawings reproduced from The Architectural Review, September 1996, EMAP Construct 1996

4.3 Internal view of 'city of mud'
© Peter Blundell Jones; photograph reproduced courtesy of the Architectural Review. September 1996, EMAP Construct 1996

4.7 Schematic of Stile Park solar housing in Stornoway – stacked sun-porches
© Comhairle nan Eilean Siar (Western Isles Islands Council)

4.16 South façade of the 'Wohnen & Arbeiten' (Living & Working) block in Freiburg
© Photograph by Guido Kirsch, Freiburg

Chapter 5 Passive Control

5.1 Cross section of roof monitor at Nordjyllands Kunstmuseum
© Drawing by Mary Patrick, Cusp Design, Glasgow

5.9 Sports 'factory' – schematic section showing system for natural light and ventilation
© David Morley Architects; cross section of the National Cricket Academy, Loughborough University, reproduced courtesy of the Architects' Journal, 11 March 2004, EMAP Construct 1996

5.19a Koster's mirror-optics – typical sections

Reproduced from Workshop Proceedings TI3, Transparent Insulation Technology for Solar Energy Conversion, 3rd International Workshop 18–19 September 1989, Tiltsee/Freiburg, FRG, ed Leslie F. Jesch, © The Franklin Company Consultants Ltd., 1989

Chapter 6 Machine Control

6.15 Double-height winter garden above plant room of solar house at Stokkan

Cross section reproduced from Proceedings North Sun 92, Trondheim, Norway
(reproduced by permission of SINTEF per Professor Anne Grete Hestnes)

6.16 The combined geothermal heat pump and solar system for Shettlestone

© John Gilbert Architects, Glasgow

Chapter 7 Green Solar Future

7.1 The concept of three overlapping dimensions of sustainability – people, place and prosperity – per William Heath Robinson

© 'An artistic way of hiding an unsightly view from a flat' from HOW TO LIVE IN A FLAT by William Heath Robinson, Hutchinson & Co, London, 1936; reproduced by permission of Pollinger Limited and the proprietor

7.8a,b The Greenwood or 'Fishbones' house on Galiano Island

© Bo Helliwell + Kim Smith: Blue Sky Architecture

7.13 Coastal House 22: architect's drawings – plans and elevations

© MacKay-Lyons Sweetapple Architects Ltd.

INDEX OF SOLAR BUILDINGS AND PROJECTS

Superscript numbers denote category of main solar attribute(s), as follows:

1 – passive solar thermal

2 – active solar thermal

3 – daylight

4 – BIPV

5 – PV

6 – environmental

Note: 'passive solar' signifies a specific design intention, sometimes linked with mechanically assisted ventilation, cf. 'environmental' where passive solar gain is usually incidental to a wider environmentally sensitive agenda; 'daylight' included as a category for non-domestic buildings (assumed for all dwellings);and distinction between BIPV and PV is that BIPV signifies integration where the PV array has another building function.

Names of architects/leaders are given in parentheses.

Culture

Art gallery – Fondation Beyeler, Basel, Switzerland[1 & 3] (Renzo Piano Workshop) 138–139

Burrell Museam, Glasgow, Scotland[1 & 3] (Barry Gasson) 173–174

Joan Miro Gallery, Barcelona, Spain[3] (Josep Lluis Sert) 24, 138

Japanese Centre for Art and Technology, Kracow, Poland (Arata Izozaki & Associates) 226, 228

Modern art gallery, Ålborg, Denmark – Nordjyllands Kunstmuseum[3] (Elissa and Alvar Aalto with Jean Jacques Baruel) 24–25, 128–135, 136, 137, 138, 139, 239

Modern art gallery (Kuntsbygning), Århus, Denmark[3] (Mads Møller) 24, 135–138, 139

Modern art gallery, Bregenz, Austria[1 & 3] (Peter Zumthor) 138

Modern art gallery, Davos, Switzerland[3] (Gijon and Guyer) 138. 139

Theatre, Parsboro, Nova Scotia, Canada[6] (Mackay-Lyons Sweetapple Architects Ltd.) 236

Education

Akademie Mont-Cenis, Herne-Sodingen, Germany[1, 4 & 6] (Jourda and Perraudin with Hegger, Hegger and Schleiff) 44, 46–47, 71, 162, 205, 206

Adult learning centre, Kirkintilloch, Scotland, UK[3] (Richard Murphy) 142–144

Community School, Benbecula, Scotland UK[1, 3 & 6] (Western Isles Islands Council) 204

College in Sönderborg, Denmark (Jean Jacques Baruel) 128

Computing technology centre, Dalhousie University, Halifax, Nova Scotia, Canada[3 & 6] (Brian MacKay-Lyons) 237

Delft Technical University library, Delft, Netherlands[3 & 6] (Mecanoo) 141–142

Jubilee Campus, University of Nottingham, Nottingham, UK[1, 3, 5 & 6] (Michael Hopkins and Partners) 194–196, 197

Junior school (St Aloysius), Glasgow, Scotland UK[3] (Elder and Cannon) 176

Kingsdale School, Dulwich, London, UK[1 & 3] (De Rijke Marsh Morgan Architects) 179

Methilhill Primary School (Building 2000 programme of the CEC Directorate General XII), Methil, Fife, Scotland[2 & 3] UK (Fife Council) 86, 187

Netley Abbey Infants' School, Hampshire, UK[1] (Dennis Goodwin, Hampshire County Council) 192–194, 196

Norwegian Institute of Technology, Trondheim, Norway[1] (Per Knudsen) 197–198

Odenwaldeschule gymnasium, Oberhambach, Germany[1 & 2] (Peter Hübner) 31–33

Queen's Building, De Montfort University, Leicester, UK[6] (Short Ford and Associates) 146–147, 148, 218

Swanlea secondary school, London UK[1 & 3] (Percy Thomas Partnership) 160

University of Strathclyde theoretical retrofit of teaching block, Glasgow, Scotland UK[1, 3 & 4] (Irena Kondratenko) 91–93, 153–154

Wolfson Medical School, University of Glasgow, Scotland UK[3?] (Reiach and Hall Architects) 180–183, 199

Environment

Brundtland Centre, Toftlund, Denmark[1, 3, 4 & 6] (KHR Architects) 160–162

De Kleine Aarde (The Little Earth), Boxtel, Netherlands[1, 4 & 6] (Tjerk Reijenga, BEAR Architecten) 144–146, 147, 198

Earth Balance project, Northumbria, UK[6] (Malcom Newton) 219

Eco-centre, Jarrow, UK[6] (Carole Townsend, Earth Sense) 146–147

Exhibition building, Earth Centre, Doncaster, UK[6] (Fielden, Clegg, Bradley Architects) 182

International Garden Exhibition, Stuttgart, Germany[1, 3 & 4] (Manfred Hegger) 162

Living Planet Report 2000 (World Wildlife Fund) 216

Exhibition

Congress and Exhibition Hall, Linz, Austria[1 & 3] (Thomas Herzog) 163

Government

ECN research campus, buildings 42 & 31, Petten, Netherlands[1, 3 & 4] (Tjerk Reijenga, BEAR Architecten) 182, 198–199

Scottish Parliament, Holyrood, Edinburgh, Scotland UK[3?] (EMBT & RMJM) 237–240

Town Hall, Nyköping, Sweden (Jean Jacques Baruel) 128

'VillaVISION', Danish Technological Institute, National Solar Test Laboratory, Taastrup, Copenhagen, Denmark[1, 2, 4 & 6] (Ivar Moltke, project manager) 14–15

Houses and Housing

Back-to-back theoretical model for atrium terraced housing[1] (Malcolm Newton) 7–11, 12–13, 219

Beddington Zero Energy Development (BedZED), London, UK[1, 2, 4 & 6] (Bill Dunster) 216–217, 218

Blue Sky Architecture house and studio, Vancouver, British Columbia, Canada[1] (Barry Downs – original house; Bo Helliwell + Kim Smith – alterations and studio) 204, 223–224, 232

Bonham House, Santa Cruz, San Fransisco, USA[6] (Charles Moore with Warren Fuller) 221

Bourneville 'solar village', Birmingham, UK 90

'Breathing Sunshine into Scottish Housing', Edinburgh, Scotland UK[1 & 5] (Kerr MacGregor) 188–189

Brown House, Tucson, Arizona, USA[1] (Arthur Brown) 87–88, 95

Budge House, Healdsburg, California, USA[6] (Charles Moore) 221

Cahn House, Lake Forest, Illinois, USA[1] (Keck & Keck) 87

Cash House, Garriston, near Dublin, Ireland[1] (Duncan Stewart) 30

Clarté apartments, Geneva, Switzerland (Le Corbusier) 116

Coastal House 22, South Coast, Nova Scotia[1 & 6] (Brian MacKay-Lyons) 157–158, 233–236

Courtyard house, Dollar, Scotland UK[1] (Andrew Whalley) 164

Delft Technical University: IEA Task XIII solar apartments, Amstelveen, Netherlands[1, 2] (Atelier Z) 206–207

Doldertal apartments, Zurich, Switzerland[1] (Marcel Breuer with Alfred and Emil Roth) 87

Duncan House, Flossmoor, Illinois, USA[1] (Keck & Keck) 9

'Ecobuild' experimental houses, Petten, Netherlands[1, 2, 4 & 6] (ECN Research Centre) 182

Edwards House (retrofit), near Kirknewton, Scotland UK[1] (Brian Edwards) 64–67, 73, 78, 110

Energiebalanswoning (energy balance house), Amersfoort, Netherlands[1, 2 & 4] (Architectenbureau Van Straalen, Zeist & BOOM) 34, 35, 39

EVA Lanxmeer eco-village, Culemborg, Netherlands (Peter van der Cammen, Orta Nova; Joachim Eble; Bart Jan van den Brink) 34–35, 37, 39, 50, 205, 216

Experimental solar house, Ayton, Scotland UK[1, 2 & 4] (Bean and Swan) 108–109, 110, 112

Experimental solar house, Bregenz, Austria[1] (Walter Unterrainer) 157, 158

Experimental solar house, Ebnat-Kappel, Switzerland[1] (Dietrich Schwarz) 165

Experimental Trombe-Michel wall, Carlow, Ireland[1] (unknown) 89–90, 154–155

Flats, Freiburg, Germany UK[1, 2 & 4] (Thomas Spiegelhalter) 51–52

Gadsby House, Hornby Island, British Columbia, Canada[1 & 6] (Bo Helliwell + Kim Smith) 229–231, 232–233

Gibson-Livingston House, Nova Scotia, Canada[2, 5 & 6] (Brian MacKay-Lyons) 204

Graham House, Hornby Island, British Columbia, Canada[1 & 6] (Bo Helliwell & Michael McNamara, Blue Sky Design) 222, 223

Graham Square urban redevelopment, Glasgow, Scotland UK[1] (McKeown Alexander) 116–117, 119–120

Gravinnehof urban infill, Haarlem, Netherlands[1] (Dolf Floors) 60–64, 67, 72, 73, 77, 218

Greenwood ('Fishbones') house, Galiano Is., British Columbia, Canada[1 & 6] (Bo Helliwell + Kim Smith, Blue Sky Architecture) 70, 225–228, 230, 231, 232

'Heatfest' community ideas competition, Glasgow, Scotland UK[1 & 2] (not applicable) 102

Hill House, South Coast, Nova Scotia, Canada[1 & 6] (Brian MacKay-Lyons) 67–68, 236

Hockerton Housing Project, Nottinghamshire, UK[1, 5 & 6] (Brenda & Robert Vale) 74–78, 85, 110, 112, 122, 128, 216, 218

Howard House, West Pennant, Nova Scotia, Canada[1] (Brian MacKay-Lyons) 31, 68, 157, 158, 174

IEA Task VIII apartments, Berlin, Germany[1/2] (Gustav Hillman) 152

IEA Task XIII apartments, Amstelveen, Amsterdam, Netherlands[1 & 2] (Atelier Z) 15, 206–207

IEA Task 28/38 Sustainable Solar Housing (monitoring of 'Wohnen + Arbeiten' below) 123

Isolated seasonal active system, Falkenborg, Sweden[2] 53

Jacobs II 'solar hemicycle', Middleton, Wisconsin USA[1] (Frank Lloyd Wright) 7–9, 11, 40, 148

Kutcher House, Herring Cove, Halifax, Nova Scotia, Canada[1] (Brian MacKay-Lyons) 68–70

Messenger II House, South Coast, Nova Scotia, Canada[6] (Brian MacKay-Lyons) 68

Moore House, Orinda, California, USA[6] (Charles Moore) 220–221

Murphy House, Gambier Island, British Columbia, Canada[1 & 6] (Bo Helliwell + Kim Smith, Blue Sky Architecture) 70–71, 203–204, 224–225, 226–228, 229

Ottrupgård Fjernewarme rural co-housing, Skörping, Denmark[2] (Per Sorenson, Plan Energi – isolated seasonal active system) 49–50, 51, 120–121, 219

Parmann House, Stavanger, Norway[1, 2, 4 & 6] (Harald Røstvik) 16

Paxton Court (Netherspring) suburban self-build, Sheffield, UK[1] (Cedric Green) 110–111, 184

Proposed floating dwellings in the Netherlands [1, 2, 4 & 6] (Bart Jan van den Brink) 205

Rothstein House, Whistler, British Columbia, Canada[6] (Bo Helliwell, Erickson-Massey) 220

Rural terraces at Ballantrae, Scotland UK[1] (Gordon Fleming, ARP Lorimer Associates) 113–115, 116, 189

Sea Ranch Condominium and Sea Ranch Swim Club, California, USA[6] (MLTW – Charles Moore, Donlyn Lyndon, William Turnbull & Richard Whittaker) 220–221

Semi-detached rural dwellings, Coldstream, Scotland UK[1] (Aitken and Turnbull) 111–112

Siedlung Halen compact rural/suburban model, Berne, Switzerland[1 7 6] (Atelier 5) 232

'Solar House', Freiburg, Germany[1, 2 & 4] (Hölken & Berghoff) 41, 42, 124, 153–154, 167, 182

'Solar Towers in Glasgow' (StinG) retrofit, Glasgow, Scotland UK[1, 2 & 4] (MEARU, Mackintosh School of Architecture) 48–49, 191

Stile Park suburban terrace, Stornoway, Scotland UK (Allan Holling, Western Isles Islands Council) 13, 95, 97–102, 106, 108, 112, 116, 185, 187

Student residence, University of Strathclyde, Glasgow, Scotland UK[1] (Kennedy and Partners) 41, 91–93, 153–154, 167, 174–175

Suburban development, Göteborg, Sweden[2] (Christer & Kirsten Nordström) 36, 37

Suburban villa at Stokkan, Trondheim, Norway[1] (Anne Grete Hestnes) 200, 201

Suburban terrace, Priesthill, Glasgow[1] (Glasgow City Council) 73–74

Suburban terrace, Zollikofen, Berne, Switzerland [1 & 5] (AARPLAN) 28–30, 31, 32, 39, 110

Terrace at Egebjerggard 'boiby' Housing Exhibition, Ballerup, Denmark[1] (Tegnestuen Vandkunsten) 110, 112

Terrace at Waterkwartier, Niewland, Amersfoort, Netherlands[1 & 5] (Galis Architectenbureau BNA and Van Straalen) 50–51

TI (transparent insulation) demonstration, Bourneville, Birmingham, UK[1] (Leslie Jesch) 175

'Trisol' rural housing, Dingwall, Scotland UK[2] (David Somerville, Ross & Cromarty District Council) 185–186, 187

Trombe-Michel (CNRS-ANVAR) experimental dwellings, Odeillo, France[1] (Jacques Michel) 88–89

Urban housing infill, Deventer, Netherlands[1] (Theo Bosch) 115–116, 206, 219

Urban housing infill, Shettlestone, Glasgow, Scotland UK[1, 2 & 6] (John Gilbert Architects) 200–201, 202, 203

Urban retrofit, Easthall, Glasgow, Scotland UK[1 & 2] (Community Architecture Scotland) 95, 102–108, 112, 115, 116, 117, 119–120, 121, 186–187, 188, 201, 206

Urban retrofit, Göteborg, Sweden[2] (Christer & Kirsten Nordström) 36, 37, 93–94, 151–152, 158, 187

Urban retrofit, Lumphinnans, Fife, Scotland UK[1] (John Gilbert Architects) 201–203

Van den Brink House 'Fantasy' competition, Almere, Netherlands[2] (Bart Jan van den Brink) 26–28, 34, 190, 204–205

Waterkwartier, Nieuwland solar suburb, Amersfoort, Netherlands[1, 2, 4 & 5] (various) 34, 50–51, 215

'Wohnen & Arbeiten' (Living & Working), Vauban, Freiburg, Germany (Michael Gies, id-architektur) 121–124, 205, 206, 216

Mixed Development

'Wasa City' urban/suburban housing and shops, Gävle, Sweden[1] (Thurfjell) 43, 146, 147

Social Care

Christopher Taylor Court, Bourneville, Birmingham, UK[1] (David Clarke Associates) 90–91, 92, 155–156

Day care centre, Alta, Norway[1] (SINTEF division 62) 14

Dementia unit, Larbert, Scotland UK[1] (Foster and Partners) 40, 41

John Darling Mall, Eastleigh, Hampshire, UK (David White, Hampshire County Council) 44, 45, 46

Söderhamn residential unit with special facilities, Sweden[1 & 3] (Jack Hanson) 43–44

Sport/leisure

Gleneagles Community Centre, Vancouver, Canada[6] (John and Patricia Patkau) 150–151

JUFO (JUgend FOrum) youth club, Möglingen, Stuttgart, Germany[1, 3 & 6] (Peter Hübner) 83–85, 86, 87

National Cricket Centre, Loughborough, UK[3] (David Morley) 140

Swimming pool retrofit, Gouda, Netherlands[2] (municipal council) 36

Transport

Nils Ericson bus station, Göteborg, Sweden[1 & 3] (Niels Torp) 140–141

Workplace

Berlingske Tidene newspaper offices, Copenhagen, Denmark[3] (Henning Larsen) 166

ECN research campus, buildings 42 & 31, Petten, Netherlands[1, 3 & 4] (Tjerk Reijenga, BEAR Architecten) 182, 198–199

Johnson Administration/Wax Building[3] 46

Okohuis, Frankfurt, Germany[1, 3 & 6] (Eble and Sambeth) 160

Photovoltaic factory, Freburg, Germany[1, 3 & 4] (Rolf and Hotz) 140, 142, 182, 205, 217

Rheinelbe Science Park research and development building, Gelsenkirchen, Germany[1, 3 & 5] (Kiessler + Partner) 174, 175, 177, 183

Rijkswaterstaat, Ijmuiden, Netherlands[1, 3, 4 & 6] (Atelier Z) 177–178, 181, 199

Strathclyde Police Traffic Division headquarters, Glasgow, Scotland UK[3] (Smith McEwan Architects) 176

INDEX OF PEOPLE, PRACTICES, INSTITUTIONS ETC.

A A5 Architects 5
Aalto, A. 24, 128, 131, 160
Aalto, E 24, 128
AARPLAN 28, 30
Aitken and Turnbull 111
Allen, G. 220, 221
Allen, R. 82, 241
Appleton, J. 59
Appropriate Energy Systems (AES) 201
Arata Izozaki & Associates 226
Arnold, D. 196
ARP Lorimer Associates 113
Atelier Z. 177, 206
Atelier 5, 232
Ayrshire Housing Association 113

B Baird, G. 177
Bak, A. 129
Baker, N. 81, 176, 192
Baker P. H. 105, 190
Balmbro, D. 4
Bartenbach, C. 160, 162
Bartholomew, D. M. L. 5
Baruel, J. J. 24, 128, 129
Bean & Swan Architects 108
BEAR Architecten 144, 198
Beck, A. 168
Beckman, W. A. 4
Bell, M. M. 17, 18
Berghoff (Hölken & Berghoff) 41
Berry, J. 195, 196
Berwickshire Housing Association 108, 111, 189

Binet, H. 129
Blair, T. 211
Blue Sky Architecture 68, 204, 220, 223, 225, 229
Blue Sky Design 222, 229
Blundell Jones, P. 84
Boddy, T. 219, 220, 229, 241
Bosch, T. 115, 206, 219
Bosselar, L. 14, 16
Botta, M. 41
Boyce, R. 9, 87, 148
Brandi, U. 162
Brawne, M. 134
Breuer, M. 87
Brown, A. 87, 95
Brown, P. 212
Brundtland, G. H. 213
Bruton, T. 215
Building Research Establishment (BRE) 190
Burke, T. 212
Busby, P. 16
Butti, K. 87, 184

C Cabot Corporation 168
Caps, R. 167, 168
Carpenter, A. M. 16
Carrell, S. 211
Carter, B. 150, 221, 233
Cerver, F. A. 140, 226
Christian Bartenbach 160, 162
Christianson, G. E. 212
Commission of European Communities 86, 90

Community Architecture Scotland 103

Compagno, A. 159, 163

Courtney-Bennett 100

Curl, J. S. 234

Currie, J. 188

D Dalenback, J.-O. 15

Daniels, K. 159, 162, 163

Danish Energy Directorate 15

Danish Technological Institute 15

Davey, P. 167, 220, 229, 241

David Clarke Associates 90

Davis, M. 162

Delft Technical University (mechanical engineering department) 141, 206

Dekker, J. E. 4

De Rijke Marsh Morgan Architects 179

Desai, P. 215, 216

Dorrel, E. 240

Downs, B. 204

Duffie, J. A. 4

Dundee Sun City 215

Dunster, B. 216

E Earth Balance 219

Earth Sense 146

Easthall Residents' Association 102, 103

Eble, J. 35, 160

Eble and Sambeth 160

Ecofys (international consultancy) 15

Ecostream (marketing arm of Ecofys) 15

Edwards, B. 64, 65, 66, 73, 78, 110

ECN Research Centre 182

Elder and Cannon Architects 176

EMBT (Enric Miralles and Benedetta Tagliabue) 238

Enconsult 200

Energy Technology Support Unit 5, 90

Erickson, A. 204, 220, 232

Erickson-Massey 220

Esbebsen Consulting Engineers 160

Etlin, R. A. 59

F Fielden, Clegg, Bradley Architects 182

Figini, L. 41

Fleming, G. 113

Floors, D. 60, 219

Fordham, M. 37, 146

Forster, W. 216

Foster and Partners 40

Fraunhofer Institut fur Solare Energiesysteme 41, 121, 123, 174

Fricke, J. 167, 168

Fulcrum (sevices consultant) 179

Fuller and Partners 192

Furbo, S. 26

G Galis Architectenbureau BNA 50

Gasson, B. 174

Gates, C. 211

Gates, M. 44

Gibson, G. 86

Gies, M. (id Architektur) 121

Gijon and Guyer 138

Gilbert, J. (John Gilbert Architects) 200

Glasgow City Council 103

Glaumann, M. 146

Goldie, S. (Community Architecture Scotland) 103

Goodwin, D. 192

Graham, J. G. 64

Grant, A. D. 153

Grassie, T. 26

Green, C. 110, 184

Greenwood, B. 228

Gregory, R. 16, 216

Guldberg, H. 212

H Hadid, Z. 59

Hagan, S. 18, 218

Hampshire County Architect's Department 44, 192

Hanna, R. 167

Hanson, J. 43, 44

Harlang, C. 129

Harris, J. 154, 160

Hastings, R. 206

Hawkes, D. 81, 182, 194, 216

Hayton, I. 116, 117, 119

Hedge, A. 72

Hegger, M. 162

Hegger, Hegger and Schleiff 44

Hegger, Hegger-Luhnen and Schleiff 162

Heideler, K. 41

Helliwell, B. (Bo Helliwell, Blue Sky Architecture) 203, 204, 219, 220, 221, 222, 229, 230

Helliwell + Smith: Blue Sky Architecture 68, 70, 204, 220, 222, 223, 224, 225, 226, 231, 232, 233, 234, 235, 240, 241

Henning Larsen (architects) 166

Herdt, J. 212, 215

Herzog, T. 163

Hestnes, A. G. 16, 200

Hicks, W. 195, 196

Hildon, A. 14

Hillman, G. 152

Ho, M. 102, 186, 190

Hopkins, M. 195

Hölken & Berghoff 41

Holling, A. 100, 185

Hollinsworth, F. 204

Howe, B. 146

Howieson, S. G. 72

Hübner, P. 31, 32, 33, 83

Hutchins, M. 162, 163

I Id-architektur 121

International Solar Energy Society (ISES) 2, 123, 175

Institute of Technology, Merrit, British Columbia 16

Irvine New Town Development Corporation 200

Izokaki, A. (Arata Izozaki Assoc.) 226

J Jacobs, H. and Jacobs K. 7, 8, 9, 148

Jacobsen, T. 200

Jbach, H. W. 167

Jensen, K. I. 168

Jesch, L. F. 159, 175

Johnstone, C. M. 91, 153

Jourda and Perraudin 44, 162

K Kahn, L. 238, 240

Keable, J. 88

Keck, G. F. 9, 87, 148

Keck and Keck 9

Kennedy, D. 190

Kennedy and Partners 92

Keren, H. 194

KHR Architects 160

Kiessler + Partners 174

Kilmartin, L. 190

King, D. (Sir) 211

Kistler, S. S. 167, 168

Knudsen, P. 197

Knudsen, S. 26

Kondratenko, I. 47, 73, 182, 190, 199, 200

Köster, H. 159, 160, 161, 162

Kugel, C. 46

L Laboratoire Energetique Solaire (at CNRS, Odeillo, France) 88

Lacy, R. E. 11

Lange, J. 123

Lean, G. 211

Lebens, R. 2, 12, 37, 38, 39, 40, 52, 53, 153, 156

Le Corbusier 116, 165, 233

Leggett, J. 211

Lewis, J. O. 90

Lewis, P. 237, 238, 242

Libby-Owens-Ford Glass Co. 9, 86

Lichtplanung Christian Bartenbach 160, 163

Liefhebber, M. 16

Link, A. 168

Linthorst, G. 15

Littlefield, D. 179

Löf, G. 184

Lomborg, B. 212

Long, G. 2, 88

Lottner, V. 14

Lowe, R. 17, 18

Lund, P. 16

Luther, J. 14

Lyndon, D. 220

Lynskey, G. 89, 155

M MacAlister, T. 17, 18

MacGregor, A. W. K. 1, 2, 4, 26, 48, 159, 188, 189, 190, 191

MacKay-Lyons, B. 31, 67, 68, 157, 158, 174, 204, 219, 220, 221, 222, 233, 240, 242

MacKay-Lyons Sweetapple Architects 220

Mackintosh School of Architecture 157

Markus, T. A. 11

Martin Centre, Cambridge 192

McEvoy, M. E. 105, 190

McKeown Alexander 116

McNamara, M. 222, 231

Mecanoo 141

Metzstein, I. 237, 238, 240, 242

Michael Hopkins and Partners 195

Michel, J. 88, 89

Mies van der Rohe, L. 160

Milner, M. 212

Miralles, E. 239

MLTW (Charles Moore, Donlyn Lyndon, William Turnbull, Richard Whittaker) 220

Molendinar Park Housing Association 116

Møller, M. 24, 135, 136

Moore, C. 220, 221, 234, 235

Morgan, M. H 241

Morley, D. 140

Morse, E. 89, 184

Murcutt, G. 220

Murphy, R. 142

N Napier University 67, 158, 180, 188, 189

Neutra, R. 57, 59, 60, 67, 78, 204, 232

Newton, M. 7, 9, 10, 11, 12, 13, 219

Niels Torp AS Arkitekter MNAL 140

Nilsson, O. 167

Nordström, C. and K. 36, 93, 94, 151, 158

Northumbria Photovoltaics Applications Centre, School of Engineering and Technology, University of Northumbria 215

Norwegian Institute of Technology (SINTEF) 197

O O'Farrell, F. 89, 155

Olgyay, V. 212, 215

Olseth, J. A. 4

Oppenheim, D. 2

Orta Nova 35, 37, 39

Ove Arup and Partners 195, 196

Oxburgh (Lord) 211

P Page, J. K. 2, 12, 37, 38, 39, 40, 52, 53, 153, 156

Palz, W. 88

Patkau, J. and K. 150

Patterson, J. 100

Pawley, M. 231

Peabody Trust 216

Pearsall, N. 215

Peebles, J. C. 9

Percy Thomas 160

Perlin, J. 87, 184

Pinna, Schwarzenbach and Süsstrunk, Architekten 167

Plant, J. A. 38

Platt, C. 116

Porteous, C. D. A. 2, 11, 12, 16, 43, 48, 49, 50, 73, 74, 98, 100, 103, 140, 142, 153, 154, 163, 164, 185, 186, 190, 191, 219, 232

Preuss, S. A. 128

R Raaen, H. 200

Radford, R. 212

Rantil, M. 15

Rees, W. 215

Reiach and Hall Architects 180

Reijenga, T. 144, 198

Renzo Piano Building Workshop 138

Richard Murphy Architects 142

Richard Rogers Partnership 162

Riddlestone, S. 215, 216

Riffat, S. B. 195, 196

Robert Matthew Johnson Marshall (RMJM) 238

Roberts, P. 17, 18

Rolf and Hotz 140, 182

Ross and Cromarty District Council 185

Røstvik, H. 16

Roth, A. and E. 87

Royal Institute of British Architects 149

Rutherford, R. 200

S Salvesen, F. 16

Saluja, G. S. 100, 185

Sambeth (Eble and Sambeth) 160

Sammonds, P. 212

Seager, A. 14

Scheer, H. 16, 17, 18

Schindler, R. 232

Schittich, C. 165

School of the Built Environment (University of Nottingham) 195

Schreck, H. 152

Schwarz, D. 165

Scottish Ecological Design Association 215

Scottish Solar Energy Group xvii, 30, 102, 215

Seager, A. 14,

Sert, J. L. 24, 138

Sharpe, S. 17

Sharpe, T. R. 48, 73, 74, 190, 191

Shigeru Ban 217

Short, Ford and Associates 146

Siemens A. G. 163

Skartveit, A. 4

Smith, K. (Kim Smith, Blue Sky Architecture) 203, 219, 220, 221, 222, 229, 230

Smith, P. F. 17, 18

Smith McEwan Architects 176

Solar Energy Systems 201

Somerville, D. 185, 186

Spiegelhalter, T. 51

Standeven, M. 81

Stansfield-Smith, C. (Sir) 44, 192

Steemers, C. 176

Steemers, T. C. 88

Stephens, M. 5, 7

Stewart, D. 30

Stillman and Eastwick-Field, Architects 5, 6

T Tagliabue, B. 238

Tait, M. 239

Talbot, R. 30

Taylor, A. 188

Taylor, W. 196

Technical Services Agency 102, 103

Thomas, R. 37

Thornton, J. 195, 196

Thurfjell arkitektkontor 43, 146

Thyholt, M. 198

Tombazis, A. H. 128

Tong, D. 72

Torp, N. 140

Townsend, C. 146

Trombe, F. 88, 89

Trumpp Ingenieurburo 174

Turnbull, W. 220

Twidell, J. W. 91, 146, 153

U University of Nottingham 194

University of Strathclyde 91

Unterrainer, W. 157

Upshall, M. 78

V Vale, B. and R. 17, 18, 74, 122

Van den Brink, B. J. 26, 34, 190, 204, 205, 214

Van den Broek and Bakema 141

Van den Cammen, P. 35

Van der Heyden, W. 23

Van Straalen 50

Van Straalen, Zeist and Boom (Architectenbureau) 34

Vector Special Projects (VSP) 179

Vitruvius, M. (Marcus Vitruvius Pollio) 241

Voss, K. 123

W Wackernagel, M. 215

Walsh, N. P. 211

West of Scotland Energy Working Group 102

Western Isles Islands Council (Comhairle nan Eilean Siar) 98

Whalley, A. 164

White, D. 44

Whittaker, R. 220

Wiggington, M. 154, 160

Wilkes, J. A. 241

Williams, A. 149, 165, 168, 241

Wilson, S. 72

Windeleff, J. 14

Wittwer, V. 154

World Commission on Environment and
Development 213

World Wildlife Fund 216

Wotton, H. 241

Wright, F. L. 7, 8, 9, 11, 40, 46, 139, 148,
160, 218, 225, 226, 233

Wundt, W. M. 78

Y Yannas, S. 90, 111, 156, 194

Younge, G. 211

Z Zumthor, P. 138

INDEX OF DEFINED TERMS AND PRODUCTS

Note: page numbers in bold used to signify some explanation of the term

A acrylic foam **167**

active/passive (solar/ventilating/servicing techniques) **xiii**, xiv, xv, xvii–xviii, **2**, 3, 4, 5–13, 14, 15, 16, 17, **23**, 24, 25, **26**, 27, 28, 29, 30, 33, 34, 35, 38, 40, 41, 42, 43, 46, 47, 50, 52, 60, 63, 64, 74, 84, 86–88, 89, 90, 92, 94, 95, 96, 98, 101, 102, 103, 104, 108, 110, 113, 115, 120, 121, 122, 123, **127**, 128, 133, 134, 138, 142, 144, 145, 146, 147, 148, 151, 153, 154, 157, 159, 160, 163, 165, 173, 174, 175, 176, 179, 182, 190, 191, 192, 193, 194, 200, 201, 204–205, 214–215, 216, 219, 237, 240, 241

adaptive control 81, **82**, 84, 85, 87, 88, 89, 90, 92, 93, 94, 95, 108, 109, 111, 143, 176

adaptive opportunity/opportunities **81**, 82

admittance xiii, 147, **149**, 150, 151, **152**, 178

aerogel (Nanogel) 41, 167–168

air-to-air heat exchanger **76**, 108, 146, 204, **205**

air-to-water heat exchanger 95, **186**, **187**

angle of incidence **23**, **39**, **88**, 176, 196, 237

angular selectivity **163**

asymmetric fluorescent light fitting 160

B black attic (solar air collector) **185**, 187

breathing solar air collectors **184**, **187**

building-integrated (e.g. photovoltaics or active solar thermal systems) xiii, 15, 25, 26, **50**, 145, 199

C climatic severity index **11**

D damping factor **152**

decrement factor **97**

degree days **2**, 3

'dendriform' **46**

direct (solar) gain 5, 6,10, 11, 12, 39, 41, **84**, 86, 87, 98, 101–102, 146, 152, 159,

double-skin façade(s) 43, 180, 182, 183, 199, 200

'Drimaster' (ventilation system by NuAire Ltd.) 114, 188, 189

'Drimaster Ecosmart' ('solar slates' ventilation system by NuAire Ltd.) 189

driving rain index (DRI) 11, 12, 101

dynamic insulation; 'dynamically insulated' wall 190

E eco-footprint **215–216**, 231

effective U-value **153**, 154, 156, 157, 158, 190,

electro-chromatic, variable-transmission glass **163**

embodied energy **217**

environmental architecture (Hagan's three criteria) **218**

equivalent outside temperature **152**, 156

'exclusive' (mode of control) **81–82**, 182, 241

F fin shades (clip fin absorber strips) **180**

fixed interstitial specular louvred blades **160**

flat-plate (solar thermal) collectors 2, 14, **25–27**, 34, 50, 123, 184, 200, 204, 205 'fluid shades' **180**

foamed acrylic 41, **167**

G geothermal heat pump/geothermal heating
150, **203–204**

global solar radiation **2**

global warming 43, **211–212**, 213

greenhouse effect 7, 62, **96**, 163, 212

H heat loss coefficient **3**, 4, 73, 111

heat pump 77, **186**, 192, **200**, **201**, **202**,
203, 204, 205, 216, 240

heliodon 131, 133

holographic diffractive film (HDF) **162**

I 'Imacryl' foam (foamed acrylic sheet) **167**

indirect (solar) gain **7**, 10, 11, 12, 29, 87,
88, 89

insolation **2**, 159, 212

Internal base temperature **3**, 73, 152, 156

'interoceptives' **57**, 59

interstitial venetian blind(s) 162, 163, 176

inverted venetian blinds **160**

irradiance **2**, 26, 154, 156, 199

irradiation **2**, 3, 11, 26, 27, 37, 38, 39, 40,
52, 53, 84, 87, 162, 165, 218

isolated (solar) systems **50**

K 'Kalwall' (transparent insulation) **167**, **168**

'Kalwall + Nanogel' **168**

Keeling curve **212**

'kinesthesis' **59**, 60, 67

Kyoto accord/protocol 211, 212

'Koolshade' (woven bronze micro-louvres)
165–166

L laser-cut panels **162**

LBL 3-pane krypton window **167**

light-grid **163**

liquefied petroleum gas (LPG) 191, **192**

low-emissivity coating/glass/surface 101,
117, 122, **163**, 164, 167, 175–176, 180,
198, 231

M 'Maxorb' (selective coating) 155, **156**, 190

McKinnel double tube 218

Mechanical/whole-house (ventilation) heat
recovery 4, 13–14, 41, **72**, 93, **108**, **122**,
200, 205

mirror-optics (optical energy transport and
optical daylight modulation) **159**, 160,
162, 163

N 'Nanogel' **168**

non-selective/selective (absorber) surfaces
26–27, 190

O 'Okalux' (transparent insulation) **167**

'Okasolar' (mirror-optics) 160, 165, 167

P parti **234**

passive heat recovery (ventilation, including
by solar ventilation preheat) **10**, **96**

passive solar architecture **127**

'passive stack ventilation' 175, 190, **192**,
218

'pedway' 43

phase-change materials **159**

photo-chromatic glass **163**

'photovoltaics in practice' **215**

'physiological psychology' **78**

primary energy 72, **191**, 194, 196

prismatic louvres **162**

proaction (relative to control systems) **82**

'proprioceptives' **57**, 59, 60

'prospect-refuge' theory (prospect and refuge) **59**, 67

PV (photovoltaic) shading lamellas 47, 198, **199**

S selective coating **156**, **167**, 176, 190

selective (mode of control) **81–82**, 182, 241

selectively coated polyester foils **167**

self-adjusting photo-chromatic glass **163**

solar air collector 28, 36, 48, 67, 73, 95, 98, 152, 173, 182, 183, **184**, **185**, **187**, **188**, **189**, **190**, 191

solar chimney **89**, **181**, 182, 199, 200

solar slates (unglazed solar air collectors) **67**, **184**, **188**, 189, 201

solar ventilation preheat (preheated supply of air) 2, **29**

'somethesis' **59**, 60, 67

specific heat capacity 93, **149**, 156, **157**

specific heat loss **3**, 73

specular louvred blades **160**

'steady state' methodology **3**

supply air windows 190

surface factor **62**

surface senses **57**

sustainability xviii, 18, 50, 64, 121, 207, 212, **213**, 214, 215, 217, 218, 229, 240, 241

sustainable development xviii, **213**

T 'teleceptives' **57**, 60

thermal admittance xiii, **149**, 150, 151, **152**, 178

thermal capacitance (storage) **10**, **73**, 74, 75, 85, 94, 145, 147, **149**, 150, 151, 156, **157**, **184**

thermal damping (factor) **97**, 147, 149, **152**

thermal diffusivity **149**

(thermal) emissivity/emittance **84**, 162 (for other references, see 'low-emissivity')

thermal response (factor) 147, 149, 151, **152**

(thermal) time lag xiii, 41, **88**, 147, **149**, **152**, 154, 156, 178

thermal transmittance coefficient (U-value) **4**, **5**, 7, 12, 41, 73, 76, 87, 90, 101, 103, 117,120. 122. 149, 151, 152, 153, 154, 155, 156, 157, 158, 159, 162, 167, 168, 190, 195, 196, 206

thermal wheel 195, **196**

thermo-chromatic gels **168**

thermo-chromatic glazing/layers **23**, **163**

thermo-chromatic, phase-change storage wall **165**

tracking collectors **26**

'translucent' PV **34**

transparent insulation (TI) **41**, 91, 153, 154, 155, 159, 160, **167**

transpired (breathing) solar air collector 67, **184**, **187**, **189**, 190, 191

transpired-plate (solar air collector) **187**, 190

Trisol (solar air collector, heat pump and brine store) **185**, **186**, 187

Trombe-Michel wall/principle **88**, 89, 91, 154, 155, 241

U 'Ultrawarm Thermascrene' (transparent insulation) 167

unglazed (transpired) solar air collector **184**, **188**, **190**

Usonia/Usonian **233**

U-value (thermal transmittance coefficient)
4, **5**, 7, 12, 41, 73, 76, 87, 90, 101, 103,
117, 120, 122. 149, 151, 152, 153, 154,
155, 156, 157, 158, 159, 162, 167, 168,
190, 195, 196, 206

V variable transmission (glazing/glass) **159**,
162, 163, 165, 179

'Visi Heat' double glazing **163–164**

Vitruvian triad **241**

volumetric thermal capacity **149**

Vostok ice core **212**

W water-to-air heat exchanger **205**

wind assisted 'passive stack ventilation'
190 (**192** for explanation of performance)

window integrated solar air collectors
(WISACs) **190**, 191

INDEX OF ACRONYMS AND ABBREVIATIONS

A AES (Appropriate Energy Systems) 27, 201

B BedZED (Beddington Zero Energy Development) 216, 217, 218

BIPV (Building Integrated Photovoltaics) 25, 46, 47, 199, 200

BMS (Building Management System) 180, 183

BRE (Building Research Establishment) 190

C CANMET (Canadian Centre for Mineral and Energy Technologies) 16

CEC (Commission of European Communities) 86, 90

CFCs (chlorofluorocarbons – also called freons) 203

CFD (Computational Fluid Dynamics) 147

CHP (Combined Heat and Power) 49, 123, 205, 217

CNRS (Centre National de la Recherche Scientifique) 88

COP (Coefficient of Performance) 203

CSI (Climate Severity Index) 11

DC (Direct Current) 26

D DHW (Domestic Hot Water) 37, 94,

DNA (deoxyribonucleic acid) 59

DRI (Driving Rain Index) 11

E ECADAP (Environmental Computer Aided Design and Performance) 147

ECN (Dutch government's energy research centre) 15, 182, 198

EMBT (Enric Miralles, Benedetta Tagliabue) 238

EPA (Energy Performance Appraisal) 90, 111

ESP/ESPr (Environmental Systems Performance) 147, 203

ETFE (ethylene-tetra-fluoro-ethylene) 179

ETSU (Energy Technology Support Unit) 5, 90, 111

EU (European Union) 14

H HDF (holographic diffractive film) 162

I IEA (International Energy Agency) 14, 15, 43, 123, 152, 206

ISE (Fraunhofer Institut fur Solare Energiesysteme) 41

ISES (International Solar Energy Society) 1, 16, 123, 175, 194

IT (Information Technology) 180

J JUFO (JUgend FOrum) 83, 85, 86, 87

L LCP (laser-cut panels) 162

LEGIS (acronym unknown for Transparent Insulation wall) 92

LPG (liquefied petroleum gas) 191, 192

LT (Light Thermal [predictive tool]) 176

M MLTW (Charles Moore, Donlyn Lyndon, William Turnbull and Richard Whittaker) 220, 221

MSP (Member of the Scottish Parliament) 239, 240

VERMONT STATE COLLEGES

0 0003 0756183 7

P PASSYS (Passive System [test cells]) 190, 191, 192

PV (photovoltaic) 1, 5, 14, 15, 16, 17, 26, 34, 37, 46, 47, 48, 50, 51, 174, 178, 182, 189, 190, 192, 195, 196, 199, 200, 204, 205, 214, 215, 216, 217

PVC (polyvinyl chloride) 44

PVT (photovoltaic thermal) 15

R RIBA (Royal Institute of British Architects) 149, 196

RMJM (Robert Matthew Johnson Marshall) 238

S SAP (Standard Assessment Procedure) 73, 117

SI (Standard International [units of measurement]) 149

SINTEF (Norwegian Solar Energy Research Centre at the Norwegian Institute of Technology, Trondheim) 14, 16, 197, 198

StinG (Solar Towers in Glasgow) 48, 49, 191

T Tardis (Time and relative dimensions in space) 85

TI (Transparent Insulation) 41, 91, 92, 153, 154, 155, 156, 157, 159, 167, 175

Trisol (triple solar system) 185, 186, 187

U UFO (Unidentified Flying Object) 83, 84

UK-ISES (UK Section of International Solar Energy Society) 2, 3, 42

V VAT (Value Added Tax) 18

VSP (Vector Special Projects) 179

W WISAC (window integrated solar air collectors') 190

WWF (World Wildlife Fund) 216